DOMESTIC VIOLENCE

Foundations of Social Work Knowledge

Foundations of Social Work Knowledge
Frederic G. Reamer, Series Editor

Social work has a unique history, purpose, perspective, and method. The primary purpose of this series is to articulate these distinct qualities and to define and explore the ideas, concepts, and skills that together constitute social work's intellectual foundations and boundaries and its emerging issues and concerns.

To accomplish this goal, the series will publish a cohesive collection of books that address both the core knowledge of the profession and its newly emerging topics. The core is defined by the evolving consensus, as primarily reflected in the Council of Social Work Education's Curriculum Policy Statement, concerning what courses accredited social work education programs must include in their curricula. The series will be characterized by an emphasis on the widely embraced ecological perspective; attention to issues concerning direct and indirect practice; and emphasis on cultural diversity and multiculturalism, social justice, oppression, populations at risk, and social work values and ethics. The series will have a dual focus on practice traditions and emerging issues and concepts.

The complete series list follows the index.

DOMESTIC VIOLENCE

INTERSECTIONALITY AND CULTURALLY COMPETENT PRACTICE

Edited by
Lettie L. Lockhart and Fran S. Danis

COLUMBIA UNIVERSITY PRESS   NEW YORK

COLUMBIA UNIVERSITY PRESS
Publishers Since 1893
New York   Chichester, West Sussex

Copyright © 2010 Columbia University Press
All rights reserved

Library of Congress Cataloging-in-Publication Data
Domestic violence : intersectionality and culturally competent practice /
edited by Lettie L. Lockhart and Fran S. Danis.
p. cm. — (Foundations of social work knowledge)
Includes bibliographical references and index.
ISBN 978-0-231-14026-3 (hard cover : alk. paper) — ISBN 978-0-231-14027-0 (pbk. alk. paper)
— ISBN 978-0-231-52137-6 (e-book)
1. Family violence. 2. Victims of family violence. I. Lockhart, Lettie L. II. Danis, Fran S.
HV6626.D666   2010
362.82'92—dc22   2009038014

Columbia University Press books are printed on permanent and durable acid-free paper.

This book is printed on paper with recycled content.
Printed in the United States of America

c 10 9 8 7 6 5 4 3 2 1
p 10 9 8 7 6 5 4 3 2 1

References to Internet Web sites (URLs) were accurate at the time of writing.
    Neither the author nor Columbia University Press is responsible for URLs
    that may have expired or changed since the manuscript was prepared.

CONTENTS

ACKNOWLEDGMENTS

TO THE abuse survivors we have known: Thank you for teaching us the meaning of resiliency and determination to survive. Although you share many common experiences, we hope this book helps us to better understand your unique circumstances and journeys to safety and community.

To our chapter contributors: Thank you for graciously sharing your passionate commitment and expertise for working with women from diverse communities who face violence and abuse. This book would not have been possible without your collaborative efforts.

To my parents, Berlin and Martha S. Lockhart, Sr., and my siblings (William Earl, Freddie Morris, Berlin, Jr., and Barbara Ann) for the perpetual love, support, and encouragement that you have shown me throughout my personal and professional adventures. Also, thanks to all my friends for their support.

For your encouragement, support, and unconditional love: My partner, Judith M. Turner, and my family: Suzanne Danis and Martin Podgainy, Elaine, Matthew and Andrew Cramer, and Bob, Mary Ann, and Sam Stillerman.

CONTRIBUTORS

Salma Elkadi Abugideiri is a licensed professional counselor, with a certification in marriage and family therapy. She has worked extensively with refugees, immigrants, and Muslim and Middle Eastern families. She is also Co-Director of the Peaceful Families Project, a Muslim organization dedicated to preventing domestic violence through education and training. She is a member of the Leadership Team of the FaithTrust Institute and serves on the Editorial Board of the *Journal of Religion and Abuse.*

Barbara Ball, Program Evaluation Specialist, received her Ph.D. in art education and art therapy from New York University. She has more than 15 years of clinical experience working with children and teens from violent homes and has integrated creative, arts-based components into school-based counseling and dating violence prevention programming. At SafePlace, she has had primary responsibility for developing the *Expect Respect Program Manual* that addresses support groups for at-risk youths, teen leadership groups, and school-wide prevention strategies. She also coordinates the program evaluation in conjunction with the Centers of Disease Control and Prevention, Research Triangle Institute, International, Georgia State University, and the University of Miami in Ohio. She has presented on the Expect Respect program and evaluation at numerous conferences.

Shreya Bhandari received her Ph.D. in social work from the University of Missouri. Her dissertation focused on coping strategies of low-income, rural, pregnant women facing intimate partner violence. She has worked as a crisis counselor for women facing domestic violence at Dilaasa, a hospital-based crisis center, in Mumbai, India. She is currently a post-doctorate fellow with

the School of Nursing at the University of Missouri working on the Domestic
Violence Enhanced Home Visitation (DOVE) Program. DOVE is testing a
research-based intervention with public health nurses/home visitors for pregnant women experiencing IPV.

Rupaleem Bhuyan is an assistant professor at the University of Toronto,
Faculty of Social Work. She is a second-generation immigrant of Assamese/
Indian heritage who was born and raised in the United States and has lived
and worked in France, Thailand, and now Canada. She has spent nearly
two decades in the anti-violence movement as a peer educator, community
organizer, and advocate. During the past six years, Dr. Bhuyan has collaborated with community-based domestic violence agencies to explore social and
political factors that impact advocacy with immigrant, refugee, and indigenous women. Her current research explores how political pressure to deny
immigrants access to public benefits influences their response to domestic
violence and related health sequelae.

Bonnie Brandl, MSW, is the director of the National Clearinghouse on
Abuse in Later Life (NCALL), a project of the Wisconsin Coalition Against
Domestic Violence (WCADV). Brandl has worked with battered women for
more than 24 years. She co-authored a book titled *Elder Abuse Detection and
Intervention: A Collaborative Approach*. Her numerous published articles and
manuals on abuse in later life have been distributed throughout the country.
For more than a decade, she has presented at national, regional, statewide,
and local conferences on domestic violence and elder abuse. Brandl has an
MSW degree from the University of Wisconsin, Madison.

Brenda Bussey, MSW (Mohawk), received her bachelor of arts degree in
American Indian studies and English from the University of Minnesota in
Duluth, MN. She received her master of social work degree from the University of Minnesota, Duluth, in 2004. Since earning her master's degree,
Brenda has worked primarily in the domestic violence/sexual assault field.
She worked for Mending the Sacred Hoop Technical Assistance Project
in Duluth as a resource coordinator for four years; there her work focused
primarily on improving the response to Native women who have been battered or sexually assaulted, by working with tribes who were implementing
tribally based domestic violence and sexual assault programs. Brenda is now
at the American Indian Community Housing Organization in Duluth as

the coordinator for Dabinoo'igan Shelter, a shelter for Native women who have been battered.

Bonnie E. Carlson, Ph.D., CSW, is currently Professor and Associate Director, School of Social Work, Arizona State University. After completing a Ph.D. at the University of Michigan in Social Work and Psychology, she served on the faculty at the University at Albany, State University of New York, from 1979 to 2007. During that time, she served in many faculty leadership roles, including Director of the Undergraduate Program (1980–84) and Associate Dean (1987–88). Her research has focused on intimate partner violence and other forms of trauma by intimates as well as public attitudes toward domestic violence. Her most recent research has addressed trauma histories and parenting strain in drug-abusing mothers. She has been the recipient of several research grants on family violence and is the author of numerous articles and book chapters. She is also on the editorial board of two professional journals, the *Journal of Interpersonal Violence* and *Trauma, Violence, and Abuse*. She has also conducted research on trauma and parenting strain in women attempting to recover from drug abuse and a group intervention on mindfulness meditation for men and women recovering from drug and alcohol abuse.

Lorraine A. Chase, DSW, has spent the last 29 years working with victims, children, and perpetrators of domestic violence. She was the director of a comprehensive, nongovernmental domestic violence program that included a shelter, hotline, and legal services; the latter provided attorneys and advocates in each courthouse, counseling services, and community outreach and education. She has done individual, group, couples, and family therapy. She has testified before Congress twice on the issue of domestic violence. Her doctoral dissertation researched gender role conflict and male domestic violence abusers. She was one of four Americans chosen to tour Pakistan, Nepal, and Bangladesh to work with advocates trying to establish domestic violence services in those countries. She was the president of the Maryland Network Against Domestic Violence (MNADV), and she remains a member after 20 of service to them. She was MNADV's representative to the National Coalition Against Domestic Violence, where she served as chair of the Women of Color Task Force. She was a volunteer for the Anne Arundel County Sexual Assault Program. She also served on boards of directors for substance abuse facility and domestic violence program, and she is currently president of the Zonta

Club of Annapolis. She is an adjunct professor at the Anne Arundel Community College. Dr. Chase received her bachelor of science degree from the State University of New York at Stony Brook; her master of social work degree from the Virginia Commonwealth University; and her doctorate degree in social work from the Catholic University of America.

Elizabeth Circo is a doctoral student at the University of Washington. Most recently a program assistant at the Annie E. Casey Foundation in Baltimore, MD, she has worked with disadvantaged populations in various positions in Washington, DC—with the Mayor's Advisory Committee on Child Abuse and Neglect; the Whitman-Walker Clinic; the Institute for Women's Policy Research; the Department of Health and Human Services Office of Minority Health; Georgetown University; the Sexual Minority Youth Assistance League; and the Little Blue House, a group home for abused, abandoned, and neglected children. Elizabeth earned her MSW degree from the Howard University School of Social Work.

Elizabeth P. Cramer, Ph.D., is a professor in the School of Social Work at Virginia Commonwealth University. Her primary practice and scholarship areas are domestic violence, lesbian and gay issues, and group work. Dr. Cramer edited a book published by Haworth Press titled *Addressing Homophobia and Heterosexism on College Campuses*. She has published a number of journal articles, a book chapter, and a CD-Rom on abuse of persons with disabilities. Dr. Cramer serves as a board member on the Chesterfield County Domestic Violence Task Force, and is a member of its DELTA committee (CDC-funded prevention project). She is the principal investigator for the I-CAN Accessibility Project, a grant-funded project by the Department of Criminal Justice Services Virginia Sexual and Domestic Violence Victim Fund, to increase accessibility to legal protections for abused persons with disabilities and to enhance the ability of disability service providers to work with abused consumers.

Fran S. Danis, Ph.D., ACSW, is Associate Professor and Associate Dean at the University of Texas at the Arlington School of Social Work. She has taught at the University of Missouri and the University of Texas at Austin. As a social work practitioner, she founded a domestic and sexual violence community-based program in Denton, Texas, served as the chair of the Texas Council on Family Violence, a state domestic violence coalition, and was staff associate at the National Association of Social Workers/Texas. Her experience in the domestic violence field includes direct services and administration, policy development and advocacy, training and technical assistance, research and evaluation, and teaching. She is a co-editor with Lettie Lockhart of *Breaking the Silence in Social Work Education: Domestic Violence Modules for Foundation Courses* published by the Council on Social Work Education (CSWE). Together they founded the CSWE Violence Against Women and Their Children annual symposium. Fran has served on the NASW Committee on Women's Issues and the CSWE Commission on the Role and Status of Women in Social Work Education. She was the principal investigator for the project "Crime Victims: A Social Work Response, Strengthening Skills to Strengthen Survivors" conducted in collaboration with NASW/Texas and funded by the U.S. Department of Justice, Office for Victims of Crime. She was the first social worker in Texas to receive the NASW Social Worker of the Year Award from two different communities. Fran earned a Ph.D. from the Mandel School of Applied Social Sciences at Case Western Reserve University and an MSW from Stony Brook University in New York. Her research interests include social work response to domestic violence, resiliency of domestic violence survivors, and adult children of battered women.

Rabbi Mark Dratch was ordained as an Orthodox Rabbi at the Rabbi Isaac Elchanan Theological Seminary of Yeshiva University and served as a pulpit rabbi for 22 years. He is Founder and CEO of *JSafe: The Jewish Institute Supporting an Abuse Free Environment* and is a member of the Leadership Team of FaithTrust Institute. He is an Instructor of Judaic Studies at the Isaac Breuer College of Yeshiva University, former Vice President of the Rabbinical Council of America and chair of its Taskforce on Rabbinic Improprieties, past member of the Jewish Advisory Committee of the FaithTrust Institute, and a member of the Clergy Task Force of Jewish Women International. He served on the Editorial Board of the *Journal of Religion and Abuse*.

Rev. Dr. Marie M. Fortune is the Founder and Senior Analyst at FaithTrust Institute since 1977. She is ordained in the United Church of Christ and is a practicing theologian and ethicist, educator, and author. She is best known for her book, *Keeping the Faith: Questions and Answers for Christian Abused Women*. Fortune was editor of the *Journal of Religion and Abuse* from 2000 to 2008. She served on the National Advisory Council to the Office on Violence Against Women in the U.S. Department of Justice (1994–2000) and the Defense Task Force on Domestic Violence for the U.S. Department of Defense (2000–2003).

Tricia B. Bent-Goodley, Ph.D., is a Professor at Howard University School of Social Work and Chair of the Community, Administration, and Policy Practice Sequence. She has numerous publications and research on the intersection of violence against women and girls with cultural competence, child welfare, health and mental health, and faith- and community-based interventions. Dr. Bent-Goodley is a Fellow with the HIV Intervention Science Training Program and a former Hartman Child and Family Scholar. Dr. Bent-Goodley serves on national boards and local planning committees providing expertise in violence against women and girls, child welfare, policy, and research. She is the editor of *African American Social Workers and Social Policy* and co-editor, with Dr. King E. Davis, of *The Color of Social Policy* and *Teaching Social Policy in Social Work Education.* Dr. Bent-Goodley received her Ph.D. from Columbia University and her MSW from the University of Pennsylvania. Prior to coming to Howard University, she was a director and clinician with several family violence prevention programs in Harlem and Queens County, New York.

Delores F. Johnson, MSW, ACSW, previously Director, Family Programs, Headquarters, U.S. Army, Family and Morale, Welfare and Recreation Command (FMWRC), is currently Director, Plan, Installation Management Command. Prior to becoming a civil service employee with the Army, Ms. Johnson held both clinical and social service management positions with local, state, and private agencies serving as a clinical social worker for the Texas Department of Mental Health and Mental Retardation, Executive Director for the El Paso, Texas, Battered Women's Shelter, and school social worker in Vernon Parish, LA. She began her tenure with the military in 1984 as the Family Advocacy Program Manager, Fort Bliss, Texas, and served as the Family Advocacy Program Manager and Army Community Service Director in Wiesbaden, Germany. Ms. Johnson joined the FMWRC staff in July 1990 as the Family Advocacy Program Manager and later served as the Chief, Army Community Service. She has served as a member of the American Bar Association Commission on Domestic Violence and the National Domestic Violence Hotline. Delores F. Johnson holds a BA degree from Averett College, Danville, Virginia. She received an MSW degree from the University of Maryland School of Social Work in Baltimore, Maryland, an MA degree in National Security and Strategic Studies from the Naval War College, is a graduate of the Senior Executive Fellows Program at John F. Kennedy School of Government, Harvard University, and the Department of Defense Leadership and Management Program (DLAMP). Delores F. Johnson is a member of the Academy of Certified Social Workers (ACSW) and a licensed clinical social worker. Delores F. Johnson has received the following awards: Department of the Army Meritorious Civilian Service Award, Superior Civilian Service Award, The Order of the White Plume, Who's Who in American Colleges and Universities, Who's Who of American Women, and Who's Who in Human Services. She has also published several articles in major publications.

Mimi Kim has worked for more than 20 years as an anti-violence advocate in Asian communities, including 10 years at the Asian Women's Shelter where she coordinated a nationally recognized multilingual access program. She is a steering committee member of the Asian and Pacific Islander Domestic Violence Institute, a national resource center. Mimi is also a founding member of Incite! Women of Color against Violence, where she has been working collectively with women of color nationally and internationally to create community-based solutions to violence. Mimi continues her domestic violence advocacy as the Founder and Executive Director of Creative Interventions, a resource center supporting community-based interventions to domestic violence and other forms of intimate violence based in Oakland. She is also a program consultant for Shimtuh: Korean Domestic Violence Program, an Oakland-based program which she co-founded in 2000. Mimi is currently a Ph.D. candidate at the School of Social Welfare at the University of California, Berkeley.

Shanti Kulkarni, Ph.D. LCSW, is Assistant Professor of Social Work at the University of North Carolina at Charlotte. Her primary research explores developmental and contextual factors within interpersonal violence theory and practice. She has worked in the sexual assault and domestic violence movement for more than a decade as an advocate, clinician, and researcher.

Taryn Lindhorst, Ph.D., LCSW, is an Associate Professor of Social Work at the University of Washington. Prior to receiving her doctorate in 2001, Dr. Lindhorst provided social work services for 15 years in public health settings in New Orleans, Louisiana, where she helped found the local chapter of ACT UP and worked with several other LGBT organizations. Her current research investigates the intersection between individuals and social institutions, particularly as this relates to issues of violence against women. Dr. Lindhorst's work on the effects of welfare reform for battered women has won two national awards, and she has received a Career Development award from the National Institutes of Health to study domestic violence and mental health outcomes. Her current projects include longitudinal analysis of the long-term impact of domestic violence on economic and mental health outcomes among adolescent mothers, a policy study of the experiences of battered women who are subject to legal action in the U.S. under the Hague Convention on the Civil Aspects of Child Abduction, and relationship violence among sexual minority youth.

Lettie L. Lockhart, Ph.D. LCSW, is currently a professor in the School of Social Work and the Director of the SSW Training Project at the University of Georgia. Lettie earned her Ph.D. from the School of Social Work from Florida State University, her MSW from Howard University in Washington, DC, and her BS in Social Work from Southern University in Baton Rouge, LA. She has been researching, teaching, and practicing in the area of domestic violence for more than 20 years. She has been a pioneer in the empirical investigation of violence in intimate personal relationships with a focus on cultural and environmental factors. Dr. Lockhart has researched and taught courses/content on domestic violence with particular attention on race, class, gender, and sexual orientation. She was one of the major community players in the development of the first Domestic Violence (Project SAFE) shelter and hotline in Athens, Georgia. She has served on Boards of Directors of Domestic Violence Programs and on national panels addressing domestic violence and she has been a juried reviewer for the U.S. Centers for Disease Control and Prevention in Atlanta. She has been an advocate for domestic violence curriculum integration with the Council on Social Work Education (CSWE) over the past nine years and an advocate for policy and funding initiatives at the national, state, and local levels to address this major social issue. She is co-editor, with Fran Danis, of *Breaking the Silence in Social Work Education: Domestic Violence Modules for Foundation Courses* published by the CSWE. Together Lockhart and Danis founded the CSWE Violence Against Women and Their Children annual symposium.

Beckie Uta Masaki is currently Co-Founder and Executive Director of the Asian Women's Shelter (AWS) in San Francisco and has served in that role since the shelter opened in 1988. She received her MSW degree from the University of California at Berkeley in 1983. In addition to her direct service and organizational development work at AWS, Beckie has provided peer-based training and technical assistance to a wide range of grassroots women's groups on local, state, national, and international levels. Beckie is an appointed representative of the California Domestic Violence Advisory Committee, one of the founding members of the Asian and Pacific Islander Institute on Domestic Violence, and currently serves on the steering committee of the National Judicial Institute on Domestic Violence. Beginning in 1983, as the first and only Asian woman in a mainstream shelter program, Beckie has continued for the past 26 years to bring the voices and experiences of marginalized groups into the center of the movement to end violence against all women.

Gita Mehrotra is currently a doctoral student in the Social Welfare Program at the University of Washington. She has been involved with domestic violence work for the past 14 years in a variety of capacities, including direct service, education/training, and program and organizational development with a focus on API and queer communities. She is a consultant with the Asian Women's Shelter, San Francisco, and is one of the lead organizers of Transforming Silence into Action, a national network of lesbian, bisexual, queer women and transgender people addressing domestic violence in queer API communities. She is also engaged with technical assistance and training with South Asian and API community-based organizations around the country. Gita's current research and teaching interests include domestic violence in South Asian and queer communities, anti-oppression/social justice education, critical theory and social work, and qualitative, community-based research.

Shawn L. Mincer, MSW, began his career 13 years ago as a prevention educator, crisis intervention staff and volunteer trainer with sexual violence and intimate partner violence (IPV) agencies in New England, and with prevention and intervention programs at the University of New Hampshire. He obtained his MSW at the University of Michigan in 2003, where he worked with the statewide Michigan Coalition Against Domestic and Sexual Violence. While there he assisted in implementing a national survey on primary prevention strategies for domestic violence, funded by the Centers for Disease Control (CDC), titled A *Vision for Prevention*. He also worked on a primary prevention program targeted at Latino youth in Southeast Michigan and a

CDC-funded program to strengthen Community Response Teams in responding to IPV and sexual violence. Currently a doctoral student in the Social Welfare Program at the University of Washington, Shawn's research interests include investigating IPV in the community of men who have sex with men, working with lesbian, gay, bisexual, transgender, and queer (LGBTQ) elders and caregiving dyads, LGBTQ youths, community organizing and social movements, and critical research methodologies.

Jacquelyn Mitchell, JD, LCISW, is a forensic social worker, attorney, and mediator. She has served on the faculty of several graduate schools and departments of social work, developing and teaching courses on social policy, diverse populations, administration, mediation, and forensic social work. Her scholarship includes empirical investigations of relationships related to noncustodial fathers, their children, and natural mothers; youth and community conflict; the impact of family formation on familial well-being; and the elderly. Her scholarship includes more than twenty juried articles and book chapters, more than 65 professional presentations, and program development activities related to the promotion of social, economic, and political justice. Her trans-disciplinary career includes positions as director of an adoptions department, a Reginald Heber Smith Fellow in legal services, a public defender, private practice of law, judicial and nonprofit administration, legislative legal counsel, and family and general mediation. She is on the editorial board of the *Journal of Values and Ethics* and has served as co-editor of the *Journal of Forensic Social Work* and as a reviewer for the *Journal of Race, Gender, and Class.* She holds a Juris doctorate degree from the University of Pennsylvania Law School and an MSW from Atlanta University.

Sara-Beth Plummer, Ph.D., MSW, is a Project Coordinator and Instructor for the Center on Violence against Women and Children at the Rutgers University School of Social Work. Her experience includes being both a social worker and an assistant director at Barrier Free Living, Inc., an agency that provides services to individuals with disabilities who have been abused. She has assisted in creating a curriculum for teachers and parents on the topic of abuse and children with disabilities. She has presented to multiple social service agencies, law enforcement personnel, and medical settings on the prevalence of abuse of individuals with disabilities. She was a research evaluator at the Partnership for People with Disabilities. Her research interests include domestic violence, criminal justice, and empowerment.

Blanca M. Ramos, Ph.D., LCSW, is currently Associate Professor of Social Work at the University of North Carolina at Charlotte. She has taught courses on clinical social work, diversity, immigrants, Hispanic cultures in the U.S., and research in Latino communities. Her research and publications have focused on health disparities, multiculturalism, international social work, and domestic violence centering on Latinos. She has served in various local, regional, and national boards and commissions, and has extensive experience as a practitioner and community advocate. She is past First Vice President of the National Association of Social Workers (NASW) and has served on the National Board of the Institute for the Advancement of Social Work Research, the editorial board of *Social Work*, and the NASW National Committee on Inquiry.

Elizabeth Randall, LICSW, Ph.D., is Associate Professor of Social Work at West Virginia University. She has 21 years of direct practice experience in the field of behavioral health, including inpatient and outpatient work with children, youths, adults, families, and groups. She is a member of Phi Kappa Phi, President of the West Virginia State Chapter of the National Association of Social Workers, and a member of the West Virginia Comprehensive Behavioral Health Advisory Board.

Selena T. Rodgers, Ph.D., LSCW-R, is an Assistant Professor of Social Work at York College, City University of New York. Prior to her fulltime appointment, she served as an Adjunct Assistant Professor for six years in the same program. She was also the Associate Vice President at Safe Horizon's Queens Criminal Justice and Community Programs; one of the nation's leading agencies in the field of victimization. Her research interests include *Posttraumatic Growth* (PTG) with multi-cultural and multi-ethnic communities. She was a recipient of the Adjunct Professional Staff Congress (PSC)/ CUNY Research Award which supported (in part) her doctoral research on PTG among Latina immigrants living in refugee-like situations. She recently received a grant from the PSC-CUNY Research Award to examine *posttraumatic growth and spiritual well-being in African-American female and male adult survivors of childhood sexual abuse*. She is a former Hartman Child and Family Services Scholar. She has a published book chapter entitled, *The Art of Healing: An Afrocentric helping guide for practitioners working with African-African families who experience intimate partner violence*. She received her Ph.D. from Adelphi University and her master's degree in social work from Syracuse University.

Barri Rosenbluth, LCSW, is Director of SafePlace's Expect Respect Program in Austin, Texas. Expect Respect provides counseling, support groups, and educational programs for youth and adults on the issues of dating and domestic violence, sexual harassment, and bullying prevention in K–12 schools. Expect Respect has gained national recognition and was selected in 2008 as one of eleven sites to participate in Start Strong, an initiative to promote healthy teen relationships funded by the Robert Wood Johnson Foundation. Barri worked closely with the U.S. Centers for Disease Control and Prevention on the development of Choose Respect, and has co-authored several curricula including the *Expect Respect Program Manual, Date Smart for the Boys and Girls Clubs of America,* and *Love All That and More* for the FaithTrust Institute. Barri, her colleagues, and youth participating in Expect Respect have been featured on *Good Morning America,* ABC News *Day One* and *World News Tonight, The Oprah Winfrey Show, Partnerships for Preventing Violence National Satellite Training, Parade* magazine, *Teaching Tolerance,* National Public Radio, and in other local and national media.

Woochan S. Shim, Ph.D., is an assistant professor in the Department of Social Welfare at Daejeon University in South Korea. Her research interests include violence against women across the life span and culture. She taught and practiced in the domestic violence field in Korea as well as in the United States. She has been dedicated to developing culturally and spiritually sensitive and effective interventions for victims of ethnic minorities in both countries. She began working toward ending violence against women in the late 1980s and she continues to work toward the same goal locally and internationally.

Deb Spangler is currently the Aging and Disabilities Program Specialist for the National Clearinghouse on Abuse in Later Life, a project of the Wisconsin Coalition Against Domestic Violence. She has provided technical assistance, training, and consultation on abuse in later life as well as abuse of persons with disabilities both in Wisconsin and nationally, for the Department of Justice, Office on Violence Against Women Training grantees, since December 2000. Prior to that, Deb was employed for ten years at the local domestic abuse program in Madison, Wisconsin. There, in addition to providing direct client services, she developed several programs including the Abuse in Later Life Program, the Rural Outreach Program, and the Health Care Advocacy Program. Deb has produced and published 11 articles, booklets, and manuals, and has facilitated trainings in the elder abuse, disabilities, and health-care fields throughout the United States.

Leslie E. Tower, Ph.D., is an Associate Professor in the Division of Social Work and the Division of Public Administration at West Virginia University. Her research interests focus on women and, in particular, on violence against women, women and work, and feminist pedagogy. She has published articles on domestic violence in the *Journal of Social Work Education*, the *Journal of Interpersonal Violence*, and the *Journal of Family Violence*. Dr. Tower is also active in community education on domestic violence, for example, updating, displaying, and producing programs around the West Virginia Silent Witness Exhibit.

Deborah D. Tucker is Executive Director for the National Center on Domestic and Sexual Violence and served as Co-Chair of the U.S. Department of Defense Task Force on Domestic Violence from 2000 to 2003. Deborah has been dedicated to ending violence against women since becoming a volunteer with the first rape crisis center in Texas in 1973. She then served as Assistant Director for the Austin Rape Crisis Center (ARCC) from 1973 to 1975. She was Co-Founder and Executive Director of the Austin Center for Battered Women from 1977 until 1982. These two agencies were combined in 1997 to become the SafePlace Survival Center. In 1982 she became the first Executive Director of the Texas Council on Family Violence, a position she held until 1996. Under her leadership, the Texas Council grew to be one of the largest state coalitions in the country with a staff of more than fifty providing training and technical assistance, public education, and advocacy, and it is home to the National Domestic Violence Hotline, 1–800–799-SAFE. She was the founding Chair of the National Network to End Domestic Violence during its development and passage of the Violence Against Women Act in 1994. The National Center on Domestic and Sexual Violence provides and customizes training and consultation, influences policy, promotes collaboration, and enhances diversity with the goal of ending domestic and sexual violence. Visit their award winning Web site at http://www.ncdsv.org. Tucker received the National Network to End Domestic Violence's Standing in the Light of Justice Award and Marshall's Domestic Violence Peace Prize in recognition of her national leadership. She has also been honored as a Public Citizen of the Year by the National Association of Social Workers.

Ann Turner has worked as an Aging and Disabilities Specialist for the National Clearinghouse on Abuse in Later Life (NCALL), a project of the Wisconsin Coalition Against Domestic Violence (WCADV) since 2002. Ms. Turner has been a grassroots organizer for the domestic violence movement in a rural area of Northwestern Wisconsin since 1981, and she opened a domestic abuse shelter in 1986. She served as Executive Director of the program for 20 years and has extensive experience in developing agency policy and procedures, including service and outreach programs. Ms. Turner's development experience also includes writing training curriculum and presenting on numerous topics including domestic violence, domestic abuse in later life, ageism, and domestic violence in the lesbian, gay, bisexual, and transgender community. Ms. Turner received the Bonnie Brandl Outstanding Systems Advocate Award from WCADV in 1991, and in 2001 she received a blanket, a symbol of honor, from the St. Croix Tribal Community for her work with that community.

Kavya Velagapudi is a graduate student and a teaching assistant in the University of Kansas, School of Social Welfare. She has worked as an advocate at a domestic violence shelter for women and children and also interned for Kansas Coalition Against Sexual and Domestic Violence during her graduate studies.

J. B. Whipple, MSW (Mi'kmaq), received her BA degree in economics from Wheaton College, Norton, MA, and her MSW degree from the University of Southern Maine, Portland, ME. She is a member of the Eskasoni Band, Mi'kmaq First Nation in Nova Scotia. Her master's research thesis explored the effect of drumming on healing from trauma in women from the tribes and bands of the Wabanaki Confederacy. JB was recently a research analyst at the Cutler Institute of Child and Family, Muskie School of Public Service, University of Southern Maine, where she had the primary responsibility for analyzing data on grants to end violence against Indian women, such as the STOP Violence Against Indian Women and the Indian Coalitions Against Sexual Assault and Domestic Violence programs, funded by the U.S. Department of Justice. In addition, she provides technical assistance to tribes on the grants which address sexual assault, domestic violence, and stalking. As a volunteer, JB works as an advocate at the Sexual Assault Services of Southern Maine (SARSSM), a local rape crisis center, staffing the hotline, responding to crisis calls, and accompanying victims to the hospital and law enforcement interviews.

INTRODUCTION

Fran S. Danis and Lettie L. Lockhart

"**DOMESTIC VIOLENCE** affects people from all ages, races and ethnicities, socio-economic classes, religions, places of origin, and sexual orientations." You have probably heard this statement or something similar countless times. It has been repeated for the past 30 years at untold public education presentations and continuing education trainings. It appears in every magazine article, on every educational video, and in all brochures and pamphlets about domestic violence. This simple statement acknowledges, of course, that there is diversity in our world, but its larger purpose is to help people understand that violence does not just happen to other women; it happens to people who look just like them. In fact, we can count among its victims our mothers, sisters, and daughters, our neighbors and cousins, even ourselves. And if it can happen to us—and to our mothers, sisters, daughters, neighbors, and cousins—and if we claim to care about the women in our lives, then we care about all battered women.

The notion of "the universal woman" was adopted to help develop public empathy for women who are often blamed for the violence—for staying and for leaving (Collins 1998). This strategy, however, has evolved, whether consciously or unconsciously, into an inadvertent barrier to addressing how a woman's culture of origin, her place in the physical, political, and social world, and the society's dominant culture come together to influence how women experience violence and the particular options available to them as a result of that violence. It is now time to move beyond this unintended barrier and to provide the field of domestic violence, social work practitioners, and others who work with survivors of violence and abuse with the necessary tools to help all women, not just those who "look like them."

Intimate partner violence against women is often experienced within the context of multiple, complex, and competing life issues that confront families grappling with the perils of domestic violence. One such important life issue is the impact of cultural values, beliefs, rituals, mores, and practices on the prevalence of domestic violence. Recognizing that domestic violence affects women of all ages, races, ethnicities, socioeconomic classes, geographical locations, residence statuses, religions, places of origin, and sexual orientations, it is imperative that social work curricula and education as well as training materials reflect the complex and diverse nature of this major problem frequently addressed by social work practitioners in all fields of practice.

This book provides social work educators and their students with a resource that uses the issue of domestic violence to meet the Educational Policy and Accreditation Standards (EPAS) of the Council on Social Work Education (CSWE) to design curricula that integrate (1) social and economic justice content grounded in an understanding of distributive justice, human and civil rights, and the global interconnection of oppression; and (2) content relating to the implementation of strategies to combat discrimination, oppression, and economic deprivations and advocate for greater social and economic justice (CSWE 2008). EPAS sets forth the purposes of social work education for preparing competent and effective professionals, developing social work knowledge, and providing leadership in developing service delivery systems that alleviate oppression and other forms of social and economic injustice, all relating to the experiences of women and their children in violent domestic living situations. Because domestic violence cuts across all fields of practice, social work students at all levels will find this material relevant to their future practices.

In addition to meeting requirements set forth in EPAS, this book will help faculty and students address the social justice values of the profession as identified through the National Association of Social Workers (NASW) Code of Ethics. The intersecting multiple layers of race, ethnicity, sexual orientation, disability, and citizenship status add to the vulnerability experienced by battered women. Thus successful culturally competent generalist social work practice that champions the cause of violence against women in intimate partner relationships requires approaches that are both flexible and respectful of the intersecting multi-categorical identities of women survivors of intimate partner violence.

This volume is the first book to focus on helping strategies and practice approaches with diverse populations—inclusive of race and ethnicity, age, place, citizenship status including immigrants, refugees, and members of our armed forces, sexual orientation, (dis)abilities, and religious tradition—as it relates to survivors of domestic violence. It represents an important developmental milestone for the field of domestic violence, the profession of social work, and other professionals that work with survivors of domestic violence. The book is a celebration of our shared commitment to culturally competent practice.

The information in this book is not just for advocates working in the domestic violence or crime victim assistance fields; it will assist professional social work practitioners in many different practice fields as well as provide the domestic violence field with a practical tool covering diverse populations affected by domestic violence. It is our hope that the book will be a unifying tool that brings together two groups committed to ending oppression: advocates for battered women and social work practitioners, many of whom are one and the same.

Practitioners, advocates, researchers, and others who work with survivors daily have long recognized that "one size does not fit all." We cannot expect the same interventions and approaches to be effective with women from different cultural backgrounds. Each domestic violence survivor brings a mix of cultural influences reflecting their own culture of origin, current status in the physical and political world, as well as the influence of the dominant social, economic, and political cultures. We know there is no such entity as the "universal victim" just as there is no "perfect client." Despite this recognition, however, information about violence against women from diverse cultural backgrounds is often difficult to find or scattered across a few specialized journals or books. With the expansion of research on specific populations, the tasks of collecting, analyzing, and disseminating this new knowledge has become ever more challenging—both from the perspective of enough hours in the day and access to scholarly journals and books. Each of the contributors to this book has collected information about a specific population, summarized important points, and applied the research to working with individuals. They have accomplished what many of us do not have the time to do. They have performed a service that will be appreciated by survivors and those who work in this field, including advocates, nurses, and criminal justice personnel.

Because of the prevalence of domestic violence and the presence of professional social workers in health, education, criminal justice, and social service settings, most social work practitioners encounter clients who have current or past involvement with violence perpetrated against them by an intimate partner (see Figure int.1). In recognition of the cross-cutting nature of the issue,

FIGURE INT.1. Domestic violence: a cross-cutting issue for social workers. Developed by Fran S. Danis, PhD.

we use a generalist practice approach that can be applied by social workers and other professionals in many different practice settings.

Embedded in the diversity content of this volume is a strong appreciation of a strengths perspective and empowerment practice. The strengths perspective can be used only if workers know the distinctive cultural packages from which their clients evolved. Armed with this knowledge, valid assessment and intervention can occur. A cornerstone of practice in both professional social work and the domestic violence field is the concept of empowerment practice (Gutierrez 1989). Within the domestic violence field, empowerment practice is addressed first as a strategy for assisting individual women to take control of their lives and, second, as a strategy for taking action against domestic violence in specific communities.

ADVOCATE AND RESEARCHER TEAMS

Most of the chapters were developed by teams of writers that included people working directly with individual survivors from specific populations as well as people conducting research about the needs of survivors from those populations. Many of the contributors are well-known experts in the domestic violence field. Researchers contribute their expertise in developing and conducting research as well as in analyzing and interpreting others' research. They usually have access to published literature in the field and have a commitment to disseminating information to practitioners through teaching and writing. Practitioners contribute practical knowledge about the diverse communities with which they work. They help researchers make sense of findings and identify ways new information can be applied in the field. We believe that these advocate–researcher teams have provided a comprehensive picture of various cultures and political statuses through working with individuals from a specific population. Although we encountered a number of areas where there were gaps on either side of the equation (a researcher or an advocate with social work backgrounds), many teams sought additional assistance from experts in their respective areas and had a strong commitment to the overall purpose of this book—aiding the provision of culturally competent services to survivors of domestic violence and abuse.

HOW TO USE THIS BOOK

Like most reference books there is no particular order in which we invite you to read the chapters of this book. We suspect that the book will be used very much like a dictionary or encyclopedia. Readers will select chapters of interest at their leisure or when they have a compelling need to do so. This interest may be sparked by having clients from specific groups or to check the facts regarding the populations to which you personally relate. Rather than attempting to organize the chapters into artificial themes, we simply ordered the chapters alphabetically, similar to any other reference book.

Although reading about each population separately may not seem congruent with an intersectionality approach, we believe that without a thorough understanding of each population, one cannot apply culturally competent practice within an intersectionality framework. For example, one cannot help an African American woman with disabilities, who lives in a small rural town, address violence from her same-sex partner without understanding the needs of African Americans, lesbians, persons with disabilities, and rural environments. The information in each of these chapters must be known and applied to the particular situation. We also recognize that by having specific chapters about specific populations there is a danger that we are creating new stereotypes and a practice cookbook. It is critical that our readers, the practice community, students, advocates, and others recognize that each client is an individual who may share many experiences in common with the groups to which he or she "belongs" but who may also have many differences. Recognition of these within-group differences is essential to culturally competent practice. That is why this book can only introduce readers to particular populations. For example, the terms "Asian and Pacific Islanders" or "Latinas" represent individuals from many different countries and cultures. It would be a mistake to think that an indigenous woman from the Hawaiian Islands would share the same cultural experiences and expectations as a woman from Taiwan. There is no way to anticipate the myriad of combinations that are potentially possible given all the diversity "factors." We wanted to be as inclusive as possible and, in doing so, made a conscious decision to sacrifice depth. We hope that by reading each individual chapter your interest is so sparked as to seek out additional sources of information about a particular population. Better yet, remember that your client is the best source of information about her life and how she perceives the cultural influences that shape her world.

Although readers may pick and choose, we suggest that you read the first two chapters to provide a context for the rest of the book. The first chapter, "Cultural Competence and Intersectionality: Emerging Frameworks and Practical Approaches," provides an overview of the mandates for the social work profession to engage in culturally competent practice, applies the elements of culturally competent practice to the field of domestic violence, and demonstrates our shared commitment to addressing social and economic oppression within a framework of intersectionality. We had many discussions about how best to reflect the concept of intersectionality, that is, moving away from a "one-size-fits-all" paradigm to a paradigm that sees women as uniquely whole with multilayered identities stemming from their race, color, age, social class, ethnicity, culture, history, geographical location, language, and citizenship status. The message of this chapter is that if we are to be effective and culturally competent in working with survivors of intimate partner violence, we must develop, adopt, and apply models and practice approaches that take into consideration the intersectionality of our multilayered identities that provide the context for one's lived experiences.

Chapter 2, "Understanding Domestic Violence: A Primer," reviews domestic violence terminology, risk and protective factors, and reasons "why women stay," and includes a discussion of the strengths of battered women. Practice issues associated with universal screening, risk assessment, and safety planning are explored as well as criminal justice interventions and contraindicated interventions.

The 12 additional chapters address specific populations: African Americans, Asian and Pacific Islanders, persons with disabilities; immigrants and refugees; women in later life; Latinas; lesbian, gay, bisexual, and transgendered persons; members of the military; Native Americans; women of different religions; rural women; and teens. Each chapter provides readers with a review of the current literature and a case study demonstrating how to apply knowledge about that particular population in a culturally competent manner. The literature review includes a general overview and demographic information, salient historical issues, and a description of cultural issues within an ecological framework. A discussion of domestic violence in that population, community reactions and resources available, barriers to using traditional domestic abuse services, differential application of policy responses, and ethical dilemmas and concerns are reviewed.

The case study for each chapter illustrates the interplay between cultural/ diversity issues and domestic violence, provides suggestions for developing a respectful collaborative working relationship between worker and client aimed at defining the issues from the victim's perspective, and demonstrates the application of generalist practice to culturally specific and sensitive intervention strategies. The case study also shows how to use interviewing skills for assessment and identification of individual strengths, selecting and implementing culturally appropriate interventions at appropriate system levels— including individual, organizational, and community levels—for both practice and policy advocacy. Each chapter ends with a resource list of national organizations that can be accessed for more information and assistance with a particular population.

We sincerely hope that Domestic Violence: Intersectionality and Culturally Competent Practice is a practical and accessible tool providing critical information and demonstrating the application of culturally competent practice skills for advocates in the field of domestic violence, as well as for social work practitioners everywhere who encounter women, children, and men who survive violence at the hands of an intimate partner. We invite our readers to join with us, the editors, and all the individuals who contributed to this volume, on this passionate quest for delivering, with sensitivity and compassion, the highest-quality services to our clients.

REFERENCES

Collins P. H. (1998). The tie that binds: Race, gender and US violence. Ethnic and Racial Studies, 21(5), 917–938.

Council on Social Work Education (CSWE). (2008). Educational Policy and Accreditation Standards. Retrieved 20 May 2008 from http://www.cswe.org/NR/rdonlyres/2A81732E-1776–4175-AC42–65974E96BE66/0/2008EducationalPolicyandAccreditationStandards.pdf.

Gutierrez, L. (1989). Working with women of color: An empowerment prospective. Social Work, 35, 149–154.

Harper, K., and J. Lantz. (1996). Cross-Cultural Practice: Social Work with Diverse Populations. New York: Lyceum Books.

Vann, A. A. (2003). Developing Culturally-Relevant Responses to Domestic Abuse: Asha Family Services, Inc. (pp. 1–48). Harrisburg, PA: National Resource Center on Domestic Violence.

DOMESTIC VIOLENCE

1

CULTURAL COMPETENCE AND INTERSECTIONALITY

Emerging Frameworks and Practical Approaches

Lettie L. Lockhart and Jacquelyn Mitchell

LONG IGNORED, the existence and impact of domestic violence in America was finally acknowledged seriously in the 1970s and 1980s. Drawing from the collective strength of our shared experience over the past thirty-five years, women have recognized that our sociopolitical demands that are voiced by millions speak more powerfully than the pleas of a few isolated voices (Crenshaw 1994). Through our collective voices and actions, advocates, practitioners, educators, and researchers have transformed our understanding of violence against women and their children. For example, no longer is battering and sexual assault of a female intimate partner seen as a private and isolated dysfunctional aggression. These acts are generally recognized as part of a broader system of domination that affects women nationally and globally (Crenshaw 1994). The persistent and diligent actions of feminist social activism laid the foundation for America's lawmakers, courts, social service providers, health care providers, and other institutional players to recognize that intimate partner violence is a major social, legal, medical, and systemic problem and can no longer be considered a private and isolated family matter.

Initially, the political and social movement of intimate partner violence against women—and, subsequently, the literature, scholarly initiatives, and intervention strategies aimed at addressing this social phenomenon—focused on abuse and violence inflicted on "the universal woman" regardless of their sociopolitical cultural context. This focus generated "one-size-fits-all" practice strategies and initiatives. The "universal woman" notion and the "one-size-fits-all" approach were dreadfully inadequate in describing the experiences and needs of diverse groups of women who were being abused (Andersen and Collins 2004; Crenshaw 1994; Collins 1998a, 1998b; Hooks 1984).

As the movement developed, however, so did our general consensus that domestic violence is a social reality that intersects with other factors—race, skin color, age, ethnicity, language, ancestry, sexual orientation, religion, socioeconomic class, ability, geographic location, and status as a migrant, indigenous person, or refugee, all interacting to determine one's social experiences and reality (Sokoloff 2005; Feinberg 2004; Sumter 2006; Warrier 2008). In addition, the definition of "survivor" of domestic violence evolved beyond relating exclusively to females in heterosexual relationships. Voices within the movement began to raise the potential of additional domestic victimization categories, including males, homosexual partners, lesbians, and unrelated cohabitants (Sumter, 2006). Consequently practice, policy, and advocacy initiatives must be sensitive to and inclusive of all the factors that shape the dynamics of the human experience.

Future practitioners and advocates must be educated and trained with theoretical models of diversity, practice skills and techniques, and research methodologies that focus on the varied lived experiences of women who are survivors of intimate partner violence and their children in order for us to be more culturally competent in assisting women address their needs and concerns. Thus it is our contention, and that of the other contributors to this volume, that variations beyond culture, gender, race, and class inequities shape the experiences of women survivors of intimate partner violence.

The aim of this chapter is to help us move away from the traditional approach of viewing diversity as based on individualize differences (e.g., culture, race, gender, age, geographical location, immigration status, sexual orientation, (dis)ability, or other variations) toward a perspective that considers all diversity factors as intersecting differentially and dynamically in each individual in any given context (Sokoloff 2005; Titterton 1992; Warrier 2008). Included is a brief overview of the changing demographics of this country; a discussion of culturally competent practice as well as competencies required for future advocates and social work practitioners who engage practice, advocacy, and research that effectively and competently responds to the diversity of the lived experiences of survivors of intimate partner violence and their children; a discussion of intersectionality and its implications for fostering a more holistic, sensitive, and inclusive understanding of, and practice with, survivors of intimate partner violence experienced by women and their children; and a transition to the remaining chapters of the book.

THE CHANGING FACE OF AMERICA: DEMOGRAPHIC TRENDS IN THE TWENTY-FIRST CENTURY AND BEYOND

Census data from the 1990s revealed an unparalleled 32.7 million increase in the U.S. population, the largest numerical increase of any decade in U.S. history, reflecting a changing American demographic mostly attributed to non-European immigration and birth rates. Persons of Hispanic or Latino and Asian heritage have emerged as the fastest growing population groups in the United States (U.S. Census 2002a, 2007a). Estimates are that "White non-Hispanics," long considered the dominant ethnic group in America, will become a statistical minority by 2050, if not sooner (Diller 2007; Okum, Fried, and Okum 1999). Beginning with the 2000 U.S. Census, respondents are permitted to categorize themselves as belonging to more than one race, and data are captured regarding disability and grandparent caregivers, further recognizing our changing demographics. The "two or more races" population category represented the highest percentage of children and the lowest percentage of persons over 65 years of age (U.S. Census Bureau 2007a). In 1990, 31.1 million elderly person 65 years of age and older were living in the United States compared to 35 million in 2000 and a projected 54 million by 2020 (ibid., 2002a). Approximately 37 million persons (12.6%) in the United States were living in poverty in 2005, revealing an increase over the number living in poverty in 2000 (11.3%). During this period women, overall, had the highest poverty rates compared to men (ibid., 2007c). Unfortunately stigma against lesbian, gay, bisexual, and transgendered individuals has prevented systematic census collection regarding this population.

Members of the domestic violence practice communities at all system levels (i.e., micro, meso/mezzo, and macro) must respond to the needs of survivors of intimate partner violence who are characterized as having varied life experiences, and different contextual values and behaviors, and who reside in demographically diverse American communities. Failure to understand the lived experiences and competently interact with survivors of intimate partner violence from a more holistic contextual framework may result in significant consequences for women who are already marginalized and oppressed. Thus a more holistic contextual understanding of the varied experiences of women from different backgrounds that examines the intersectionality of all forms of inequalities and oppression (i.e., gender, race, class privilege, geographical location, immigration status, sexuality, abilities) of survivors of intimate partner violence will help us become more culturally sensitive and competent practitioners (Sokoloff and Dupont 2005; Brah and Phoenix 2004; Richie 2000).

CULTURAL COMPETENCE IN THE FIELD
OF DOMESTIC VIOLENCE

WHAT IS CULTURAL DIVERSITY?

Although "cultural diversity" has no standard definition, it is generally agreed that the term refers to a variety and a richness of communities with distinct norms, beliefs, practices, and values. In addition to the obvious cultural similarities and differences that exist between peoples, such as language, dress, and traditions, societies also vary significantly in their shared moral values, their interactions with and within their environment, and the ways in which individuals and groups of people view the universe in forming values about their lives and the world around them. The aspects contributing to cultural diversity are the following:

- **Age:** including a recognition of the different realities, needs, and issues facing young girls and boys, adolescent girls and boys, adult women and men, and older women and men.
- **Ethnicity/Race:** including different realities related to racial and ethnic group and subgroup identification, skin color, cultural practices, particularly those that facilitate or support, or impede or undermine, efforts to end violence against women.
- **Immigration/Citizenship Status:** including individuals who are refugees, asylees, and immigrants.
- **Religion:** including religious/cultural practices and beliefs that facilitate or support, or impede or undermine, efforts to end violence against women.
- **Sexual Orientation/Identity:** including lesbian, gay, bisexual and transgendered individuals, communities, and organizations.
- **Disability:** including the increased vulnerability of persons with physical and developmental disabilities.
- **Language:** including linguistic ability, cultural dialects, and accents that facilitate or support, or impede or undermine, individual and community access to services and other resources. Other recognized forms of language that individuals use to communicate with others may include, for example, sign language and the use of pictorial images in art therapy by children surviving or witnessing abuse.
- **Education/Literacy:** Literacy is an important subset of education and includes, for instance, being able to read a protective order and write

notes about an incident shortly after it occurs. Education, the broader category, includes, but is not limited to, the development of skills enabling one to calculate the amount of emergency financial support that is available, and so on.

- **Economic Status:** including access to financial and other support, particularly a livable income, shelter and housing, food, clothing and other necessities.

Competent cultural social work practice also compels practitioners to expand their understanding of the meaningful events in their clients' lives as well as in their own lives (Gutierrez, Yeakley, and Ortega 2000; Devoe and Schlesinger 1999). Openness and respect of cultural differences, culturally sensitive assessment of life experiences, and genuine openness to the uniqueness of cultural psychosocial development in a client's life are essential for viewing another's approach to making daily life events meaningful. To cross the threshold into the cross-cultural helping process, practitioners must be aware and free of bias so that the common human condition can be promoted through well-informed practice initiatives (Harper and Lantz 1996, p. 4).

WHAT IS CULTURAL COMPETENCY?

According to Lum (2007), the social work profession, other applied social sciences, and even the federal government have developed a number of working definitions of cultural competent practice. The definitions, though varied, are all premised on an understanding that contextually cultural competent practice requires the acquisition of knowledge, skills, attitudes, and values that will enable individuals, organizations, and societal institutions to respond effectively to a diverse society. Generally "cultural competence" is defined as a process by which individuals and systems respond respectfully and effectively to people of all cultures, languages, classes, races, ethnic backgrounds, religions, and other diversity factors in a manner that recognizes, affirms, and values the worth of individuals, families, and communities, and protects and preserves the dignity of each (Diller 2007; Lum 2007; Davis and Donald 1997; Cross et al. 1989).

Cultural competence requires the implementation of congruent behaviors, attitudes, and policies that come together in a system or agency or among professionals and enable the system, agency, or professionals to work effectively in cross-cultural situations (Diller 2007; Lum 2007; Pederson 2002; Davis and Donald 1997; Cross et al. 1989). As evident in this definition, cultural competence is more than being politically correct or tolerating diversity; it is a sincere commitment, active engagement in, and dedication to a lifelong learning process to enrich the delivery of services to domestic violence survivors and other persons seeking the services of helping professionals (Diller 2007; Lum 2007).

SOCIAL WORK MANDATES FOR CULTURAL COMPETENT PROFESSIONALS

Continuous enhancement of services that are culturally sensitive is an ethical imperative for all social work practice, including work in the domestic violence community. Generally, social workers are ethically required to pursue social justice and, more specifically, to fight against discrimination in our practice, practice communities and environments, and society as a whole (National Association of Social Workers [NASW], 1999). In our continual pursuit of our professional mission to abide by the ethical dictates of our six core values (service, social justice, dignity and worth of the person, importance of human relationships, integrity, and competence), NASW carefully reviewed the social work literature and the diversity agendas in practice communities, and concluded that cultural competency standards needed to be incorporated into social work practice to help social workers respond knowledgeably, sensitively, and skillfully to the diverse populations they serve (NASW 1999, p. 2).

As a result, NASW (2001) developed standards for cultural competence in social work practice that address such key areas as ethics, values, self-awareness, cross-cultural knowledge and skills, empowerment and advocacy, workforce diversity, professional education, language diversity, and cross-cultural leadership. According to NASW (2001, p. 2), "cultural competence in social work practice implies a heightened consciousness of how clients experience their uniqueness and deal with their differences and similarities within a larger social context." The drafters of the NASW *Standards for Cultural Competence in Social Work Practice* (see Table 1.1) recognized the need to measure and evaluate these competencies. In other words, the development of standards goes hand in hand with the development of measures to evaluate the implementation of these standards in preparing culturally competent professionals (Lum 2007; NASW 1991).

TABLE 1.1 NASW Standards for Cultural Competence in Social Work Practice

STANDARD 1. ETHICS AND VALUES

Social workers shall function in accordance with the values, ethics, and standards of the profession, recognizing how personal and professional values may conflict with or accommodate the needs of diverse clients.

STANDARD 2. SELF-AWARENESS

Social workers shall seek to develop an understanding of their own personal, cultural values and beliefs as one way of appreciating the importance of multicultural identities in the lives of people.

STANDARD 3. CROSS-CULTURAL KNOWLEDGE

Social workers shall have and continue to develop specialized knowledge and understanding about the history, traditions, values, family systems, and artistic expressions of major client groups that they serve.

STANDARD 4. CROSS-CULTURAL SKILLS

Social workers shall use appropriate methodological approaches, skills, and techniques that reflect the workers' understanding of the role of culture in the helping process.

STANDARD 5. SERVICE DELIVERY

Social workers shall be knowledgeable about and skillful in the use of services available in the community and broader society and be able to make appropriate referrals for their diverse clients.

STANDARD 6. EMPOWERMENT AND ADVOCACY

Social workers shall be aware of the effect of social policies and programs on diverse client populations, advocating for and with clients whenever appropriate.

STANDARD 7. DIVERSE WORKFORCE

Social workers shall support and advocate for recruitment, admissions and hiring, and retention efforts in social work programs and agencies that ensure diversity within the profession.

STANDARD 8. PROFESSIONAL EDUCATION

Social workers shall advocate for and participate in educational and training programs that help advance cultural competence within the profession.

STANDARD 9. LANGUAGE DIVERSITY

Social workers shall seek to provide or advocate for the provision of information, referrals, and services in the language appropriate to the client, which may include use of interpreters.

STANDARD 10. CROSS-CULTURAL LEADERSHIP

Social workers shall be able to communicate information about diverse client groups to other professionals

Source: NASW 2001.

The educational arm of the profession, the Council on Social Work Education (CSWE), has also embraced a commitment to preparing culturally competent professionals to serve a constantly changing, diverse service community. Two decades ago, the CSWE-Commission on Accreditation initially adopted *Standards* on preparing culturally competent professionals that include outcome measures, curriculum methodology, and course-learning objectives (CSWE 2001). The newly adopted CSWE (2008) *Educational Policy and Accreditation Standards* reflect further development of the commitment to ensuring that professionals are prepared for culturally competent practice in a diverse society (for the content of these two standards, see Table 1.2). In fact, both explicit and implicit curriculum Educational Policy and Accreditation Standards address our commitment to preparing culturally competent professionals, the intersectionality of multiple forms of identities, and the need to advance human rights and social and economic justice across systems, practice levels, and practice approaches, as we champion our mission to educate culturally competent professionals (Compton and Galaway 1999).

PUTTING CULTURAL COMPETENCE INTO DOMESTIC VIOLENCE PRACTICE

In addition to the mandates from the National Association of Social Workers (1999, 2001) and the Council on Social Work Education (2008) requiring social workers to be culturally competent, several models have been advanced to guide us in how best to incorporate cultural sensitivity in our professional mission of providing social and economic justice for the people we serve. Though varied, models address cultural competence from the perspective of the practitioner, the organization, and community involvement. These models also have been adopted by the domestic violence practice community (see Figure 1.1).

THE PRACTITIONER PERSPECTIVE

As noted, cultural competence is a developmental process that requires a long-term commitment. It is not achieved simply by attending a one-day cultural sensitivity workshop but is an active process of learning and practicing over time. Given the multilayered diversity of our practice communities, becoming and continuing to be culturally competent is easier to talk about

TABLE 1.2 CSWE Educational Policy and Accreditation Standards—Diversity

EXPLICIT CURRICULUM

Educational Policy 2.1.4—Engage diversity and difference in practice.

Social workers understand how diversity characterizes and shapes the human experience and is critical to the formation of identity. The dimensions of diversity are understood as the intersectionality of multiple factors including age, class, color, culture, disability, ethnicity, gender, gender identity and expression, immigration status, political ideology, race, religion, sex, and sexual orientation. Social workers appreciate that, as a consequence of difference, a person's life experiences may include oppression, poverty, marginalization, and alienation as well as privilege, power, and acclaim. Social workers

- recognize the extent to which a culture's structures and values may oppress, marginalize, alienate, or create or enhance privilege and power;
- gain sufficient self-awareness to eliminate the influence of personal biases and values in working with diverse groups;
- recognize and communicate their understanding of the importance of difference in shaping life experiences; and
- view themselves as learners and engage those with whom they work as informants.

Educational Policy 2.1.5—Advance human rights and social and economic justice.

Each person, regardless of position in society, has basic human rights, such as freedom, safety, privacy, an adequate standard of living, health care, and education. Social workers recognize the global interconnections of oppression and are knowledgeable about theories of justice and strategies to promote human and civil rights. Social work incorporates social justice practices in organizations, institutions, and society to ensure that these basic human rights are distributed equitably and without prejudice. Social workers

- understand the forms and mechanisms of oppression and discrimination;
- advocate for human rights and social and economic justice; and
- engage in practices that advance social and economic justice.

IMPLICIT CURRICULUM*

Educational Policy 3.1—Diversity

The program's commitment to diversity—including age, class, color, culture, disability, ethnicity, gender, gender identity and expression, immigration status, political ideology, race, religion, sex, and sexual orientation—is reflected in its learning environment (institutional setting; selection of field education settings and their clientele; composition of program advisory or field committees; educational and social resources; resource allocation; program leadership; speaker series, seminars, and special programs; support groups; research and other initiatives; and the demographic make-up of its faculty, staff, and student body).

Accreditation Standard 3.1—Diversity

3.1.1 The program describes the specific and continuous efforts it makes to provide a learning environment in which respect for all persons and understanding of diversity and difference are practiced.

3.1.2 The program describes how its learning environment models affirmation and respect for diversity and difference.

3.1.3 program discusses specific plans to improve the learning environment to affirm and support persons with diverse identities.

* "The implicit curriculum refers to the educational environment in which the explicit curriculum is presented. It is composed of the following elements: the program's commitment to diversity . . . The culture of human interchange; the spirit of inquiry; the support for difference and diversity; and the values and priorities in the educational environment, including the field setting, inform the student's learning and development. The implicit curriculum is as important as the explicit curriculum in shaping the professional character and competence of the program's graduates. Heightened awareness of the importance of the implicit curriculum promotes an educational culture that is congruent with the values of the profession" (CSWE, 2008, p 10).

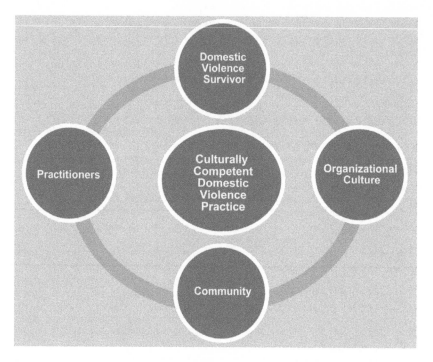

FIGURE 1.1. Systems level of culturally competent practice and domestic violence.

than to accomplish. Generally, models for the culturally competent practitioner working with diverse practice communities prescribe six core values:

- Respect and appreciation of diversity, consistent with social work values and ethics
- Awareness of the dynamics of one's own diversity
- Engagement of continuous professional education on cultures other than one's own
- Advocacy for marginalized populations and work for their empowerment
- Support of an appropriately diversified workforce and organizational culture
- Engagement of leadership roles in celebrating diversity

The model advanced by Cross et al. (1989) suggests that culturally competent practice requires the following "Individual Cultural Competence Skill Areas."

- Awareness and acceptance of cultural differences and use of that active appreciation to service delivery
- Practitioner **self-awareness** of, and work on, the impact of their own cultural, ethnic, and racial predispositions in the helping relationship
- Practitioner dedication to the need for continuing education on the **dynamics of difference** and consultation with experts from diverse cultures, for the purpose of enhancing contextual understanding of clients
- Use of **knowledge of clients' cultures** in practice to adapt intervention approaches to better meet clients' needs
- **Adaptation of skills** to better meet the needs of clients of different cultures

The Lum (2007, pp. 64–65)[1] model prescribes competence indicators for both generalist and advanced practitioners, and it includes four core competencies for practitioners:

- **Cultural Awareness**

   Generalist level: Consciousness of one's own experiences related to cultural diversities; contact with, and awareness of, other cultures/ ethnicities (e.g., positive and negative experiences); vigilance of one's own "isms" such as racism, ageism, sexism, classism, ableism, heterosexism/ homophobia, prejudice, and discrimination

   Advanced level: Assessment of involvement with people from diverse cultural backgrounds with multilayered identities throughout the life span; completion of course work, internship, and research focused on cultural diversity; employment experiences with culturally diverse consumers and programs; academic and employment evaluation of progress on attaining academic material; and professional cultural diversity experience

- **Knowledge Acquisition**

   Generalist level: Understanding cultural diversity terms; demographic knowledge of culturally diverse populations; critically thinking about cultural diversity; understanding the history of oppression and of sociopolitically diverse groups; knowledge of the strengths of people from culturally diverse backgrounds including the intersecting, multilayered diversity within groups; and knowledge of the values of culturally diverse groups that provides group solidarity, group networks, and group identification

Advanced level: Use of systems and psychosocial theory in practice with consumers of diverse backgrounds; knowledge of theories on ethnicity, culture, minority identity, and social class; mastery of applied cross-cultural social science theories and disciplines to construct relevant intersecting knowledge systems of sociopolitically diverse groups with all their multilayered complexities and richness

- **Skill Development**

Generalist level: Overcoming consumer resistance to acknowledgment of culturally diverse backgrounds and experiences; understanding the variations among individuals from diverse backgrounds in self-disclosure, open and positive styles of communication, discrimination of problem identification, assessment of stressors, strengths, and client dimensions (e.g., biological, psychological, social, cultural, and spiritual), establishment of culturally acceptable goals, multi-systemic interventions, and culturally sensitive termination

Advanced level: Designing programs in culturally diverse communities; understanding the importance of accessible services, belief in recruiting a diverse workforce, participation in community outreach, and establishment of collaboration with other agencies; fostering a conducive agency setting; engaging cultural skill development research

- **Inductive Learning**

Generalist level: Participating in continuing discussions with culturally diverse educators, practitioners, students, and consumers on topics such as cultural competence issues, emerging cultural trends, and future directions for culturally diverse practice aimed at fostering new knowledge and insight on culturally diverse social work practice

Advanced level: Engaging in inductive research on cultural competences and disseminating new information via publishing and presentations on cultural competence and culturally diverse practice

To apply these principles and skills to working with women survivors of intimate partner violence, social workers and other human service practitioners must do the following:

- Acquire core knowledge about women from culturally diverse groups (including one's own) and inquire about the diversity within these groups to attain a more holistic understanding of how violence in intimate personal relationships is supported or opposed within the multilayered diverse sector of this group

■ Assess and understand verbal and nonverbal cues of survivors of intimate partner violence, that is, determine what works and what does not; how the beliefs and behaviors of the cultural group affect women survivors of intimate partner violence and their children; and one's own personal feelings and reactions to women survivors of intimate partner violence from an array of cultural backgrounds with all their multilayered complexities

■ Create and evaluate culturally relevant and appropriate materials, interventions, and programs; and devise community resource guides containing cultural competency policies and values sensitive to the multilayered diversity presented by female survivors of intimate partner violence

GUIDANCE FOR ORGANIZATIONS

Cross et al. (1989) also offer cultural competence guidance for social service organizations, suggesting "anchor points" along a continuum against which organizational cultural competence is evaluated according to the extent to which organizational attitudes, practice, and policies reinforce:

■ The superiority of the dominant culture and its "destructive" effect on cultures that differ; this represents the most negative end of the continuum, where culture is viewed as a problem and efforts are deliberately made to suppress or destroy non-dominant cultures

■ Segregated, ostensibly equal services and practices that mark the organization's "incapacity" to help individuals from diverse cultural backgrounds; an adherence to separate but "equal treatment"

■ The promotion of cultural assimilation by advocating "cultural blindness" that does not incorporate the multiple, layered, and differentiated identities of consumers and assumes that culture makes no difference and thus all people are the same

■ Organizational "cultural pre-competence" in which an organization is aware and sensitive to the needs of culturally diverse individuals and groups but often takes no specific or concrete actions to improve cultural competence at all levels using protocols such as staff hiring, training, and board representation, or only makes sporadic or inconsistent efforts in this direction

- Organizational "cultural competence" by continually demonstrating respect for the input of individuals, organizations, and communities representing different cultures and other constructed groups, and incorporating those suggestions into organizational operations and practices
- Organizational "proficiency and responsiveness" by actively enhancing culturally competent services based on research initiatives and disseminating the findings, fostering diversity relationships, and acting as an advocate

The literature reflects several core strategies that the staff of domestic violence organizations may engage in to begin, maintain, or enhance their organizations' cultural proficiency. All are designed to facilitate the creation of an organizational culture that actively values and respects the diversity of women who are survivors of domestic violence and members of a historically marginalized population. Examples of these strategies include:

- Maintaining an atmosphere that welcomes women from diverse cultural backgrounds
- Conducting periodic self-assessments of cultural competency
- Developing an action plan for achieving cultural competency with clearly defined goals, objectives, benchmark competencies, and implementation and evaluation plans
- Institutionalizing cultural competency knowledge and practices
- Developing participatory, collaborative partnerships with communities and tribes
- Utilizing various formal and informal mechanisms to facilitate community and consumer involvement in designing, implementing, and planning service delivery systems and cultural competency standards
- Ensuring that staff members at all levels and across all disciplines receive ongoing cultural diversity education and training
- Exploring and adopting service delivery models that reflect a solid understanding and appreciation of cultural diversity, so that service is responsive to clients' needs and are delivered in a manner compatible with their cultural beliefs and practices, physical abilities, and preferred language (Diller 2007; Lum 2007; Cross et al. 1989).

COMMUNITY INVOLVEMENT

Although perhaps not readily apparent, significant diversity is also present in communities. Indeed, a major principle of cultural competence and community engagement is the recognition that communities determine their own needs. The National Association of Black Social Workers' (2002) "Position Statement on Domestic Violence," based on the premise of "collective work and responsibility," reflects a similar paradigm. The Statement asserts that the African American community has a collective responsibility to eradicate domestic violence and that culturally competent community intervention must be aimed at helping African Americans find solid mechanisms to fortify healthy and stable relationships. Organizational staff may use "asset mapping" to identify community members who are domestic violence survivors or advocates against intimate partner violence and have the interest and ability to listen to, lead, and organize their fellow peers (Diller 2007; Lum 2007; Cross et al. 1989).

According to Symington (2004, p. 7), when working in a diverse community one needs to assess the various forms of identity that are critical organizing principles for a community, and often cue the extent to which women and girls in the community are oppressed and marginalized. Culturally competent organizational personnel are aware of the influence of a community's historical intersection of social, economic, generational, race, gender, disability, social class, and sexuality in the development of members' self-identity. Therefore, to be effective in advancing the safety and security of women and girls in the community, culturally competent staff, organizations, and agencies must be attentive to the community's influence on identity. Knowledge of and respect for community dynamics is essential to culturally competent domestic violence practice in communities (Diller 2007; Lum 2007; Cross et al. 1989).

Domestic violence staff and organizations should carefully consider the values and principles shaping their approaches to providing services and support and governing their participation in, and engagement of, the diverse communities where they are located. Culturally competent staff and organizations must understand that citizens and women from these communities are inherently able to recognize their own problems and intervene appropriately on their own behalf (Goode 2001; Diller 2007; Lum 2007; Cross et al. 1989). Consequently asset mapping helps communities focus on the strengths of the residents rather than their needs (Kretzman and McKnight 1993).

When working in diverse communities, culturally competent staff and organizations must also allow women survivors of domestic violence to:

- Determine their own needs based upon their particular diverse intersectional contextual realities
- Fully participate in, and benefit from, decision making, problem solving, and planning initiatives, as well as implementing these strategies
- Transfer the knowledge and skills gained from collaboration with domestic violence organizations
- Engage in collaborative working relationships with natural, informal support and helping networks such as advocacy associations (Diller 2007; Lum 2007; Cross et al. 1989).

INTERSECTIONALITY: AN ENHANCING FRAME FOR CULTURAL COMPETENCY

In the earlier years of the feminist movement's quest for acceptance and its desire that all women speak collectively and in unison about their oppression and marginalization, pioneering feminists promoted the idea that gender was the linchpin of oppression, regardless of one's membership in multiple and layered categorical communities (Symington 2004; Collins 1998a, 1998b; hooks 1984). This "universal woman" perspective merely promoted a gender identity and an anti-categorical identity for other sociopolitical groups. Although the "universal woman" campaign may have been needed for sociopolitical reasons, women from other oppressed and marginalized groups challenged its assertion of sameness. As a result, the concept of intersectionality surfaced, as a group of black revisionist feminists challenged the assertion of radical white feminists that "gender" was the primary factor determining a woman's fate and that women were a homogeneous category sharing essentially the same life experiences (hooks 1984; Collins 1998a, 1998b; Appleby, Colon, and Hamilton 2007; Hall 2000; Schiele 2007).

As early as 1977 the Combahee River Collective, a black lesbian feminist organization, pointed out the futility of privileging a single dimension of our lives as if it constituted all life experiences. These women expressed their awareness that their lives were profoundly shaped by the simultaneous (an earlier term for intersectionality) influences of race, class, gender, and sexuality and their commitment to struggle against racial, sexual, sexual orientation, and class oppression (Brah and Phoenix 2004). Thus these women advanced intersectionality to encourage a deeper understanding of the experiences of African American women by looking at the intra-categorical variations of their identities as well as our inter-categorical variations. The intersectionality framework challenged analyses and conclusions of more limited dimensions that emerged from African American-centered, male-centered, and White, middle-class, feminist movements (Chronister 2006; Mann and Huffman 2005; Collins 2000). Thus a culturally competent practitioner working with individuals from diverse sociopolitical backgrounds and identities must understand and appreciate that our lived experiences are influenced by the multilayered variations of our human existence. Further, the intersection of these multilayered variations of one's existence influences the nature and extent of one's sociopolitical oppression or marginalization. Based on this notion, culturally competent practitioners must understand the variations within, as well as between, groups of women survivors of intimate partner violence.

WHAT IS INTERSECTIONALITY?

Intersectionality is a conceptual framework, a methodology for practice and research, and a catalyst for social and economic justice agendas to address social issues, such as those affecting women in our society who experience intimate partner violence. The intersectionality framework acknowledges that women have multiple and layered identifies derived from biological inheritance, social relations, political struggles, economic status, and societal power structure. For example, the framework helps us to be aware that a woman who suffers domestic violence at the hands of her intimate partner at home may be a well-respected surgeon in the community (McCall 2005; Brah and Phoenix 2004; Symington 2004; Collins 1998a, 1998b; Crenshaw 1994; hooks 1984).

Thus, through this framework, we can examine and describe the ways in which various socially and culturally constructed categories interact on multiple levels and how these intersections contribute to unique experiences of oppression and marginalization, as well as privilege in society (Symington 2004). Intersectionality does not regard traditional factors or premises of oppression and marginalization within society (e.g., those based on race and ethnicity, gender, religion, nationality, sexual orientation, class privileges, and physical ability) as independently instructive. Instead, those factors are viewed as intersecting with one another at multiple points, creating systemic oppression and marginalization that reflects the "intersection" of multiple forms of discrimination (McCall 2005; Crenshaw 1994; Collins 1998a, 1998b; hooks 1984).

Crenshaw (1994) and Collins (2000) contend that social and cultural patterns of oppression are not only interrelated but are bound together and influenced by the intersectional systems of society, such as race, gender, socioeconomic status, and ethnicity. Therefore, simple acknowledgment that a woman lives in a sexist society is insufficient information to describe her experience; instead, it is essential to know the total dimensions of her reality, including, for example, her cultural orientation, race, sexual orientation, age, socioeconomic status, and so on. Moreover, intersectionality suggests that the woman consequently experiences discrete forms of expressed oppression, shaped by interactional relationship among and between these categorical factors.

A woman's lived experiences, therefore, reflect the complex, irreducible realities that result when multiple social, political, cultural, and experiential axes of differentiation interact in shaping our lived experiences (Collins 2000; Crenshaw 1994; Collins 1998a, 1998b; Brah and Phoenix 2004, p. 76; Sokoloff and Dupont 2005). In other words, an intersectional perspective suggests that to fully understand the oppression of women, one must understand the multidimensional, socially constructed categorization that influenced the experiences of women in general, but, specifically, those experienced by each woman who is a survivor of intimate partner violence.

An intersectionality conceptual framework promotes greater emphasis on multilayered variations within a group as opposed to the traditional focus on variations between groups which all too often stifles a holistic multidimensional understanding of one's lived experiences. The traditional approach that compares differences between groups reinforces the notion that one group may be used as the criterion against which another group is compared. This approach continues the oppression and marginalization of those who are different from the dominant criterion comparative group. As discussed in the next section, an intersectionality conceptual framework enhances one's understanding and cultural competence in our practice with diverse communities in general but especially women and particularly women survivors of intimate partner violence as opposed to the continued oppression and marginalization of women.

WHY AN INTERSECTIONALITY CONCEPTUAL FRAMEWORK?

Using intersectionality as a framework helps us recognize and understand multiple categorical identifiers and uncover the various forms of discrimination and oppression that result from the interactional combination of these categorical identities so that we can work competently with women in domestic violence situations (Symington 2004). We view the interaction of multilayered categorical identities as producing substantively distinct differences between and within those identities, as well as producing variable increases in discrimination and oppression. For example, the lived experiences of an African American mother with five children who is unemployed, has limited education, and is living in a rural southern community are substantively different from her African American counterpart who has no children and is employed as a bank teller in an urban city in Michigan.

When examining and understanding within-group (intra-categorical) and between-group (inter-categorical) variations, the aim is to reveal meaningful distinctions and similarities for the purpose of addressing the oppression and discrimination of women victimized by domestic violence. Equally important, an intersectionality perspective helps us to better understand and assess the impact of these converging identities on access to opportunities, which is further complicated by the impact of laws, policies, programs, and practice initiatives on the aspects of our lives that are inextricably linked together to form our identity (Symington 2004; McCall 2005). Consider, for example, an undocumented immigrant female non-English-speaking domestic worker from El Salvador, who is sexually assaulted and physically and financially abused by a husband who is a naturalized U.S. citizen. It is the intersectionality of her multilayered identities (female, poor, foreign citizen, non-native language speaker) that place her in a vulnerable position to incur abuse and oppression. The additional intersection of the policies and laws (e.g., public housing policies, employment policies, citizenship laws, policies of shelters for abused women) that further define the identity and vulnerability of this particular female immigrant, based on the extent of responsiveness to her specific needs. A change in one identity layer—for instance, citizenship status rather than undocumented immigrant—would likely alter how the woman would be effectively served by a domestic violence organization, resulting in a different intersection with policies and socioeconomic dynamics (eligibility for legal employment with at least a minimum wage) (Symington 2004; Brah and Phoenix 2004; Sokoloff and Dupont 2005; McCall 2005).

The intersectionality conceptual framework replaces dichotomous, binary thinking about power by focusing on specific contexts, distinct experiences, and the qualitative aspects of equality, discrimination, and justice, permitting us to work simultaneously on behalf of ourselves and others (Symington 2004). Intersectionality is an important conceptual paradigm for helping us appreciate the need for more competent professionals, services, and programs when working with women victimized by intimate partner violence. Intersectionality, therefore, is an indispensable conceptual paradigm to guide our future practice, policy, advocacy, and research agendas and actions, enabling us to become competent practitioners in our fight to eradicate violence against women and their children within all the dimensions of diversity (Symington 2004: Sokoloff and Dupont 2005; McCall 2005).

Competence to work effectively with survivors of intimate partner violence within the context of their particular individual diversity depends on a thorough assessment that initially and continuously captures the complexity of the interwoven issues of their multilayered categorical identification. All aspects of professional practice must be based on a complete picture of the social, economic, political, and cultural realities of women in domestic violence situations. Without an intersectional perspective, our advocacy, interventions, and program initiatives cannot and will not achieve their full intended potential (Symington 2004: Sokoloff and Dupont 2005; McCall 2005).

INTERSECTIONALITY: AN ESSENTIAL DIMENSION OF CULTURAL COMPETENCY

A major axiom of the intersectionality conceptual framework is that what we think determines what we do and how we do it. Thus the application of an intersectionality conceptualization in our quest to become more culturally sensitive and competent in our domestic violence work requires us to think differently about identity and the multilayered intersection of identity, equality, and power (Symington 2004). For example, when working with female survivors of intimate partner violence, advocates and social work practitioners must focus on all the points of intersection, complexity, dynamic processes, and structures that define these women's access to rights and opportunities rather than on one definitive category or isolated issue. We must view the eradication of oppres-

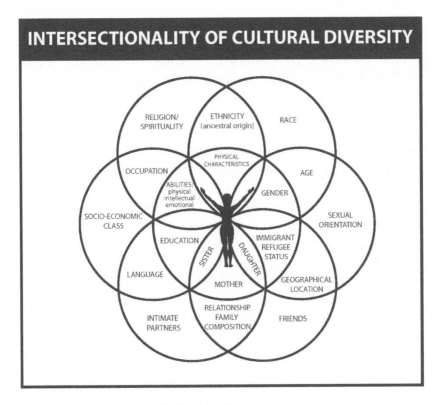

FIGURE 1.2. Intersectionality of cultural diversity.

sion, marginalization, and discrimination and the celebration of diversity in all its complexities as fundamental to a culturally competent practice.

Additionally, this conceptual framework must permeate all aspects of practice, advocacy, and policy initiatives, beginning with the initial assessment. Faulty assessment leads to faulty planning, programming, policies, and practice initiatives. For instance, a researcher using an intersectionality approach incorporates the qualitative personal accounts and testimonies from survivors of domestic violence as well as a quantitative multivariate analysis of disaggregated data to reflect the multilayered identities of women. Our assessment and research analysis should aim to reveal how practices and policies shape the lives of women impacted by domestic violence rather than exaggerating the differences between women from different social and political realities. Therefore, when analyzing the impact of socioeconomic status on the contextual experiences of women in domestic violence situations, we would not stop at a finding that domestic violence is disproportionately higher among the poorest groups of women; instead, we would explore the historical policies and practices that have contributed to life experiences fostering intimate partner victimization, including limited economic privileges, political dynamics, policy, practice, and programmatic designs and implementation (Symington 2004; McCall 2005).

As illustrated in Figure 1.2, women must be viewed as having multilayered, sociopolitical identities and dimensions stemming from race, color, age, social class, sexual orientation, abilities, religion, spirituality, ethnicity, nationality, physical characteristics, culture, history, geographical location, language, and migrant status, and yet still be seen as uniquely whole. Thus women survivors of intimate partner violence must be viewed as exhibiting complex, interlocking sociopolitical identities and group memberships that are all equally important in shaping women's lived experiences. The impact of these multilayered identities on women's lived experiences is not simply cumulative; each sociopolitical multilayered identity cannot be extracted from all the other dimensions of identity (Lum 2007). As stated by Brah and Phoenix, (2004, p. 76), our diverse identities cannot be separated out into discrete and pure strands; they all intersect and interlock to define who we are and how the dominate society interacts with individuals—in this case, women survivors of intimate partner violence. In other words, does the dominate society value and respect, oppress and marginalize, or accept and prize diversity among its citizens? When a society is reluctant to acknowledge and celebrate diversity, members of multilayered diverse groups and of dominant societal groups both suffer. When members of diverse groups live in a society that promotes policies, laws, and practices that discriminate, oppress, and marginalize people who are different from the dominant society, they often struggle with both externalized and internalized oppression.

CONCLUDING THOUGHTS

The ubiquity of domestic violence virtually assures that it will appear with different actors, in different forms, and in different contexts. It is not surprising, therefore, that the domestic violence movement, as in other professional arenas, is engaging in dialogue around the development of strategies and profiles that address those dynamics and variations. This area of practice is clearly not a one-size-fits-all endeavor. The issue is complex and not easily resolved, and the challenge is how best to accommodate all the possible sizes.

We have suggested enhancing the cultural competence paradigm by adding an intersectionality framework to better meet the needs of the diverse population of domestic violence survivors. Women come to us with multilayered identities that are shaped, reshaped, and sometimes dismantled by individual factors intersecting with one another and with political and socioeconomic issues that often precipitate marginalization, oppression, and discrimination. These intersections create dynamics beyond the individualized factors and are different for each domestic violence survivor. Therefore, effective practices with women survivors of intimate partner violence seeking our assistance deserve this more nuanced, reality-based approach. As you read the following chapters on diverse groups of women survivors of intimate partner violence, continue to apply your intersectionality-infused cultural competence lens to further promote your understanding of these women's lived contextual experiences.

RESOURCES AND WEB SITES

Many resources on the Internet provide information on cultural competence, and they come from various disciplines including social work, education, medicine, public health, and mental health.

INCITE! Women of Color Against Violence
P.O. Box 226
Redmond, WA 98073
Phone: (484) 932–3166
INCITE! Women of Color Against Violence is a national activist organization of radical feminists of color advancing a movement to end violence against women of color and our communities through direct action, critical dialogue, and grass-roots organizing.

National Association of Social Workers
750 First Street, NE • Suite 700 •
Washington, DC 20002–4241
Phone; (202) 408–8600
Web site: http://www.socialworkers.org/pressroom/2002/020502.asp
NASW cultural competency standards; requires membership for access.

National Center for Cultural Competence
Georgetown University Center for Children and Human Development

Mailing Address	Address for Visitors and Delivery
Box 571485	3300 Whitehaven Street, NW, Suite 3300
Washington, DC 20057–1485	Washington, DC 20007

Voice: (202) 687–5387 or
Phone: (800) 788–2066;
TTY: (202) 687–5503
Fax: (202) 687–8899
E-mail: cultural@georgetown.edu
Web site: http://www.georgetown.edu/research/gucdc/nccc/
Resource site with self-assessments for organizational cultural competence that contains a comprehensive searchable resource database.

National Consumer Supporter
2000 N. Beauregard Street, 6th Floor
Alexandria, VA 22311
Phone: (800) 969–6642
Fax: (703) 684–5968
E-mail: ConsumerTA@nmha.org
Web site: http://www.ncstac.org/content/culturalcompetency/
A review of best practices for culturally competent consumer self-help programs.

U.S. Department of Health and Human Services
Office of Minority Health
Tower Building
1101 Wootton Parkway, Suite 600
Rockville, Maryland 20852
Web site: http://www.omhrc.gov/clas/index.htm
National standards for culturally and linguistically appropriate services (CLAS) in health care.

Women of Color Network
6400 Flank Drive, Suite 1300
Harrisburg, PA 17112
Phone: (800) 537–2238, ext 137
Fax: (717) 545–9456
E-mail: wocn@pcadv.org
The mission of the Women of Color Network (WOCN) is to provide and enhance leadership capacity and resources that promote the activities of women

of color advocates and activists within the Sovereign Nations, the United States, and U.S. Territories to address the elimination of violence against women and families.

REFERENCES

Andersen, M. L., and P. H. Collins. (2004). *Race, Class, and Gender: An Anthology* (6th Ed.). Belmont, CA: Wadsworth.

Appleby, G. A., E. Colon, and J. Hamilton. (2007). *Diversity, Oppression, and Social Functioning* (2nd Ed.). New York: Pearson Education.

Brah, A. and Phoenix, A. (2004) Ain't I a woman? Revisiting intersectionality. *Journal of International Women's Studies*, 5(3), 75–86.

Carpenter-Song, E. A., M. N. Schwallie, and J. Longhofer. (2007). Cultural competence reexamined: Critique and directions for the future. *Psychiatric Services*, 58(10), 1362–1365.

Chronister, K. M. (2006). The intersection of social class and race in community intervention research with women domestic violence survivors. *American Journal of Community Psychology*, 37, 175–182.

Collins, P. H. (1998a). Intersections of race, class, gender, and nation: Some implications for black family studies. *Journal of Comparative Family Studies*, 29(1), 27–36.

——. (1998b). The tie that binds: Race, gender, and U.S. violence. *Ethnic and Racial Studies*, 21(5), 917–938.

——. (2000). *Black Feminist Thought: Knowledge, Consciousness, and the Politics of Empowerment* (2nd Ed.). New York: Routledge.

Compton, B. R., and B. Galaway. (1999). *Social Work Processes* (6th Ed.). Pacific Grove, Calif.: Brooks/Cole.

Council on Social Work Education. (2001). *Educational Policy and Accreditation Standards*. Alexandria, VA: Author.

Council on Social Work Education. (2008). *Educational Policy and Accreditation Standards*. Retrieved May 20, 2008, from http://www.cswe.org/NR/rdonlyres/2A81732E-1776–4175-AC42–65974E96BE66/0/2008EducationalPolicyandAccreditationStandards.pdf.

Crenshaw, K. W. (1994). Mapping the margins: Intersectionality, identity politics, and violence against women of color. In M. Fineman and R. Mykitiuk (Eds.), *The Public Nature of Private Violence* (pp. 93–118). New York: Routledge.

Cross, T., B. Bazron, K. Dennis, and M. Isaacs. (1989). *Towards a Culturally Competent System of Care*, Vol. 1. Washington, DC: Georgetown University Child Development Center, CASSP Technical Assistance Center.

Davis, P., and B. Donald. (1997). *Multicultural Counseling Competencies: Assessment, Evaluation, Education and Training, and Supervision.* Thousand Oaks, CA: Sage.

Devoe, W., and E. G. Schlesinger. (1999). *Ethnic-sensitive Social Work Practice* (5th Ed.). Boston: Allyn and Bacon.

Diller, J. V. (2007). *Cultural Diversity: A Primer for the Human Services* (3rd Ed.). Belmont, CA: Brooks/Cole.

Eiser, A. R., and G. Ellis. (2007). Viewpoint: Cultural competence and the African American experience with health care: The case for specific content in cross-cultural education. *Academic Medicine,* 82(2), 176–183.

Feinberg, C. (2004). Improvement in the legal response to domestic violence. In L. Volpe (Ed.), *Contemporary Issues Companion: Battered Women* (pp. 43–74). San Diego: Greenhaven.

Goode, T. (2001). *Policy Brief 4: Engaging Communities to Realize the Vision of One Hundred Percent Access and Zero Health Disparities: A Culturally Competent Approach.* Washington, DC: National Center for Cultural Competence, Georgetown University Center for Child and Human Development.

Guadalupe, K. L., and D. Lum. (2005). *Multidimensional Contextual Practice: Diversity and Transcendence.* Belmont, CA: Brooks/Cole.

Gutierrez, L., A. Yeakley, and R. Ortega. (2000). Educating social workers for practice with Latinos: Issues for a new millennium. *Journal of Social Work Education,* 36, 541–560.

Hall, R. E. (2000). The racial canons of American sociology: Identity across the lifespan as biracial alternative. *American Sociologist,* 31(1), 86–93.

Harper, K. and J. Lantz. (1996). *Cross-Cultural Practice: Social Work with Diverse Populations.* New York: Lyceum Books

hooks, b. (1984). *Feminist Theory: From Margin to Center* (2nd Ed.). Cambridge, MA: South End, 1984.

Kelly, J. B., and M. P. Johnson. (2008). Differentiation among types of intimate partner violence: Research update and implications for interventions. *Family Court Review,* 46(3), 476–499.

Kretzman, J. R., and J. L. McKnight. (1993). *Building Communities from the Inside Out: A Path Toward Finding and Mobilizing a Community's Assets.* Chicago, IL: ACTA.

Lo, H., and K. P. Fung. (2003). Culturally competent psychotherapy. *Canadian Journal of Psychiatry,* 48(3), 161–170.

Lum, D. (2007). *Culturally Competent Practice: A Framework for Understanding Diverse Groups and Justice Issues* (3rd Ed.). Belmont, CA: Brooks/Cole.

McCall, L. (2005). The complexity of intersectionality *Journal of Women in Culture and Society,* 30(3), 1771–1800.

National Association of Social Workers. (1999). *Code of Ethics*. Washington, DC: Author.

——. National Association of Social Workers. (2001). NASW *Standards for Cultural Competence in Social Work Practice*. Washington, DC: Author.

Okum, B. F., J. Fried, and M. L. Okum. (1999). *Understanding Diversity: A Learning-as-Practice Primer*. Pacific Grove, CA: Brooks/Cole.

Pederson, P. B. (2002). The making of a culturally competent counselor. In W. J. Lonner, D. L. Dinnel, S. A. Hayes, and D. N. Sattler (Eds.), *On-line Readings in Psychology and Culture* (Unit 10, Chapter 2). Retrieved May 31, 2006, from http://www.ac.wwu.edu/~culture.

Richie, B. (2000). A Black feminist reflection on the antiviolence movement. *Signs*, 25, 1122–1137.

Savory, V. (2007). Racial indigestion: Black immigrant identities in late 19th and early 20th century America. *International Journal of Diversity*, 6(4), 69–74.

Sokoloff, N. J. (2005). Alternative visions to ending domestic violence: Using a race, class, gender, sexuality perspective Paper presented at the Annual Meeting of the American Sociological Association, Marriott Hotel, Loews Philadelphia Hotel, Philadelphia, PA. Retrieved April 22, 2008, from http://www.allacademic.com/meta/p18990_index.html.

Sokoloff, N. J., and I. Dupont. (2005). Domestic violence at the intersections of race, class and gender: Challenges and contributions to understanding violence against marginalized women in diverse communities. *Violence Against Women*, 11(1), 38–64.

Sumter, M. (2006). Domestic violence and diversity: A call for multicultural services. *Journal of Health and Human Services Administration*, 29(2), 173–190.

Symington, A. (2004). Intersectionality: A tool for gender and economic justice: Facts and issues. *Women's Rights and Economic Change*, no 9 (August): 1–8. Ontario, Canada: Association for Women's Rights in Development (Retrieved March 4, 2008, from http://www.awid.org).

Titterton, M. (1992). Managing threats to welfare: The search for a new paradigm. *Journal of Social Policy*, 21, 1–23.

U.S. Census Bureau. (2002a). *Census Basics*. Washington, DC: U.S. Government Printing Office.

——. (2002b). *Demographic Trends in the 20th Century*. Washington, DC: U.S. Government Printing Office.

——. (2007a). Population profile of the United States: Dynamic version: Race and Hispanic origin in 2005. Retrieved May 10, 2008, from http://www.census.gov/population/pop-profile/dynamic/RACEHO.pdf.

——. (2007b). Population profile of the United States: Dynamic version: Families and living arrangements in 2005. Retrieved May 10, 2008, from http://www.census.gov/population/pop-profile/dynamic/FamiliesLA.pdf.

——. (2007c). Population profile of the United States: Dynamic version: Poverty in 2005. Retrieved May 10, 2008, from http://www.census.gov/population/pop-profile/dynamic/poverty.pdf.

Vann, A. A. (2003). *Developing Culturally-Relevant Responses to Domestic Abuse: Asha Family Services, Inc.* (Pp 1–48). Harrisburg, PA: National Resource Center on Domestic Violence.

Warrier, S. (2008). "It's in their culture": Fairness and cultural considerations in domestic violence. *Family Court Review, 46*(3), 537–542.

2

UNDERSTANDING DOMESTIC VIOLENCE

A Primer

Fran S. Danis and Shreya Bhandari

THE SECOND wave of the feminist movement that began in the late 1960s created opportunities for women to share their personal life stories with one another. Women learned that the experiences they thought were unique to them were, in fact, also happening to other women. As women shared with one another, they also learned that the physical, sexual, and emotional abuse they experienced was not only done by total strangers but also by their intimate partners. The "personal" became "political," and feminist activists opened rape crisis hotlines, safe houses, and shelters for women who had been physically, sexually, or emotionally battered by their male partners. Advocates also spoke publicly to raise awareness and to establish laws holding abusers accountable and to increase safety for battered women and their children. The modern battered women's movement was born (Schechter 1982).

We have learned much in the years since domestic violence was defined and recognized as a social problem. Researchers and advocates for abused women continue to explore the experiences women share, the risk factors for abuse, factors protecting against abuse, the consequences for women who are abused, how they seek help, what help is available, and what help is most effective.

This book recognizes that not all abused women are alike. Women's perceptions and reactions to abuse, as well as the help available to them, are influenced by the lens through which they see the world and the intersectionality of the different cultural influences on their lives. These cultural influences include race, ethnicity, age, citizenship status, (dis)ability, sexual orientation, religion, military involvement, and geographical location. Each of these will influence a woman's reactions to abuse, and the personal and institutional resources available to assist her. This book investigates these differences and examines how women call upon the strengths of their cultures, religion, and experience of the world to assist in their survival and resiliency.

This chapter addresses the prevalence and consequences of abuse, policy, and practice issues, including the basic questions of why men hit and why women stay, and provides social workers, advocates, and other health and human services workers with a framework for understanding domestic violence so that the differences and commonalities highlighted within each chapter have greater clarity and clearer context. As readers learn about the different issues that may be unique to persons in various "categories" it is important to understand that, even within these categories, not all women's situations are the same.

DEFINITIONS AND TERMINOLOGY

Most experts define "domestic violence" as a pattern of coercive behaviors to control one's partner through physical abuse, the threat of physical abuse, repeated psychological abuse, sexual assault, progressive social isolation, deprivation, intimidation, or economic coercion. Domestic violence is perpetrated by adults or adolescents against their intimate partners in current or former dating, married, or cohabiting relationships of heterosexuals, gay men, lesbians, bisexuals, and transgendered persons.

The terms "domestic violence," "domestic abuse," and "intimate partner violence" are often used interchangeably. "Interpersonal violence" can refer to any violent act between individuals, irrespective of their relationship. "Family violence" refers to violence perpetrated between family members and includes child abuse, domestic abuse, sibling abuse, and elder abuse. Violence against women or gender-based violence targets girls and women throughout the life span and includes sexual assault and female genital mutilation. International organizations, including the United Nations, refer to violence against women as "gender-based" violence and view this behavior as a human rights violation. Although this terminology identifies women as the primary victims of violence, it does not take into account the violence that women perpetrate against other women in lesbian relationships, or that women use against male partners, or that men perpetrate against male partners. The term "intimate partner violence" has been promoted as a more inclusive way to describe domestic violence, but its obvious drawback is the failure to acknowledge the gendered nature of the violence. Because this is a multifaceted problem requiring the focus of many different disciplines, consensus on the terminology has not yet and may never be achieved.

TACTICS OF ABUSE: POWER AND CONTROL

The definitions discussed above refer to domestic violence as being a "pattern of coercive control including physical abuse or the threat of physical abuse." Physical abuse includes hitting, shoving, pushing, punching, kicking, tripping, biting, twisting arms, beating, throwing or pushing people out of cars, throwing or causing people to fall down stairs, pulling hair, choking, and using or threatening to use a weapon such as a gun, knife, baseball bat, car, or lit cigarette. Many people may not consider that a push or a shove is an act of violence, yet it may represent an escalation of an attempt to gain power and control over a partner.

The Power and Control Wheel (see Figure 2.1) was developed in Duluth, Minnesota, by a support group for women who were being abused by their partners (Minnesota Program Development, Inc. n.d.). The women wanted to share their experiences of how their partners used violence to wield power over them and control their behavior. Besides physical abuse, the women had been subjected to emotional abuse including constant belittling and being called derogatory names, as well as financial abuse such as keeping the women from getting and keeping jobs or the money earned from jobs, and giving the victims small allowances and making them beg for money. I once had a client with a law degree, and the night before a job interview her husband would beat her severely around her face so that she always had to cancel her appointment. This happened time and again, and she never worked as an attorney. In fact, she never worked at all.

Sexual violence, which women often hesitate to disclose, is often the most severe example of domestic violence and involves forcing a partner to have sex against her will, penetrating her with objects, or forcing her to have unsafe and unprotected sex with the abuser and others.

Batterers often use their children as weapons by threatening to take them away from their mothers or reporting the mothers as unfit to child welfare authorities. Batterers are also adept at isolating women from their families and social support networks by sabotaging their partner's relationships with friends and family or making others feel unwanted and unwelcome around them. Male abusers often believe that they are lords or masters over women and deserve to be waited on. It is their responsibility, they claim, to correct their wives' and children's bad behavior: "I wouldn't have to hit you if only you would do such and such or if only you didn't do such and such." The woman often feels like a servant who is always walking on eggshells, fearing that her partner may harm her or her children, pets, family, or even himself to get her to do what he wants. Listening to the experiences of women who are abused is often painful and angering, as it is hard to fathom how people can be so callous and harmful to those who love them.

Although the Power and Control Wheel has become a standard way of explaining the tactics of abuse, it does not capture the experiences of all women. For example, the wheel does not include spiritual or religious abuse (Bent-Goodley and Fowler 2006). Women have reported that abusers may prevent them from attending church and church events, interpret certain scriptures to justify their abuse, or manipulate the women's status within their church community (ibid.).

FIGURE 2.1. Domestic Violence Power and Control Wheel developed by Domestic Abuse Intervention Project (Duluth, MN).

PREVALENCE AND INCIDENTS OF DOMESTIC ABUSE

It is difficult to get a precise picture of the prevalence of domestic abuse in the general population and the number of violent incidents that occur each year. Only a few studies, such as the National Violence Against Women Survey (Tjaden and Thoennes 1998) and the National Crime Victimization Survey (Bachman and Saltzman 1995), use samples representative of the general population. These studies offer insight into the prevalence of abuse as well as information about the specific incidents of abuse in a given time period or across a lifetime. Many other studies examine the prevalence of domestic violence in certain categories of the population, such as people seeking public assistance through Temporary Aid to Needy Families (Brandwein 1998; Lyon 2002) or the number of families referred for child abuse services that also involve abuse of the mother (Edleson 1999).

At the local level, law enforcement may keep track of the number of calls related to domestic violence that they respond to as well as the number of arrests made in these cases. Law enforcement statistics are compiled by states and submitted to the FBI for inclusion in the Uniform Crime Report. Hospitals and public health clinics may keep records on the number of people that enter their emergency rooms seeking care for injuries that resulted from violence. Injuries that were incurred through domestic violence are categorized as intentional injuries by state health departments and the CDC Office of Injury Prevention. Local domestic violence shelters keep data on the number of telephone hotline calls they receive, the number of women and children they shelter, and the number of people who receive nonresidential counseling. They may report this information to their funding sources and to state coalitions of community-based domestic violence service providers. State-level data may also be compiled and shared with national domestic violence organizations so that they may share these facts with Congress and the national media on the number of women and children that have sought help for this problem each year.

Because much of this violence occurs in the privacy of the home, it is important to recognize that many incidents go unreported, and therefore incident reports do not reveal all the cases. Prevalence studies using representative samples provide a better sense of how many people are directly affected by the problem. Listed below are statistics that every social worker and advocate should know. The Family Violence Prevention Fund Web site (www.endabuse.org) maintains a list of the most recent prevalence information.

- At least one in every three women worldwide has been beaten, coerced into sex, or otherwise abused during her lifetime (Heise, Ellsberg, and Gottemoeller 1999).
- Approximately one in five female high school students in the U.S. report being physically or sexually abused by a dating partner (Silverman et al. 2001).
- The Bureau of Justice Statistics indicate that intimate partner violence is primarily a crime against women; in 2001, for example, women accounted for 85 percent of the victims of intimate partner violence (588,490 total) and men accounted for approximately 15 percent of the victims (103,220 total). Females are five to eight times more likely than males to be victimized by an intimate partner (Rennison 2003).
- The National Violence Against Women Survey estimates that 5.9 million physical assaults against women occur annually, with approximately three-quarters (76 percent) of those incidents perpetrated by current or former husbands, cohabiting partners, or dates (Tjaden and Thoennes 1998).
- The National Violence Against Women Survey also reported that one-quarter of surveyed women, compared to 8 percent of surveyed men, said they were raped or physically assaulted by a current or former spouse, cohabiting partner, or date at some time in their life (Tjaden and Thoennes 1998).
- The National Crime Victimization Survey found that nearly 30 percent of all female homicide victims were killed by their husbands, former husbands, or boyfriends, in contrast to just over 3 percent of male homicide victims killed by their wives, former wives, or girlfriends (Bachman and Saltzman 1995).
- Domestic violence incidents involving emergency room treatment were four times higher than the estimates of domestic violence that come to the attention of law enforcement agencies (Rand 1997).
- With only 69 percent of eligible U.S. domestic violence programs reporting in one 24-hour period (September 25, 2007), 53,203 adult women were living in shelters and 19,432 women called crisis telephone hotlines. Programs also reported the inability to accommodate 7,707 requests for assistance because of lack of resources. During the same reporting period, the National Domestic Violence Hotline answered 1,150 calls (National Network to End Domestic Violence 2008).

WHAT ARE THE CONSEQUENCES OF DOMESTIC VIOLENCE?

Abuse has been linked to negative health outcomes, including reduced general health, digestive problems (diarrhea, spastic colon, constipation, irritable bowel syndrome, nausea, loss of appetite, eating binges, and abdominal and stomach pain), urinary tract infection, kidney infection, and problems in urination, as well as severe menstrual problems, dysmenorrhea, sexual dysfunction, headaches, migraines, fainting , seizures, convulsions, back pain, chronic neck pain, influenza or cold, stuffy or runny nose, and hypertension (Campbell, Dienemann, and Jones 2002; Coker et al. 2002; McCauley, Kern, and Kolodner 1995).

Forced sex particularly may result in vaginal infection causing discharge and itching, sexually transmitted diseases, vaginal bleeding, fibroids, reduced sexual desire, painful intercourse, chronic pelvic pain, and urinary tract infection (Campbell and Soeken 1999; Koss, Koss, and Woodruff 1991; Leserman et al. 1998). The correlation between intimate partner violence and unintended pregnancies, as well as sexually transmitted diseases including HIV, can be explained through men's control over women's sexuality and verbal sexual degradation resulting in women's lower negotiating power in the use of condoms or contraception (Campbell and Soeken 1999).

Apart from the physical symptoms, a range of negative mental health outcomes result from abuse, including post-traumatic stress disorder (PTSD), suicidal tendencies (Golding 1999), depression, anxiety, and insomnia (Mercy et al. 2003). People suffering from post-traumatic stress disorder may exhibit symptoms such as difficulty falling asleep or staying asleep, irritability or outbursts of anger, difficulty concentrating, hypervigilance, exaggerated startle response, diminished interest or participation in events, detachment, restricted range of affect, and a sense of foreshortened future.

Immediate reactions to abuse may be shock, fear for safety, immobilization owing to terror, shame, low self-esteem (Fischbach and Herbert 1997), emotional numbness, withdrawal, and denial. Women might have painful images and dreams, flashbacks, anger, constant feeling of vulnerability, low self-esteem, self-blame, and loss of control (American Medical Association Council on Scientific Affairs 1992). Some women may also resort to substance abuse as a method to cope with abuse and avoid facing the reality of abuse in their lives (Kilpatrick et al. 1997).

These negative outcomes present serious challenges to women and may have fatal consequences for them. It is important to know, however, that women do survive abusive relationships. In the aftermath of stressful or trau-matic life experiences, many abuse victims report personal growth in the midst of coping with their adversity (Saakvitne, Tenne, and Affleck 1998). These positive changes are often referred to as "posttraumatic-" or "stress-related" growth and highlight the human capacity for transformation in even the most ominous circumstances.

IMPACT ON CHILDREN

Another serious consequence of domestic violence is the impacts on children residing in the household. No exact data exist, but it is estimated that 3.3–10 million children each year are exposed to violence involving seeing, hearing, or otherwise knowing about the abuse (Fantuzzo et al. 1997). Of these chil-dren, 30–60 percent will also be physically abused by the batterer, who may be their own parent, stepparent, or mother's intimate partner (Edleson 1999). Children 0–5 years of age may be present in the room when abuse takes place (Fantuzzo et al. 1997).

The impact of abuse on an individual child depends on the severity of the abuse, how long it continues, how frequently it occurs, and the age, gender, and temperament of the child (Edleson 2006). Responses may vary among children in the same household. Children exposed to domestic vio-lence compared to children who have not been exposed to violence may experience physical aggression, antisocial behavior, low self-esteem, anxi-ety, and depression (Cummings, Peplar, and Moore 1999; Jaffe, Wolfe, and Wilson 1990; Kolbo, Blakely, and Engelman 1996). PTSD symptoms such as the inability to concentrate and poor attention span may negatively affect a child's cognitive progress in school (Kilpatrick, Litt, and Williams 1997). Exposed children may become victims of abuse or perpetrators of abuse themselves when they get older. Men who were both abused and exposed may be 3.8 times more likely than other men to perpetrate domestic violence (Whitfield et al. 2003).

Children also have the capacity for resilient responses to living in an abu-sive and oppressive family environment. Adults who as children were exposed to their mothers' abuse report using various protective strategies to withstand and oppose a sense of powerlessness (Anderson and Danis 2006). Strategies of "withstanding" were focused on building support networks with adults at schools, churches, and in extended families, and creating mental or physical escapes and trying to create order out of chaos. Strategies of actively working to prevent or stop the violence included intervening directly with the batterer, developing their own safety plan, and physically protecting their mothers.

WHAT CAUSES DOMESTIC VIOLENCE?

Three theories that have been used to explain domestic violence include social learning (Bandura 1973; Widom 1989), feminist (Yllo 1993), and social exchange (Gelles 1993). As in most attempts to address human behavior, none of these theories or other proposed theories explain and predict all domestic violence. Most researchers have adopted an ecological framework to fit together all the influences causing domestic violence (Carlson 1984; Crowell and Burgess 1996; Edleson and Tolman 1992; Heise 1998). The ecological framework considers the influences on individuals at the individual or micro level, the relationship itself (think of two micro levels interacting with each other as well as with all the other levels), the community level (neighborhoods and local institutions, usually referred to as the meso or mezzo level), and the broader socio-cultural influences that are part of the macro level. Factors at each level contribute to the risk of perpetrating abuse. Many of these factors are considered correlates of abuse; for example, although a high correlation exists between alcohol and violence, alcohol is not considered the cause of violent behavior (Bennett and Williams, 2003). The Centers for Disease Control (n.d.) list the following risk factors for abuse:

- At the individual level, certain biological or individual experiences increase the possibility of an individual becoming an abuser. This includes exposure to violence as a child, either through witnessing male parent on female parent abuse, being directly abused, or alcohol or drug use. Persons with a history of arrest are also more likely to use violence with their intimate partner.
- At the relationship level, adherence to rigid traditional gender roles and unhealthy relationships are considered risk factors. Having peers that engage in violent behavior may normalize the use of violence against a partner.
- At the community level, exposure to violence, poverty, and low socioeconomic status are considered risk factors. Easy access to guns and unemployment are also contributors.

- At the societal level, norms granting men control over female behavior, acceptance of violence as a way to resolve conflict, the idea that masculinity is linked to dominance, honor, or aggression, and mass media and culture including films, music, advertising images all contribute to perpetuating an environment that allows for the violence against women.

While these are risk factors for perpetrating abuse, some of the risk factors for being a victim include being female, having been previously assaulted either as a child or adult, and being isolated.

BARRIERS TO SAFETY: WHY DO WOMEN STAY?

The most frequently asked question about domestic violence from the general public and social work students alike is why women stay. Many women who ask themselves if they would "put up with" violence and abuse invariably answer with a resounding no. However, the answer to why women stay reveals a complexity of influences that would inhibit anyone from just walking out the door. These influences may be rooted in the individual herself, the batterer, the culture of origin, her location, socioeconomic status, religion, and military service. The concept of "intersectionality" explains how each of these influences becomes either a junction for safety or a barrier that must be addressed.

Women are constantly engaged in assessing the risks to their personal safety (Davies, Lyon, and Monti-Catania 1998). Decisions regarding staying or leaving whether at the time of a violent incident or because of the violent relationship itself often depend on whether the woman believes she can overcome the factors that keep her with an abuser. These issues may be personal, such as how the woman will support herself and her children? Where will she go? Who will help her? What will her family and friends think of her? How will the children react? Will she be able to find a safe place or will her abuser come and find her? Some institutional factors women encounter are lack or inadequate services, affordable legal services, child care, housing, transportation, public-assistance benefits, and job-training programs. Other influences on her decision to stay or leave may be the societal messages that children should be raised in two-parent families; the stigma of being a single mother; and religious messages that marriage means "till death do you part." I often ask my classes to think of as many four-letter words that might relate to the reasons why women would stay. Table 2.1 lists some of the most common reasons why women stay.

TABLE 2.1 Reasons Women Stay

CASH	The number one reason why women stay is the economic dependency they have on the abuser (Raphael and Tolman 1997). Because batterers know that an independent income or the education to prepare for a career provides women with the option of economic self-sufficiency they often interfere with their female partners' employment or interest in gaining employment such as going back to school (Lloyd and Taluc 1999). Women who do not have a marketable work history or who have not completed a high school education may have difficulties getting employment that will provide them with a living wage. If they have children younger than school age, the costs of child care alone may significantly impact their ability to stretch their paycheck to cover the basic necessities. Women may decide to choose the economic stability of their husband's paycheck over the uncertainty of their own economic self-sufficiency. The batterer's paycheck may also come with some "perks" that the woman may not be able to provide. These "perks" may include health insurance for her and the children and a decent place to live in a safe neighborhood with good schools. Upper- and middle-class women may be particularly reluctant to lose their source of income. Along with the loss of their partner's paycheck may be the loss of a place to live. Homelessness can be a very real outcome of domestic violence (Browne and Bassuk 1997).

The Role of Public Assistance

One alternative that many women do consider is the option of welfare. The rolls of the federal Temporary Aid to Needy Families (TANF) program are filled with many abused women and their children (Lyon 2002). Federal laws allow each state the option to provide time waivers to battered women who may have difficulty finding employment by the five-year lifetime benefit cap (Postmus 2000).

KIDS	The presence of children greatly increases the complexity of the options women must consider. Having children in common insures ongoing interaction with the children's father. There are strong societal norms that support "staying together for the sake of the children." Many people believe that children need their fathers and should grow up in two-parent families. Will leaving with the children stop the abuse? Women have reported continual assaults when interacting with their ex-husbands regarding visitation (Saunders 2007). Abusers may threaten to sue for custody of the children, thereby restricting the mother's access to her children. Courts may award custody to abusers who can prove they can provide better for their children (Bancroft and Silverman 2002). The abuser may also threaten to call child welfare and report the woman for being a "bad mother." Some child protection offices have pursued removal of the children and have charged mothers with the failure to protect her children from witnessing abuse which may do more harm to children and their mothers (Spears 2000). The age of the children also influences women's decisions to stay or leave. Women with younger children who are not yet in school and unable to care for themselves are more likely to stay. As children age, enter school, and become more self-sufficient, women are more apt to leave (Kelley 2003).
HOPE	One reason women stay or return to their abuser is that he promises he will get counseling and change (Gondolf and Fisher 1988). A woman wants to believe that change is possible.
LOVE	The abuser doesn't always beat the woman. She has an investment in the relationship and still holds on to the memories of the man she fell in love with.

CONTINUED

FEAR	Leaving does not stop the abuse (Fluery, Sullivan, and Bybee 2000). The most dangerous time for a woman is when she leaves an abuser. Women are more likely to be killed when they leave (Campbell 1995). The fear of death or threats of harming her, her children, family, and pets keep women who are subjected to severe violence in the relationship. When a batterer threatens, "If I can't have you, nobody can," he should be taken seriously.
VOWS	The woman may have been raised in a tradition that does not believe in separation and divorce. She took marriage vows "for better or for worse" and believes she must endure the abuse to save her marriage at all costs.
PETS	Pets are often thought of as members of the family and abusers have manipulated women by threatening to kill their pets. Women may not want to leave their pets behind if they leave the abuser; not having a safe place to leave their pets may be a deterrent to leaving (Arkow 1996).
LOST	In long-term cases of abuse, where the abuser has isolated the woman from her family and friends, she may feel so lost that she cannot identify places where she can go for safety.
LOSS	We all have been in relationships that we knew were over but we stayed longer than we would have liked because we were waiting for the right time to discuss breaking up, or we were not ready to accept the loss of the relationship. Avoiding the inevitable grief and loss associated with leaving a relationship may be a contributing factor to women staying.
SHAM(E):	Women feel an incredible sense of shame and stigma associated with being abused. These feelings may immobilize women who do not want their families, friends, neighbors, or co-workers to know about their experience (Brown 2006). Women are socialized to believe that they are responsible for the emotional health of their marriages and families. Consequently they blame themselves when things go wrong within the family. To admit that there are problems is to admit to failure. When working with an abused woman, it is essential to reduce shame and stigma by helping her see that the abuse is not her fault. Shame may be the abuser's ultimate tool of internalized oppression. If he can get the victim to blame herself for the abuse, she is easier to control and manipulate. She may not leave because she believes that the abuse is her fault and she is too embarrassed to ask for help.

STRENGTHS OF ABUSED WOMEN

When one recognizes the obstacles to women leaving abusers and what women face in staying, it is important to help women identify their strengths. Social workers and other advocates must look below surface issues and help women recognize the ways they have survived the abuse. Help them to identify their strengths and survival skills and, indeed, to understand that these strengths are part of their coping skills. These skills, however, are not responsible for the abuser's behavior. Only the abuser is responsible for the abusive behavior.

Contrary to the earliest theories explaining that women stay in abusive relationships as a result of "learned helplessness" (Walker 1979), women in abusive relationships are not totally immobilized by abuse. Research has shown that women seek help increasingly as the violence escalates (Gondolf and Fisher 1988). They are not passively sitting at home waiting for their partners to kill them.

Social workers and other advocates can use these strengths by helping women see them as skills they can use to survive and potentially thrive. Some of these strengths may include:

- *Assessment skills.* Most abused women can tell as soon as their partners get home from work what type of day he has had, the mood he is in, and how close he is to becoming violent. Women describe this as "walking on eggshells." However, another way to view this is to help women see that they have skills in assessing his emotions. The woman may have high "emotional intelligence" that can help her succeed in the workplace as well as in other interpersonal relationships (Salovey and Mayer 1990).

- *Protective of their children.* Many women delay getting help and often assume that as an adult they can choose to handle the violence. However, when a batterer turns his attention to the children, an abused mother may decide to seek help and look for ways to protect her children. Acknowledging her love and protectiveness toward her children may help to empower a woman to take further steps to protect them and herself.

- *Informal support networks.* Only a small percentage of abused women actually go into shelters. Although women might be initially embarrassed to ask for help from their family and friends, informal support networks are great sources of strength for women and their children. The role of a social worker or other advocate is to help women identify who they might ask for help, get them past their reluctance to ask for and accept help, and, if necessary, help them rehearse asking for assistance.

- *Perseverance.* It takes perseverance to live with abuse. The woman may be waiting for the "right time" to leave or may feel that the risks of leaving outweigh the risks of staying. She is determined to survive and persevere. Acknowledging her perseverance lets her know that you value her ability to survive violence and abuse.

Other strengths that abused women may have include:

- Endurance
- Loyalty
- Love for others
- Creativity
- Courage
- Persistence
- Humor
- Spirituality
- Connection with others

POLICY RESPONSES

Besides the criminal and civil justice policies described in the practice issues section, specific policy responses to domestic violence are found at the federal, state, local, and organizational levels. Several federal policies have become important tools for advocates for abused women. The federal Violence Against Women Act (VAWA) provides funding for domestic violence shelters and state coalitions, the national domestic violence hotline, law enforcement and prosecution programs, rural programs, child visitation/exchange programs, university and college violence-against-women programs, transitional housing programs, specialized programs in Indian country, and specific funding targeting marginalized communities such as women with disabilities. Besides providing needed funding for domestic violence service providers, VAWA also addresses important issues in service provision. One very significant issue was the difficulty of enforcing protective orders across state lines. VAWA allows for full faith and credit of protective orders across jurisdictions. This means that a protective order issued in Kansas City, Missouri, is enforceable in Kansas City, Kansas. For thousands of women who live in one state but work in another, or who seek safety in a different state from their abuser, law enforcement agencies must honor the protective order or be in violation of federal law. Another section of VAWA is the provision that respondents to a protective order or those found guilty of domestic assault are prohibited from owning firearms. Unfortunately this provision has met with much resistance, and judges are often reluctant to take away firearms from an abuser. VAWA also makes provisions for battered immigrant women to stay in the United States. This provision is addressed in chapter 6, which focuses on the needs of immigrant and refugee women.

The Victims of Crime Act (P. L. 98–473) also created two very important programs that assist victims of domestic violence: The Crime Victims Compensation program provides monetary assistance directly to victims to reimburse them for expenses incurred as a result of the crime. These may include medical expenses, the costs of mental health counseling, loss of wages, and funeral expenses. Other expenses that may be covered are eyeglasses and other corrective lenses, dental services and devices, and prostheses. Recently expanded coverage includes relocation expenses for battered women (Office for Victims of Crime 2001). Each state has different rules for expenses covered and the amount of coverage. The Victim Assistance Program also provides funding to states that subsequently finance local victim-assistance programs. Eligible for these funds are community-based organizations that provide services for victims of domestic violence.

The other federal policy to be aware of is the ability of states to offer waivers, in two important ways, to TANF (Temporary Assistance to Needy Families) recipients. One of these waivers may allow the recipient additional time to receive benefits given the barriers she may have in gaining and keeping employment. Typically the waiver is for six months. The second waiver relates to child support enforcement requirements. If the woman believes that her life and the lives of her children will be endangered by state involvement in seeking child support, she can request a waiver so that the state agency will not contact the father of the children. To learn if your state provides TANF waivers, contact your state welfare office or visit the Web site of Legal Momentum at www.legalmomentum.org.

Legal Momentum also compiles a comprehensive review of other state laws addressing issues such as employment and housing rights. Some states protect battered women from discrimination in the workplace, allow for time off for attending civil and criminal justice hearings, and provide eligibility for unemployment compensation if leaving one's job is a result of safety issues. Some states have also passed laws addressing housing discrimination. Specific statues may prohibit landlords from terminating a lease early or not renting to someone who has been abused. Women seeking a safer place to live are also given the right to terminate a lease early without penalty. Because each state is different, it is important to know the laws that are available in your own state.

A number of states have also adopted workplace violence policies that apply to their own state agencies and serve as models for private businesses. The Corporate Alliance to End Partner Violence suggests that businesses provide education on domestic violence to their own employees, train supervisors to be alert for signs of abuse, develop policies and procedures for addressing safety and security on the job, provide time off for abused employees to attend court or look for a new place to live, and have specific policies that address employees who are abusers.

SOCIAL WORK PRACTICE ISSUES

Social work in the field of domestic violence offers practitioners an opportunity to make a difference in the lives of woman, children, and men directly through clinical practice or indirectly through community and organizational practice. Social workers involved in the domestic violence field may work in community-based domestic violence programs with a wide range of services, including emergency shelters, crisis telephone hotlines, transitional housing programs, individual and group nonresidential counseling, hospital- and court-based advocacy, school-based programs with children and teens, children's programs in shelters, batterer intervention programs, teen dating violence prevention and intervention programs, and community education.

Social workers who work in other practice fields will also encounter women and children whose lives are impacted by domestic violence. For example, school social workers will work with children exposed to domestic abuse and also adolescents involved in teen dating violence. Child protective workers will work with maltreated children whose mothers are also being abused. Hospital social workers may be asked to help women who present at emergency rooms with serious physical injuries. Social workers serving homeless populations will encounter women and their children who are fleeing abusive partners and fathers. Social workers in public social services will meet women seeking assistance so they can leave an abusive partner. Adult protective workers will be asked to investigate the abuse of older women. The figure in the introduction (fig. int.1) shows the linkages between various social work fields of practice and domestic violence.

SOCIAL WORK PRACTICE AT THE INDIVIDUAL AND FAMILY LEVELS

Since social workers will encounter individuals and families impacted by domestic violence in many different fields of practice, it is important that all social workers screen for past and current abuse, assess risk for homicide, and help women develop short- and long-term safety plans. This section provides information on these important practice tasks, and also addresses criminal and civil justice interventions and contraindicated interventions that may be harmful to women.

UNIVERSAL SCREENING

Because of the prevalence of domestic violence, social workers should include questions about past or current abuse in all bio-psycho-social-spiritual assessments. Asking all clients about abuse is called "universal screening." The Family Violence Prevention Fund (2002) recommends that all females, ages 14 years of age and older, be screened for victimization during all intakes. Although it is recommended that questions about abuse be included on intake forms, women are more likely to disclose abuse when asked questions face to face (McFarlane et al. 1991). Social workers should establish rapport and trust with clients before asking domestic violence screening questions. Questions about past and current abuse should be behaviorally oriented and conducted in a nonjudgmental and confidential manner. Any limits to confidentiality should be discussed beforehand, for example, disclosing whether the social worker is mandated to report abuse of the woman or maltreatment of children in the home. Only very few states mandate reporting domestic violence; however, most require reporting child and elder abuse. Never ask about abuse in the presence of an intimate partner, children, or other family members. To overcome language barriers, use professional interpreters to ask about this issue. Do not ask members of the family, especially children and adult partners, to interpret. Always interview partners in a relationship separately, especially if they are seeking couples counseling.

One way to frame questions about abuse is to acknowledge the prevalence of the problem. Thus, because it is so prevalent, it is your or your agency's policy to ask all women about the past and current situation. Framing questions in this way communicates the importance of this issue in women's lives and your concerns about the problem; it also conveys to women who are being abused that they are not alone. Here are some screening questions that can be used:

- Have you ever been hit, kicked, slapped, pushed, punched, or shoved by your current or past boyfriend, husband, or partner?
- Has anyone ever used or threatened to use a weapon against you (knife, gun, car, or something like a baseball bat)?
- Are you in a relationship with a person who physically hurts or threatens you?
- Do you ever feel afraid of your partner?
- Has your partner ever forced you to have sex when you do not want to?
- Do you feel isolated or controlled by your partner?

RISK ASSESSMENT FOR HOMICIDE

When clients report that they are in an abusive relationship, social workers should assess the level of danger the client currently faces. Although neither the social worker nor the woman can predict with absolute certainty that someone else (the abusive partner) is likely to become homicidal, women's perceptions about the level of their danger have been shown to be more accurate than any predictive test given to the abusive partners themselves (Heckert and Gondolf 2004). Working in collaboration with the client, social workers can explore risk factors for homicide. The Danger Assessment instrument, developed by the eminent nurse researcher Jackie Campbell (2003), is based on her study of women murdered by an intimate partner (Table 2.2). Information regarding training in the use of the instrument can be found at http://www.dangerassessment.org/WebApplication1/. To assess homicide risk, social workers should ask questions related to the abuse itself, the abuser's behavior and situation, and the woman's situation, and they should assess the level of danger the woman is facing. Each of these questions can be thought of as a "red flag" for subsequent abuse.

After completing a thorough assessment, social workers should discuss with the woman the number of "red flags" there may be for homicide and the woman's perception of the level of danger she is facing. Homicide assessment is not an exact science, and the presence of several red flags does not mean the woman is definitely going to be killed. Nor does the absence of red flags mean she is absolutely safe from danger. However, affirmative answers to several of these questions should spark additional discussion of the various options that may be available to the woman and her children, which can include staying with family and friends, going to an emergency shelter, leaving the area, or staying with the abuser. It is important to help women identify risks generated

TABLE 2.2 Danger Assessment

Several risk factors have been associated with increased risk of homicides (murders) of women and men in violent relationships. We cannot predict what will happen in your case, but we would like you to be aware of the danger of homicide in situations of abuse and for you to see how many of the risk factors apply to your situation.

Using the calendar, please mark the approximate dates during the past year when you were abused by your partner or ex-partner. Write on that date how bad the incident was according to the following scale:

1. Slapping, pushing; no injuries and/or lasting pain
2. Punching, kicking; bruises, cuts, and/or continuing pain
3. "Beating up"; severe contusions, burns, broken bones
4. Threat to use weapon; head injury, internal injury, permanent injury
5. Use of weapon; wounds from weapon
(If any of the descriptions for the higher number apply, use the higher number.)

Mark Yes or No for each of the following. ("He" refers to your husband, partner, ex-husband, ex-partner, or whoever is currently physically hurting you.)

___ 1. Has the physical violence increased in severity or frequency over the past year?
___ 2. Does he own a gun?
___ 3. Have you left him after living together during the past year?
      3a. (If you have never lived with him, check here___.)
___ 4. Is he unemployed?
___ 5. Has he ever used a weapon against you or threatened you with a lethal weapon? (If yes, was the weapon a gun? ____)
___ 6. Does he threaten to kill you?
___ 7. Has he avoided being arrested for domestic violence?
___ 8. Do you have a child that is not his?
___ 9. Has he ever forced you to have sex when you did not wish to do so?
___ 10. Does he ever try to choke you?
___ 11. Does he use illegal drugs? By drugs, I mean "uppers" or amphetamines, "meth," speed, angel dust, cocaine, "crack," street drugs, or mixtures.
___ 12. Is he an alcoholic or problem drinker?
___ 13. Does he control most or all of your daily activities? For instance: does he tell you who you can be friends with, when you can see your family, how much money you can use, or when you can take the car? (If he tries, but you do not let him, check here: ____)
___ 14. Is he violently and constantly jealous of you? (For instance, does he say "If I can't have you, no one can"?
___ 15. Have you ever been beaten by him while you were pregnant? (If you have never been pregnant by him, check here: ____)
___ 16. Has he ever threatened or tried to commit suicide?
___ 17. Does he threaten to harm your children?
___ 18. Do you believe he is capable of killing you?
___ 19. Does he follow or spy on you, leave threatening notes or messages on answering machine, destroy your property, or call you when you don't want him to?
___ 20. Have you ever threatened or tried to commit suicide
___   Total "Yes" Answers
      Thank you. Please talk to your nurse, advocate, or counselor about what the Danger Assessment means in terms of your situation.

Source: Jacquelyn C. Campbell, Ph.D., R. N. Copyright, 2003; www.dangerassessment.com

by the batterer himself and the risks generated by the women's life circumstances (Davies et al. 1998). Batterer-generated risks include repeated and
severe physical violence posing the possibilities of death, permanent injuries,
and disabilities. Repeated sexual violence may also result in physical injuries and HIV and other sexually transmitted diseases; repeated psychological
harm may include the possibility of PTSD, increased risk of drug and alcohol
abuse, and suicidal ideation. Women may also consider the increased risk of
both physical and emotional harm to their children—including kidnapping,
child custody disputes, and the involvement of Children's Protective Services
(Davies et al. 1998).

Social workers should also explore clients' perceptions of their life-
generated risks, which include financial limitations because of employment
history, poor credit history, as well as loss of access to transportation, housing, and health care (Davies et al. 1998). Women may be unable to recover
their own personal resources and material goods if they choose to leave. They
may face discrimination based on race, ethnicity, gender, sexual orientation,
(dis)ability, and citizenship status, all of which are discussed more thoroughly
in subsequent chapters in this book.

Given this risk analysis, women may choose to stay with an abuser, particularly if they think the partner will find and kill them if they leave. They may
also be afraid that he will hurt family members and friends who try to help. If
the woman is afraid that she may not be safe at a local emergency domestic
violence shelter, the shelter can arrange for her to stay at another shelter in a
different community.

Situations where clients choose to return to the abuser, especially when
the woman's safety is a matter of concern, can be frustrating and ethically
challenging for social workers. Although we claim to respect our clients' self-
determination, these situations question our values and professional competence. The woman chooses to go back not because you were unable to
convince her that she is in mortal danger, nor because she is necessarily in
denial or minimizing her danger. She chooses to return because she would
rather see what is coming than constantly look over her shoulder and live in
fear. She may also choose to go back at this time because the cost of leaving
outweighs the costs of staying. It is essential that social workers pay attention
to their own verbal and nonverbal communication at this time. We do not
want to give the impression that we are disappointed by our client's decision
to return to the abuser. We want her to know that we are concerned for her
safety and that if she ever wants us to help make other arrangements for her,

we will be there to do so. Whether a woman chooses to leave or stay, the next important practice task social workers should do is safety planning.

SAFETY PLANNING

One of the most significant interventions social workers can do with someone in an abusive situation is helping them identify short- and long-term strategies for their safety. Safety planning is about building a partnership with a survivor so that together you can identify her strengths and help her access her own personal power. This is the heart of empowerment practice.

Although there are many reasons women may stay in relationships with someone who can be abusive, they all want the abuse to stop and want to identify ways they can increase their safety. Before discussing concrete safety strategies, it is important to acknowledge that no one strategy can keep women safe (Goodkind, Sullivan, and Bybee 2004). Whether they are abused in the future depends on the batterer's behavior, not the women's.

Researchers find that abused women use strategies that include placating the abuser, actively resisting violence, seeking help from both formal and informal sources of support, and having an emergency safety plan (Goodkind et al. 2004). Strategies used for placating the abuser included trying to avoid him at certain times, not resisting his demands, keeping the kids quiet, and avoiding family and friends. They reported actively resisting the abuse by fighting back physically or using or threatening to use a weapon in self-defense. Many women seek formal help from religious organizations, health-care providers, domestic violence programs, mental health counselors, criminal and civil justice agencies, and legal assistance. Their informal help-seeking strategies included staying and talking with family and friends (Goodman et al. 2003). Although none of these strategies are completely effective, plans such as actively resisting the violence are considered largely ineffective and may be met with retaliatory violence.

Short-term or emergency strategies are actions women take during a violent incident. This is a very scary time, but if the woman has arranged a plan to go to a safe place where the abuser can't find her, and a back-up destination in case the first is unavailable, she may be able to focus on going somewhere safe rather than feel helpless. It is important to process these action plans with her so she can be ready to implement the plan at a moment's notice.

In addition to exploring a safe place she can go, does she have a suitcase packed with emergency essentials? Has she made copies of important papers, and put aside some money and extra keys and left these items with trusted family members or friends? During the violent incident, it is important to move to the safest part of the house and away from the kitchen, garage, bathroom, or any other room with sharp tools that could be used as weapons. She can also alert her children and neighbors who might overhear the violence to call the police. She can practice having a code word or phrase to signal children to call the police. Children should also have a safety plan that might include going to a neighbor's house during a violent incident, where they can call police from a safe location (Hart 1990). Women with pets may also want to have arrangements for taking care of their animals if they cannot take them to a safe place and fear for their safety if they are left behind.

Women can use many longer-term strategies to plan for their safety that may include subsequently leaving the abuser. These strategies include increasing their economic independence by opening their own bank account; having bills sent to a different address, particularly bills for cell phones; going back to school to prepare for a career; and seeking employment if they are currently not working and if it is feasible given their circumstances. She may also change locks on doors and install security systems.

One of the most important telephone numbers social workers can give their clients is the number for the National Domestic Violence Hotline, 1–800–799–SAFE and 1–800–787–3224 (TTY). The hotline is available 24 hours, 7 days a week, has Spanish-speaking advocates and other language interpreters available, and can connect women with resources anywhere in the United States.

CRIMINAL JUSTICE INTERVENTIONS

During or immediately after a violent incident, women often turn to the criminal justice system for help. Police intervention is commonly used during a violent incident when a woman feels her life is in danger. Most states and many local communities have adopted pro or mandatory arrest policies that require responding officers to arrest the person identified as the primary aggressor. It is important to note that implementation of state laws varies among jurisdictions. The potential unintended consequences of involving the police, however, include retaliation against victims and the arrest of both the abuser and the victim. The abuser may also flee before police can arrive. However, arrest marks the entrance into the criminal justice system and may lead to prosecution.

TABLE 2.3 Items to Take When Leaving

PERSONAL INFORMATION	CHILDREN'S PAPERS
■ Birth certificates	■ Birth certificates
■ Social security cards	■ School records and vaccination records
■ Passports	■ Medical records
■ Green cards and Work Permits	■ Passports
■ Credit cards	
■ Savings and checking-account information	**CHILDREN'S ITEMS**
	■ Favorite pictures
IMPORTANT PAPERS	■ Children's favorite toys
	■ Blankets
■ Divorce papers	■ Medical prescriptions
■ Protective orders	
■ Medical records	**PETS AND PET ITEMS**
■ Insurance papers	
■ Lease or mortgage papers	■ Toys, bedding, and food
■ Address books	■ Vet records
OTHER ITEMS INCLUDING THOSE OF SENTIMENTAL VALUE	**IMPORTANT TELEPHONE NUMBERS**
	■ People they can stay with
■ Jewelry	■ Work and school
■ Photographs	■ Local domestic violence program
■ Medical prescriptions	■ Medical doctors
	■ Attorney

Criminal charges may vary depending on the severity of the injuries sustained and the presence of weapons. Laws vary between states, so social workers should become knowledgeable about criminal laws in the states where they practice. Information about state laws can be found at the Web site of the American Bar Association Commission on Domestic Violence. Successful prosecution of an assault may lead to mandated batterer intervention counseling in areas where programs exist, and where the criminal justice system and services for both victims and perpetrators have developed coordinated community responses to domestic violence. The goal of a coordinated community response is to enhance safety for victims and hold batterers accountable for their behavior (Hart 1995); it is typically marked by regular communication between primary stakeholders in the field.

Women are often reluctant to participate in the prosecution of their partners. Victims and offenders often have strong emotional and financial ties, including the sharing of children, and many women want their partners to get counseling instead of going to jail (Hart 1993). Recognizing these dynamics, many prosecutors use evidence-based prosecution techniques that do not require victims to testify against abusers. Local domestic violence programs may provide victim advocates to help victims feel empowered to pursue prosecution (Weisz 1999). Many prosecutors also employ victim advocates to provide services such as helping victims apply for protective orders, information gathering regarding the nature, severity, and prior violence by the offender, explaining the criminal justice system, keeping victims informed of key events (Healey, Smith and O'Sullivan 1998), as well as accompanying victims to courtroom appearances. Despite women's fears about sending their partner to jail, judges have shown a preference for using court-mandated batterer's treatment as a condition of probation, with little interest in using incarceration as a possible deterrent (Hanna 1998).

CIVIL JUSTICE INTERVENTIONS

Protective or restraining orders are civil court orders prohibiting offenders from contacting victims or their children, using physical abuse or the threat of physical abuse, or damaging the victim's personal property (Postmus 2007). The order may provide for custody, visitation, support of minor children, and living arrangements; violation of protective orders is now a criminal offense (Finn and Colson 1990). A protective order issued in one jurisdiction is enforceable in all U.S. jurisdictions, but protective order remedies may vary between states. Social workers can learn more about the protective order policies in the states where they practice through the Web site of the American Bar Association Commission on Domestic Violence or by contacting their state domestic violence coalition or local domestic violence service provider.

Women can obtain applications for protective orders through local domestic violence programs and county and municipal courts. Application for protective orders can be made without an attorney (pro se) and social workers can help clients fill out the paper work. People who apply for a protective order are called "petitioners." The application is then given to a judge to approve the order. A copy of the protective order is served to the other party, the "respondent." The protective order is usually good on an emergency basis, typically lasting 30 days. To make the protective order permanent, with extensions typically lasting six months to a year, petitioners must appear before a judge to affirm that they are still concerned for their safety and want the protective order to be extended.

The respondent must be given notification of the court date but is not mandated to appear. The respondent has the right to dispute the need for a protective order, and the judge hearing the case determines the disposition of the request. Social workers should be wary when exploring the protective order option, as it does not prevent violence from occurring. It can only hold an abuser responsible for committing subsequent violence. A woman may choose not to go forward with a request to extend the protective order beyond its 30-day emergency status if she feels that the threat of violence has lessened or if she fears severe retaliation if she proceeds with the court date.

CONTRAINDICATED INTERVENTIONS

A number of intervention modalities that social workers have traditionally used are contraindicated in situations where violence is present. Those interventions typically involve couples counseling, marriage counseling, divorce mediation, and family therapy. Many experts in the field believe that interventions involving joint counseling may be dangerous, unfair, and ineffective (New York State Office for the Prevention of Domestic Violence n.d.). Since abusive partners often warn their partners against disclosing their violence to others, they may also retaliate against their female partners for violating another of their "rules." Requiring a woman to attend counseling with someone who has victimized her is unfair; victims often take responsibility for the violence and consequently, the focus of the counseling session shifts away from the abuser. This only reinforces the batterer's belief that he can use violence to discipline his partner's misbehavior. Because of the ever present threat of retaliation, abused women often are afraid to disclose the power and control issues within the relationship. Neither well-trained professional social workers nor other mental health professionals believe that they can restore the balance of power between abusive partners and their victims in 50-minute sessions and then have the couple maintain that balance after they leave the office. When contacted for couples counseling, social workers should always screen each partner separately for violence before contracting for subsequent intervention. When violence is disclosed, social workers should explore other options such as group programs specifically geared toward abusive partners. Couples counseling may be appropriate after completion of a batterer intervention program. However, completing a batterer intervention program does not guarantee that the abusive partner is no longer using violence or other forms of coercive control. Family therapy interventions that require the presence of an abusive partner, abused partner, and their children are also contraindicated for the same reasons. In this case, not only is the abused partner at risk for subsequent violence, but their children are also at risk.

Interventions such as the ones mentioned above may rely on family systems theory as its foundation. Under family systems theory each member of the family interacts with all others in order to form the whole system. Individual problems are a result of a dysfunctional family unit, where each member contributes to the problem. From this perspective, violence is produced by the interactions between people, so no one is responsible for the violence. Thus interventions using family systems theory may create opportunities for blaming the victims. It is important, however, to hold abusers responsible for their own behavior.

When making recommendations for programs that target batterers your local programs should be investigated before making referrals. If your state has developed standards for practice in this area, look for programs that have been certified by a state agency or your state domestic violence coalition. Programs focusing on anger management have not been found to be effective in stopping violence. Focusing on anger as an issue implies that someone is unable to control his anger or behavior, but the fact is that abusers are quite able to control their anger depending on the situation. Abusers rarely target people whom they perceive to have power over them, such as their employers, and may in fact appear cool, calm, and collected when the police show up. Anger management programs, therefore, may not address the coercive tactics that batterers use. Referring batterers to an anger management program may give the abused partner a false sense of safety.

Divorce mediation or child custody investigations are other approaches that may risk the safety of children (Imbrogno and Imbrogno 2000), as an abusive partner may use divorce proceedings to gain custody of the couple's children. Because domestic violence is strongly correlated with child abuse, it is important that social workers conducting child custody investigations are trained in assessing for violence and abuse and for the impact of a batterer's violence on children (Bancroft and Silverman 2002). The use of a standardized instrument such as the Child Exposure to Domestic Violence Scale can help determine the level of impact on youngsters (Edleson, Shin, and Johnson-Armendariz 2008).

Because allegations of domestic violence are not generally more common in disputed custody cases, social workers must question claims of the so-called parental alienation syndrome (PAS) (Saunders 2007), which is often used to accuse women of alienating their children from their fathers. PAS has been discredited by various experts as lacking any scientific basis or data to support it (Meier, 2009). Although PAS has been found to be unscientific, some judges have awarded sole custody of children to abusive fathers on the basis of its use in the courtroom (Bancroft and Silverman 2002); thus, having the effect of prohibiting mothers from legitimately protecting the safety of their own children

Awarding batterers joint or sole custody of children reinforces their power over mothers and children, and puts the children's safety and mental and physical health at risk for further abuse (Bancroft and Silverman 2002). Even if custody is awarded to the nonabusive parent, divorce and separation does not mean that the abuse has ended. Children should be taught safety planning for both unsupervised and supervised visitations with an abusive parent (Saunders 2007). The use of community supervised visitation/exchange programs, many of which were developed to increase the safety of abuse survivors and their children (McMahon, Neville-Sorvilles, and Schubert 1999), can be an important recommendation for child custody evaluators to make.

SOCIAL WORK MACRO PRACTICE: ORGANIZATIONS, COMMUNITIES, AND PUBLIC POLICY LEVELS

Social work practice at the organizational, community, and local, state, national, and international levels is rich with challenges and opportunities. Social workers involved with state coalitions, national organizations, and state and local agencies may be developing training programs, enhancing the ability of their member organizations to provide effective services.

ORGANIZATIONAL LEVEL   At the organizational level, social work practice should include the development and implementation of policies that require screening and the creation of tracking systems to maintain consistent data regarding the percentage of the caseload involving domestic violence. Regular training programs for employees on domestic violence issues should also be developed and implemented. Further, social service agencies should have workplace policies that address the needs of workers personally affected by domestic violence.

COMMUNITY LEVEL At the community level, social workers can participate in local domestic violence task forces or coordinating councils and should seek ways to keep women safe and hold abusers accountable. Social workers should plan and participate in multi-agency community awareness events that provide information to the public about topics that reach all clients and also look for ways to collaborate with other agencies in the community. For example, an agency providing alcohol and drug treatment may develop a Memorandum of Understanding (MOU) with a local domestic violence program that addresses domestic violence screening among alcohol- and drug-treatment clients, and alcohol and drug screening among domestic violence clients.

LOCAL, STATE, NATIONAL, AND INTERNATIONAL PUBLIC POLICY LEVELS
At all public policy levels social workers should advocate for better funding of programs that meet the needs of families where violence is present. Funding is needed for emergency and transitional housing programs for abuse survivors, as many domestic violence shelters turn away women and children because of overcrowding. Funding is also needed for primary prevention programs targeting teens and for therapeutic programs for children exposed to violence. These programs are critical for breaking the intergenerational transmission of violence. Joining state domestic violence coalitions will connect social workers with valuable training opportunities and help keep them informed about changes in state policies. Social workers can also advocate for specific policy changes through testimony, letters, and telephone calls to elected officials.

SUMMARY

Social workers in all areas of practice can benefit from understanding the prevalence, consequences, and dynamics of domestic violence. Minimally, social workers should be able to screen for past and current abuse, assess for risk, be able to discuss potential options, and conduct safety planning with persons who are being abused. The ability to identify the strengths of battered women will help advocates elicit the natural resiliency within each woman and assist her in making her own reasoned decisions about her own safety and that of her children.

RESOURCES

HOTLINES

The National Domestic Violence Hotline
Phone: 1 (800) 799–SAFE or 1 (800) 787–3224 (TTY)
Links individuals to help in their area using a nationwide database that includes detailed information on domestic violence shelters, other emergency shelters, legal advocacy, and social service programs.

Teen Dating Violence Hotline
Phone: 1 (866) 331–9474 or 1 (866) 331–8453 (TTY)

Rape Abuse and Incest National Network (RAINN)
Phone: 1 (800)–656-HOPE
Automatically transfers the caller to the nearest rape crisis center anywhere in the nation. It can be used as a last resort if people cannot find a domestic violence shelter.

NATIONAL ORGANIZATIONS AND WEB SITES

American Bar Association Commission on Domestic Violence
Web site: http://www.abanet.org/domviol
Maintains a Web site with state specific laws, and provides individualized support to attorneys representing victims of domestic violence, sexual assault, and stalking

Statutory Summary Charts
Web site: http://www.abanet.org/domviol/statutorysummarycharts.html\

The Battered Women's Justice Project
2104 4th Ave. South
Suite B
Minneapolis, MN 55404
Phone: 1 (800) 903–0111, ext. 1

Web site: http://www.bwjp.org
Primarily provides support and technical assistance to organizations and professionals engaged in the criminal and civil justice system's response to domestic violence.

Bureau of Justice Statistics Clearinghouse
Web site: http://www.ojp.usdoj.gov/bjs
Provides statistics on intimate partner violence in the United States

Corporate Alliance to End Partner Violence
Web site: http://www.caepv.org/
Focuses on workplace violence policies

Danger Assessment Website
Web site: http://www.dangerassessment.org/WebApplication1/default.aspx
Provides information on using the Danger Assessment model developed by Jackie Campbell

EconEmpowerment
Web site: http://www.econempowerment.org
Provides financial empowerment resources to domestic violence survivors

Family Violence Prevention Fund (FVPF)
Web site: http://www.endabuse.org
A national nonprofit organization focusing on domestic violence education, and on prevention and public policy reform; videos, curriculum, posters, and other tools are available for download or purchase

Legal Momentum
Web site: http://www.legalmomentum.org
The nation's oldest legal advocacy organization dedicated to advancing the rights of women and girls; the Web site has a database of state-specific laws regarding housing, employment and immigration issues, and violence against women

Minnesota Center Against Violence and Abuse (MINCAVA)
Web site: http://www.mincava.umn.edu
A comprehensive electronic clearinghouse that provides quick access to more than 3,000 resources centered on the topics of violence

National Center on Domestic and Sexual Violence
Phone: 1 (512) 407–9020
Web site: http://www.ncdsv.org

Offers consulting, training, and advocacy on issues relating to domestic violence and sexual abuse

National Center for Injury Prevention and Control
(Centers for Disease Control and Prevention)
Phone: 1 (800) CDC–INFO (232–4636)
Web site: http://www.cdc.gov/ncipc
The lead federal agency for injury prevention, NCIPC works closely with other federal agencies; national, state, and local organizations; state and local health departments; and research institutions focusing on intimate partner violence and sexual violence topics

National Center for Victims of Crime
Web site: http://www.ncvc.org
The nation's leading resource and advocacy organization committed to helping crime victims rebuild their lives

National Coalition Against Domestic Violence (NCADV)
Web site: http://www.ncadv.org
Dedicated to the empowerment of battered women and their children and therefore committed to the elimination of personal and societal violence in the lives of battered women and their children

National Criminal Justice Reference Service (NCJRS): Domestic Violence
Web site: http://www.ncjrs.gov
Provides a Web site listing domestic violence-related publications, frequently asked questions, and related links

National Network to End Domestic Violence
Web site: http://www.nnedv.org
A membership and advocacy organization of state domestic violence coalitions, allied organizations, and supportive individuals that works with city and state domestic violence survivors and their advocates to ensure that their needs are heard and understood by policymakers at the national level

National Online Resource Center on Violence
Against Women (VAWnet)
Web site: http://www.nnedv.org
A comprehensive collection of full-text, searchable electronic resources developed to assist those working to end domestic and sexual violence by increasing access to timely, reliable, and relevant information and materials

National Resource Center on Domestic Violence (NRCDV)

Web site: http://www.nrcdv.og

Provides support to all organizations and individuals working to end violence in the lives of victims and their children through technical assistance, training, and information on responding to and preventing domestic violence.

National Sexual Violence Resource Center

Web site: http://www.nsvrc.org

The nation's principle information and resource center regarding all aspects of sexual violence

Office for Victims of Crime, U.S. Department of Justice

Web site: http://www.ojp.usdoj.gov/ovc/

Provides resources, grant programs, and federal funding opportunities

Office on Violence Against Women, U.S. Department of Justice

Web site: http://www.ovw.usdoj.gov/

Provides resources, grant programs, and federal funding opportunities

REFERENCES

American Medical Association Council on Scientific Affairs. (1992). Violence Against Women. *JAMA, 267*, 3184–3189.

Anderson, K. M., and F. S. Danis. (2006). Adult daughters of battered women: Resistance and resiliency in the face of danger. *Affilia: Journal of Women and Social Work, 21(4)*, 419–432.

Arkow, P. (1996). The relationship between animal abuse and other forms of family violence. *Family Violence and Sexual Assault Bulletin 12(1/2)*, 29–34.

Bachman, R., and L. E. Saltzman. (1995). Violence against women: Estimates from the redesigned survey. *Bureau of Justice Statistics Special Report*. Washington, DC: U.S. Department of Justice.

Bancroft, L., and J. G. Silverman. (2002). *The Batterer as Parent: Addressing the Impact of Domestic Violence on Family Dynamics*. Thousand Oaks, CA: Sage.

Bandura, A. (1973). Aggression: A Social Learning Analysis. Englewood Cliffs, NJ: Prentice Hall.

Bennett, L., and O. Williams. (2003). Substance abuse and men who batter: Issues in theory and practice. *Violence Against Women, 9(5)*, 558–575.

Bent-Goodley, T., and D. Fowler. (2006). Spiritual and religious abuse, *Affilia: Journal of Women and Social Work, 21(3)*, 282–295.

Brandwein, R. (Ed.) (1998). *Battered Women, Children, and Welfare Reform: The Ties That Bind.* Thousand Oaks, CA: Sage.

Brown, B. (2006). Shame resilience theory: A grounded theory study on women and shame. *Families in Society: The Journal of Contemporary Social Service,* 87(1), 43–52.

Browne, A., and S. Bassuk. (1997). Intimate violence in the lives of homeless and poor housed women: Prevalence and patterns in an ethnically diverse sample. *American Journal of Orthopsychiatry,* 67, 261–277.

Campbell. J. C. (1995). Prediction of homicide of and by battered women. In J. C. Campbell (Ed.), *Assessing Dangerousness: Violence by Sexual Offenders, Batterers, and Child Abusers* (pp. 96–113). Thousand Oaks: CA: Sage.

Campbell, J. C., J. Dienemann, and A. Jones. (2002). Intimate partner violence and physical health consequences. *Archives of Internal Medicine,* 162, 1157–1163.

Campbell, J. C., and K. Soeken. (1999). Forced sex and intimate partner violence: Effects on women's health. *Violence Against Women,* 5, 1017–1035.

Carlson, B. E. (1984). Causes and maintenance of domestic violence: An ecological analysis. *Social Service Review,* 58, 569–587.

Coker, A., K. Davis, I. Arias, S. Desai, M. Sanderson, H. Brandt, and P. H. Smith. (2002). Physical and mental health effects of intimate partner violence for men and women. *American Journal of Preventive Medicine,* 23(4), 260–268.

Crowell, N. A., and A. W. Burgess. (1996) (Eds.). *Understanding Violence Against Women.* National Research Council, Washington, DC: National Academy Press.

Cummings, J., D. Peplar, and T. Moore. (1999). Behavior problems in children exposed to wife abuse: Gender differences. *Journal of Family Violence,* 14(2), 133–156.

Davies, J., E. Lyon, and D. Monti-Catania. (1998). Safety Planning with Battered Women: Complex Lives/Difficult Choices. Thousand Oaks, CA: Sage.

Edleson, J. L. (1999). The overlap between child maltreatment and woman battering. *Violence Against Women,* 5(2), 134–154.

——. (2006). *Emerging Responses to Children Exposed to Domestic Violence.* Harrisburg, PA: VAWnet, a project of the National Resource Center on Domestic Violence/Pennsylvania Coalition Against Domestic Violence, Retrieved June 9, 2008, from http://www.vawnet.org.

Edleson, J. L., and R. M. Tolman. (1992). *Intervention for Men Who Batter: An Ecological Approach.* Newbury Park, CA: Sage.

Edleson, J. L., N. Shin, and K. K. Johnson-Armendariz. (2008). Measuring children's exposure to domestic violence: The development and testing of the Child Exposure to Domestic Violence (CEDV) Scale. *Children and Youth Services Review,* 30, 502–521.

Family Violence Prevention Fund (2002). *National Consensus Guidelines on Identifying and Responding to Domestic Violence Victimization in Health Care Settings.* Retrieved June 3, 2008, from http://www.endabuse.org/programs/healthcare/files/Consensus.pdf.

Fantuzzo, J., R. Boruch, A. Beriama, M. Atkins., and S. Marcus. (1997). Domestic violence and children: Prevalence and risk in five major U.S. cities. *Journal of the American Academy of Child and Adolescent Psychiatry,* 36(1), 116–122.

Finn, P., and S. Colson. (1990). Civil Protection Orders: Legislation, Current Court Practice, and Enforcement. Washington DC, U.S. Department of Justice, National Institute of Justice NCJ 123263. Retrieved June 3, 2008, from http://www.ncjrs.gov/App/Publications/abstract.aspx?ID=123263.

Fischbach, R., and B. Herbert. (1997). Domestic violence and mental health: Correlates and conundrums within and across cultures. *Social Science and Medicine,* 45(8), 1161–1176.

Fluery, R. E., C. M. Sullivan, and D. I. Bybee (2000). When ending the relationship doesn't end the violence: Women's experiences of violence by former partners. *Violence Against Women,* 6(12), 1362–1383.

Gelles, R. J. (1993). Through a sociological lens: Social structure and family violence. In R. J. Gelles and D. R. Loseke (Eds.), *Current Controversies on Family Violence* (pp. 31–46). Newbury Park, CA: Sage.

Golding, J. (1999). Intimate partner violence as a risk factor for mental disorders: A meta-analysis. *Journal of Family Violence,* 14, 99–132.

Gondolf, E. W., and E. R. Fisher. (1988). Battered Women as Survivors: An Alternative to Treating Learned Helplessness. Lexington, MA: Lexington Books.

Goodman, L., M. Dutton, K. Weinfurt, and S. Cook. (2003). The Intimate Partner Violence Strategies Index. *Violence Against Women,* 9(2), 163–186.

Goodkind, J. R., C. M. Sullivan, and D. I. Bybee. (2004). A contextual analysis of battered women's safety planning. *Violence Against Women,* 10 (5), 514–533.

Hanna, C. (1998). The paradox of hope: The crime and punishment of domestic violence. *William and Mary Law Review,* 39, 1505.

Hart, B. (1990). Safety Planning for Children: Strategizing for unsupervised visits with batterers. Retrieved June 3, 2008, from http://www.mincava.umn.edu/documents/hart/hart.html#id2307114.

——. (1993). Battered women and the criminal justice system. *American Behavioral Scientist,* 36(5), 624–638.

——. (1995). Coordinated community response research themes. Washington, DC: National Research Council.

Healey, K., C. Smith, and C. O'Sullivan. (1998). *Batterer Intervention: Program Approaches and Criminal Justice Strategies.* Washington, DC: National Institute of Justice.

Heckert, D.A., and W. W. Gondolf. (2004). Battered women's perceptions of risk versus risk factors and instruments in predicting repeat reassault. *Journal of Interpersonal Violence* 19(7), 778–800.

Heise, L., M. Ellsberg, and M. Gottemoeller. (1999). *Ending Violence Against Women. Population Reports*, series 50, no. 11.

Heise, L. L. (1998). Violence against women: An integrated, ecological framework. *Violence Against Women* 4 (3), 262–290.

Imbrogno, A. I., and S. Imbrogno. (2000). Mediation in court cases of domestic violence. *Families in Society: The Journal of Contemporary Human Services*, 81(4), 392–401.

Jaffe, P. G., D. A. Wolfe, and S. K. Wilson. (1990). *Children of Battered Women.* Newbury Park, CA: Sage.

Kelley, M. (2003). Concerns for children as a factor in battered mothers' decision making about change. Ph.D. diss., Catholic University of America, Washington, DC

Kilpatrick, D., R. Acierno, H. Resnick, B. Saunders, and C. Best. (1997). A two-year longitudinal analysis of the relationships between violent assault and substance use in women. *Journal of Consult Clinical Psychology*, 65, 834–847.

Kilpatrick, K., M. Litt, and L. Williams. (1997). Post-traumatic stress disorder in child witnesses to domestic violence. *American Journal of Orthopsychiatry*, 67(4), 639–644.

Kolbo, J. R., E. H. Blakely, and D. Engelman. (1996). Children who witness domestic violence: A review of empirical literature. *Journal of Interpersonal Violence*, 11(2), 281–293.

Koss, M., P. Koss, and W. Woodruff. (1991). Deleterious effects of criminal victimization on women's health and medical utilization. *Archives of Internal Medicine*, 151, 342–347.

Leserman, J., D. Li, D. Drossman, and Y. Hu. (1998). Selected symptoms associated with sexual and physical abuse among female patients with gastrointestinal disorders: The impact on subsequent health care visits. *Psychological Medicine*, 28, 417–425.

Lloyd, S., and N. Taluc. (1999). The effects of male violence on female employment. *Violence Against Women*, 5, 370–392.

Lyon, E. (2002). *Welfare and Domestic Violence: Lessons from Research.* Harrisburg, Pa.: VAWnet, a project of the National Resource Center on Domestic Violence/ Pennsylvania Coalition Against Domestic Violence. Retrieved June 3, 2008, from http://www.vawnet.org.

McCauley, J., D. Kern, and K. Kolodner. (1995). The "battering syndrome": Prevalence and clinical characteristics of domestic violence in primary care internal medicine practices. *Annuals of Internal Medicine*, 123, 737–746.

McFarlane, J., K. Christoffel, L. Bateman, V. Miller, and L. Bullock. (1991). Assessing for abuse: Self-report vs. nurse interview assessments. *Public Health Nursing,* 8(4), 245–250.

McMahon, M., J. Neville-Sorvilles, and L. Schubert. (1999). Undoing harm to children: The Duluth family visitation center. In M. F. Shepard and E.L. Pence (Eds.), *Coordinating Community Responses to Domestic Violence: Lessons from Duluth and Beyond* (pp. 151–167). Thousand Oaks, CA: Sage.

Meier, J. (2009). Parental alienation syndrome and parental alienation: Research reviews. Harrisburg, PA. VAWnet, a project of the National Resource Center on Domestic Violence/Pennsylvania Coalition Against Domestic Violence. Retrieved, March 15, 2009, from http://www.vawnet.org.

Mercy, J., A. Butchart, L. Dahlberg, A. Zwi, and E. Krug. (2003). Violence and mental health. *International Journal of Mental Health,* 32(1), 20–35.

Minnesota Program Development, Inc. (N.d.). The Domestic Abuse Intervention Project. Retrieved May 25, 2008, from http://www.duluth-model.org/.

National Network to End Domestic Violence. (2008). *Domestic Violence Counts 07: A 24-Hour Census of Domestic Violence Services.* Washington, DC: National Network to End Domestic Violence.

New York State Office for the Prevention of Domestic Violence. (N.d.). *Guidelines for Mental Health Professionals.* Retrieved April 10, 2008, from http://www.opdv .state.ny.us/health_humsvc/mental_health/guidelines.html#counseling.

Office for Victims of Crime (2001). Report to the nation 2001: Fiscal years 1999 and 2000. Washington, DC Department of Justice, Office of Justice Programs.

Postmus, J. L. (2000). Analysis of the family violence option: A strengths perspective. *Affilia: Journal of Women and Social Work,* 1(2), 244–258.

——. (2007). Challenging the negative assumptions about civil protective orders: A guide for advocates. *Affilia: Journal of Women and Social Work,* 22(4), 347–356.

Rand, M. R. (1997). *Violence-related Injuries Treated in Hospital Emergency Departments.* Washington, DC: U.S. Department of Justice.

Raphael, J. and R. M. Tolman. (1997). *Trapped by Poverty, Trapped by Abuse: New Evidence Documenting the Relationship between Domestic Violence and Welfare.* Chicago: Project for Research on Welfare, Work, and Domestic Violence, Taylor Institute and University of Michigan Research Development Center on Poverty, Risk, and Mental Health.

Rennison, C. M. (2003). Intimate Partner Violence, 1993–2001. Washington, DC: U. S. Department of Justice Bureau of Justice Statistics. NCJ 197838. Retrieved May 15, 2008, from http://www.cdc.gov/ncipc/dvp/IPV/ipv-risk_protective.htm.

Saakvitne, K. W., H. Tennen, and G. Affleck. (1998). Exploring thriving in the context of clinical trauma theory: Constructivist Self Development Theory. *Journal of Social Issues*, 54(2), 279–299.

Salovey, P., and J. D. Mayer. (1990). Emotional intelligence. *Imagination, Cognition, and Personality*, 9, 185–211.

Saunders, D. (2007). Child custody and visitation decisions in domestic violence cases: Legal trends, risk factors, and safety concerns. Harrisburg, PA: VAWnet, a project of the National Resource Center on Domestic Violence/Pennsylvania Coalition Against Domestic Violence. Retrieved June 3, 2008, from: http://www.vawnet.org.

Schechter, S. (1982). *Women and Male Violence: The Visions and Struggles of the Battered Women's Movement*, Boston: South End.

Silverman, J. G., A. Raj, A., L. Mucci, and J. Hathaway. (2001). Dating violence against adolescent girls and associated substance use, unhealthy weight control, sexual risk behavior, pregnancy, and suicidality. *Journal of the American Medical Association*, 286(5), 572–579.

Spears, L. (2000). *Building Bridges Between Domestic Violence Organizations and Child Protective Services*. National Resource Center on Domestic Violence, Child Welfare League of America, Inc., National Council of Juvenile and Family Court Judges, Resource Center on Domestic Violence: Child Protection and Custody, and Family Violence Prevention Fund. Retrieved June 3, 2008, from http://www.vaw.umn.edu/documents/dvcps/dvcps.html

Tjaden, P., and N. Thoennes. (1998). *Prevalence, Incidence, and Consequences of Violence Against Women: Findings from the National Violence Against Women Survey*. Washington, DC: National Institute for Justice and Centers for Disease Control and Prevention.

Victims of Crime Act of 1984. P.L. 98–473, 42 U.S.C. 10601 et seq.

Victims of Crime Act, P. L. 98–473, 98 Stat. 4792.

Victims' Rights and Restitution Act of 1990. P.L. 98–473, 98 Stat. 2170, 42 U.S.C. 10601.

Violence Against Women Act of 1994. P.L. 98–473, 42 U.S.C. 13931–14016.

Walker, L. (1979). The Battered Woman. New York: Harper and Row.

Weisz, A. N. (1999). Legal advocacy for domestic violence survivors: The power of an informative relationship. *Families in Society*, 80(2), 138–147.

Whitfield, C. L., R. F. Anda, S. R. Dube, and V. J. Felitti. (2003). Violent childhood experiences and the risk of intimate partner violence in adults. *Journal of Interpersonal Violence*, 18, 166–185.

Widom, C. S. (1989). Does violence beget violence? A critical examination of the literature. *Psychological Bulletin*. 106(1), 3–28.

Yllo, K. A. (1993). Through a feminist lens: Gender, power, and violence. In R. J. Gelles and D. R. Loseke (Eds.), *Current Controversies on Family Violence* (pp. 31–46). Newbury Park, CA: Sage.

3

OUR SURVIVAL, OUR STRENGTHS

Understanding the Experiences of African American
Women in Abusive Relationships

Tricia B. Bent-Goodley, Lorraine Chase, Elizabeth A. Circo,
and Selena T. Antá Rodgers

DOMESTIC VIOLENCE reportedly is the primary public health issue facing African American women (Joseph 1997). Even so, limited resources have been provided to address this issue. Although the general public has started to view domestic violence as a serious problem, resulting in the criminal justice system enacting laws and procedures to assist survivors of domestic violence, government policies lack consistent plans for providing shelters, services, and assistance for abused women, particularly those who choose to remain in the relationship (Bent-Goodley 2004a). These facts, combined with the sheer numbers of African American women who experience domestic violence annually, underscore the necessity for culturally competent services for this group of African American women.

The Centers for Disease Control estimates that five million women report for medical treatment annually as a result of intimate partner violence (National Center for Injury Prevention and Control [NCIPC] 2003). African American women continue to suffer from domestic violence at disproportionate levels compared to other groups of women, except for Native American women, who have also been recognized as experiencing high levels of domestic violence (Lee, Thompson, and Mechanic 2002). Despite this, we still have limited culturally competent domestic violence interventions, few community-based services or health campaigns in the African American community focusing on domestic violence, and persistent barriers that often discourage African American women from obtaining services (Bent-Goodley 2001; West 2002, 1999). This chapter examines how African American women experience domestic violence, offers strategies to address the identified issues from a generalist practice perspective, and identifies selected resources specific to domestic violence in the African American community.

LITERATURE REVIEW

African American women comprise 13 percent of women and 54 percent of all African Americans in the United States (U.S. Census Bureau 2004). An estimated 26 percent of African American women experience domestic violence over their lifetime (Taggart and Mattson 1996). According to the National Crime Victims Survey (NCVS), the domestic violence rate among African American women is 35 percent higher than among Caucasian women and nearly three times higher among women of other races (Bureau of Justice Statistics [BJS] 2006). African American women are more likely to suffer exacerbated mental and physical health issues related to domestic violence (Schollenberger et al. 2003), and are more likely to receive more serious injuries as a result of domestic violence compared to other women, largely because of delays in reporting abuse (Campbell 2002; Lee, et al. 2002). In fact, domestic violence is the leading cause of death among African American women between the ages of fifteen and forty-four (Office of Justice Programs 1998), and African American women are seven times more likely than Caucasian women to be killed as a result of domestic violence (Barak, Flavin, and Leighton 2001). African American women are also more than 14 times more likely than women in other racial groups to be murdered by a man the woman knows, as opposed to a stranger (Violence Policy Center 2003).

DIVERSITY WITHIN THE AFRICAN AMERICAN COMMUNITY

Women of African ancestry born in Africa, the United States, the Caribbean, and throughout the diaspora have unique experiences but also share commonalities and differences (Davis and Cloud-Two Dogs 2004; Devore and Schlesinger 1996; Lewis 1999). Each ethnic group has a rich history and stories that must be heard and understood. To best serve these varied groups, the diversity within the African American population needs to be acknowledged and emphasized, and ways must be found to respond accordingly.

Differences in age, class, sexual orientation, and geographical region also cannot be ignored, as they are manifested in domestic violence incidents. The Bureau of Justice Statistics (2006) posits that African American women aged 20 to 34 are at particularly high risk of nonfatal domestic violence incidents. African American women in rural communities are also at great risk of domestic violence because of poor transportation systems, profound isolation, and higher poverty rates (Sullivan et al. 2005). African American women in same-sex relationships not only experience discrimination through social isolation owing to their race and gender, but they are further isolated from their race-based communities, receiving virtually no assistance from traditional and nontraditional sources because of their sexual orientation (Bent-Goodley and Williams 2005; Kanuha 2005; McClennen 2005; Robinson 2002). Acknowledging that domestic violence is not the same for every African American woman is critical, as different responses are needed in each instance. This diversity must be understood, acknowledged, and utilized in practice.

THE HISTORICAL CONTEXT OF DOMESTIC VIOLENCE AMONG AFRICAN AMERICANS

Understanding the historical context of domestic violence among African Americans is essential to provide services to this diverse community. No existing documents have been identified to suggest that domestic violence was prevalent in ancient African countries (Bent-Goodley 2005a; Dennis et al. 1995). As a result, discussions about domestic violence in the African American community generally begin with an examination of African peoples' enslavement and its impact on gender relationships (Bent-Goodley and Williams 2005; Dennis et al. 1995; Franklin 2001). Slavery's high rates of rape and sexual violence against African American women, slaves' inability to control or determine their own relationships, and slave owners' refusal to acknowledge the validity of African American marriages are viewed as having had a profound impact on the degree of violence in African American intimate relationships (Bent-Goodley 2005; Franklin 2001; Myers 1995). Post-Traumatic Slave Syndrome (PTSS) is described as "a condition that exists when a population has experienced multigenerational trauma resulting from centuries of slavery and continues to experience oppression and institutionalized racism today . . . [and] benefits of the society in which they live are not accessible to them" (DeGruy-Leary 2005, p. 125). Research reinforces the need to examine history's impact on contemporary relationships. Raj and colleagues (1999) found an increased risk of violence toward African American women linked to jealousy and low empathy for the woman, as well as having children too early in the relationship and the lack of male income. Wingood and DiClemente (1996) found that many African American women choose to stay in abusive relationships because of the scarcity of available, marriageable African American men. This information was confirmed in a study by Wyatt et al. These historical experiences resonate within the communal consciousness from generation to generation.

STRUCTURAL DISADVANTAGES

African Americans in poor communities (making $5,999 or less annually) are more likely to experience domestic violence than African Americans above that income range (Bent-Goodley 2001). In fact, low socioeconomic status is a risk factor for domestic violence for all populations of women (Williams and Mickelson 2004; Wyatt, et al. 2000). African American women earning less than $50,000 are more likely to experience domestic violence compared to those making more than $50,000 (Schollenberger et al. 2003). When income is controlled, the rates of domestic violence among African Americans compared to Caucasians are comparable (Campbell 2002; Hampton and Gelles 1994; Lockhart 1985; Lockhart and White 1991; Walton-Moss et al. 2005). One could argue that domestic violence is a problem of African Americans in poor communities, but it has also been found among middle-class Americans; African American middle-class families are more likely to experience domestic violence compared to Caucasian middle-class families (Lockhart and White 1989). It is unclear if the reason for this difference stems from witnessing violence in the family of origin (Uzzell and Peebles-Wilkins 1989). Because much of the research among African Americans has been conducted only within poor communities, it is difficult to form conclusions related to the influence of socioeconomic status.

Purportedly communities where more children and nonrelated adults live together have less of a support network and experience greater isolation and vulnerability to domestic violence because of short-term residence and fewer community anchors (Cazenave and Straus 1979). Network embeddedness (the number of adults and children in a home and the number of years an individual or family has lived in a neighborhood) has not been sufficiently studied to support its importance in explaining domestic violence among African Americans. New research exploring this factor is warranted, but studies so far do show that the risk for violence increases when partners are not living together and the children have no blood relationship to the male (Campbell 2002). Issues with housing and population density could also be further studied under this construct.

Employment and occupational status has been linked to domestic violence as well; studies have found that unemployment and blue-collar occupations are associated with a greater prevalence of domestic violence (Cazenave and Straus 1979; Jasinski 1998; Uzzell and Peebles-Wilkins 1989; West 1998). Unemployment, of course, is linked to lower incomes, so it is difficult to differentiate between the influences of these two variables. Examination of the connections between class, income, employment, occupation, and network embeddedness clearly indicates that African Americans are greatly affected by these issues and that further research should explore how they impact domestic violence within this community (Hampton, Carrillo, and Kim 2005; West 2005).

SEXISM AND SEX-ROLE PERCEPTIONS

Domestic violence occurs within a context of sexism that permeates all aspects of life, and so it cannot be fully understood without a critical examination of sexism and the systems supporting it (Hill-Collins 2000). Patriarchal systems, supported by laws and societal expectations in their use of power and control, dominate and immobilize women (Dietz 2000; Guy-Sheftall 1995). Sexism continues to be evidenced by lower pay scales for women, laws that disproportionately impact and focus on women, and expectations that women carry greater responsibility for child rearing and for maintaining the home environment. Rigid sex-role perceptions have been linked to a greater acceptance of domestic violence among African Americans, including women (Bent-Goodley 2001; Lockhart 1985). More information is needed on this topic to fully determine its impact, however. The ways in which sexism and sex-role perception are linked to domestic violence must be understood to fully contextualize domestic violence in the African American community.

THE IMPACT OF TRAUMA

The key to understanding traumatic events is that no clear division exists between stress that leads to trauma and stress that leads, instead, to adaptation (Giller 1999). For African American women, this distinction is important because, depending on the circumstances in their lives, the degree to which structural racism and sexism impact their lives—and the level of understanding of their options—many African American women may not view the resultant emotions of being abused as trauma. Whether African American women react to victimization as trauma or adaptation depends on many factors, including childhood experiences, peer input, and environmental and community circumstances. Trauma associated with growing up in violent communities also should not be overlooked (Jenkins 2002; Richie 1996; West 2005).

The high rates of trauma associated with child sexual abuse and child abuse within the African American community reveals histories of violence, oppression, and abuse from childhood to adulthood (Ramos, Carlson, and McNutt 2004; Wingood and DiClemente 1997b; Wyatt et al. 2000; Wyatt et al. 2002). African American women with histories of child abuse are more vulnerable to experiencing domestic violence and other forms of abuse during adulthood than others (Wyatt et al. 2002). One-third of African American women have reported experiencing childhood sexual abuse and one-fourth have reported experiencing childhood physical abuse. These high rates of victimization are most evident in populations of incarcerated African American women (Richie 1996).

DISPARITIES IN DOMESTIC VIOLENCE SERVICES

African American women at every level have experienced discriminatory treatment within the domestic violence service system. Evidence suggests that not only does discriminatory treatment impact help-seeking among African American women but there is a link between perceived racism, intimate partner violence, and negative health outcomes among African American women (Waltermaurer, Watson, and McNutt 2006). In the health-care arena, African American women have found health professionals to be disinterested, judgmental, insensitive to the unique circumstances of being a woman of color, disrespectful, and inattentive when dealing with domestic violence and other health-related issues (Bent-Goodley 2007; Campbell 2002; McNutt et al. 2000; Plichta 2004). Within the mental health arena, African American women are more likely to suffer from undiagnosed or mis-diagnosed stress-related symptoms—depression and anxiety—resulting from domestic violence (Humphreys and Joseph 2004). Within the child welfare arena, African American women in abusive relationships are more likely to have their children removed from the home compared to Caucasian women (Bent-Goodley 2004b). Within the criminal justice system, African American women are more likely to experience dual arrests under the mandatory arrest policy, which requires that the primary aggressor in a domestic violence situation must be arrested (Mills 1998), as these women are often regarded by law enforcement officers as uncooperative, too loud, out of control, and equally capable of abuse (Melton 1999; Richie 2005). Within the court system, African American women are more likely to be prosecuted for having defended themselves against a batterer (Bent-Goodley 2004a; Richie 1996). Within the domestic violence service provision system, African American women have been turned away from shelter services based on stereotypical assumptions that they are strong enough to handle the abuse, they do not appear sufficiently upset, or they are physically big enough to fight back against the abuser (Hill-Collins 2000; Richie 2005; West 1999). These areas of disparate treatment are rarely recognized or fully understood. The cultural convention of protecting and sustaining women becomes irrelevant when considering that discrimination, stereotypes, and racism can be used to justify the negative treatment of African American women. The insult of such treatment discourages many African American women from reaching out for help, even when they need it.

THE INTERSECTIONALITY OF OPPRESSION

The issues above are sufficiently interconnected to make the lives of African American women much more complex and difficult, causing this issue to be harder to understand than if we were only examining a single form of oppression (Allard 2005; Crenshaw 1991). The intersection of different kinds of oppression for African American women is key to understanding their unique position and experiences (Crenshaw 1991; Sokoloff 2005). Issues of race/ethnicity, gender, and class oppression pose independent individual threats; when considered together the challenges are even more profound. "These systems are not mutually exclusive, static or abstract. They operate independently or simultaneously, and the dynamics of each may exacerbate and compound the consequences of another" (Bograd 2005, p. 26). It could be argued that none of these issues alone, but how they *intersect*, warrants greater understanding. Continuing to offer fragmented services, wherein issues are individually treated and not considered within the context of their intersections, is an inefficient, and ultimately *ineffective*, means of providing services.

CULTURALLY SENSITIVE PRACTICE AND DOMESTIC VIOLENCE

The emphases on family, community, and spirituality are important elements of the African American experience. In addition, the role of religious institutions, matters of racial loyalty, and help-seeking are critical when examining cultural dimensions relevant to African Americans.

FAMILIAL INFLUENCES

Intergenerational transmission of violence among African Americans has been found to be a key factor for adult intimate partner violence (Huang and Gunn 2001). It is within the family unit that our understandings of appropriate behavior, relationships, love, identity, and social obligations are formed. Family is described as more than the immediate nuclear family, and includes the extended family and those regarded as family members.

Even though the family is the system within which abuse occurs, service provision typically centers on the woman, with limited regard for the family. Yet, family is critical to African Americans (Boyd-Franklin 2003; Hill 1997). African American women strongly hold the value of maintaining the family. The family unit can be helpful or harmful, but it must be considered. To provide services to the woman without considering and providing services for her family creates conflict. For example, the major source of service to survivors of domestic violence is to provide shelters, and many shelters do not accept children older than a certain age. In many instances, adolescent males are not allowed in a shelter, and so women must choose between either continuing to live in violence or separating from their adolescent sons. This consideration limits their ability to access shelters and lowers the possibility that a shelter program could be of assistance. Rodgers (2006) contends that *separate but treatable* interventions, essentially separating culture from the treatment of the problem, guarantee an unsuccessful healing process for African American women.

COMMUNITY INFLUENCES

Community is viewed as an extension of the family, and there is a notion that individuals and families cannot thrive when the community itself is in disarray (Carlton-LaNey 2001). The community is a part of the life of the family, impacting opportunities for socialization, mentorship, informal guidance, and support. The community represents the larger context for family life, for it is where behaviors are reinforced—deemed appropriate or inappropriate— and where individuals and families share common stories and experiences to access support and resources. Consequently, addressing the needs of families without addressing the needs of the community is antithetical to engaging African Americans.

SPIRITUAL AND RELIGIOUS INFLUENCES

Spirituality and religion are critical constructs for African Americans (Billingsley 1999; Hill 1997; Martin and Martin 2002). Spirituality refers to one's belief in a "higher" power, whereas religion refers to the practice of one's faith (Martin and Martin 2002). The importance of prayer among African American survivors of domestic violence has been documented (Abernethy et al. 2006; Bent-Goodley and Fowler 2006; Davis 2002; El-Khoury et al. 2004; Hassouneh-Phillips 2003; Senter and Caldwell 2002; West 1999). With their history of lending support to the community, African American faith-based communities (FBC) are recognized for providing food, shelter, and clothing, as well as counseling, education, and financial and supportive services (Billingsley 1999). In the past the FBC provided resources to African Americans when mainstream society would not (Billingsley 1999; Carlton-LaNey 2001). As a result, African Americans and others view FBCs as an indispensable, powerful influence in their lives. Providing a moral code of conduct, reinforcing inner strength and spiritual beliefs, and attending to sensitive personal issues unknown to others, the FBC represents a viable venue for addressing domestic violence. In fact, African American women are known to seek help from their FBC before reaching out to formal service providers (Bent-Goodley 2006; Bent-Goodley and Fowler 2006; Neighbors, Musick, and Williams 1998). Simultaneously, however, FBCs have also been places of bondage for women seeking help to get out of abusive relationships. Rigid interpretation of scripture, sexism within the FBC, lack of understanding about domestic violence, and an unwillingness to address the issue have all conspired to limit the church as a resource to many African American women seeking shelter, counseling, and care (McClure and Ramsay 1998; Nason-Clark 2004). It remains important, at any rate, to appreciate the possible influence of the FBC on African American women's thinking in order to serve them well.

RACIAL LOYALTY

Racial loyalty occurs when an "African American woman may withstand abuse and make a conscious self-sacrifice for what she perceives as the greater good of the community, but to her own physical, psychological, and spiritual detriment" (Bent-Goodley 2001. p. 323). Racial loyalty occurs when a woman wants to receive help for domestic violence but sacrifices herself to protect an African American man from further abuse and discriminatory treatment within the criminal justice and court systems (Bent-Goodley 2004b; Richie 1996). Historical challenges to ensure the safety of African American males are heightened for many African American families (Boyd-Franklin and Toussaint 2001), especially for women. African American women may feel pressured to keep the family together, fearing that they will be considered disloyal to their race should they reveal the abuse they suffer (Fraser et al. 2002; Richie 1996; West 1999; White 1994). African American women may also choose not to report domestic violence to avoid feeding negative stereotypes about African American relationships. For these reasons, African American women may withstand the violence, trying to protect and maintain the family at great personal cost. This decision can also increase their sense of isolation (Taylor 2000). As a result, racial loyalty takes place within a larger context of discriminatory treatment.

HELP SEEKING

Increasing data have emerged regarding help-seeking behavior among African American women who have experienced domestic violence. Compared to other women, African American women are most likely to turn first to family and friends, and then to their faith-based community (Herbert and Gunn

2001; Lipsky et al. 2006). It has been stated that African Americans turn to law enforcement officers for support to address domestic violence more than others (Lee et al. 2002; Yoshioka et al. 2003), which might reflect a scarcity of resources available for addressing the issue within their respective communities. The literature, however, has also discussed the resistance that many African American women have to contacting the police to address domestic violence (Campbell 2002; Pyles and Kim 2006). Many African American women fear the police because of perceived police brutality and unfair treatment, and possible dual arrests. Often African American women contact the police only to stop a particular violent episode, rather than seeking to have the abuser incarcerated or mistreated by the police. It is unclear, moreover, how income is related to this issue. For example, poor communities of color have an increased police presence, whereas more dense housing in these communities may account for neighbors hearing the violence more readily and then contacting the police. It is uncertain, therefore, if phone calls for police assistance are associated with issues of class and poverty or with issues of race and culture. Greater research is warranted to tease out these relationships.

CULTURAL COMPETENCE

Cultural competence can be defined as "the process used by individuals and systems to respectfully integrate and transform knowledge of culture and language, the cultural strengths of people and their communities, the assessment of cross-cultural relations, vigilance to dynamics in cultural and linguistic differences, and the adaptation of services to meet culturally unique needs" (Cross et al. 1989). Cultural competence addresses every level of performance within a program and its systems of care (Almeida and Lockard 2005). Staffing should be examined—from the direct-level practitioners to the senior administrative staff and board members—to reflect the clients being served. Many agencies serving African American women have direct-service providers indigenous to the population, but their senior-level managers are not African American and may be unfamiliar with the African American experience. This is not to suggest that just because someone is African American that he or she will be culturally competent; cultural competence is reflected through knowledge, values, and skills. Culturally competent programs should involve African American women and their communities in the decision making regarding everything from the program's philosophy to its components. Without these assurances, the inclusion of one aspect of African American culture is ineffective at best, and insulting at worst. Programs receiving public funds should especially be required to show evidence of cultural competence.

SHORTCOMINGS OF TRADITIONAL APPROACHES

Existing models for responding to domestic violence among African American women are predicated on oppressive organizational structures that continue to mirror the institutionalized racism within non-black organizations (Asbury 1987; Hampton and Yung 1996). Failure to address the larger racial context, the power of language, the lack of comprehensive and holistic services, and the geographic inaccessibility of services ignores the underlying influences shaping the experiences of African American women who are survivors of domestic violence (Pyles and Kim 2006).

FAILURE TO ADDRESS THE LARGER CONTEXT

Too many programs continue to function from a culturally neutral perspective, where violence is believed to be similar across all groups and thus consider that tailoring unique approaches to race, ethnicity, or culture is unwarranted. As a result, services are offered and provided in the same fashion to everyone, without recognizing the diverse and unique factors that lead women to have to seek services. When interventions are not designed to be relevant to any particular group, the outcome is ineffective services, skepticism about a program's effectiveness, and mistrust in the helping relationship.

THE POWER OF LANGUAGE

Too many programs attempt to impose their definitions and terminology for abuse with African Americans. Some African American women object to the term "battered woman," and many African American women also find it difficult to be called a victim, noting that the term does not acknowledge the strength it took for them to survive. Practitioners who try to force their program's definitions and terminology for domestic violence on African American women might find that domestic violence unwittingly goes unidentified.

LACK OF COMPREHENSIVE SERVICES

Domestic violence clearly does not take place within a vacuum. For example, substance abuse and HIV/AIDS further complicate issues of treatment. Women with addiction problems are often turned away from receiving shelter services for domestic violence, and substance abuse counselors often do not explore whether the addiction is linked to the violence the woman is experiencing. This is an especially important point, as HIV/AIDS is the second leading cause of death of African American women between 25 and 44 years of age (Center for Disease Control and Prevention 2001; Fullilove and Fullilove 2005). African American women are the greatest number of newly diagnosed HIV cases compared to all other groups of women; domestic violence enhances the risk for contracting HIV/AIDS (Wingood and DiClemente 1997a; Wyatt et al. 2002). The reason is that African American women generally have reduced ability to negotiate safer sex, and the increased risks of sexual assault and violence obviously increase the likelihood of contracting HIV (Wyatt et al. 2002). Treating these issues in isolation diminishes the effectiveness of the intervention. These two issues illustrate the need for more comprehensive services that address the link between domestic violence and other critical health and mental health issues. To continue to isolate treatment shows a blatant disregard for the complexity of the lives of the women experiencing these difficult issues.

GEOGRAPHIC INACCESSIBILITY OF SERVICES

The geographic inaccessibility of domestic violence services is also a barrier for African American women (Bent-Goodley 2001, 2004a). Several components contribute to the inaccessibility of services, including location, funding, and transportation limitations. Transportation problems also make it difficult to receive services. A woman with two children, for example, may have difficulty managing her children when they have to take a train and a bus to get to services, particularly when those services are dispersed throughout the week and compete with the children's needs. Navigating public transportation is challenging enough, but it becomes almost impossible when negotiating with tired children, late buses and trains, crowds, poor weather, and restricted budgets. Many African American women lack the financial resources to be able to go from place to place outside the community for services. Even if an agency helps a woman by providing transportation tokens or a reimbursement card, the agency might neglect to provide her with resources for babysitting or funds needed to travel with children, such as money for snacks. Finally, having to travel to a Caucasian community to obtain services could be a major deterrent for an African American woman, who might perceive the environment as potentially hostile. The woman may feel unaccepted and uncomfortable in the

Caucasian environment or fear for her safety. Clearly not having services in the woman's immediate geographic community constitutes many service barriers.

CULTURALLY SENSITIVE DOMESTIC VIOLENCE INTERVENTION AND PREVENTION

Domestic violence within the African American community requires a comprehensive, holistic approach sensitive to diversity that is organic and innovative in service delivery. What may be unacceptable to the larger community of domestic violence service providers, such as emphasizing the need to find solutions for men who batter while working with the woman, is critical for serving the needs of African American women. *Stopping the violence and maintaining the physical and mental health of the woman and her children is clearly the first and primary priority.* However, without including a renewed emphasis on finding solutions to curtail battering within the African American community from a holistic perspective, we will continue to struggle with this issue.

CULTURAL COMPETENCE IN LANGUAGE AND DEFINITIONS

How the community defines domestic violence is critical to our discussion. Without understanding the definition of domestic violence, we cannot build a relationship based on a common understanding. We should not assume that any particular woman views pushing, shoving, or punching as domestic violence, and practitioners must discuss the issues in order to understand the individual's concept of domestic violence. Once identified and once there is an understanding—not necessarily a shared definition—professionals can build on understanding their clients' perceptions. Further, the definition of domestic violence often contains an implied solution. While identifying the definition, it is paramount that the solution be as multifaceted as the definition. For many African American women, the primary option that professionals offer is terminating the relationship, but this may be viewed as destroying the African American family and supporting negative images of the African American family as "dysfunctional." Another concern about the definition of domestic violence relates to who is named the primary aggressor or person responsible for the abuse. The facts of who hit first, who started the argument, who is the aggressor are resolved within the criminal justice system. These issues warrant greater attention; the different ways that systems identify domestic violence is an important consideration for clients.

Many interpret the consideration of language differences to imply that a person is not a native English speaker. Language, however, also includes nuance and the meaning ascribed to words. The vernacular is critical to understanding and building communication (Bent-Goodley 2005a, 2005b; Sokoloff 2005).

PROVIDING HOLISTIC PREVENTION AND INTERVENTION

As we consider the strategies needed in working with African American women, we must also develop an understanding of what works to help African American children who have witnessed violence. The intervention strategies required should focus on maintaining safety, healing, parenting consider-ations, and finding ways to include the extended family in services. There must be an emphasis on encouraging men not to be abusive toward their part-ners. Nonviolent men must be a part of this movement for it to succeed. It is essential to find ways to help men take greater responsibility for this problem and link it to the preservation and sustenance of the community.

Next, it is vital to create safe spaces for African American women who experience domestic violence. Besides having services available outside the community, African American women should have the option of utilizing services within their community. Creative solutions must be developed to address issues holistically, not in isolation.

INVOLVING THE COMMUNITY

Community involvement is crucial and includes creating public health cam-paigns on domestic violence. The Family Violence Prevention Fund has developed a public health campaign on this topic for African Americans. However, more targeted involvement is needed. We continue to have too few public health endeavors that focus on identifying and publicizing healthy relationships. Education and services for domestic violence may be better uti-lized were they situated within community organizations, without ties to law enforcement or the criminal justice community. If the group has credibility in the community, a program in a local nonprofit organization may be more acceptable than one housed within a child welfare agency or welfare office. Educating communities and faith-based organizations on how to respond to the issue is essential. Many in the community want to respond to domestic violence but do not know how to or fear for their own safety. It is important to provide community members with succinct and realistic tools on how to address domestic violence.

FOCUSING ON STRENGTHS

Domestic violence services are often seen as focusing on the victim and exploring the pathology of abuse (Danis 2003). Despite these perceptions, African American women continue to exert resistance strategies that allow them to survive (Taylor 2002a, 2002b; West 1999). Every person has a particular strength, even if it is that the person chose to wake up at all and face the day. Focusing on strengths allows practitioners to help clients identify areas to address and their corresponding mechanisms for change. Elements of both domestic violence activism and cultural diversity are important to African American women, but they are not integrated with the strength- and culturally based philosophies of African centered (Asante 1980; Bent-Goodley 2005a; Karenga 1980; Myers 1995), black feminist (Allard 2005; Collins 2000a), and womanist (Eugene 1995; Sanders 1995; Walker 1983) principles.

GENERALIST PRACTICE AND CULTURALLY SPECIFIC STRATEGIES FOR AFRICAN AMERICAN WOMEN

Generalist practice uses a holistic approach in service provision that spans the individual level to the societal level. Reflecting on different elements of generalist practice, here we discuss how one can use a generalist approach to respond to an African American woman dealing with domestic violence.

Mona is referred to you because her eight-year-old son, John, is not attending school. As a family preservation specialist assigned to her case, you discover that John is not going to school because he wants to protect his mother. When you confront Mona, she tells you that John has heard some of his parents' arguments, but that there isn't any abuse—just two married folks trying to work out their problems.

Not until three months later, during a parent support group, does Mona admit that Gerald, her husband of 15 years, has been physically abusive toward her but never abusive to John. Mona shares pictures of herself to show what she looked like prior to the abuse. You are astonished to the see the significant difference in her physical appearance. She has lost 30 to 40 pounds, has missing teeth, and her hair is falling out. She tells you that the abuse began when her husband suffered a head injury

"CONTINUED"

and lost his job. Once a vibrant working-class family, Mona states that her family is now poor and relying on public assistance. Mona tells you that she wants to get out of the relationship but is fearful of what her husband will do to her and to himself. She admits that he stalks her and has often threatened to kill her if she ever leaves him. She tells you that she "just doesn't want to see another African American man go into the system," but she wants the violence to stop. She also tells you that she doesn't believe that she can raise a black boy to be a man by herself, and that too many black families are led by single mothers. She tells you that she doesn't want her family to be another statistic, showing that black people can't stay together. She insists on staying in the marriage, at least until John is 18. When asked if her family is aware of the violence, she says that they live in a different state and that her sister got tired of her leaving and returning to her husband, so they have not been in touch with each other in three years. She also states that her mother and father told her to work it out because they have a child together—"at least she has a man"—and that this is a part of being married.

After an abusive incident that led to an overnight hospital stay, Mona tells you that she is ready to leave the relationship for good and that she and her son can move in with her sister. Through careful safety planning, you help Mona prepare to leave. On the day she is to depart, you don't hear from her and cannot find her or her son at home. Two days later, John explains to you that his mother decided not to leave and that last night she tried to overdose on medication but saw him looking at her and stopped.

The practitioner's approach to assisting Mona requires, first, establishing a working relationship with her, and then proceeding to an assessment of her situation and setting up goals for a course of action.

THE WORKING RELATIONSHIP

Establishing the working relationship includes forming a partnership, identifying challenges and strengths, being genuine and reliable, and demonstrating integrity. Most important, workers need to be aware of their own biases and beliefs about domestic violence and the African American community. "The process of forming professional relationships sets the tone for the entire interaction between clients and practitioners. Empowerment-oriented social workers respect clients' perspectives and recognize the positive contribution of working collaboratively" (DuBois and Miley 1996, p. 216). In a study of welfare reform among survivors of domestic violence, the researchers found that "[the] women expected their workers to be genuine, empathetic, concerned, and nonjudgmental. . . . [T]hey also expected their workers to be knowledge-able about the multiple difficulties of their lives . . . [and] expect[ed] their workers to understand the continuing risk of violence by their perpetrators" (Busch and Wolfer 2002, pp. 577–578). To meet these expectations, workers need to be well trained about the dynamics of domestic violence, available services, and community support networks. Beginning with the initial meet-ing, workers need to be careful about their own nonverbal and verbal behav-iors. They should be welcoming and listen to the survivor, and the setting should be a safe space. The worker's bias can undermine the establishment of rapport and trust in the helping relationship. Female workers who are sur-vivors of domestic violence themselves need to be aware of any unresolved issues of their own that can impact the helping relationship. In the event of such issues, they should actively seek supervision and consultation to ensure that the working relationship remains professional.

ASSESSMENT STRATEGIES

"Empowerment-based social work practice reframes assessment from a process that gathers information to detect problems to one that focuses on gathering information to discover resources that will strengthen solutions" (DuBois and Miley 1996, p. 226). The first level of assessment is to listen to the woman and establish *her view of her world and her thoughts about possible options*. Under-stand that it may take time for her to reveal the violence. Only when workers understand the survivor's point of view can any assistance be rendered. The survivor's viewpoint also gives workers information about the services that may be needed to assist the victim. In the above scenario, Mona made many statements that constitute her view of her world. She is concerned about her son, financial issues, fear of her husband but concerns about his medical condition, racial loyalty, disparate support from her family of origin, concerns about child rear-ing, and emotional distress. She minimizes the abuse. Some of her statements expose conflicting beliefs about her current situation. The worker needs to assess her stress level, strengths, and resources to ascertain her ability to take action of any kind. Assessment questions need to be open-ended, giving Mona the ability to define her situation in her own words and from her own experiences.

The worker must be patient. Mona has endured this situation for 15 years. She has developed coping mechanisms and strengths that have sustained her through many crises. The worker has to identify how she has coped, what strategies she has used, and may need to explain to her how these strategies are her *strengths*. The next level of assessment is to ascertain her understanding of her life. Does she identify herself as abused? Why does she think the abuse occurs? What is her definition of safety, and what will help her feel safe? What does she think about her son's situation or her husband's medical situation? Has she ever attempted to connect to services? If so, were they helpful? What does she think may be helpful to her? What is the outcome she wants? In many situations, the woman wants to end the violence in her life but not necessarily end the relationship. The worker must be aware of the available services within the community, from financial and educational services to emotional services. The more aware the worker is about available services, the more useful she will be to Mona.

GOAL SETTING AND CONTRACTING

"The goal-setting process involves negotiating agreements about the course of action" (DuBois and Miley 1996, p. 233). Contracting is viewed "as living agreements that evolve as interactions with clients proceed" (DuBois and Miley 1996, p. 235). Goal setting can be very difficult in Mona's current emotional state and stress level. Short-term goals may be preferred, as they create a sense of accomplishment and more immediately demonstrate progress. Setting weekly attainable goals, such as attending church services regularly or finding information about possible options, could be helpful. Setting small, attainable exercises can help Mona realize that she can make changes, which is the steppingstone to further progress, and working together to develop these changes is important to affirm her sense of control over her life. How will she get through today? What services does she need? What does she need to secure a degree of safety in her life? Has she been evaluated by a medical doctor? Does she want mental health treatment? The social worker must be careful not to overwhelm her. For an African American woman, assessing how she will handle the community's response to her changes is also important. If Mona considers filing for the civil protection order that could remove her husband from the home for a time, how will her neighbors, her support system, and her community view her after that decision? Will this create more stress in her life? How will this impact her son and his life with his peers? These are all questions that need to be asked and discussed for Mona to feel comfortable enough to take such an action.

As part of contracting to work together, agreements are needed about when the worker can collaborate or share information with other agencies or persons who may also be working with Mona. Whether this is in the form of a signed release of information agreement or an agreement to meet together to discuss progress, some form of collaborative agreement is helpful.

ALTERNATIVE INTERVENTIONS

To consider alternative interventions, "social workers and clients consider the information they've gathered to discover resources and strengths that they can build upon" (DuBois and Miley 1996, p. 229). Traditional programs may not alleviate some of Mona's concerns in that they may not address the racial loyalty or the unique issues of raising an African American son as a single mother (Bent-Goodley and Williams 2007; Tubbs and Williams 2007). Mona's daily living activities need to be understood. Is her husband home all day with her? Does she have the ability to move freely? The answers to these questions give a better understanding of what options can be discussed. Getting her husband involved is an avenue that would need to be addressed, since Mona stated that things changed after he sustained a work-related injury and lost his job. Working with formal service providers that might help him with his injury might alleviate some stress in her life. What about her husband's family? Can they be of assistance? Becoming more involved in her son's school and having him in extracurricular activities or a mentoring program may alleviate some parenting concerns. Collaborating with other agencies and having regular, collaborative meetings to monitor her progress and ensure that all helping agencies are progressing along the same path might also help Mona. Attempting to involve her family members as a unified support system would be helpful as well. Increasing her exposure to others, including informal providers, through religious activities could be helpful. Women who have survived abusive situations over time have a much better understanding of what strategies could be useful to them as well as their ability to make changes. When workers have a predetermined set of steps to take, they leave little room for discussion with the woman and lessen the chance that she will move forward with the plan.

RESOLVING ETHICAL DILEMMAS

"Ethical behavior is based on an interpretation of the application of values" (DuBois and Miley 1996, p. 123). The social worker can minimize ethical dilemmas when working with a new client by stating, at the outset, the values and mission of the helping agency and the profession. The value of "self-determination," which is highly respected in the profession of social work, must be kept in focus. Many times women will have concerns and make decisions that workers may not view as the best choice. However, workers must remember that self-determination is about the client making decisions and workers assisting them to make those decisions successfully, as the clients define success.

As noted earlier, many African American survivors of domestic violence want the violence in their lives to end, but they do not necessarily want to have the abuser mistreated by police or incarcerated. If the worker believes that the only way to end the violence is within the criminal justice system and that incarceration is possible, many African American women, not wanting to take that step, will feel that the helping relationship is actually not helping them. The survivor may decide not to move forward with a protection order, or she may totally withdraw from services. There are times when the worker will still have to contact these resources, but this should be done with consultation and care. Talking with the client about strategies that can help alleviate the violence, getting families involved, working with the woman's faith community, or even taking the civil legal route (which does not involve incarceration) may support her concerns. If the selected strategy does not result in the desired end, then the woman will recognize that some of the options she thought would work are not beneficial. If the worker has supported and assisted as much as possible, then the woman might become more open to other strategies.

SELECTING APPROPRIATE INTERVENTIONS

Selecting appropriate interventions involves "plans of action [that] draw upon the formal provisions of the social service delivery system as well as the informal resources in clients' social networks" (DuBois and Miley 1996, p. 233). Although evidence-based practice currently has a significant presence in social work interventions, to date, there are limited evidence-based practices in domestic violence upon which to draw (Wathen and MacMillan 2003). Promising approaches are being developed and tested, but right now workers must become familiar with the aforementioned issues and consider interventions that reflect the needs of the population.

Individual- and group-level services should be assessed for the entire family. In Mona's case, for example, in addition to counseling services, the worker might consider play therapy for John, a women's support group for Mona, and a batterer's intervention program for Gerald. The worker should assess the support from community partners, such as religious institutions and the extended family. Perhaps the religious institutions have ministries to address or support change regarding the identified issues. If culturally competent services are not available, inaccessible, or fragmented, the social worker or the agency or both are expected to engage in community education and advocacy to promote the need for these services in the community.

The purpose of monitoring and evaluating the outcomes are to "validate clients' achievements and substantiate the usefulness of social service strategies, programs, and policies" (DuBois and Miley 1996, p. 239). Mona herself must define success. What does she believe will alleviate the violence in her life and help her feel safe and productive again? We have to support her choices. We cannot define success for her, but we can assist her in constructing a realistic, attainable goal in her life. Perhaps she will never leave the relationship, so we cannot set that as a goal. However, intervention from the church, counseling, or involvement in other supportive associations may alleviate the violence, which is a shared goal. As stated before, African American women are cautious about discussing their lives with strangers and in public. Therefore, methods of assessment must be both culturally competent and sensitive to the context of domestic violence.

ENDINGS

"Endings are also beginnings" (DuBois and Miley 1996, p. 245). Once a survivor has achieved a level of safety or has made the changes *she* wanted to make, the formal helping relationship may end. Termination should occur over several sessions and stretch over longer periods of time. Sessions could be held bi- monthly or monthly, instead of weekly, giving the client more time between sessions to evaluate her progress and decide whether to end formal services. It is important that women know they can always return for more support or further assistance if changes occur in their situation. Helping the woman become involved in some kind of social action or community education to assist victims or to obtain increased services may also be useful for her ongoing growth and continued health. Many African American women have become involved in their state's chapter of the domestic violence coalition Women of Color Task Force to continue their own growth, receive ongoing going support, and work on increasing the understanding of domestic violence in their communities. Equally critical is the need for more mezzo-level interventions such as the development of local task forces on domestic violence, as well as the building of collaborative partnerships with local African American community-based and domestic violence programs.

These can assist us with developing post-shelter and post-services in critical and meaningful ways (Sullivan et al. 1994).

CONCLUSION

This chapter has explored the experiences of African American women subject to domestic violence. Domestic violence occurs within a range of sociocultural factors that must be fully considered when addressing the needs of African American women. Comprehensive and holistic services draw on cultural strengths and recognize barriers and limitations, and are critical in providing meaningful and useful services to a group of diverse women. As this area of social work evolves, we must find solutions that help address the context of these women's lives, not just the individual circumstances. Only with a comprehensive understanding of the circumstances of the lives of African American women can we acknowledge their profound strength and resilience, and fortify the groundwork for their survival.

RESOURCES

Africentric Personal Development Shop, Inc.
1409 East Livingston Avenue
Columbus, OH 43205
Phone: (614) 253–4458
E-mail: apds@apdsinc.org
Web site: http://www.apdsinc.org/

ASHA Family Services
3821 W. North Avenue
Milwaukee, WI 53208
Phone: (414) 875–1511
Web site: http://www.ashafamilyservices.com/

Black Church and Domestic Violence Institute
2740 Greenbriar Pkwy., Suite 256
Atlanta, GA 30331
Phone: (770) 909–0715
E-mail: bcdvorg@aol.com
Web site: http://www.bcdvi.org/

Black Women's Health Imperative
1726 M. Street, NW, Suite 300
Washington, DC 20036
Phone: (202) 548–4000
Email: info@BlackWomensHealth.org
Web site: http://www.blackwomenshealth.org/

Incite! Women of Color Against Violence
E-mail: incite_national@yahoo.com
Web site: http://www.incite-national.org/

Institute on Domestic Violence in the African American Community
University of Minnesota, School of Social Work
290 Peters Hall
1404 Gortner Avenue
St. Paul, MN 55108-6142
Phone: 1 (877) NIDVAAC (643–8222)
E-mail: nidvaac@che.umn.edu
Web site: http://www.dvinstitute.org/

Men Can Stop Rape
1003 K Street, NW, Suite 200
Washington, DC 20001
Phone: (202) 265–6530
Email: info@mencanstoprape.org
Web site: http://www.mencanstoprape.org/

Men Stopping Violence
2785 Lawrenceville Highway, Suite 112
Decatur, GA 30033
Phone: (404) 270–9894
Email: msv@menstoppingviolence.org
Web site: http://www.menstoppingviolence.org/index.php

National Coalition Against Domestic Violence
(Houses data about state coalitions and services in every state, as well as a Women of Color [WOC] Caucus that can be helpful.)
1120 Lincoln Street, Suite #1603
Denver, CO 80203
Phone: (303) 839–1852

TTY: (303) 839-8459
Fax: (303) 831-9251
E-mail: gshaw@ncadv.org
Web site: http://www.ncadv.org/takeaction/CaucusInformation_156.html

National Domestic Violence Hotline
1 (800) 799–SAFE (7233)
Web site: http://www.ncadv.org

REFERENCES

Abernethy, A. D., T. R. Houston, T. Mimms, and N. Boyd-Franklin. (2006). Using prayer in psychotherapy: Applying Sue's differential to enhance culturally competent care. *Cultural Diversity and Ethnic Minority Psychology*, 12, 101–114.

Allard, S. A. (2005). Rethinking battered women's syndrome: A Black feminist perspective. In N. Sokoloff and C. Pratt (Eds.), *Domestic Violence at the Margins: Readings on Race, Class, Gender, and Culture* (pp. 194–205). New Brunswick, NJ: Rutgers University Press.

Almeida, R. V., and J. Lockard. (2005). The cultural context model: A new paradigm for accountability, empowerment and the development of critical consciousness against domestic violence. In N. Sokoloff and C. Pratt (Eds.), *Domestic Violence at the Margins: Readings on Race, Class, Gender, and Culture* (pp. 301–320). New Brunswick, NJ: Rutgers University Press.

Asbury, J. (1987). African Americans in violent relationships: An exploration of cultural differences. In R. Hampton (Ed.), *Violence in the African American Family: Correlates and Consequences* (pp. 89–104). Lexington, MA: Lexington |Books.

Asante, M. (1980). *Afrocentricity and Knowledge.* Trenton, NJ: African World Press.

Barak, G., J. Flavin, and P. Leighton. (2001). *Class, Race, Gender and Crime: Social Realities of Justice in America.* Cary, NC: Roxbury.

Bent-Goodley, T. B. (2001). Eradicating domestic violence in the African American community: A literature review, analysis and action agenda. *Trauma, Violence, and Abuse*, 2, 316–330.

——. (2004a). Policy implications of domestic violence for people of color. In K. E. Davis and T. B. Bent-Goodley (Eds.), *The Color of Social Policy* (pp. 65–80). Alexandria, VA: CSWE Press.

——. (2004b). Perceptions of domestic violence: A dialogue with African American women. *Health and Social Work*, 29, 307–316.

——. (2005a). An African centered approach to domestic violence. *Families in Society*, 86, 197–206.

——. (2005b). Culture and domestic violence: Transforming knowledge development. *Journal of Interpersonal Violence 20,* 195–203.

——. (2006). Domestic violence and the Black church: Challenging abuse one soul at a time. In R. L. Hampton and T. P. Gullotta (Eds.), *Interpersonal Violence in the African American Community* (pp. 107–119). New York: Springer.

——. (2007). Health disparities and violence against women: Why and how cultural and societal influences matter. *Trauma, Violence and Abuse, 8,* 90–104.

Bent-Goodley, T. B., and D. Fowler. (2006). Spiritual and religious abuse: Expanding what is known about domestic violence. *Affilia, 21,* 282–295.

Bent-Goodley, T. B., and O. J. Williams. (2005). *Community Insights on Domestic Violence among African Americans: Conversations about Domestic Violence and Other Issues Affecting Their Community, Seattle, Washington.* St. Paul, MN: Institute on Domestic Violence in the African American Community.

——. (2007). Box: Fathers voices on parenting and violence. In J. L. Edleson and O. J. Williams (Eds.), *Parenting by Men Wwho Batter: New Directions for Assessment and Intervention* (pp. 32–44). New York: Oxford University Press.

Billingsley, A. (1999). *Mighty Like a River: The Black Church and Social Reform.* New York: Oxford University Press.

Bograd, M. (2005). Strengthening domestic violence theories: Intersections of race, class, sexual orientation and gender. In N. Sokoloff and C. Pratt, (Eds.), *Domestic Violence at the Margins: Readings on Race, Class, Gender and Culture* (pp. 25–38). New Brunswick, NJ: Rutgers University Press.

Bolles, A. (2001). Seeking the ancestors: Forging a black feminist tradition in anthropology. In McClaurin (Ed.), *Black Feminist Anthropology* (pp.24–48). New Brunswick, NJ: Rutgers University Press.

Boyd-Franklin, N. (2003). *Black Families in Therapy: A Multisystems Approach* (2nd ed.). New York: Guilford.

Boyd-Franklin, N., and P. Toussaint. (2001). *Boys into Men: Raising Our African American Teenage Sons.* New York: Plume.

Bureau of Justice Statistics. (2006). Intimate partner violence. Retrieved January 10, 2007, from http://www.ojp.usdoj.gov/bjs.

Busch, N. B., and T. A. Wolfer. (2002). Battered women speak out. *Violence Against Women, 8,* 566–584.

Campbell, J. C. (2002). Health consequences of intimate partner violence. *Lancet, 359,* 1331–1336.

Carlton-LaNey, I. B. (Ed.). (2001). *African American Leadership: An Empowerment Tradition in Social Welfare History.* Washington, DC: NASW Press.

Cazenave, N. H., and M. A. Straus. (1979). Race, class, network embeddedness, and family violence: A search for potent support systems. *Journal of Comparative Family Studies, 10,* 281–299.

Center for Disease Control and Prevention, National Center for HIV, STD, and TB Prevention, Divisions of HIV/AIDS Prevention. (2001). *HIV/AIDS among US Women: Minority and Young Women at Continuing Risk.* Retrieved January 9, 2007, from http://www.cdc.gov/hiv/pubs/facts/women.htm.

Collins, P. H. (2000a). *Black Feminist Thought: Knowledge, Consciousness, and the Politics of Empowerment* (2nd ed.). London: Routledge.

Collins, P. H. (2000b). The social construction of Black feminist thought. In J. James and T. D. Sharpley-Whiting. *The Black Feminist Reader* (pp. 183–207). Walden, MA: Blackwell.

Crenshaw, K. (1991). Mapping the margins: Intersectionality, identity politics and violence against women of color. In L. M. Alcoff and E. Mendieta (Eds.), *Identities: Race, Class, Gender and Nationality* (pp. 175–200). Malden, MA: Blackwell.

Cross, T. L., B. J. Bazron, K. W. Dennis, and M. R. Isaacs. (1989). *Toward a Culturally Competent System of Care* (Vol. 1). Washington, DC: Child and adolescent services system, program technical assistance center.

Danis, F. S. (2003). Social work response to domestic violence: Encouraging news from a new look. *Affilia, 18*, 177–191.

Davis, K. E., and I. Cloud-Two Dogs. (2004). The color of social policy: Oppression of indigenous tribal populations and Africans in America. In K. E. Davis and T. B. Bent-Goodley (Eds.), *The Color of Social Policy* (pp. 3–20). Alexandria, VA: Council on Social Work Education Press.

Davis, R. E. (2002). The strongest women: Exploration of the inner resources of abused women. *Qualitative Health Research, 12*, 1248–1263.

DeGruy-Leary, J. D. (2005). *Posttraumatic Slave Syndrome: America's Legacy of Enduring Injury and Healing.* Milwaukie, OR: Upton.

Dennis, R. E., L. J. Key, A. L. Kirk, and A. Smith. (1995). Addressing domestic violence in the African American community. *Journal of Health Care for the Poor and Underserved, 6*, 284–293.

Devore, W., and E. G. Schlesinger. (1996). *Ethnic-Sensitive Social Work Practice* (4th ed.). Needham Heights, MA: Allyn and Bacon.

Dietz, C. A. (2000). Responding to oppression and abuse: A feminist challenge to clinical social work. *Affilia, 15*, 369–389.

DuBois, B., and K. K. Miley. (1996). *Social Work: An Empowering Profession* (2nd ed.). Boston: Allyn and Bacon.

El-Khoury, M., M. A. Dutton, L. A. Goodman, L. Engel, R. J. Belamaric, and M. Murphy. (2004). Ethnic differences in battered women's formal help-seeking strategies: A focus on health, mental health and spirituality. *Cultural Diversity and Ethnic Minority Psychology, 10*, 383–393.

Eugene, T. M. (1995). "Swing low, sweet chariot": A womanist response to sexual violence and abuse. In C. J. Adams and M. M. Fortune (Eds.), *Violence against*

Women and Children: A Christina Theological Sourcebook (pp. 185–200). New York: Continuum.

Franklin, D. L. (2001). *What's Love Got to Do with It?: Understanding and Healing the Rift between Black Men and Women.* New York: Simon and Schuster.

Fraser, I. M., L. McNutt, C. Clark, D. Williams-Muhammed, and R. Lee. (2002). Social support choices for help with abusive relationships: Perceptions of African American women. *Journal of Family Violence,* 17, 363–375.

Fullilove, R. E., and M. T. Fullilove. (2005). HIV/AIDS in the African American community: The legacy of urban abandonment. *Harvard Journal of African American Public Policy,* 11, 33–41.

Giller, E. (1999). What is psychological trauma? The Annual Conference of the Maryland Mental Hygiene Administration, May 1999. The Sidran Foundation.

Guy-Sheftall, B. (Ed.). (1995). *Words of Fre: An Anthology of African American Feminist Thought.* New York: New Press.

Hampton, R. L., R. Carrillo, and J. Kim. (2005). Domestic violence in African American communities. In N. Sokoloff and C. Pratt (Eds.). *Domestic Violence at the Margins: Readings on Race, Class, Gender and Culture* (pp. 127–141). New Brunswick, NJ: Rutgers University Press.

Hampton, R. L., and B. Young. (1996). Violence in communities of color: Where we were, where we are, and where we need to be. In R. L. Hampton, P., Jenkins, and T. P. Gullotta (Eds.), *Preventing Violence in America* (pp. 53–86). Thousand Oaks, CA: Sage.

Harris, A. (1997). Race and essentialism in feminist legal theory. In A. Wing (Ed.), *Critical Race Feminism* (pp. 11–18). New York: New York University Press.

Hassouneh-Phillips, D. (2003). Strength and vulnerability: Spirituality in abused American Muslim women's lives. *Issues in Mental Health Nursing,* 24, 681–694.

Herbert, C., and T. Gunn. (2001). An examination of domestic violence in an African American community in North Carolina: Causes and consequences. *Journal of Black Studies,* 31, 790–811.

Hill, R. B. (1997). *The Strengths of African American Families: Twenty-five Years Later.* Washington, DC: R and B Publishers.

Hill-Collins, P. (2000). *Black Feminist Thought: Knowledge, Consciousness and Empowerment* (2nd ed.). New York: Routledge.

hooks, b. (2000). Black women: Shaping feminist theory. In J. James and T. D. Sharpley-Whiting (Eds.), *The Black Feminist Reader* (pp. 131–145). Walden, MA: Blackwell.

——. (2005). *Sisters of the Yam: Black Women and Self-Recovery.* Cambridge, MA: South End.

Humphreys, C. H., and S. J. Joseph. (2004). Domestic violence and the politics of trauma. *Women's Studies International Forum, 27,* 559–570.

Jasinski, J. L. (1998). The role of acculturation in wife assault. *Hispanic Journal of Behavioral Sciences 20,* 175–191.

Jenkins, E. J. (2002). Black women and community violence: Trauma, grief and coping. In C. M. West (Ed.), *Violence in the Lives of Black Women: Battered, Black and Blue* (pp. 29–44). New York: Haworth.

Joseph, J. (1997). Woman battering: A comparative analysis of Black and White women. In G. Kantor and J. L. Jasinski (Eds.), *Out of Darkness: Contemporary Perspectives on Family Violence* (pp. 161–169). Thousand Oaks, CA: Sage.

Kanuha, V. K. (2005). Compounding the triple jeopardy: Battering in lesbian of color relationships. In N. Sokoloff and C. Pratt (Eds.), *Domestic Violence at the Margins: Readings on Race, Class, Gender and Culture* (pp. 71–82). New Brunswick, NJ: Rutgers University Press.

Karenga, M. (1980). *Kawaida Theory.* Los Angeles, CA: Kawaida.

Koenig, H. G., and D. B. Larson. (2001). Religion and mental health: Evidence for an association. *International Review of Psychiatry, 13,* 67–78.

Lawrence-Lightfoot, S. (2000). *Respect: An Exploration.* New York: Perseus Books.

Lee, R. K., V. L. Thompson, and M. B. Mechanic. (2002). Intimate partner violence and women of color: A call for innovations. *American Journal of Public Health, 92,* 530–534.

Lewis, E. (1999). Staying the path: Lessons about health and resistance from women of the African Diaspora in the United States. In L. M. Gutierrez and E. A. Lewis (Eds.), *Empowering Women of Color* (pp. 150–166). New York: Columbia University Press.

Lipsky, S., R. Caetano, C. A. Field, and G. L. Larkin. (2006). The role of intimate partner violence, race, and ethnicity in help-seeking behaviors. *Ethnicity and Health, 11,* 81–100.

Lockhart, L. L. (1985). Methodological issues in comparative racial analyses: The case of wife abuse. *Research and Abstracts, 13,* 35–41.

Lockhart, L. L., and B. White. (1989). Understanding marital violence in the Black community. *Journal of Interpersonal Violence, 4,* 421–436.

Martin, E. P., and J. M. Martin. (2002). *Spirituality and the Black Helping Tradition in Social Work.* Washington, DC: NASW Press.

McClaurin, I. (2001). Theorizing a black feminist self in anthropology: Toward an auto ethnographic approach. In I. McClaurin (Ed.), *Black Feminist Anthropology* (pp. 49–76). New Brunswick, NJ: Rutgers University Press.

McClennen, J. C. (2005). Domestic violence between same-gender partners: Recent findings and future research. *Journal of Interpersonal Violence, 20,* 149–154.

McClure, J. S., and N. J. Ramsay (Eds.). (1998). *Preaching about Sexual and Domestic Violence: Telling the Truth.* Cleveland, OH: United Church Press.

McNutt, L. A., M. van Ryn, C. Clark, and I. Fraiser. (2000). Partner violence and medical encounters: African American women's perspectives. *American Journal of Preventive Medicine, 19,* 264–269.

Melton, H. C. (1999). Police response to domestic violence. *Journal of Offender Rehabilitation, 29* (1/2), 1–21.

Mills, L. G. (1998). Mandatory arrest and prosecution policies for domestic violence: A critical literature review and the case for more research to test victim empowerment approaches. *Criminal Justice and Behavior, 25,* 306–318.

Myers, L. J. (1995). *Understanding of Afrocentric World View: Introduction to an Optimal Psychology.* Dubuque, IA: Kendall/Hunt.

Nason-Clark, N. (2004). When terror strikes home: The interface between religion and domestic violence. *Journal for the Scientific Study of Religion, 43,* 303–310.

National Association of Social Workers. (2001). *NASW Standards for Cultural Competence in Social Work Practice.* Washington, DC: Author.

National Center for Injury Prevention and Control (NCIPC). (2003). *Costs of Intimate Partner Violence against Women in the United States.* Atlanta, GA: Centers for Disease Control and Prevention.

Neighbors, H. W., M. A. Musick, and D. R. Williams. (1998). The African American minister as a source of help for serious personal crises: Bridge or barrier to mental health care? *Health Education and Behavior, 25,* 759–778.

Office of Justice Programs. (1998). *Bureau of Justice Statistics Factbook: Violence by Intimates—Analysis of Data on Crime by Current or Former Spouses, Boyfriends, and Girlfriends* (NCJ No. 167237). Washington, DC: Department of Justice.

Plichta, S. B. (2004). Intimate partner violence and physical health consequences. *Journal of Interpersonal Violence, 19,* 1296–1323.

Pyles, L., and K. M. Kim. (2006). A multilevel approach to cultural competence: A study of the community response to underserved domestic violence victims. *Families in Society, 87,* 221–229.

Raj, A., J. G. Silverman, G. M. Wingood, and R. J. DiClemente. (1999). Prevalence and correlates of relationship abuse among a community-based sample of low-income African American women. *Violence Against Women, 5,* 272–291.

Ramos, B. M., B. E. Carlson, and L. A. McNutt. (2004). Lifetime abuse, mental health, and African American women. *Journal of Family Violence, 19,* 131–164.

Richie, B. E. (1996). *Compelled to Crime: The Gender Entrapment of Battered Black Women.* New York: Routledge.

——. (2005). A Black feminist reflection on the antiviolence movement. In N. Sokoloff and C. Pratt, (Eds.). *Domestic Violence at the Margins: Readings on*

Race, Class, Gender and Culture (pp. 50–55). New Brunswick, NJ: Rutgers University Press.

Robinson, A. (2002). "There's a stranger in this house": African American lesbians and domestic violence. In. C. M. West (Ed.), *Violence in the Lives of Black Women: Battered, Black and Blue* (pp. 125–132). New York: Haworth.

Rodgers, S. (2006). The art of healing: An Afrocentric helping guide for practitioners working with African American families who experience intimate partner violence. In R. L. Hampton and T. P. Gullotta (Eds). *Interpersonal Violence in the African American Community: Evidence-based Prevention and Treatment Practices* (pp. 121–147). New York: Springer-Verlag.

Sanders, C. J. (1995). (Ed.). *Living the Intersection: Womanism and Afrocentricism in Theology* (pp. 67–80). Minneapolis, MN: Fortress Books.

Schollenberger, J., J. Campbell, P. Sharps, P. O'Campo, A. Gielen, J. Dienemann, and J. Kub. (2003). African American HMO enrollees: Their experiences with partner abuse and its effect on their health and use of medical services. *Violence Against Women, 9,* 599–618.

Senter, K. E., and K. Caldwell. (2002). Spirituality and the maintenance of change: A phenomenological study of women who leave abusive relationships. *Contemporary Family Therapy, 24,* 543–564.

Sokoloff, N. J. (Ed.). (2005). *Domestic Violence at the Margins: Readings on Race, Class, Gender, and Culture.* New Brunswick, NJ: Rutgers University Press.

Sullivan, C., R. Campbell, H. Angelique, K. Eby, and W. Davidson. (1994). An advocacy intervention program for women with abusive partners: Six-month follow-up. *American Journal of Community Psychology, 22,* 101–122.

Sullivan, M., R. Bhuyan, K. Senturia, S. Shiu-Thornton, S. and Ciske. (2005). Participatory action research in practice: A case study in addressing domestic violence in nine cultural communities. *Journal of Interpersonal Violence 20,* 977–995.

Taylor, J. Y. (1998). Womanism: A methodological framework for African American Women. *Advances in Nursing Science 21,* 53–64.

——. (2002a). "The straw that broke the camel's back": African American women's strategies for disengaging from abusive relationships. In. C.M. West (Ed.), *Violence in the Lives of Black Women: Battered, Black and Blue* (pp. 79–94). New York: Haworth.

——. (2002b). Talking back: Research as an act of resistance and healing for African American women survivors of intimate male partner violence. In. C.M. West (Ed.), *Violence in the Lives of Black Women: Battered, Black and Blue* (pp. 145–160). New York: Haworth.

Tubbs, C. Y., and O. J. Williams. (2007). Shared parenting after abuse: Battered mothers' perspectives on parenting after dissolution of a relationship. In J. L. Edleson and O. J. Williams (Eds.), *Parenting by Men Who Batter: New Directions for Assessment and Intervention* (pp. 19–44). New York: Oxford University Press.

Uzzell, O., and W. Peebles-Wilkins. (1989). Black spouse abuse: A focus on relational factors and intervention strategies. *Western Journal of Black Studies, 13,* 10–16.

Violence Policy Center. (2003). *Women and Firearms Violence [Fact Sheet].* Washington, DC: Author.

Walker, A. *In Search of Our Mother's Gardens: Womanist Prose.* New York: Harcourt Brace Jananovich.

Waltermaurer, E., C. A. Watson, and L. A. McNutt. (2006). Black women's health: The effect of perceived racism and intimate partner violence. *Violence Against Women, 12,* 1214–1222.

Waltington, C. G., and C. M. Murphy. (2006). The roles of religion and spirituality among African American survivors of domestic violence. *Journal of Clinical Psychology, 62,* 837–857.

Walton-Moss, B., J. Manganello, V. Frye, and J. C. Campbell. (2005). Risk factors for intimate partner violence and associated injury among urban women. *Journal of Community Health, 30,* 377–389.

West, C. M. (1998). Lifting the "political gag order": Breaking the silence around partner violence in ethnic minority families. In J. L. Jasinski and L. M. Williams (Eds.), *Partner Violence: A Comprehensive Review of 20 Years of Research* (pp. 184–209). Thousand Oaks, CA: Sage.

—— (Ed.). (2002). *Violence in the Lives of Black Women: Battered, Black and Blue.* New York: Haworth.

——. (2005). Domestic violence in ethnically and racially diverse families: The "political gag order" has been lifted. In N. Sokoloff and C. Pratt (Eds.), *Domestic Violence at the Margins: Readings on Race, Class, Gender and Culture* (pp. 157–173). New Brunswick, NJ: Rutgers University Press.

West, C. M., G. K. Kantor, and J. L. Jasinski. (1998). Sociodemographic predictors and cultural barriers to help-seeking behavior by Latina and Anglo American battered women. *Violence and Victims, 13,* 361–375.

West, T. C. (1999). *Wounds of the Spirit: Black Women, Violence, and Resistance Ethics.* New York: New York University Press.

White, E. (1994). *Chain, Chain, Change: For Black Women in Abusive Relationships.* Washington, DC: Seal.

Williams, S. L., and K. D. Mickelson. (2004). The nexus of domestic violence and poverty: Resilience in women's anxiety. *Violence Against Women, 10,* 283–293.

Wingood, G. M., and R. J. DiClemente, (1996). HIV sexual risk-reduction interventions for women: A review. *American Journal of Preventive Medicine, 12* 209–217.

——. (1997a). Child sexual abuse, HIV sexual risk, and gender relations of African American women. *American Journal of Preventive Medicine, 13,* 380–384.

——. (1997b). The effects of an abusive primary partner on the condom use and sexual negotiation practices of African American women. *American Journal of Public Health, 87,* 1016–1018.

Wyatt, G. E., J. Axelrod, D. Chin, J. V. Carmona, and T. B. Loeb. (2000). Examining patterns of vulnerability to domestic violence among African American women. *Violence Against Women, 6,* 495–514.

Wyatt, G. E., H. F. Myers, and T. Loeb. (2004). Women, trauma and HIV: An overview. *AIDS and Behavior Special Issue, 8,* 401–403.

Wyatt, G. E., H. F. Myers, J. K. Williams, C. R. Kitchen, T. Loeb, J. V. Carmona, L. E. Wyatt, D. Chin, and N. Presley. (2002). Does a history of trauma contribute to HIV risk for women of color? Implications for prevention and policy. *American Journal of Public Health, 92,* 660–665.

Yoshioka, M. R., L. Gilbert, N. El-Bassel, and M. Baig-Amin. (2003). Social support and disclosure of abuse: Comparing South Asian, African American and Hispanic battered women. *Journal of Family Violence, 18,* 171–180.

4

A LILY OUT OF THE MUD

Domestic Violence in Asian and Pacific Islander Communities

Mimi Kim, Beckie Masaki, and Gita Mehrotra

The lotus lily is a symbol of beauty and tranquility that rises up and breaks through the muddy darkness. Like the flower, we can break through the destructive cycle of domestic violence.

—ASIAN WOMEN'S SHELTER, LOTUS PROJECT, 1999

ASIAN AND Pacific Islander (API) women remain silent survivors of intimate partner violence. Hidden in violence statistics, unheard over crisis lines, unseen in mainstream shelters, the invisibility of API women is captured in the phrase "violence does not happen to them." Conversely, when situations of domestic violence in API communities do become public, we may hear the opposite—"those women always face violence; it's part of their culture."

Between the myths of the peaceful and harmonious API family and that of the patriarchal violent API man coupled with a passive, obedient wife, there is a complex truth. This chapter provides social workers for domestic violence survivors, advocates for abused women, and other human service providers with a framework for understanding the realities of domestic violence in the API communities in the United States, and it also offers guidelines for working effectively with these families and survivors of domestic violence.

I am from a traditional family with many children, a family of survivors and visionaries, a family of fearful immigrants

I am from strong but reserved women.

I am from heritage, many of which are unspoken.

I am from a family that is matriarchal and patriarchal, that is from the old world and the new world, a world that is strong and fragile.

I am from Laos, DC, Iowa City, a small town in Thailand, Vietnam, Dallas, Mumbai.

I am from always having to define Hmong, since people only associate countries with people.

I am from the "ghetto," poor neighborhood, many family gatherings, 5 feet fenced in yard.

I am from a hateful class system.

I am from my land where 200 tons of bombs landed, a land of many, a land of opportunity.

I am from breathtaking natural beauty and shocking poverty.

I am from no country to call my own. I am from everywhere and nowhere. I am here.

I am from chocolate and champagne, kimchee, hot papaya salad that burns my tongue. I am from tom yum goong, chicken over rice, watermelon juice, lychees, rambutan, mirchi, biryani, I am from rice, the staple of my life.

I am from celebrations of the Lunar New Year, of birth, death and marriages that last. I am from togetherness with family, eating good food, being generous and giving.

I celebrate epiphany, holi, diwali, harvest moon. I worship ancestors.

I celebrate Christmas, sunrise service at Easter, Norooz, Chahar Shanbeh Soori.

I bow down to seek the blessings of my elders, and they lift me in a warm embrace.

I am a china doll, geisha girl, yellow, old maid, fat.

I am a person stuck in a hole, and I cannot dig myself back out.

I have fear, but I will face the fear.

I am a descendant of a long line of resistance and revolutionaries.

I am valuable to my children, my family, and my community.

I am a building block that can support anything.

I am from the passage from dark to light and new beginnings.

I am a woman, a girl, a child. I am a lily out of the mud. I am me.[1]

DEFINING API COMMUNITIES

The category of Asian and Pacific Islander (API) is largely a political construct, shifting and evolving historically with changes in political climate
and the pressures of advocacy groups. The Asian and Pacific Islander American Health Forum (APIAHF) (2008), a national health advocacy institute,
offers a broad definition of the API category that includes Asian and Pacific
Islander national identities as well as ethnic identities that do not necessarily fall within national boundaries. (Asian and Pacific Islander Domestic
Violence [APIDV] 2008a) These include people who trace their origins (or
diasporic communities) to many different nations in the East, including East
Asian nations such as Japan, China, and South and North Korea; Southeast
Asian nations including Vietnam and Laos and ethnic entities such as Mien
and Hmong (the latter groups having emigrated primarily from Laos, Vietnam, and China); South Asian nations of India, Pakistan, and Nepal, among
others; and newly independent Central Asian nations such as Kazakhstan
and Uzbekistan; or West Asian (nations as far as Afghanistan, Lebanon, and
Palestine). The U.S. Census follows a narrower definition that generally
excludes West Asia from the Asian category.[2] Pacific Island nations and peoples include native Hawaiians, Samoans, Fijians, Nieuese, and Chamorro,
to name just a few.

In the 2000 U.S. Census, the broad category of Asian and Pacific Islander
which had been historically unified was separated for the first time. Pacific
Islanders were also redefined as Native Hawaiians and Other Pacific Islanders
(NHOPI) (Grieco 2002). For the purposes of this chapter, the broader categorization of the APIAHF will be assumed.

Demographic factors reflect some of the diversity of the API population. The categorization itself is an artificial boundary around a grouping
that covers an area from Hawaii to Afghanistan. Most API people would, in
fact, identify more with their particular ethnicity or nationality than with
the category of Asian or Pacific Islander. Even those from the same ethnic
community have enormous diversity based on gender, region, class, religion,
sexual orientation, and so on. A recently arrived Chinese immigrant woman
who works in a factory in New York City and an older Chinese woman living in suburban California who has been in the United States for 20 years
each have very different experiences of "Chinese" culture; an Indian Muslim woman may identify more strongly in some settings with other Muslims
and in another setting with other South Asians; and a Vietnamese lesbian

woman may identify more strongly at times with the lesbian-gay-bisexual-transgender-queer (LGBTQ) community than she does with the mainstream Vietnamese community.

DEMOGRAPHIC CHARACTERISTICS OF THE API POPULATION

The Asian population comprises many racial and ethic groups that differ in language, culture, and length of residence in the United States. Some Asian groups, such as the Chinese and Japanese, have lived in the United States for several generations. Other groups, such as the Hmong, Vietnamese, Laotians, and Cambodians, tend to be comparatively recent immigrants. During the last two decades of the twentieth century, the Asian and Pacific Islander population tripled because of large-scale immigration (Hobbs and Stoops 2002). Between 2005 and 2006 the Asian population increased by 3 percent, becoming the second fastest-growing minority group in the United States (U.S. Census Bureau News 2007).

According to the 2000 Census, some 12.7 million Asian and Pacific Islanders were living in the United States, constituting almost 5 percent of the total population (Reeves and Bennett 2005; Harris and Jones 2005). Among the 12 million self-identified Asians, almost 2 million are multiracial (Reeves and Bennett 2004; U.S. Census-American Community Survey Report 2007; Smelser, Wilson, and Mitchell 2001). According to Reeves and Bennett (2004), the Chinese population make up the highest percentage of Asians (24 percent), followed by Filipino (18 percent), Asian Indian (16 percent), Vietnamese (11 percent), and Korean (11 percent). Almost 1 million are Pacific Islanders (PI), and more than half of this number identified as multiracial in the 2000 census (Harris and Jones 2005); the three largest subgroups were Native Hawaiians, Samoans, and Guamanians, accounting for three-quarters of the PI population (Harris and Jones 2005).

GEOGRAPHIC DISTRIBUTION

In March 2002, just over half the API population lived in coastal or metropolitan areas in the West (51 percent), followed in concentration by the South and Northeast (19 percent in each region), and the Midwest (12 percent). According to the 2000 U.S. Census, the ten states with the largest Asian populations were California, New York, Hawaii, Texas, New Jersey, Illinois, Washington,

Florida, Virginia, and Massachusetts. Combined, these states represented three-quarters of the Asian population (Reeves and Bennett 2004; Barnes and Bennett 2002).

Native Hawaiian and Other Pacific Islander respondents to the 2000 census indicated a similar profile, with almost three-quarters residing in the West (73 percent), followed by the South (14 percent), Northeast (7 percent), and Midwest (6 percent). The ten states with the largest NHOPI populations in 2000 were Hawaii (0.28 million), California (0.22 million), Washington (0.04 million), Texas (0.03 million), New York (0.03 million), Florida (0.02 million), Utah (0.02 million), Nevada (0.016 million), Oregon (0.016 million), and Arizona (0.013 million). Together these states represented 80 percent of the NHOPI population (Grieco 2001).

EDUCATION

API women were less likely to have earned a bachelor's degree or higher compared to API men (44 percent vs. 51 percent) (Reeves and Bennett 2003). Despite great variation within the API population, they are still more likely than non-Hispanic whites to have earned at least a college degree; they also are more likely to have less than a ninth-grade grade education. Although the aggregated level of Asian educational attainment is relatively high, figures vary widely by ethnicity. For example, the Cambodian (9.2%), Hmong (7.5%), and Laotian (7.7%) ethnic groups had the lowest proportion of college graduates (Reeves and Bennett 2004).

SOCIAL ECONOMIC STATUS

Based on the 2000 census data, roughly three-quarters of Asian men 16 years old and older were employed in the civilian labor force compared to almost two-thirds of Asian women of the same age; 41 percent of the men and 37 percent of the women were employed in managerial and professional positions (Reeves and Bennett 2003).

In 2001, 40 percent of the API families had incomes of $75,000 or more, primarily among API families maintained by men—31 percent vs. 17 percent for families with a female as head of the household. Further, API female-headed households without a spouse are almost twice as likely as male-headed households to be living in poverty (14.6 percent vs. 9.1 percent) (Reeves and Bennett 2003).

As seen with all demographic data discussed so far, when income data are disaggregated, specific API groups vary widely. For example, the per capita income for the total U.S. population is $21,587 compared to $26,415 for Asian Indian, $13,532 for Bangladeshi, $6,613 for Hmong, and $11,191 for Samoan populations (APIAHF 2008). Thirteen percent of Asians and 18% of Pacific Islanders live below the federal poverty level compared to 12 percent in the total U.S. population.

IMMIGRANTS AND LANGUAGE STATUS

A significant proportion of the Asian population in the United States consists of native born or naturalized citizens (63%), leaving 35 percent foreign born and not citizens. The Pacific Islander population is predominantly (87 percent) born in the United States.

In 2000, 18 percent of the total population five years of age and older, or 47.0 million people, reported that they spoke a language other than English. Most of the people (92 percent) who spoke a language other than English at home reported that they spoke English "very well" or had difficulty speaking English. On the other had, the proportion of the population aged five years of age and older that spoke English less than "very well" grew from 4.8 percent in 1980 to 6.1 percent in 1990 to 8.1 percent in 2000. Roughly three-quarters (77.5 percent) of the API population indicated that they spoke English "very well" or "well." As reflected in Table 4.1, the four API groups with the largest percentage of respondents who indicated that they did not speak English at all or not very well were of Asian descent: Vietnamese (32.4%), and Korean (29.6%), Mon-Khmer, Cambodian (28.9%) and Chinese (28.2%) (Shin and Bruno 2003).

PREVALENCE AND TYPE OF DOMESTIC VIOLENCE IN API COMMUNITIES

Since research began on this salient issue, our knowledge and understanding of the realities of victims of intimate partner violence from smaller census ethnic and racial groups (such as Asian and Pacific Islanders and Native Americans) have not appreciably increased over the past three decades (Tjaden and Thoennes 2000; Grossman and Lundy 2007;). National domestic violence prevalence studies have failed to adequately capture statistics regarding API

TABLE 4.1 Ability to Speak English by Language Spoken at Home by Asian and Pacific Islanders Five Years Old and Older

	TOTAL NUMBER	LANGUAGE SPOKEN AT HOME "VERY WELL"		SPEAK ENGLISH "WELL"		SPEAK ENGLISH "NOT WELL"		SPEAK ENGLISH "NOT WELL AT ALL"	
		NUMBER	%	NUMBER	%	NUMBER	%	NUMBER	%
	6,960,065	3,370,045	48.4	2,023,310	29.1	1,260,260	18.1	306,455	4.4
Chinese	2,022,145	855,690	42.3	595,330	29.4	408,595	20.2	162,525	8.0
Japanese	477,995	241,705	50.6	146,615	30.7	84,020	17.6	5,660	1.2
Korean	894,065	361,165	40.4	268,475	30.0	228,390	25.6	36,030	4.0
.Mon-Khmer, Cambodian	181,890	77,620	42.7	51,650	28.4	41,460	22.8	11,160	6.1
Miao, Hmong	168,065	65,865	39.2	55,910	33.3	34,405	20.5	11,885	7.1
Thai	120,465	57,630	47.8	43,250	35.9	17,635	14.6	1,950	1.6
Laotian	149,305	67,565	45.3	43,175	28.9	32,100	21.5	6,465	4.3
Vietnamese	1,009,625	342,595	33.9	340,060	33.7	270,950	26.8	56,020	5.6
Other Asian Languages	398,435	282,565	70.9	81,740	20.5	28,000	7.0	6,135	1.5
Tagalog	1,224,240	827,560	67.6	311,465	25.4	79,720	6.5	5,495	0.5
Other Pacific Island Languages	313,840	190,085	60.6	85,640	27.3	34,985	11.2	3,130	1.0

Source: U.S Census Bureau, Internet Release Date: October 29, 2004 (revised 2/2006); Census 2000, http://www.census.gov/population /cen2000/phc-t37/tab01a.xls.

domestic violence (Grossman and Lundy 2007; Yick 2000; Yoshioka et al. 2001). The results of Tjaden and Thoennes's (2000) national study indicated significantly lower rates of sexual (4%) and physical (13%) assault for API women compared to other women. On the other hand, data from community surveys and police reports indicate higher rates. The discrepancy between relatively low disclosures of violence from national samples and the stark reality of community surveys and police reports illustrate the wide gap in knowledge about prevalence within API communities.

Studies on the prevalence of violence are rare, and existing API research tends to focus on localized settings and specific API ethnic groups. In Santa Clara County, in Northern California's Silicon Valley, Asians made up 30 percent of domestic violence deaths from 1993 to 2001 (Santa Clara County Domestic Violence Council 2002). Yoshioka et al. (2001) collaborated with a local API program, the Asian Task Force against Domestic Violence in Boston, to conduct a survey among Chinese, Vietnamese, Korean, and Cambodian women. The survey found that a range of 24 percent (Chinese) to 48 percent (Cambodian) respondents knew someone who had been subjected to intimate partner violence. A community survey of the Korean community in the San Francisco Bay Area found that 42 percent of respondents know a Korean woman who has been "slapped, hit, kicked, or suffered any physical injury" by a male partner (Shimtuh 2000, p. 10). In a telephone survey among Chinese respondents conducted by Yick (2000), 7 percent disclosed physical violence in the past 12 months and 18 percent over their lifetime, a figure the author found surprisingly low. A study of South Asian women in Greater Boston found that the rate of physical violence was 30 percent and was 18.8 percent for sexual abuse (Raj and Silverman 2003); 15.4 percent of these women reported injuries requiring medical attention. A study of Korean women in Chicago found a lifetime prevalence of 60 percent among the women sampled (Song 1996).

CULTURAL BELIEFS AND DOMESTIC VIOLENCE IN API COMMUNITIES: AN ECOLOGICAL APPROACH

Like all survivors of domestic violence, API victims experience physical, emotional, sexual, and economic abuse, and commonly feel such emotions as shame, guilt, isolation, anger, confusion, fear, and helplessness. Social workers should be aware, however, of the particular factors influencing the type of, and vulnerability to, domestic violence that survivors may face; the barriers and obstacles survivors and abusers may have in seeking support, safety, and services; and the strengths and resources to which individuals, families, or communities may have access.

For API women and families, the beliefs and practices embedded in their culture, the social assets of family and community, and the resources available from community-based resources and mainstream society are important factors in their vulnerability to domestic violence as well as their ability to resist violence (Campbell et al. 1997; Yick 2000; Yoshihama 2002; Chantler 2006; Yoshioka 2001). The central role of the individual and the self in Western culture may not be a meaningful starting point for API women, as they construct individual identities based on social roles and collective communities (Chantler 2006; Sastry and Ross 1998; Yick 2000; Yoshihama 2002). In this section we focus on the spheres of cultural beliefs, family, and community institutions, and examine the barriers and strengths of some of the important characteristics of and resources accessible to API women, families, and community.

THE IMPACT OF CULTURAL CONCEPTS

SHAME AND SAVING FACE   Shame and "saving face" are often raised when API women talk about domestic violence. A strong sense of shame that she somehow deserved the violence, that she was not a good wife or mother, that she is unsuccessful in marriage, or that she may face the stigma of divorce or separation are all common themes among women experiencing violence. Another side of shame is "saving face," protecting the reputation and dignity not only of oneself but of one's family. These cultural values are not unique to API populations, but they are key features of API communities. A woman may not even fear for her loss of face but may be more concerned about her family or her children. She may also want the violence to end but not at the expense of her abuser's reputation. Shame and the need to "save face" may be factors that cause abused women to endure or to find solutions that will not risk violating these important values (Lee and Bowman 2007; Yoshihama 2002). Certain cultural concepts may cause her to blame herself or keep silent. Clearly shame that an individual feels may be linked to concern for family and community.

COLLECTIVISM   One major characteristic of API cultures is that, in contrast to the individualism typical of Western cultures, they are inclined to collectivism (Sastry and Ross 1998). The degree of collectivism varies across gender, ethnicity, length of time in the United States, and personal history, but many advocates working with API survivors note the importance of family and community (Chantler 2006; Kim 2002). Collectivism not only provides a strong, interdependent identity for API individuals but also offers a sense of belonging, reciprocal services such as child care, and material benefits such as shared housing or access to culturally familiar foods. For immigrant women, the family or community can literally ensure survival, particularly if they do not speak English, lack marketable skills, or hold no legal documentation in the United States. For women in abusive relationships, collectivism can offer social sanctions against abusive partners or a sense of community to mitigate the alienation and fear they might feel in the abusive relationship (Chantler 2006; Kim 2005).

On the other hand, however, collectivism can mete out social sanctions against women seeking help, deciding to divorce, or otherwise resisting violence (Gill 2004; Yoshioka et al. 2001). If an API woman is in a same-gender relationship, the collective of her LGBTQ community may offer sanctuary to her as a lesbian but also may pressure her to remain silent regarding the abuse. In focus groups and interviews of API women also in the category of LGBTQ, survivors stated that they were just as fearful, or even more so, of family and community reactions if they disclosed than they were of their abusive partner (Chung and Lee 2001). For many API women, the stakes are high for risking disclosure. Women who seek outside help risk rejection, discredit, and blame from members of the close-knit community. Breaking free from an abusive relationship can also mean losing the safe space created by the collective (Chantler 2006). For immigrant women, this loss can be equally life-threatening as the abuse of her partner (Kim 2002).

Within some families and cultures, the family system accentuates the abuse against women by participating directly in the violence. Mothers-in-law, for example, may share in physical abuse, and fathers-in-law and brothers-in-law may add further abuse or condone their family member's abusive behavior (Gill 2004; Kim 2002; Yoshioka et al. 2003). One's own family members may collude in violence or blame survivors for their own abuse. The "coiled spring of violence" developed by advocates and activists in India replaces the stages more familiarly associated with the U.S. "cycle of violence" with that of the increasing vulnerability of abused women as they move between a violent husband's family and the escalating victim-blaming of her own family (APIDV 2008b).

STATUS AND ROLES OF WOMEN   Asia is home to some of the oldest continuous civilizations in the world. In China, India, and other Asian countries, patriarchal relationships have historically defined the role of women in society, which is reinforced through language, laws, religion, daily customs, and beliefs. For API women, the expected roles of women as daughters, wives, and mothers persist, providing both a place of meaning and belonging with the family and community as well as contributing toward entrapment and violence (Chantler 2006). As in most cultures, a static view of women's roles can be used to constrain women's choices and control those who would veer from these expectations. API women exhibit internalized and social pressures to endure violence or find ways to resist violence that do not upset the family's status quo or risk public shame (Yoshihama 2002). Even for API women who have followed less traditional trajectories, these culturally proscribed values of sacrifice and endurance can remain powerful influences (Shimtuh 2000).

API cultural histories have condoned domestic violence in many ways, but each culture also contains values condemning domestic violence and empowering women. Every community throughout time has had at least one survivor, one mother, one grandmother, or one community member brave enough to escape, speak out, or resist domestic violence. Studies of API attitudes toward domestic violence reveal differences across ethnicities and age (Yoshioka et al. 2001) but finds that a significant sector of API women and men denounce violence against women. A Korean community study found that 97 percent of respondents advocated for a Korean domestic violence program (Shimtuh 2000).

FAITH   API populations also come with a rich history of religious practice from their home countries as well as transplanted and newly developed practices in the United States. The religious diversity across API communities is rich and complex with faiths as varied as Christianity, Buddhism, Islam, Hinduism, Confucianism, Jainism, shamanism, the Ba'hai faith, and many indigenous faiths (Yoshioka et al. 2000). For much of the API immigrant population, religious institutions are also important for maintaining community identity, gathering information, and finding social supports. Immigrants may also choose a different religious institution in the United States because of convenience or availability within their local community or to benefit from the particular resources these institutions provide (Portes 2004; Shimtuh 2000).

Faith and religious institutions have been influential for API survivors of domestic violence in both positive and negative ways. All religious doctrines have been used to condone and condemn domestic violence, and all institutions have been used as refuges for abused women and children or to support violence and patriarchy. As early as the thirteenth century in Japan, the Kakekomidera (refuge temple) was essentially a battered women's shelter. Documentation shows that only women could go there and live at the temple in safety and peace. Despite the stigma of divorce, this temple offered a culturally sanctioned way to escape an abusive marriage. After three years an abused woman could file for divorce, and the Buddhist priest would sanction her life free from her abusive husbands. The temple still remains today in Kamakura prefecture (Wright 1997).

CHILDREN   API children witnessing domestic violence and living in an abusive environment, like all children, suffer trauma and fear. The trauma for API children is often compounded by having to interpret for their non–English-speaking parents. API adult survivors also face other additional challenges such as racism, poverty, cultural adjustment, and extreme isolation. A Korean community study revealed the concern that abused women had not only for themselves but for their children (Shimtuh 2000). In some cases women reported that the harm done to their children by either being directly abused or witnessing abuse caused them to leave. Others who chose to stay in abusive relationships cited concern for their children as well but also the perceived need for a father or the stigma that divorce would bring to their children. In the same study, adults who experienced domestic violence as children spoke of the fear, isolation, and shame they felt as young witnesses to violence. For many of these adults, emotional problems and issues of distrust followed them into later years.

THE IMPACT OF CULTURAL BELIEFS ON DOMESTIC VIOLENCE IN API COMMUNITIES

Cultural identities can vary depending on the setting, life experience, and the broader context of oppression. It is important to note, however, that cultural commonalities do exist among members of a group and affect violence, survival, services, and support, but their role is often oversimplified. Making generalizations and cultural assumptions are commonly rooted in unequal power and privilege, and they can have serious consequences for domestic violence survivors. Recognizing our own cultural attitudes and biases, and being constantly open to learning and questioning our assumptions, are key to successful social work across cultural differences. Some questions that social workers and advocacy workers may want to ask themselves include:

1. What countries and ethnicities are you familiar with? Which ones are unfamiliar?
2. If you know something about these ethnicities, did you learn it from the media, from studies, from your community, coworkers, or friends? Do you belong to any of these groups?
3. Which API communities are in your city or your region? What do you know about their ethnicity, their income or educational level, their immigration history, their community institutions, or other specific factors that describe these populations?

TWO CASE STUDIES

The following case studies of Farah and Eun Jung illustrate how specific cultural influences impact the experience of domestic violence.

FARAH

Farah is a Pakistani woman who recently immigrated to the United States to be with her husband, Rahul, who has been living in the United States for five years and has permanent resident status. She has no family or friends in the United States and speaks very limited English. Upon arrival, she asks her husband if she can take ESL (English as a Second Language) classes. He tells her that she cannot take classes because Americans think that Pakistanis are terrorists, and were she to take the class she would be harassed and treated badly. Rahul leaves the house early in the morning and does not return home until late at night. Every day he calls several times to check on her and becomes very upset if she does not pick up the phone immediately. Sometimes when he comes home he brings her sweets and compliments her cooking—Farah wishes he could always be like this. Other days he comes home angry, is rough with her, and pressures her to have sex with him. When he is angry, he threatens to call immigration authorities to deport her.

Farah's only contact with the outside world is through her husband. The only people she knows are the friends her husband brings to their home. Rahul often criticizes Farah in front of his friends and tells them she is crazy. Farah is very embarrassed by this, but she fears that no one would believe her if she tried to refute her husband's claims. When she calls her family back home, her husband listens in on their conversation.

Farah feels that Rahul's behavior is unfair, but she is afraid to discuss her relationship with anyone. She thinks that if she tried harder, maybe Rahul would treat her better. She worries that if she tells anyone about her troubles with Rahul, one or both of them could be deported. She also fears that Rahul might harm her family back in Pakistan. She has recently learned that she is pregnant but has not yet told Rahul for fear of his reaction.

EUN JUNG

Eun Jung and Lucy have had an intimate relationship for three years. Lucy's parents have not spoken to her in five years; when Lucy and Eun Jung moved in together, they told Eun Jung's parents that they were roommates. Lucy is a well-known immigration attorney in town. Eun Jung is still on a student visa that will expire in a year, but she is hoping to obtain work with an employer that will sponsor her to stay in the United States. Eun Jung's parents know nothing of her relationship with Lucy and expect that she will either marry a Korean American man or return to Korea to marry

"CONTINUED"

after her visa expires. Eun Jung loves Lucy, but she is also afraid of what might happen if her family learns that she is in a lesbian relationship.

Starting in the second year of their relationship, Lucy and Eun Jung increasingly began to argue, causing greater tension in their relationship. Lucy began to criticize Eun Jung often and disapprove of the amount of time Eun Jung spends with her friends from the Korean Student's Association (KSA). She is also jealous of the relationships Eun Jung has with the other Korean graduate students in her department. Lucy wants Eun Jung to quit her job at the department so that she can spend more time at home. Eun Jung is determined to keep her job, as her student visa does not allow her to work off-campus and it would be difficult for her to find other work.

One night last week when Eun Jung came home from a KSA meeting, Lucy and Eun Jung got into an argument. During their fight, Lucy accused Eun Jung of having a crush on one of the men in the group and threatened to attend the next KSA meeting and tell everyone about their relationship. Lucy also reminds Eun Jung constantly that, because her parents are not speaking to her, Eun Jung is the only family she has.

Eun Jung is terrified of what will happen if her KSA friends know about her relationship with Lucy. She knows that many of her KSA friends are religious and believe that lesbian relationships are sinful and abnormal. Eun Jung is also very worried about Lucy's temper and well-being, and wants her to go to counseling, but Lucy refuses.

Let us first consider the case of Farah. Although she is from Pakistan, which is 97 percent Muslim, we cannot assume that she is a Muslim or presume to know how she practices her faith. The social worker, in addition to examining her own cultural assumptions, will also want to understand Farah's perception of the cultural, religious, and family values impacting her situation and her options. We learn that Farah is embarrassed and afraid of discussing her relationship with anyone. She also is concerned that Rahul may harm her family back in Pakistan. The values of saving face and collectivism are important factors for Farah. She may fear for her own safety, but she also fears for her family's safety in Pakistan and also for Rahul's reputation among his friends.

Many of the traditional options for women survivors of domestic violence in the United States are centered on the individual rather than the collective, such as an individual woman seeking safety at a shelter. This may not seem to be a viable option for Farah, because although it would help her safety, it could heighten the risk for her family and would affect Rahul's reputation with his friends. Starting from Farah's cultural perspective, the worker can help Farah explore possible alternatives and also find ways to utilize existing resources, such as the shelter, while acknowledging and mitigating the possible other consequences, such as planning for the safety of her family in Pakistan.

In Eun Jung's case, family and community are also important factors. Eun Jung is fearful about her family and KSA student colleagues discovering her sexual orientation. For the social worker helping Eun Jung, it would be important to understand the severe consequences of any options that would jeopardize her relationship with her KSA colleagues, and the magnified isolation and vulnerability that Eun Jung faces without the support of her family of origin. Confidentiality and nonjudgmental acceptance of Eun Jung's sexual identity are key elements for setting the tone and building a working relationship between the social worker and Eun Jung.

Because of their own cultural perceptions and isolation, Farah and Eun Jung may not identify themselves as being in an abusive relationship. The social worker can play a vital role in ending the isolation by giving clients information about the dynamics of domestic violence, and assisting them with safety planning and resources. On a community level, the experiences of Eun Jung, Farah, and others in similar situations can highlight gaps in domestic violence services, and this information can help shape future program development and prevention strategies.

EXTERNAL FACTORS AFFECTING DOMESTIC VIOLENCE IN API COMMUNITIES: AN ECOLOGICAL APPROACH

For API communities, the values of "saving face," collectivism, and women's sacrifice and concern for children over self not only can leave API women vulnerable to violence but also can promote resilience in the face of hardship. API women and communities are also subject to the social, political, and economic realities of the United States, and the ways in which API communities are differentially subjected to these conditions. Because social workers, including those from API communities, are often bridges to external systems such as schools, public assistance, and immigration or are perceived to be agents of these systems, it is important for social workers to be aware of the impact of these factors. It is also critical for social workers to act as advocates for API people to ensure that their rights are protected.

Those working with abused API women may easily understand the dynamics of violence. But beyond the cultural entrapment, API women also are subjected to other systems of oppression within the United States: sexism, racism, classism, nativism, homophobia, and ableism. They influence women's vulnerability to intimate violence as well as violence inflicted by other intersecting systems of oppression (Crenshaw 1994; Incite!/Critical Resistance 2005; Kanuha 1990; Ritchie 2006). It is important to understand the multiple ways in which API women are vulnerable to violence and to stand in solidarity with their attempts to gain integrity and safety while maintaining connections to family and community even when they may be participating in her abuse (Chantler 2006).

IMPACT OF IMMIGRATION STATUS AND LANGUAGE

For Farah and Eun Jung, immigration status is a significant factor in their domestic violence situations, as Farah fears that if she discloses her husband's abusive behavior, they both could be deported. Batterers, in fact, often use immigration status as a control tactic. If you were the social worker meeting with Farah, it would be important to let her know that there are immigration remedies that might be available to her, such as the self-petition provision of the Violence Against Women Act (VAWA). Utilize the immigration resources at the end of this chapter to connect her with an immigration attorney and provide more information. Eun Jung is in the United States on a foreign student visa, so if you were working with Eun Jung, you should understand her immigration status and the impact it may have on her options. For example, Eun Jung's visa allows her to study and work at the university, but her visa status would change if she left her relationship and moved. The social worker can explore options together with Eun Jung, such as safety planning, restraining orders, and other protective measures she can take while remaining on campus. She could also consult with an immigration attorney or campus resources to find options for changing schools.

Farah is described as speaking very limited English. If you were the social worker for Farah and did not speak her language, a first step would be to determine what language(s) she speaks. The national language in Pakistan is Urdu, but she may speak a regional language such as Punjabi. Using a telephone language-interpretation service is one way to communicate and ensure confidentiality. Some limitations of interpretation services are the potential for misinterpretation, especially concerning specific terminology such as "domestic violence," and also the possibility of an insensitive interpreter. In some close-knit communities, few options are available for interpretation, and it is important to find out whether the interpreter knows the client.

A more sustainable solution to language access is to build a pool of trained bilingual social workers. Working with an interpreter or bilingual advocate trained in domestic violence is also an effective way to communicate. For more information, refer to the section below titled "Innovative Strategies within API-Specific Domestic Violence Programs."

LIMITATIONS OF CONVENTIONAL INTERVENTIONS MODELS

"Cultural competency" and "language access" have become familiar terms in all areas of human services, particularly in urban areas with diverse and growing immigrant communities. Many domestic violence programs and social service agencies, TANF programs, child welfare agencies, schools, and the criminal legal system have been faced with increased demands for services accessible to growing immigrant populations. Over time, the model of more extensive "cultural competence" training has become more common, as mainstream domestic violence and social service programs have become more aware of the multifaceted meaning of language accessibility and cultural competence, the diverse needs within communities of color, and the need for these competencies to be integrated into multiple levels of programs and related institutions.

Many mainstream social service and domestic violence programs have filled this gap by hiring a particular staff person to provide language accessibility, culturally competent services, and outreach. Many bilingual, bicultural workers who have occupied this ethnic-specific staff position can attest to the structural deficiencies of this model. API advocates within mainstream organizations often find that they are the only people of color or of a specific ethnic group within an otherwise white-dominated organization. Although this advocate may indeed be able to become the conduit for language accessibility and culturally competent services, the position is often accompanied by isolation and the overwhelming burden of meeting all the needs of a particular community. Added to these multiple roles may be the task of providing cultural competency training for outside advocates and policymakers. Many of those with the skills to provide services also act as advocates for their own family and community members on and off the job, thereby adding to an unsustainable position (Asian Women's Shelter 1994).

Despite years of determined work by many Asian and Pacific Islanders, immigrants, people of color, and white advocates to increase accessibility based on language and culture to API communities, the concrete impact on many mainstream domestic violence and social service programs has remained surprisingly low. High staff turnover and lack of structural support necessitating continuous orientation, training, and integration of language accessibility and cultural competence into all areas of program services are common reasons for this phenomenon. Relying on specific grant initiatives for these services and treating them as special projects instead of integrating them into basic programming is another common reason why many mainstream programs have failed to effectively institutionalize language accessibility and cultural competence (Asian Women's Shelter 1994).

THE NEED FOR LANGUAGE ACCESSIBLE AND CULTURAL COMPETENT SERVICES

It is estimated that there are more than 300[3] API-specific programs in the United States. These programs are created by, based in, and led by API communities, and have emerged as a response to the limitations of traditional anti-violence programs and approaches. Earlier demands by API immigrant women and advocates primarily targeted the expansion of accessible resources by domestic violence and legal institutions (Kim 2002). This included greater language and cultural access to mainstream institutions for API survivors of violence. In recent years, growing numbers of advocates have seriously questioned the nature of the programs and remedies provided for survivors of domestic violence.

The contemporary U.S. anti-violence movement is rooted in second-wave feminism of the 1960s and 1970s, giving rise to the movement's focus on power, control, and the privileging of gender hierarchy over other systems of oppression and interventions based on survivor-centered empowerment (Schechter 1982). Although these remain powerful conceptual frameworks, the white Western dominance of U.S. feminism also greatly influenced the evolution of the anti-violence movement, as it focused on the experience and needs of white, heterosexual, U.S.-born women. These factors have further shaped the intervention options now dominating the array of choices available for women and children escaping violence. This framework, combined with the growing professionalism within the anti-violence sector and the increased reliance upon legal remedies, has created a relatively standardized system and violence intervention practices and policies characterized by hotlines, shelters, restraining orders, and criminal penalties for domestic violence and sexual assault.

The assumed universality of Western feminism has long been subject to criticism, particularly by women from the global South and women of color within Western nations (i.e., Crenshaw 2001; Kanuha 1996; Razack 1998). In recent years, anti-violence activists and advocates have increasingly revealed the cultural and political biases embedded within these assumptions. Insisting on an expansion of the patriarchal framework to embrace the intersection of racism, nativism, classism, heterosexism, ableism, and ageism, people from the margins, largely women of color, immigrant women, and LGBTQ people have argued for a more accurate analysis of violence against women and children (Bhattacharjee 1997, 2001; Crenshaw 2001; Incite!/Critical Resistance 2005; Kanuha 1990, 1996; Kim 2009; Richie 1996, 2000, 2006; Smith 2006; Sokoloff and Dupont 2005).

An "intersectional" framework more adequately captures the multiple systems of oppression, including the state violence that marginalized people face, and demands an accompanying reformulation of responses to intimate forms of violence (Crenshaw 2001; Sokoloff and Dupont 2005). This radical critique of the mainstream anti-violence movement has emerged with increasing frequency in conferences, journal articles, and books. Even movement leaders most associated with conventional remedies have become similarly ambivalent or have been pressured by critics to reexamine some of their fundamental assumptions under mounting evidence of unintended consequences (Das Gupta 2003; Schneider 2000).

THE API ADVOCACY RESPONSE: FINDING OUR OWN SOLUTIONS

This critique, however, is not new. Much of it has been formulating unrecognized and undocumented within the margins of the anti-violence movement and among the many survivors who have found that available remedies were unable to meet their needs. In one study of the API anti-violence movement, a survey of key informants, consisting of long-time advocates and leaders in programs serving diverse API communities, revealed the Western biases embedded in the conventional violence intervention model (Kim 2002). The focus on individualized services for survivors, reliance on criminal legal interventions for perpetrators of violence, and the promotion of individual empowerment and separation as the solution to violence were cited as characteristics of conventional responses not necessarily suited for immigrant women and families. The study further identified traditional social service norms such as strict professional boundaries between advocates and clients as antithetical to more familial relationships of help-seeking and help-giving within API immigrant communities.

For API communities, traditional domestic violence interventions may appear equally as alienating and isolating as the domestic violence that women and children endure. Separation from family or community may tear women and children from valuable intimate resources, language and cultural familiarity, exposing them further to poverty and racism. For immigrants, the engagement of perpetrators with the criminal legal system could lead to conditions not only for loss of family livelihood but for deportation. And, in an

---

ORGANIZING IN THE HMONG COMMUNITY

The organizing work among Hmong women throughout the United States is one example of the ways in which new organizations are addressing the multiple, complex conditions of oppression that collude with and perpetuate domestic violence and sexual assault in their communities. Hmong women have organized resistance to male domestic violence and sexual assault through the establishment of anti-violence programs in high density Hmong communities in Minneapolis/St. Paul and the Wisconsin cities of Madison, Wausau, and Milwaukee. Hmong advocates are often identified or emerging leaders of all ages within their communities and have creatively negotiated these informal positions with their formal roles as domestic violence advocates. With a framework of community accountability rather than individualized services, Hmong advocates have provided safety and support for individual women and children facing violence while recognizing that physical escape from communities is often not feasible or desired. Creating safe spaces *within* communities rather than outside of communities requires long-term commitment to community engagement, credibility with grassroots community members, and skillful advocacy with the multiple systems influencing the lives of Hmong women, children, and men. Challenges and accommodations to indigenous clan leadership and laws are critical to individual and collective advocacy. Complex negotiations with local criminal legal systems, which routinely racially profile Hmong adults and youth and regularly contribute to the deportation of Hmong Americans convicted of felonies add to the innovative strategies necessary to effective domestic violence advocacy within the Hmong community.

alarming new trend, many immigrant women have found themselves wrong-fully arrested for domestic violence owing to the failure of police to provide proper interpretation, legal manipulation by violent partners, or overzealous law enforcement policies of arrest and prosecution.[4]

Here follows an example of community-based anti-violence strategies.

INNOVATIVE STRATEGIES WITHIN API-SPECIFIC DOMESTIC VIOLENCE PROGRAMS

Domestic violence and sexual assault programs and organizations established to serve primarily API immigrant populations since the 1980s have negoti-ated culturally specific needs with mainstream violence intervention models and legal standards. Created to address the gap in services to the API com-munity, these programs often created innovative features to more adequately meet the needs of the populations they were addressing. The Multilingual Access Model of Asian Women's Shelter is a replicable language-access pro-gram developed to meet the needs of more than 40 API language groups and cultures in the San Francisco Bay Area (Asian Women's Shelter 1999). Ke Ala Lokahi (Natural Order of Things) in Hilo, Hawaii, is a model of domestic violence intervention based on the foundations of Hawaiian cosmology and the reversal of the alienation and trauma of colonization (Kim 2005). Free-dom, Inc., an intergenerational advocacy program in Madison, Wisconsin, has built gender equity and accountability into its youth organizing program resulting in an everyday practice of accountability among the young men and women in its program (Kim 2005).

CASE ILLUSTRATION

The frequent necessity to challenge state initiatives and mandates regulat-ing intimate forms of violence illustrates the conflicting realities of those in marginalized communities. For example, advocates within API organizations actively fought against the passage of California's Proposition 187, which proposed the denial of social services, health care, and public education to undocumented immigrants. When Proposition 187 passed in 1994, many of these same advocates spread fliers throughout the community, informing fear-ful immigrants that domestic violence programs would not report them to the Immigration and Naturalization Service (INS). Following anti-immigrant sentiment and unquestioned compliance with criminal legal systems, some other domestic violence programs vowed to adhere to this new law.

Advocates serving API communities similarly struggle to negotiate legal compliance with child-abuse reporting laws while maintaining the need to build immigrant mothers' capacities to protect their children (Pennell and Kim 2009). Avidly pro-criminalization policies such as mandatory arrest—the result of the anti-violence movement's strong efforts to demand police accountability—were questioned early in the movement particularly by advocates from marginalized communities routinely subject to police surveillance and abuse. One consequence of the rapid enactment of these laws across the United States has been the increasing arrest of women—10 percent of domestic violence arrests in some cases (Pence 1999)—and the rising wrongful arrests of immigrant women.

As the API anti-violence sector has grown and matured, it has increasingly created networking and organizing opportunities to identify common concerns and develop new strategies to address the complexity of violence in API communities. Two national organizations promoting the interests of API immigrant advocates and survivors are the National Network to End Violence against Immigrant Women, which organizes providers and survivors working with all immigrant communities, and the Asian and Pacific Islander Institute on Domestic Violence, which focuses on API advocates and programs. These national coalitions and other local and regional coalitions organizing around immigrant women—particularly ethnic communities or specific interests—have provided valuable spaces to create new conceptual frameworks, policy agendas, and innovative practices that better meet the needs of immigrant communities.

CONCLUSION

In striving to meet the material, emotional, and cultural needs of immigrant survivors who seek to end domestic and sexual violence, activists and community advocates have created new strategies that extend beyond the confines of conventional violence intervention options. These strategies, developed and led by API community members, advocates, and survivors, often bridge the boundaries between individual services and community organizing; they address the intersection of race, gender, and other factors influencing domestic and sexual violence; and they provide API women and families the connection of culture and community while loosening the bonds of relationships based upon abuse and violence.

The sparse literature on both API domestic violence and innovative solutions to violence neglects the importance of API anti-violence programs not only to immigrant communities but to the broader anti-violence movement. The achievements and challenges of this sector needs to be documented and analyzed to build a body of literature. Historically underrepresented, the uniqueness of the Pacific Islander or NHOPI population warrants its own chapter as well as further research.

By building a critical understanding of culture and cultural competency, developing a more comprehensive understanding of domestic violence in API communities, and supporting and learning from the analysis building and work of API anti-violence advocates and allies, social workers can play a valuable role in addressing domestic violence in API communities. We hope that this chapter, as well as the rest of the book, challenges and inspires each of us to do our part in ending domestic violence, rising up like lilies out of the mud.

RESOURCES

Asian and Pacific Islander Institute on Domestic Violence
450 Sutter St., Suite 600
San Francisco, CA 94108
415–954–9988 ext. 315
http://www.apiahf.org/apidvinstitute
apidvinstitute@apiahf.org

Asian Women's Shelter
National Technical Assistance and Training Project
Transforming Silence Into Action/Queer Asian Women's Services
3543 18th Street, #19
San Francisco, CA 94110
Phone: (415) 751-7110 (business line); 1 (877) 751-0880 (crisis line)
Web site: http://www.sfaws.org

Creative Interventions
1904 Franklin Street, #200
Oakland, CA 94612
Phone: (415) 593-5330

E-mail: info@creative-interventions.org
Web site: http://www.creative-interventions.org

Incite! Women of Color Against Violence
PO Box 226
Redmond, WA 98073
Phone: (484) 932-3166
E-mail: incite_national@yahoo.com
Web site: http://www.incite-national.org

National Network to End Violence Against Immigrant Women
Web site: http://www.immigrantwomennetwork.org

REFERENCES

Asian and Pacific Islander American Health Forum (APIAHF). (2008). APPI's Population, Growth and Socioeconomic Status. Retrieved March 2, 2008, from http://www.apiahf.com/cic/index.asp.
Asian and Pacific Islander Institute on Domestic Violence (APIIDV). (2008a). *Asian and Pacific Islander Identities.* Retrieved March 2, 2008, from http://www.apiahf.org/apidvinsittute/definition.htm.
——. (2008b). *Coiled Spring of Violence.* Retrieved March 2, 2008, from http://www.apiahf.org/apidvinstitute/GenderViolence/analyze_b.htm.
Asian Women's Shelter. (1999). *The Multilingual Access Model: A Model for Outreach and Services in Non-English Speaking Communities.* Harrisburg, PA: National Resource Center on Domestic Violence.
Barnes, J. S., and C. E. Bennett. (2002). *The Asian Population: 2000. Census 2000 Brief.* Washington, DC: U.S. Census Bureau.
Bhattacharjee, A. (1997). A slippery path: Organizing resistance to violence against women. In S. Shah (Ed.), *Dragon Ladies* (pp. 29–45). Boston: South End.
——. (2001). *Whose Safety? Women of Color and the Violence of Law Enforcement.* Philadelphia: American Friends Service Committee and Committee on Women, Population, and the Environment. Retrieved December 9, 2007, from http://www.afsc.org/community/WhoseSafety.pdf).
Campbell, D. W., B. Masaki, and S. Torres. (1997). "Water on rock": Changing domestic violence perceptions in the African American, Asian American and Latino communities. In E. Klein, J. Campbell, E. Soler, and M. Ghez (Eds.), *Ending Domestic Violence: Changing Public Perceptions/Halting the Epidemic* (pp. 64–87). Thousand Oaks, CA: Sage.

Castles, S. (2006). Global perspectives on forced migration. *Asian and Pacific Migration Journal,* 15(1), 7–28.

Chantler, K. (2006). Independence, dependency and interdependence: Struggles and resistances of minoritized women within and leaving violent relationships. *Feminist Review,* 82, 27–49.

Chung, C., and S. Lee. (2001). *Raising Our Voices: Queer Asian Women's Responses to Relationship Violence.* Edited by L. Marin. San Francisco: Family Violence Prevention Fund.

Communities Against Rape and Abuse (CARA). (2006). Taking risks: Implementing grassroots community accountability strategies. In Incite! Collective (Ed.), *Color of Violence: The INCITE! Anthology* (pp. 250–266). Cambridge, MA: South End.

Crenshaw, K. (1994). Mapping the margins: Intersectionality, identity politics, and violence against women of color. In M. Fineman, and R. Myktiuk (Eds.), *The Public Nature of Private Violence* (pp. 93–118). New York: Routledge.

Das Gupta, S. (2003). *Safety and Justice for All: Examining the Relationship between the Women's Anti-Violence Movement and the Criminal Legal System.* New York: Ms. Foundation

Dixon, D. (2006). *Migration Immigration Source: Characteristics of the Asian Born in the United States.* Retrieved December 26, 2007, from http://www.migrationinformation.org/USfocus/print.cfm?ID=378.

Edleson, J. L. (2006). *Emerging Responses to Children Exposed to Domestic Violence.* Retrieved December 27, 2007, from http://new.vawnet.org/SpecialDocs/Documents.php?docid=585.

Faist, T. (2000). Transnationalizaiton in international migration: Implications for the study of citizenship and culture. *Ethnic and Racial Studies,* 23(2), 189–222.

Foster, R. M. P., M. Moskowitz, and R. A. Javier. (1996). *Reaching across Boundaries of Culture and Class: Widening the Scope of Psychotherapy.* Northvale, NJ: Jason Aronson.

Gill, A. (2004). Voicing the silent fear: South Asian women's experiences of domestic violence. *Howard Journal,* 43(5), 465–483.

Grieco, E. M. (2001). *The Native Hawaiian and Other Pacific Islander Populations: 2000. Census 2000 Brief.* Washington, DC: U.S. Census Bureau.

Grossman, S. F., and M. Lundy. (2007). Domestic violence across race and ethnicity: Implication for social work practice and policy. *Violence Against Women,* 13(10), 1029–1052.

Harris, P. M., and N. A. Jones. (2005). *We the People: Pacific Islanders in the United States . Census 2000 Special Report.* Washington, DC: U.S. Census Bureau.

Hobbs, F., and N. Stoops. (2002). *Demographic Trends in the 20 th Century: Census 2000 Special Reports.* Washington, DC: U.S. Census Bureau.

Incite!/Critical Resistance. (2005). Gender violence and the prison industrial complex: Interpersonal and state violence against women of color. In N. J. Sokoloff and C. Pratt (Eds.), *Domestic Violence at the Margins: Readings in Race, Class, Gender and Culture* (pp. 102–114). New Brunswick, NJ: Rutgers University Press.

Kanjanapan, W. (1995). The immigration of Asian professionals to the United States: 1988–1990. *International Migration Review*, 29(1), 7–32.

Kanuha, V. K. (1996). Domestic violence, racism, and the battered women's movement. In J. L. Edleson and Z. C. Eisikovits (Eds.), *Future Interventions with Battered Women and Their Families* (pp. 34–50). Thousand Oaks, CA: Sage.

Kanuha, V. K. (1990). Compounding the triple jeopardy: Battering in lesbian relationships. In L. S. Brown and M. P. P. Root (Eds.) *Diversity and Complexity in Feminist Therapy* . New York: Haworth .

Kim, M. (2002). *Innovative Strategies to Address Domestic Violence in Asian and Pacific Islander Communities: Examining Themes, Models and Interventions.* San Francisco: Asian and Pacific Islander Institute on Domestic Violence.

Kim, M. (2005). *The Community Engagement Continuum: Outreach, Mobilization, Organizing and Accountability to Address Violence against Women in Asian and Pacific Islander Communities.* San Francisco: Asian and Pacific Islander Institute on Domestic Violence.

Kwong, D. (2002). Removing barriers for battered immigrant women: A comparison of immigrant protections under VAWA I and II. *Berkeley Journal of Gender, Law and Justice*, 17, 137–152.

Lee, J., E. C. Pomeroy, and T. M. Bohman. (2007). Intimate partner violence and psychological health in a sample of Asian and Caucasian women: The roles of social support and coping. *Journal of Family Violence*, 22, 709–720.

Orloff, L., D. Jang, and C. F. Klein. (1995). With no place to turn: Improving legal advocacy for battered immigrant women. *Family Law Quarterly*, 29, 313–329.

Paisano, E. (1993). *We the Americans: Pacific Islanders.* Washington, DC: U.S. Department of Commerce.

Pence, E. (1999). Some thoughts on philosophy. In M. F. Shepard and E. L. Pence (Eds.), *Coordinating Community Responses to Domestic Violence: Lessons from Duluth and Beyond* (pp. 25–40). Thousand Oaks, CA: Sage.

Pennell, J., and M. Kim. (2009). Opening conversations across cultural, gender, and generational divides: Family and community engagement to stop violence against women and children. In J. Ptacek (Ed.), *Feminism and Restorative Justice*. New York: Oxford University Press.

Portes, A. (2004). Introduction: The debates and significance of immigrant transnationalism. *Global Networks*, 1(3), 181–193.

Raj, A., and J. Silverman. (2002). Violence against immigrant women: The roles of culture, context, and legal immigrant status on intimate partner violence. *Violence Against Women*, 8(3), 367–398.

——. (2003). Immigrant South Asian women at greater risk for injury from intimate partner violence. *American Journal of Public Health*, 93(3), 435–437.

Razack, S. H. (1998). *Looking White People in the Eye: Gender, Race, and Culture in Courtrooms and Classrooms*. Toronto: Toronto University Press.

——. (2004). Imperiled Muslim women, dangerous Muslim men and civilized Europeans: Legal and social responses to forced marriage. *Feminist Legal Studies*, 12, 239–174.

Reeves, T. J., and C. L. Bennett. (2004). *We the People: Asians in the United States. Census 2000 Special Report*. Washington, DC: US Census Bureau.

Richie, B. E. (2000). A Black feminist reflection on the antiviolence movement. *Signs*, 25(4), 1133–1137.

——. (1996). *Compelled to Crime: The Gender Entrapment of Battered, Black Women*. New York: Routledge and Kegan Paul.

Ritchie, A. J. (2006). Law enforcement violence against women of color. In Incite! Collective (Ed.), *Color of Violence: The INCITE! Anthology* (pp. 138–156). Cambridge, MA: South End.

San Francisco Department on the Status of Women (SFDOSW). (2007). *Safety for All: Identifying and Closing the Gap in San Francisco's Domestic Violence Criminal Justice Response*. San Francisco, CA: T. Erwin.

Santa Clara County Domestic Violence Council. (2002). *Domestic Violence in Santa Clara County . Annual Data Report*. San Jose: Author.

Sastry, J., and C. E. Ross. (1998). Asian ethnicity and the sense of personal control. *Social Psychology Quarterly*, 61(2), 101–120.

Schechter, S. (1982). *Women and Male Violence: The Visions and Struggles of the Battered Women's Movement*. Cambridge, MA: South End.

Schneider, E. (2000). *Battered Women and Feminist Lawmaking*. New Haven, CT: Yale University Press.

Schor, E. (2000). Domestic abuse and alien women in immigration law: Response and responsibility. *Cornell Journal of Law and Public Policy*, 9(3), 697–713.

Shimtuh. (2000). *Korean American Domestic Violence Needs Assessment Report*. Oakland, CA: Korean Community Center of the East Bay.

Shin, H. B., and R. Bruno. (2003).*Language Use and English-Speaking Ability: 2000. Census 2000 Brief*. Washington, DC: U.S. Census Bureau.

Smelser, N. J., W. J. Wilson, and F. Mitchell. (2001). *America Becoming: Racial Trends and Their Consequences*. Vols. 1 and 2. Washington, DC: National Academy Press

Smith, A. (2006). Looking to the future: Domestic violence, women of color, the state, and social change. In N. J. Sokoloff, and C. Pratt (Eds.), *Domestic Violence at the Margins: Readings on Race, Class, Gender, and Culture*. New Brunswick, NJ: Rutgers University Press.

Sokoloff, N. J., and I. Dupont. (2005). Domestic violence at the intersections of race, class, and gender: Challenges and contributions to understanding violence against marginalized women in diverse communities. *Violence Against Women*, 11(1), 38–64.

Song, Y. I. (1996). *Battered Women in Korean Immigrant Families: The Silent Scream.* New York: Garland.

Tjaden, P., and N. Thoennes. (2000). *Extent, Nature, and Consequences of Intimate Partner Violence: Findings from the National Violence against Women Survey.* Washington, DC: U.S. Department of Justice.

U.S. Census Bureau. (N.d.). American factfinder: Asian in combination with one or more other races. Retrieved March 20, 2008, from http://www.census.gov/population/socdemo/education/cps2007/Table1–09.xls.

U.S. Census Bureau News. (2007). Minority population tops 100 million. Retrieved March 20, 2008, from http://www.census.gov/population/www/socdemo/race/ppl-184_aoic.html.

U.S. Department of Health and Human Services. (N.d.). Fact Sheet on Guidance to Federal Financial Assistance Recipients Regarding Title VI Prohibition Against National Origin Discrimination Affecting Limited English Proficient (LEP) Persons. Retrieved April 16, 2009, from http://www.hhs.gov/ocr/civilrights/resources/specialtopics/lep/factsheetguidanceforlep.html.

Volpp, L. (1994). (Mis)Identifying culture: Asian women and the "cultural defense." *Harvard Women's Law Journal*, 17, 57–101.

Warrier, S. (2005). *Culture Handbook*. San Francisco: Family Violence Prevention Fund.

Weil, J. M., and H. H. Lee. (2004). Cultural considerations in understanding family violence among Asian American Pacific Islander families. *Journal of Community Health Nursing*, 27(4), 217–227.

Wright, D. E. (1997). Severing the karmic ties that bind. The "divorce temple" Mantokuji. *Monumenta Nipponica*, 52(3), 357–380.

Yick, A. G. (2000). Predictors of physical spousal/intimate violence in Chinese American families. *Journal of Family Violence*, 15(3), 249–267.

Yoshihama, M. (2002). Battered women's coping strategies and psychological distress: Differences by immigration status. *American Journal of Community Psychology*, 30(30), 429–452.

Yoshioka, M., Q. Dang, N. Shewmangal, C. Chan, and C. I. Yan. (2000). *Asian Family Violence Report: A Study of the Chinese, Cambodian, Korean, South Asian and Vietnamese Communities in Massachusetts.* Boston: Asian Task Force Against Domestic Violence, Inc.

Yoshioka, M. R., J. DiNoia, and K. Ullah. (2001). Attitudes toward marital violence: An examination of four Asian communities. *Violence Against Women*, 7(8), 900–926.

5

SOCIAL WORK PRACTICE WITH ABUSED PERSONS WITH DISABILITIES

Elizabeth P. Cramer and Sara-Beth Plummer

DISABILITY: DEFINITIONS, PREVALENCE, AND THEORIES

ACCORDING TO the National Violence Against Women Survey, three times as many women as men experience physical assault by an intimate partner during their lifetime (21% vs. 7%, respectively) (Tjaden and Thoennes 2000). Depending on its definition, annual incidents of violence toward women range from 837,899 (National Crime Victim Survey) to 6.25 million (National Family Violence Survey) (Gelles 2000). When one considers nonphysical abuse—emotional abuse, threats, and controlling behaviors—the numbers increase for both men and women. When one includes abuse directed toward the disabled, the number rises. Until recently, little research or scholarship has focused on a population of women and men who are at great risk of being abused: persons with disabilities.

The term "disability" has many definitions. Some consider "disability" within a medical-diagnostic context, which generally implies medical or psychological treatment as well as accommodations for activities of daily living. Those that view disability as a medical condition (within and outside the disability community) adopt particular terms: "people with X," with X referring to the condition (e.g., people with multiple sclerosis, people with a hearing impairment). They also may use the disability as a noun to describe the person, particularly regarding mental illness (e.g., "He's a schizophrenic"). Others view disability as a "set of limitations imposed on individuals (with or even without diagnosed medical conditions) from external factors such as social, cultural, and other environmental influences" (DePoy and Gilson 2004, p. 4). Those adhering to the second or constructed view of disability may choose, for example, to refer to people as disabled—not because the person has an intrinsic condition but rather because the environment disables people from functioning to their fullest potential.[1] Others may reject the idea that a disability needs to be "fixed" or "cured" in order for individuals to live good and meaningful lives (e.g., cochlear implants for deaf children).

The Americans with Disabilities Act defines a person as having a disability "if s/he has a physical or mental impairment that substantially limits one or more major life activities, has a record of such impairment, or is regarded as having such an impairment" (U.S. Equal Employment Opportunity Commission 2002, p. 6). According to the 2000 U.S. Census (Waldrop and Stern 2003), 49.7 million noninstitutionalized civilians aged 5 and over reported some type of enduring condition or disability; this represents one-fifth of the population. The percentage of persons reporting disabilities is highest for adults 65 years old and older, who account for 42 percent of the disabled.

One theory about disability is referred to as Explanatory Legitimacy Theory (ELT) (DePoy and Gilson 2004; Gilson, DePoy, and Cramer 2003). Three interactive elements comprise this theory: "description," "explanation," and "legitimacy." To illustrate, we provide two hypothetical situations, using Ed and Becky. "Description" includes what people do and do not do, and how they do it. Ed and Becky both slur their words when they speak. This type of speaking would be considered "atypical" (not of the norm or considered normal) and observable. The "explanation" for why each individual slurs his or her words, however, may differ. Ed's word slurring may be explained by his cerebral palsy, a medical diagnosis, whereas Becky's slurring is explained by blood-alcohol levels. Ed's slurring his words fits within a "legitimate value framework" (i.e., caused by a medical condition through no fault of his own). Consequently, the responses to him may focus on what treatments or therapies may enable him to communicate slurring fewer words (i.e., more "normally"). The judgment and response to Becky from some individuals, however, may be quite different based on the explanation for Becky's word slurring—her misuse of alcohol. Whereas Ed may be viewed as a person with a disability (CP) whose condition causes various atypical characteristics, Becky may be termed a "drunk," engendering a response such as removing her from the premises. In this example, one person (Ed) would be legitimized as disabled, and the other (Becky) would not be considered disabled.

PREVALENCE OF ABUSE OF PERSONS WITH DISABILITIES

The number of men and women with disabilities who are abused appears similar to or higher than others. One U.S. study comparing lifetime prevalence rates of emotional, physical, and sexual abuse of women with disabilities with other women found that both groups had experienced such abuse—62 percent, respectively (Young et al. 1997); husbands or live-in partners were most commonly the perpetrators. Compared to other women, women with disabilities experience abuse for a longer duration, by a greater number of perpetrators, and more frequently at the hands of health-care workers and personal care attendants. They also have fewer options for leaving the abusive situation (Young et al. 1997).

A study of women attending family practice clinics in the U.S. reported that women with disabilities were more than twice as likely to report intimate partner violence (IPV) than women without disabilities (Coker, Smith, and Fadden 2005). A recent study of women in North Carolina found similar rates of physical assault for women with and women without disabilities, although those with disabilities had four times the odds of experiencing sexual assault in the past year than others (Martin et al. 2006).

A Canadian study demonstrated higher rates of physical, sexual, emotional, and financial abuse among women with activity limitations compared to other women (Cohen et al. 2006). Persons with activity limitations were defined as "those with difficulties in activities of daily living or persons who have a physical or mental condition or health problem that limits the kind or amount of activities they can perform" (p. 1). In this same study, men with activity limitations showed greater rates of physical, emotional, and financial abuse than other men. Women who had activity limitations were more likely to experience a form of intimate partner violence, and more frequently and severely, compared to men who had activity limitations. This difference, however, disappeared when factoring in sociodemographic variables for the analysis (i.e., age, marital status, income, and self-rated health status).

A recent Canadian study of 7,027 women found that disabled women had 40 percent greater odds of experiencing violence (physical assault, physical threat, or sexual assault) committed by a marital or common-law partner in the preceding five years compared to other women. Furthermore, the disabled women were more at risk for severe violence (Brownridge 2006). The author identified patriarchal dominance and sexual jealousy and possessiveness as perpetrator characteristics, or risk markers, for violence against this female population.

It has also been suggested that the risks of abuse increase for women living in institutional settings (Chenoweth 1996; Sobsey 1994). Personal Assistance Service providers are also known to abuse women and men with disabilities (Oktay and Tompkins 2004; Saxton et al. 2001).

Being abused may cause short- or long-term disabling conditions for men and women, such as head and traumatic brain injuries (Banks and Acker-man 2002; Jackson et al. 2002); chronic pain syndromes (Kendall-Tackett, Marshall, and Ness 2003); and neurological impairments as a result of stran-gulation (Wilbur et al. 2001). Coker et al. (2005) found that all types of IPV (physical assault, sexual assault, and psychological/emotional abuse) were associated with having a disability. They note that IPV may lead to disabilities "indirectly through distress and adverse lifestyle or coping strate-gies. . . . Some IPV-associated disability is the result of an injury, but most IPV-associated disability results from women's long-term exposure to chronic abuse. . . . [I]ndirect effects of both physical and psychological IPV may be more important than the direct physical injuries that many abused women experience" (p. 834).

CONCEPTUAL FRAMEWORKS FOR UNDERSTANDING ABUSE OF PERSONS WITH DISABILITIES

Several researchers have offered conceptual frameworks for understanding abuse of persons with disabilities. An ecological model helps us to understand and address the abuse of the disabled population (Sobsey 1994). This model includes the vulnerability of persons with disabilities to be abused, partly owing to limited physical and cognitive skills; increased isolation because of interactions and relationships that encourage physical and emotional depen-dency; and the tendency of those who work with persons with disabilities to exhibit a need for power and control, and to take positions intentionally in institutions that offer opportunities to abuse. Dehumanization, depersonal-ization, and devaluation of persons with disabilities add to the continuation of abuse.

The concepts "silence" and "paradox" have also been used to help explain the abuse of individuals with disabilities (Chenoweth 1996). "Silence" is based on the overall societal denial of the prevalence of abuse of the disabled population. Abuse of these individuals is often not discussed and, when encountered, is routinely ignored. The "paradoxes" include the overprotection, segregation, and trained compliance of individuals with disabilities, with the simultaneous expectations of either asexual or promiscuous behavior among disabled women. In an attempt to protect individuals with disabilities, we inadvertently facilitate situations that increase the potential for abuse by fostering vulnerability through isolation, limiting autonomy, and encouraging learned compliance.

Another construct for understanding abuse of persons with disabilities is "limitation" (Cramer, Gilson, and DePoy 2003; DePoy, Gilson, and Cramer 2003; Gilson, Cramer, and Depoy 2001; Gilson, DePoy, and Cramer 2003; Gilson, DePoy, and Cramer 2001). Researchers facilitated focus groups of persons with disabilities who had been abused and service providers in rural and urban locations in Virginia, from which the theoretical construct of limitation emerged. This construct includes abuse expressed through restraint and control, including withholding medication, neglecting personal care, and blocking accessibility to mobilization devices specifically targeted to one's disability. The participants identified the limiting experience of perpetrators' paternalistic attitude, shared by human service providers as well as law enforcement and court personnel, and its effects on their self-esteem and resilience. Abused persons with disabilities are limited in their efforts to obtain services because of inaccessible buildings, written information in inaccessible formats, and the lack of communication aids in the courthouse. Inaccessible means something different than obscure in the disability community.

Explanatory Legitimacy Theory, described earlier in this chapter, can also be applied to domestic violence through a discussion of harm: "harm activity" and "harm consequences" (Gilson, DePoy, and Cramer 2003). Actions that produce negative consequences constitute "harm activity." These "harm consequences" are the observable and reportable outcomes. A "harm threshold" is the point at which the harm consequences are unacceptable and require intervention. The extent to which harm activity and harm consequences fit into current legal and value parameters influences the policy and system response to domestic violence. If, for example, removing a battery from a motorized wheelchair is viewed as "mean" but not "abuse," the response to such an act falls outside the legal realm. If such an act was considered "assault" or "battery" under state codes, then the response would legitimately involve the criminal justice system.

POLICY AND SERVICES RESPONSES TO ABUSE OF PERSONS WITH DISABILITIES

Research has shown that many individuals with disabilities often do not report abuse or neglect to the authorities (Sobsey and Doe 1991). Those who attempt to report abuse are often met with disbelief by the authorities (Mitchell and Buchele-Ash 2000) or insensitive behavior by service providers and first responders (Swedlund and Nosek 2000). Additionally, those individuals who have sought help in the form of counseling, medical assistance, and legal aid found that service providers did not offer adequate accommodations (Sobsey and Doe 1991). In most states, personal assistance providers who are not family or household members are excluded from family abuse statutes, which influence how an assault is categorized and the availability of Family Abuse Protective Orders.[2]

According to the Americans with Disabilities Act of 1990, public entities must not exclude persons with disabilities from their services, programs, and activities. Public entities are responsible for "program accessibility," meaning that the state's programs must be made accessible to persons with disabilities, which could include altering existing facilities, acquiring or constructing new facilities, relocating services to an accessible site, or providing services at alternative accessible locations (U.S. Equal Employment Opportunity Commission 2002). Although the buildings in which courts are held may themselves be accessible for persons with disabilities, the service for which a disabled person is going to the courthouse may not be so. For example, one study of people with disabilities and people who accompanied them to court reported various problems, including the lack of appropriate communication devices for women who are deaf or hard of hearing; one locale reported the lack of any certified American Sign Language interpreters in the community (Gilson, Cramer, and DePoy 2001).

The legal arena has begun to address the issue of abuse and neglect of individuals with disabilities (e.g., American Bar Association 1992; Crime Victims with Disabilities Awareness Act 1998; Developmental Disabilities Assistance and Bill of Rights Act 1994. 1998; Office of Victims of Crime 2002a, 2002b, 2002c). Comprehensive and enforceable policies and programs that specifically address this issue remain lacking, however. Current policies and laws are difficult to enforce, and protection is often elusive for those in institutions and group homes, largely because of a separation or isolation of services. Few programs exist that adequately address individuals with disabilities that have experienced abuse or neglect or both. Currently there are concerns that domestic violence program workers are not adequately trained to work with individuals with disabilities; many need training on disability issues, including the unique types of abuse experienced by individuals with disabilities (Chang et al. 2003). Further, many of these programs are not financially equipped to make their centers physically accessible to a wide range of disabilities (Chang et al. 2003; Nosek, Howland, and Young 1997; Swedlund and Nosek 2000).

Swedlund and Nosek (2000) found that most of the surveyed independent living centers[3] (ILCs) referred clients to domestic violence clinics. The study respondents suggested that the option of referring individuals with disabilities to domestic violence clinics is flawed. ILC providers identified many barriers encountered when referred individuals attempted to access domestic violence shelters and programs; leading the list was inaccessibility, including limited physical access to programs and shelters, and lack of interpreters and adequate transportation. Attitudinal barriers were also identified, including insufficient understanding and insensitivity to disability-related issues. In order to better serve individuals with disabilities who may experience abuse or neglect, ILC providers suggested increased coordination between service providers, specifically between ILCs and abuse intervention services.

In addition to the problems noted above with service provision, insufficient accessible and affordable housing, inadequate transportation, and employment discrimination are significant concerns for abused persons with disabilities who want to leave the abusive relationship. People choosing between leaving an accessible home that maximizes autonomy and independence and availing services at inaccessible shelters may choose to remain in the situation because of a shortage of reasonably priced, accessible housing (National Coalition Against Domestic Violence 1996). The ability to manage one's financial needs also influences the decisions of abused, disabled individuals regarding the abusive relationship. People with disabilities are less likely to be employed compared to nondisabled persons.[4] Persons with more severe disabilities are even less likely to be employed, which also applies to those with inadequate transportation, and as many as 31 percent of disabled individuals lack adequate transportation (Virginia Board of People with Disabilities, "Community Participation and Disability," 2006).

In this technological age, computers and the Internet offer people with disabilities greater access to information and services than existed in the past.

According to a survey of more than 10,000 households, however, the use of computers and the Internet consistently lagged among people with disabilities compared to the general population. One-quarter of the individuals who identified as having a disability reported owning a computer, and only one-tenth reported that they had Internet access (Kaye 2000). For disabled persons with Web access, navigating Web sites can be a challenge because of inaccessible Web pages (Choi and Rajikumar 1996; Kautzman 1998).

Articles detailing the lack of coordinated service systems to respond to abused, disabled persons abound in the literature (Gilson et al. 2001; Nosek et al. 1997). Disabled victims have recommended better coordination of services between domestic violence/sexual assault programs, disability services, and the criminal justice system. Therefore, a collaborative approach between service providers is needed so that abused persons with disabilities can successfully access legal protections and support services.

IMPROVING POLICY AND SERVICE PROVISION: A CULTURALLY INFORMED, INTERSECTIONAL APPROACH

We prefer to use the term "culturally informed" rather than "culturally competent": "Competence" implies the capacity to master all the values, knowledge, and skills needed to serve various cultural, racial, or ethnic groups. "Culturally informed," in contrast, suggests the systematic gathering of data about different cultural groups and communities (including the tensions within communities), useful for informing oneself when filtered through the critical lens of interpretation, including the influence of one's own social location. Dean (2001) suggests that, instead of striving for cross-cultural competence based on knowledge about particular cultures, practitioners should engage in understanding and building a relationship through "respectful, nonjudgmental, and deeply interested questioning and the exchange of beliefs" (p. 628). We believe that Dean's advice is appropriate when working with persons with disabilities.

We also suggest that intersectionality (see chapter 1 in this volume) might be a particularly useful framework for understanding the help-seeking and help-receiving behaviors of abused, disabled individuals. Historical and contemporary power relationships between persons with disabilities and service providers provides a lens through which critical questions about seeking and receiving help can be posed. These critical questions examine how social, economic, political, and cultural contexts influence the construction of multiple identities/selves, and how these contexts influence decisions about seeking help as well as the experience of receiving help. Race, gender, ethnicity, class, disability, and so on, are viewed as social, political, economic, and cultural constructs or *"positionalities"* (e.g., social locations) that classify, categorize, and construct the social value that is assigned to individuals according to various components (e.g., beliefs, concepts, and structures that define social practice)" (Harley et al. 2002, p. 216).

Frameworks derived from the constructs of intersectionality, ELC, and the "informed, not-knowing" stance advocated by Dean (2001) assist in critically analyzing the abuse of persons with disabilities, and may lead us to ask the following questions: How does the intertwining of race, gender, class, and disability affect poor African American women with disabilities who are being battered when they seek assistance from the police? What types of harm are legitimated as criminal assault for which one can receive intervention from law enforcement and the courts? When and according to whom is an action viewed as criminal versus mean behavior?

CASE STUDY: TONYA

Tonya is an African American woman in her mid-fifties. She met her ex-husband (whom we call J) when she was in her early twenties, working in Europe as an au pair. J was also an American visiting abroad. Immediately upon meeting Tonya, he began courting her, buying gifts, and taking her out several times a week. At the end of the summer, Tonya decided to stay with the family throughout the school year. J called and wrote continually, begging her to return to the States to be with him. She finally gave in to his requests and subsequently flew to the U.S. expecting to begin a wonderful life with him.

Tonya reported that the abuse began immediately, as soon as she arrived at the airport. After departing the plane she saw that J was not at the airport to pick her up as promised. She took a cab to his home, and when she arrived he was drunk and belligerent. She ignored this behavior and assumed it was a one-time occurrence, but this was not to be. She reported that throughout their relationship he would vacillate between kind and attentive behavior to abusive and degrading acts. During a period of calm, they married. Tonya hoped that the marriage would encourage peace and security in their relationship. Her husband increased his alcohol abuse and began using drugs. Tonya was unaware of his illicit drug use. She reported punching her and forcing her to use cocaine. Fearing another assault, she relented; arriving home one day from work and witnessing J using cocaine. She was shocked

"CONTINUED"

and expressed her feelings of anger and betrayal. J responded to Tonya's anger by she became addicted soon after. The drug use and physical abuse continued during their marriage.

A few years later, while walking across the street, Tonya was hit by a car. She fell into a coma and awoke a month later. Once out of the coma, she discovered that her leg had been amputated. She returned home to her husband, although at this point they were living less as a married couple and more like roommates. Tonya had successfully stopped using drugs. Her husband continued his drug use and increased the number of substances he abused. Tonya reported feeling trapped in the marriage, unable to go off on her own. She was now financially dependent upon her husband. Although he frequently abused drugs, he remained successfully employed. She, however, lost her job and applied for Social Security Disability (SSD). Tonya reported feeling increasingly isolated and depressed. She was fitted for a prosthetic leg and given a scooter through her insurance company. Her husband immediately took control of her SSD checks, cashing them as soon as they arrived at their home. His verbal and physical assaults began to increase, as Tonya was less able to help around the home. J's abusive acts began to target Tonya's disability. Recognizing how Tonya relied on both her prosthetic leg and her scooter, J used this dependence to his advantage. Tonya discussed how her husband would take her leg and hide it. In one instance he used the leg as his weapon, hitting Tonya with her own prosthesis. At other times he would tamper with her scooter, remove the battery and hide it as well.

Tonya began working part-time at a credit card company. Hiding her paychecks, she slowly saved her money until she had enough to leave her husband. She answered an advertisement for a rented room and applied for a home health aide. After leaving her husband and settling into the apartment, she called a hotline number she saw listed in the phonebook for people with disabilities. She needed help to find a subsidized and wheelchair accessible apartment. Her current apartment was not accessible, and she relied on her home health aide to help her up and down the stairs to her new home. Soon after, she began weekly individual and group sessions at an out-patient mental health clinic.

Tonya's social worker helped her set manageable goals and timelines to increase her independence regarding both her physical functioning and her husband's controlling and abusive behaviors. Early on in their work together, the social worker and Tonya created a personalized safety plan.[5] Discussion of Tonya's activities of daily living (ADLs) and instrumental activities of daily living (IADLs) assisted with identifying areas where Tonya would need assistance from informal or formal help providers. The social worker helped Tonya prepare to interview potential care providers who could meet her needs and how to look for "red flags" signaling possibly abusive providers. The counselor also monitored Tonya's depression by periodically administering the Beck Depression Inventory (Beck 2007).

In the following sections Tonya's story is integrated into a discussion of recommended social work practice values and skills for working with abused persons with disabilities. Our discourse begins by addressing a major ethical dilemma that social workers often face when working with this population: mandatory reporting of abuse or neglect of persons with disabilities.

GENERALIST PRACTICE PRINCIPLES FOR WORKING WITH ABUSED, DISABLED PERSONS

The very nature of social work implies that workers in the field will encounter ethical situations daily. Social work is a value-based profession attracting practitioners from a variety of backgrounds who have their own individual beliefs and ideas. This diversity inevitably creates conflict over values, customs, even law. When social workers serve individuals with disabilities who have been abused, conflict between the law and professional social work ethics arises in multiple ways, one of which, described below, relates to mandatory reporting of abuse or neglect of persons with disabilities. Social workers are encouraged to reflect upon their own values prior to serving others. We also recommend that they review their attitudes relating to domestic violence as well as their own preconceived views, and those of the greater society, regarding individuals with disabilities.

MANDATORY REPORTING REQUIREMENTS AND SELF-DETERMINATION

Self-determination—the right of individuals to make their own decisions—is primary among social work's principal values (Lowenberg, Dolgoff, and Harrington 2000). Laws and policies surrounding domestic violence, however, are filled with questions regarding safety versus self-determination. A social worker may be in a situation where he or she must ask, "When should I step in as a professional and make a decision that may conflict with my client's wishes?" This dilemma occurs, for example, when an abused client with a disability reports the abuse but does not wish to leave the situation. Current literature about domestic violence counseling often stresses the importance of respecting the victim's choice, regardless of whether the victim remains in the abusive relationship (Danis 2003). We also know that an abusive situation can become more dangerous, even deadly, when a victim chooses to leave. Yet in some states, Virginia among them, reporting abuse of individuals with disabilities is mandatory (Code of Virginia §63.2–1606). This statute requires that a mandatory reporter contact Adult Protective Services if a person 18 years of age or older and incapacitated[6] is believed to be abused. This may inherently cause a conflict between the legal requirements, the desire to keep a client safe, and the social work value of client self-determination.

EXAMINING ONE'S VALUES REGARDING PERSONS WITH DISABILITIES

Social workers must always reassess their personal values before beginning work with clients, including individuals with disabilities. Society tends to marginalize and isolate this population. Many believe that individuals with disabilities, regardless of the disability, cannot accomplish anything for themselves, an infantilizing perspective. Succumbing to antiquated views about people with disabilities, or other negative values, can quickly hamper one's relationship with a client and destroy any possibility of a collaborative relationship. In Tonya's case, for example, a worker who disapproved of substance use, or one who was repulsed by the use of prostheses, may have had difficulty establishing rapport and warmth with Tonya. Furthermore, a worker may try to plan a disabled client's goals, conduct all necessary calls, and complete the essential paperwork to accomplish these goals. This could easily impede a client's self-determination and sense of empowerment. We suggest that workers ask themselves these questions: "Is this what the client wants?" "Are there things I am doing that the client could do?"

Working with individuals with disabilities requires social workers to view the world through a new lens that enables them to see life through their clients' eyes. This difference in worldviews suggests that before beginning a discussion around the issue of abuse and neglect, workers must make every effort to learn and absorb all the information they can about a client's specific disability or disabilities. In order to become a skilled social worker, one must exhibit a willingness to learn from one's clients. "Becoming competent in working with diversity involves extensive self-knowledge along with an openness that accompanies inductive learning" (Johnson and Yanca 2004, p. 115). We also suggest that workers approach their clients with interest, openness, and tentativeness about what they think they know, a recommendation echoed by Dean (2001).

Gaining knowledge about disabilities and related abuse grows with experience. Each client offers new insight into his or her specific disability and experience with abuse. Broadly attempting to learn about disabilities in general will not suffice. Although some scholars argue that disability is a culture (Mitchell 1996), it is important to remember that people who self-identify as disabled may not feel that they belong to a disability community or culture. For example, a person who is D/deaf may believe that he or she has little in common with an individual with a mobility-limiting disability. We recommend, therefore, that social workers learn about various types of disabilities and inquire as to how the individual describes him- or herself (What terms are used? Does the person believe in the medical-diagnostic view of disability or the constructed perspective? Does he or she identify with a community or communities?). For example, Tonya, who had not been born with her disability, expressed anger and frustration adapting to life with one leg. She exhibited great difficulty connecting to other individuals with disabilities who attended a weekly domestic violence support group. She discussed her struggles with DLAs owing to the limitations she experienced as an amputee. She made the worker aware during the session when she was physically uncomfortable and sometimes asked to leave the session early because she was in pain.

DEVELOPING RESPECTFUL COLLABORATIVE WORKING RELATIONSHIPS: USE OF EMPOWERMENT THEORY

In generalist social work practice, social workers are encouraged to define the initial concerns from the clients' perspectives, including successfully identifying all potential strengths of clients and their surrounding systems (Johnson and Yanca 2004). Taking the time to learn as much as one can from a client encourages a positive and effective collaboration and also provides a strong foundation for future steps to successful outcomes. A major principle of empowerment practice is the use of collaboration between worker and client. This emphasis on a cooperative relationship is based on social workers withdrawing from the role of an authoritarian expert (Perkins and Zimmerman 1995). Clients should be considered experts about their concerns and, as such, wield the power in the client-worker relationship. The client is the one who identifies the "concern" and provides the directive on creating goals and objectives (Lee 1996). Focusing on how the client describes the problem or concern also establishes a worker's commitment to view the client as the "expert" on his or her own life, which is consistent with empowerment theory. We strongly suggest that social workers who serve this population integrate and utilize empowerment theory throughout the client-worker relationship. This is especially important because of the patronizing attitude that many individuals with disabilities encounter. Using these skills can also help minimize perceived struggles between client and worker, and also eliminate misunderstandings.

Tonya was a strong, independent woman who made it clear at the start of the working relationship that she was not a victim. She spoke for hours about her past accomplishments and her future goals. Early on, she identified the goals and objectives she wanted to address. Before Tonya wanted to discuss her history of abuse, her priority was to find an accessible and affordable home and hire a reliable home health aide. In the initial sessions, discussions about the abuse she experienced were minimal and largely related to her lack of financial independence. Concerns about the impact of abuse on her mental health were addressed through conversations around her battles with depression and anxiety. Although the worker may have felt that placing the abuse and addiction issues in the forefront was important, she respected Tonya's desire to address the other issues first.

COLLECTING AND ASSESSING DATA

Building a collaborative relationship begins the moment the client and worker sit down together to complete an assessment. This is the first opportunity for the social worker to connect with the client and build a relationship that will progress through treatment. First and foremost, clients must feel safe to share their thoughts and emotions related to the abusive situation. Social workers are responsible to create a safe atmosphere by encouraging a sense of security and trust. The agency Tonya attended tried to create a safe haven for its clients by refusing to publicize the office address, providing it only to clients and ambulette companies. The agency also worked hard to make the facilities as accessible as possible. Tonya immediately reported feeling safe and comfortable at the agency, because she saw how dedicated the workers were to individuals with disabilities. She was able to use her scooter or braces to enter the building, thereby functioning independently at the agency.

Once a client feels safe and begins to share his or her story, a worker's focus should be on the client's strengths (Johnson and Yanca 2004), which includes recognizing the client's accomplishments in the face of an abusive situation. Tonya rebounded from drug abuse and a life- threatening accident to leave an ongoing abusive situation. Rather than feeling trapped by her disability, she persevered, maintaining her sobriety and finding a way to move out on her own.

We suggest that the social worker, using an ecological approach, obtain information about the client's thoughts and emotions regarding the abusive situation and also about the client's interactions with his or her environment (Johnson and Yanca 2004). This enables the worker and client to determine the next steps to take once the client is ready to set goals. Reviewing how the client interacts with the environment, and making note of any deficits, is essential for individuals with disabilities because of the often inhospitable nature of the outside community to this population (e.g., a disregard for accessibility). This gathering of data informs the worker about how the environment itself may need to be changed to improve the client's situation. Tonya was aware of her limited surroundings and the lack of affordable and accessible homes. When she first came to the agency, she was residing in a basement apartment that necessitated walking down a flight of steps to enter. Therefore, she could not leave her home without another person assisting her. She had taken the apartment initially in order to leave her abusive husband. At the time she could not afford any other housing; the waiting lists for subsidized housing were very long. Tonya also needed to hire a reliable aide. She had gone through several aides who at various times were neglectful, unreliable, and inconsistent. The worker and Tonya discussed the accessibility inside her home and the current condition of both her electric scooter and braces.

Some individuals born with a disability are isolated intentionally from the surrounding world for their own protection. Families who do so, however, are in fact insulating the disabled family member from the world and encouraging possible opportunities for abuse. Clients' abilities vary based on their environment, familial customs, culture, and socioeconomic status, and so an assessment should include questions about everyday living skills. Examples include the following; "Are you aware of the monthly amount of your Social Security Disability checks?" "Have you ever had a checking account?" "Do you pay your own bills?" Answers to these questions provide a history of possible abusive acts, and also inform the client and worker of potential goals. Steps toward a life free from intentional abuse and neglect begin with increasing independence and self-esteem. Learning about the level to which clients live an independent life helps gauge their sense of empowerment and autonomy in the world. Tonya arrived at the agency free from her abusive husband, finally in control of her finances, but in the past she had experienced various forms of isolation, neglect, and abuse by her husband when she first lost her leg. After she returned home from the hospital, his abuse began immediately when he began to pilfer her SSD check. As for her current situation, the worker and Tonya explored activities that she was able to complete on her own (toileting and showering) and those for which she needed assistance (cleaning and cooking). This helped identify her needs and provided clear expectations for the new home health aide. It also opened up a discussion around possible goals and objectives related to occupational and physical therapy, which might enable her to expand the activities she could complete on her own.

Once abuse-related concerns are voiced, a comprehensive assessment targeting abuse-related questions is needed. The ability to identify unique forms of abuse that disabled persons face is a critical first step in increasing safety for this population. Common standardized abuse questionnaires may fail to uncover these forms of abuse. Focus group participants in the study by Gilson et al. (2001) recommend questions to use as probes to identify abuse: Has someone ever withheld something from you such as medication or an assistive device that you needed? Has someone ever said that you cannot do something, for example, get a job or find housing? Has someone ever just walked out of the room when you said that you needed to use the restroom or left you in your chair knowing that you could not transfer out of it without assistance? What level of respect do you feel people give you? Do you feel in control of your life? Who controls your activities, your medication, and your health? Have you ever experienced anything that made you uncomfortable?

Two additional screening tools have been developed to assess abuse of women with disabilities: the Abuse Assessment Screen-Disability (AAS-D) (McFarlene et al. 2001) and a screening questionnaire focusing on Personal Assistance Service providers developed by the Center on Self-Determination, Oregon Health Sciences University (Curry and Oswald 2000; Saxton et al. 2001). Screening tools specifically designed for the disabled population are a relatively recent development that requires additional testing with various populations of abused persons with disabilities and with service providers who work with this population. Although Tonya no longer lived with her abusive husband, she remained in jeopardy of being neglected or abused by a home health aide or an ambulette driver. Tonya completed a screening in order to identify other possible abusive persons in her life. As an amputee she almost always had to rely on others for assistance in daily living skills, so completing a screening helped determine if she was at risk of abuse by those in her life upon whom she relied. It also provided an educational component around potential "red flags" for the future.

SETTING GOALS

Setting goals *with* the client, rather than *for* the client maintains a collaborative relationship. Goals vary widely with each client depending on the situation not only because the client will have a voice in choosing the weekly or monthly objectives, but also because the goals need to be tailored to the client's unique needs and issues. The client's disability, assessment information, environmental stressors, culture, age, and personal goals need to be considered in order to incorporate an intersectional lens.

As mentioned, in addition to collaboration and intersectionality when working with a client, we recommend incorporating empowerment theory when setting goals. Scholars have identified three levels of empowerment (Gutierrez and Ortega 1991). Although different authors use varying terms to define these levels of empowerment, they all capture similar concepts. Gutierrez et al. (1998) employ the terms "personal," "interpersonal," and "environmental" to distinguish three levels of power, whereas Zimmerman (1995) uses "intrapersonal," "interactional," and "behavioral." Making use of three levels of empowerment promotes the idea that social workers should not focus solely on issues pertaining to the personal level (intra-psychic issues) impacting the client's problem or concern. The person's interpersonal relationships (e.g., social supports and familial conflicts) as well as the interactions between the individual and the community (e.g., lack of services) also influence the client's situation and should be addressed in counseling.

On a personal/intrapersonal level, the goal is for individuals to exhibit a reduction of self-blame and express feelings of self-worth. Goals on this level may include discussions around the abuse, emotions related to their disability, or tangible steps toward independence. With the practitioner's help, the client may shed self-blaming thoughts sometimes voiced by survivors of domestic violence. Other individuals may use this as an opportunity to discuss their feelings about their disability. Clients may express feelings of low self-worth related to their disability, which may have an enormous effect on how they feel about the abuse. Women with disabilities, such as Tonya, have expressed a sense of "not being good enough" to leave an abusive relationship. Because she became disabled later in life, Tonya had difficulty accepting her disability. She shared her feelings of anger and depression around losing her leg and, because of her perceived inadequacies, expressed concern about finding love. Tonya described herself after the accident as "damaged goods," believing at times that it would be impossible to find another intimate relationship. These concerns were addressed through her goals and objectives surrounding her bouts of depression. Objectives were based on self-care, self-encouragement, and keeping a journal.

On an interpersonal/interactional level, an individual attempts to exhibit an increased ability to interact and influence others as well as his or her environment. This also includes the ability to obtain information, knowledge, and skills. Clients who depend on others for daily care may set a goal relating to how their ADLs might be met if others refuse to help. Goals can also address the extent to which clients begin to advocate for themselves, such as calling Section 8 about housing or scheduling a doctor's appointment. Tonya had immediately identified the lack of support she experienced with her current home health aides. She expressed her desire to interview and to hire her aides in order to be in control of her own needs. She also created goals around obtaining and completing the necessary forms for Section 8 housing.

On the environmental/behavioral level, the client can influence the community, become involved in social change, and help others. Goals may include participating in a support group, contacting local politicians about new legislation, and speaking out about abuse at domestic violence conferences or marches. Tonya began a support group for women at the agency soon after she arrived. She also participated in conferences in the area during Domestic Violence Awareness Month. At one conference she was invited to take the podium and tell her story.

THE IMPORTANCE OF FLEXIBILITY AND ADVOCACY WHEN WORKING WITH PERSONS WITH DISABILITIES

Because of the diversity of individuals a social worker encounters, flexibility is definitely in order. One social worker, who served women with disabilities who had been abused stated, "Being creative and being open to the disability and the circumstances of the abuse means getting out of the traditional idea of mental health help" (Kim Ahearn, personal communication, September 27, 2006). The use of arts and crafts, often saved for children, can be useful with some clients with disabilities, such as individuals with developmental disabilities. The use of drawing, writing, or dictating their story can be used as an alternative to traditional "talk therapy." One of the authors remembers a client with a diagnosis of mild mental retardation with a history of abuse, who often drew pictures and then described the picture, relating it to her abusive relationship. These pictures would also identify the client's goals and hopes for the future. This alternative is good for clients with limited verbal capacity or those less able to express themselves in a conversation. Tonya preferred to use narrative therapy during her sessions. Uncomfortable with sharing her feelings at times, she requested to dictate her story to the social worker who typed it on a computer. After dictating her story for a while, the worker would then review her words and begin discussing what the client had expressed.

Social workers may also find that they do less "traditional therapy" and serve more as advocates with this population.[7] "Advocacy was important—I never did so much advocacy in so many systems because these places were not set up to adequately help the client" (Kim Ahearn, personal communication, September 27, 2006). Social workers who serve this group of individuals will have to redefine what they believe is therapy. In order to help clients reach a goal, social workers may accompany clients to agencies, businesses, or hospitals. For example, a worker may go to the bank and help the client get a bank order; another day, a worker might accompany a client to the courthouse to advocate for a Protective Order or for child support. These out-of-agency meetings may also be connected to a client's personal goals pertaining to self-esteem and confidence. One of the authors would regularly take two sisters, both with cerebral palsy, to a local fast-food restaurant and then to get manicures and pedicures. These sessions not only helped establish a trusting relationship between client and worker but also addressed the goal of self-worth and a feeling of belonging in the world.

Creativity is not restricted to in-session skills and one's social work repertoire. Sometimes getting clients to attend sessions is itself a hurdle. Because of the reliance on ambulette services, difficulties and inconsistencies around client pick-up time and late arrivals to sessions are the norm. One of the authors found that most women did not attend sessions on time. Workers would therefore do well to remain open about session times, making sure they provide additional time in their schedules for such mishaps. Illness is also part of the attendance issue. Sessions are often missed because of sickness, relapse, doctor's appointments, and hospitalizations. Alternative types of sessions need to be incorporated so as to remain connected to one's client and continue the client's progress. Flexibility around phone sessions, or limiting sessions to once or twice a month rather than weekly, is sometimes more feasible. We also suggest encouraging phone discussions between clients to offer additional support outside the agency. This may spark a support group in which participants can call one another and be a part of one another's safety plan. Recognizing that accessibility may be an issue, home visits may be necessary as well as meetings in alternative places such as hospitals, courtrooms, and doctors' offices. Tonya was not always able to attend sessions in person either because of a failed ambulette trip or excessive pain. To maintain consistency and support, Tonya and the worker engaged in periodic phone sessions.

EVALUATING THE PROCESS OF CHANGE

As stated, empowerment is identified at three levels: personal/intrapersonal, interpersonal/interactional, and environmental/behavioral. Just as the goals address each level, so should the evaluation. Using empowerment as the basis for goals and objectives, an evaluation relies on a review of individually created treatment plans. Evaluation also includes a discussion with clients about their personal goals and objectives. On the simplest level, the worker and client can ask, "Have the goals been attained?" Just as clients were equal partners in creating goals, they are the most reliable sources as to whether these goals were accomplished (Johnson and Yanca 2004). Hepworth, Rooney, and Larsen (2002) suggest that client goals should be evaluated throughout the treatment process and not only when termination is near. Client and worker can discuss specific objectives as well as feelings related to personal development. This periodic review encourages clients to recognize steps they have already accomplished and establish whether any goals need to be rewritten or rejected. Although much advancement has been made related to evaluation, for example, single-subject design and computer programs that track goals, we suggest a qualitative approach in assessing client improvement (Johnson and Yanca 2004). Encouraging feedback from clients about their progress helps maintain an empowering stance. In Tonya's situation, weekly sessions included a discussion about her goals and objectives. Together client and worker reviewed Tonya's objectives and mapped her progress through a number system, rating her progress on a scale from 1 to 5 for each objective. Decisions were then made about those goals, including deleting accomplished goals and adding new ones. Lastly, as noted, a Beck Depression Scale was administered monthly to track Tonya's symptoms.

COMMUNITY-LEVEL STRATEGIES AND POLICY ADVOCACY

Social workers are expected not only to address client needs through micro-level practice but also through mezzo and macro levels. Advocacy, in particular, is essential when working with diverse and oppressed groups. For example, social workers can be a part of court-watch groups to make sure women's needs are met in the judicial system. One social worker reported, "I testified at city hall for a couple of clients, mothers who had their children taken away by the city and how her disability [had not been] taken into account" (Kim Ahearn, personal communication, September 27, 2006). Workers can also join local and state domestic violence councils, which are available in each state, and use the time to raise issues related to disability. It is also important to advocate at conferences and interdisciplinary meetings related to disability and domestic violence. One can also advocate at local, state, and federal levels for improved policies and adequate funding, especially related to accessible domestic violence programs, accessible and affordable housing, and adequate transportation. Finally, social workers can increase public knowledge about this issue by offering training sessions at various agencies that may interact with individuals with disabilities who have been abused.

Abuse of persons with disabilities is an important concern for social work practitioners. In summary, we recommend that workers be aware of their own biases and values related to disabilities, and strive for collaborative, respectful relationships with abused persons with disabilities. We also suggest that social workers use a culturally informed, intersectional approach, along with tenets of ELT theory, when working with abused, disabled persons, and encourage the inclusion of flexibility, creativity, and empowerment. On the macro level, workers can effect change in laws and policies that ignore the unique needs of abused, disabled persons or that create negative consequences for this population. Social workers can work to improve a coordinated service response to victims with disabilities.

The following resources are from Gilson, E. DePoy, and Cramer (2003).

RESOURCES

WEB SITES

Center for Applied Special Technology: www.cast.org

Center for Research on Women with Disabilities (CROWD): www.bcm.tmc .edu/crowd

Center for Universal Design: www.design.ncsu.edu/cud/

Family Violence Prevention Fund (FVPF): www.endabuse.org

Minnesota Center Against Violence and Abuse (MINCAVA): www.mincava .umn.edu

National Coalition Against Domestic Violence (NCADV): www.ncadv.org

U.S. Census Bureau: factfinder.census.gov

Census 2000 Brief series: http://www.census.gov/population/www/cen2000/briefs .html

Web Content Accessibility Guidelines: http:www.w3.org/TR/1999/WAI-WEBCON-TENT-19990505/

TRAINING MANUALS FOR SERVICE PROVIDERS

National Coalition Against Domestic Violence. (1996). *Open Minds, Open Doors.* Denver, CO. To order, go to www.ncadv.org/products/productshome.htm.

Office for Victims of Crime Resource Center. (2002). *First Response to Victims of Crime Who Have a Disability.* To order or download, go to www.puborder.ncjrs.org.

SafePlace, Disability Services ASAP. (2002). *Stop the Violence, Break the Silence: A Training Guide.* Austin, TX. To order, go to www.austin-safeplace.org, or call Wendie Abramson, Director of Disability Services ASAP at 512–356–1599; or e-mail her at wabramson@austin-safeplace.org.

VIDEOS AND DVDS

Office of Victims of Crime. *Serving Crime Victims with Disabilities: Meet Us Where We Are.* 14 minutes (closed-captioned, open-captioned, and visually described). Discussion guide included. To order, call OVC Resource Center, 800–627–6872 (voice) or 877–712–9279 (TTY).

Office of Victims of Crime. Serving Crime Victims with Disabilities: The Time is Now. 17 minutes, 30 seconds (closed-captioned, open-captioned, and visually described). Discussion guide included. To order, call the OVC Resource Center, 800–627–6872 (voice) or 877–712–9279 (TTY).

Partnership for People with Disabilities, Virginia Commonwealth University. (2006). *Access to Justice* (closed-captioned). DVD geared toward judges regarding an enhanced response to abused women with disabilities. To order, call the Partnership for People with Disabilities, 804–828–3876 or 800–828–1120 (TDD Relay), or go to their Web site: www.vcu.edu/partnership.

SafePlace. (2003). *Disability, Violence and Survival: A Personal Story* [part of the Stop the Violence, Break the Silence training materials]. 11 minutes (closed-captioned version available). Facilitator's guide included. To order, go to www .austin-safeplace.org; or call Wendie Abramson, Director of Disability Services ASAP at 512–356–1599 (voice), 512–482–0691 (TTY); or e-mail her at wabramson@ austin-safeplace.org.

REFERENCES

American Bar Association. (1992). *Opening the Courthouse Door: An ADA Access Guide for State Courts*. Washington, DC: Author.

Banks, M. E., and R. J. Ackerman. (2002). Head and brain injuries experienced by African American women victims of intimate partner violence. *Women and Therapy*, 25(3/4), 133–143.

Beck, A., (2007). *Introduction to Beck Scales*. Aaron T. Beck Web site. University of Pennsylvania Health Systems. Retrieved May 14, 2007, from http://mail.med .upenn.edu/~abeck/scaleintro.htm.

Brownridge, D. A. (2006). Partner violence against women with disabilities: Prevalence, risk, and explanations. *Violence Against Women*, 12, 805–822.

Chang, J. C., et al. (2003).Helping women with disabilities and domestic violence: Strategies, limitations, and challenges in domestic violence programs and services. *Journal of Women's Health*, 12(7), 699–708.

Chenoweth, L. (1996). Violence and women with disabilities. *Violence Against Women*, 2(4), 391–411.

Choi, W., and T., Rajikumar. (1996). Computing for the disabled. *Journal of Computer Information Systems*, 36(4), 77–85.

Cohen, M. M, T. Forte, J. Du Mont, I. Hyman, and S. Romans. (2006). Adding insult to injury: Intimate partner violence among women and men reporting activity limitations. *Annals in Epidemiology*, 16(8), 644–651.

Coker, A. L., P. H. Smith, and M. K. Fadden. (2005). Intimate partner violence and disabilities among women attending family practice clinics. *Journal of Women's Health*, 14(9), 829–838.

Collins, P. H. (1998a). Intersections of race, class, gender, and nation: Some implications for black family studies. *Journal of Comparative Family Studies*, 29(1), 27(10). Retrieved April 20, 2005, from InfoTrac.

——. (1998b). The tie that binds: Race, gender and U.S. violence. *Ethnic and Racial Studies*, 21, 917–938.

Cramer, E. P., S. F. Gilson, and E. DePoy. (2003). Women with disabilities and experiences of abuse. *Journal of Human Behavior in the Social Environment*, 7(3/4), 183–199.

Crenshaw, K. W. (1994). Mapping the margins: Intersectionality, identity politics, and violence against women. In M. A. Fineman and R. Mykitiuk (Eds.), *The Public Nature of Private Violence* (pp. 93–118). New York: Routledge. Retrieved April 18, 2005, from http://www.hsph.harvard.edu/grhf/WoC/feminisms/crenshaw.html.

Crime Victims with Disabilities Awareness Act, Pub L. No. 105–301, 112 Stat. 2838. (1998).

Curry, M. A., and M. Oschwald. (2000). *Personal Assistance Services Providers Abuse of Women with Disabilities Project.* Presentation at the National Conference on Health Care and Domestic Violence, San Francisco, CA.

Danis, F. S. (2003). The criminalization of domestic violence: What social workers need to know. *Social Work*, 48(2), 237–246. Retrieved April 27, 2004, from http://web1.infotrac.galegroup.com.proxy.library.vcu.edu.

Dean, R. G. (2001). The myth of cross-cultural competence. *Families in Society*, 82, 623–630.

DePoy, E., and S. F. Gilson. (2004). *Rethinking Disability: Principles for Professional and Social Change.* Belmont, CA: Brooks/Cole.

DePoy, E., S. F. Gilson, and E. P. Cramer. (2003). Understanding the experiences of and advocating for the service and resource needs of abused, disabled women. In A. Hans and A. Patri (Eds.), *Women, Disability and Identity* (pp. 177–187). Thousand Oaks, CA: Sage.

Developmental Disabilities Assistance and Bill of Rights Act, 42 U.S.C.S. Sec. 6000 et seq. (2000).

Gelles, R. J. (2000). Estimating the incidence and prevalence of violence against women. *Violence Against Women*, 6, 784–804.

Gilson, S. F., E. P. Cramer, and E. DePoy. (2001). Redefining abuse of women with disabilities: A paradox of limitation and expansion. *AFFILIA: Journal of Women and Social Work*, 16(2), 220–235.

Gilson, S. F., E. DePoy, and E. P. Cramer. (2001). Linking the assessment of self-reported functional capacity with abuse experiences of women with disabilities. *Violence Against Women*, 7(4), 418–431.

——. (2003). *Violence Against Women with Disabilities.* CD-Rom. Funded by the Office of Women's Health, U.S. Department of Health and Human Services. Available from Elizabeth Cramer, Virginia Commonwealth University School of Social Work: ecramer@vcu.edu.

GlenMaye, L. (1998). Empowerment of women. In L. M. Gutierrez, R. J. Parsons, and E. O. Cox (Eds.), *Empowerment in Social Work Practice: A Sourcebook* (pp. 29–50). Pacific Grove, CA: Brooks/Cole.

Gutierrez, L. M., L. GlenMaye, and K. A. DeLois. (1995). The organizational context of empowerment practice: Implications for social work administration. *Social Work,* 40(2), 249–258.

Gutierrez, L. M., and R. Ortega. (1991). Developing methods to empower Latinos: The importance of groups. *Social Work with Groups,* 14(2), 23–43.

Gutierrez L. M., R. J. Parsons, and E. O. Cox. (1998). *Empowerment in Social Work Practice: A Sourcebook.* Pacific Grove, CA: Brooks/Cole.

Harley, D. A., K. Jolivette, K. McCormick, and K. Tice. (2002). Race, class, and gender: A constellation of *positionalities* with implications for counseling. *Journal of Multicultural Counseling and Development,* 30, 216–238.

Hepworth, D. H., R. H. Rooney, and J. Larsen. (2002). *Direct Social Work Practice: Theory and Skills* (6th Ed.). Pacific Grove, CA: Brooks/Cole.

Jackson, H., E. Philp, R. L. Nutall, and L. Diller. (2002). Traumatic brain injury: A hidden consequence for battered women. *Professional Psychology,* 33(1), 39–45.

Johnson, L. C., and S. J. Yanca. (2004). *Social Work Practice: A Generalist Approach* (8th ed.). Boston: Pearson and AB.

Kautzman, A. M. (1998). Virtuous, virtual assess: Making Web pages accessible to people with disabilities. *Searcher,* 6(6), 42.

Kaye, S. H. (2000). *Computer and Internet Use among People with Disabilities: Disability Statistics Report* 13. National Institute on Disability and Rehabilitation Research, U.S. Department of Education. Retrieved March 11, 2005, from ERIC at http://firstsearch.oclc.org.

Kendall-Tackett, K., R. Marshall, and K. Ness. (2003). Chronic pain syndromes and violence against women. *Women and Therapy,* 26(1/2), 45–56.

Lee, J. A. B. (1996). The empowerment approach to social work practice. In F. J. Turner (Ed.), *Social Work Treatment: Interlocking Theoretical Approaches* (pp. 218–249). New York: Free Press.

Lowenberg, F. M., R. Dolgoff, and D. Harrington. (2000). *Ethical Decisions for Social Work Practice* (6th ed.) Itasca, IL: F. E. Peacock.

Martin, S. L., et al. (2006). Physical and sexual assault of women with disabilities. *Violence Against Women,* 12, 823–837.

McFarlene, J., R. B. Hughes, M. A. Nosek, J. Y. Groff, N. Swedlund, and P. D. Mullen. (2001). Abuse Assessment Screen-Disability (AAS-D): Measuring frequency, type, and perpetrator of abuse toward women with physical disabilities. *Journal of Women's Health and Gender-Based Medicine,* 10(9) 861–866.

Mitchell, D. (1996). *Vital Signs: Crip Culture Talks Back.* Videorecording. Marquette, MI: Brace Yourselves Productions.

Mitchell, L. M., and A. Buchele-Ash. (2000). Abuse and neglect of individuals with disabilities: Building protective supports through public policy. *Journal of Disability Policy Studies,* 10(2), p. 225. Retrieved August 23, 2001, from InfoTrac.

National Association of Social Workers. (1999). *Code of Ethics of the National Association of Social Workers.* Washington, DC: Author.

National Coalition Against Domestic Violence. (1996). *Open Minds, Open Doors.* Denver, CO: Author.

——. (2007). *Safety Plan.* Retrieved March 6, 2007, from http://www.ncadv.org/protectyourself/SafetyPlan_130.html.

Nosek, M. A., and C. A. Howland. (1998). *Abuse and Women with Disabilities.* Retrieved April 18, 2005, from http://www.vam.umn.edu/Vawnet/disab.htm.

Nosek, M., C. Howland, and M. Young. (1997). Abuse of women with disabilities: Policy implications. *Journal of Disability Policy Studies,* 8(1/2), 157–175.

Office for Victims of Crime. (2002a). *First Response to Victims of Crime Who Have a Disability.* Washington, DC: U.S. Department of Justice.

——. (2002b). Serving crime victims with disabilities: Meet us where we are. [Videotape and companion guide]. Washington, DC: U.S. Department of Justice.

——. (2002c). Serving crime victims with disabilities: The time is now. [Videotape and companion guide]. Washington, DC: U.S. Department of Justice.

Oktay, J. S., and C. J. Tompkins. (2004). Personal assistance providers' mistreatment of disabled adults. *Health and Social Work,* 29(3), 177–188.

Perkins, D. D., and M. A. Zimmerman. (1995). Empowerment theory, research, and application. *American Journal of Community Psychology* 23(5), 569–580. Retrieved February 4, 2005, from http://web2.infotrac.galegroup.com.proxy.library.vcu.edu.

Rappaport, J. (1987). Terms of empowerment/exemplars of prevention: Toward a theory for community psychology. *American Journal of Community Psychology* 15(2), 121–147.

Safe Place, Disability Services ASAP. (2002). *Stop the Violence, Break the Silence: A Training Guide.* Austin, TX. Retrieved May 15, 2007, from www.austin-safeplace.org.

Saxton, M., M. A. Curry, L. E. Powers, S. Maley, K. Eckels, and J. Gross. (2001). "Bring my scooter so I can leave you": A study of disabled women handling abuse by personal assistance providers. *Violence Against Women,* 7(4), 393–417.

Sobsey, R. (1994). *Violence in the Lives of People with Disabilities: The End of Silent Acceptance?* Baltimore, MD: Paul H. Brookes.

Sobsey, D., and T. Doe. (1991). Patterns of sexual abuse and assault. *Sexuality and Disability,* 9(3), 243–259.

Solomon, B. (1976). *Black Empowerment: Social Work in Oppressed Communities.* New York: Columbia University Press.

Swedlund, N. P., and M. A. Nosek. (2000). An exploratory study on the work of independent living centers to address abuse of women with disabilities. *Journal of Rehabilitation,* 66(4), 57–71.

Tjaden, P., and N. Thoennes. (2000). Full report of the prevalence, incidence, and consequences of violence against women: Findings from the National Violence Against Women Survey. U.S. Department of Justice, Office of Justice Programs.

U.S. Equal Employment Opportunity Commission. (2002). *Americans with Disabilities Act: Questions and Answers*. Retrieved November 19, 2004, from http://www.ada.gov/q%26aeng02.htm.

Virginia Board of People with Disabilities. (2006). *Community Participation and Disability*. Retrieved May 9, 2006, from http://www.vaboard.org.

Virginia Department of Social Services. (N.d.). *Who Are Mandatory Reporters for APS?* Retrieved October 6, 2006, from http://www.dss.state.va.us/pub/pdf/aps.pdf#search=%22mandatory%20reporting%20in%20va%22.

Waldrop, J., and S. M. Stern. (2003). *Disability Status: 2000*. Census 2000 Brief. Washington, DC: U.S. Census Bureau.

Wilbur, L., et al. (2001). Survey results of women who have been strangled while in an abusive relationship. *Journal of Emergency Medicine, 21*, 297–302.

Young, M. E., M. A. Nosek, C. Howland, G. Chanpong, and D. H. Rintala. (1997). Prevalence of abuse of women with physical disabilities. *Archives of Physical Medicine and Rehabilitation, 78*, Suppl 5, S34-S38.

Zimmerman, M. A. (1995). Psychological empowerment: Issues and illustrations. *American Journal of Community Psychology, 23*(5), 581–600. Retrieved February 4, 2005, from http://web2.infotrac.galegroup.com.proxy.library.vcu.edu.

6

DOMESTIC VIOLENCE ADVOCACY WITH IMMIGRANTS AND REFUGEES

Rupaleem Bhuyan, Woochan Shim, and Kavya Velagapudi

EVER SINCE the Immigration and Nationality Act of 1965 lifted the national-origin quotas on immigration, which eased migration for family reunification and skilled labor, immigration to the U.S. has increased steadily, reaching a high of 37.9 million people in 2007. Removing the national quotas also lifted more than forty years of racial discrimination in U.S. immigration policy, facilitating new waves of immigration from countries in Central and South America, Asia, and Africa. The foreign-born population now accounts for one in eight U.S. residents, with an estimated one in three immigrants living in the U.S. without legal documentation (Camarota 2007). The changing demographics of immigrants, coupled with increased attention to cultural competence, requires domestic violence advocates to attend to complex cultural, social, and political dynamics when working with foreign-born survivors of domestic violence.

Immigrants are diverse by ethnicity and national origin. They migrate to the United States because of various push-and-pull factors including job losses in their country of origin, economic restructuring of labor worldwide, economic opportunity, family reunification, and to flee political and social turmoil. Culturally competent practice requires that advocates are able to function effectively amid cultural differences (Cross et al. 1989) while addressing the structural factors associated with migration. Engaging in culturally competent practice with immigrants and refugees thus requires a critical consciousness of the political and social position of immigrant groups within the society.

In this chapter we draw on theories of intersectionality and anti-oppression to address structural power dynamics impacting immigrant survivors of domestic violence. Intersectionality is a framework for addressing the interconnectedness of characteristics such as gender, ethnicity, race, and class when addressing immigrants' experiences with battery (Crenshaw 1995; Kanuha 1996). An intersectionality analysis of gender recognizes that sexism affects everyone but has differential effects in concert with the influences of other forms of oppression (e.g., classism, racism, and homophobia). This chapter focuses on advocacy with women in response to the majority of domestic violence perpetration by men abusing their female partners. We also address how immigration policies impact advocacy with immigrants in same-sex relationships, for whom there are often fewer social and legal rights.

Anti-oppression perspectives draw attention to social policy and institutional practices that pose barriers to survivors of abuse. Institutional forms of oppression become manifest for immigrant survivors as they interact with the criminal justice system, the legal system, and health and social services. A common challenge facing advocates who work with immigrants is the need to know about immigration laws and immigrant rights. Since the 1990s, antiviolence and immigrant rights activists have worked closely on behalf of immigrant survivors of domestic violence (Chen 2000). These collaborations have resulted in legislation for battered immigrants, national conferences to train advocates working with immigrants, and stronger community-based services for immigrants and refugees. This chapter draws on this work to provide domestic violence advocates and social workers who engage in advocacy with a basic understanding both of immigration policy and of how public policy shapes an individual's response to abuse. We begin with an overview of how different groups of immigrants are classified in the United States. We then discuss provisions offered through the Violence Against Women Act and related legislation for battered immigrants. Finally, we present three case studies that illustrate advocacy with domestic violence survivors with different immigration histories.

WHO IS AN IMMIGRANT?

IMMIGRANT CATEGORIES

Immigration status is an important factor in domestic violence advocacy, as it determines an individual's social and political rights. Both domestic violence and immigrant advocacy groups use the term "immigrant" to refer broadly to foreign-born persons who have migrated to and settled in the United States for work, refuge, or to join their families. U.S. immigration law, however, employs a stricter classification system, designating the term "immigrant" exclusively for persons who are lawful permanent residents (LPRs) or natural- ized citizens of the United States. Everyone else who is not a U.S. citizen is considered to be an "alien." Most immigrant families in the United States are "mixed-status" families—they include both citizen and noncitizen members (Dinan 2005). Thus many children of immigrants who are born in the United States are U.S. citizens but have parents or guardians who may be undocu- mented, reside in the U.S. on temporary visas, or have established lawful permanent residency. Owing to incredible backlogs in processing immigra- tion applications, thousands of immigrants are in the process of adjusting their status to lawful permanent resident and have a quasi-legal or liminal status (e.g., characterized by ambiguity and indeterminacy) while they wait for their LPR status to be processed. The 2007 U.S. Census estimate of 37.9 million immigrants includes people who have naturalized, legal permanent residents, temporary visa holders, and undocumented immigrants (see Table 6.1 for more detail on each of these immigrant categories).

Refugees and asylum seekers form a special class of nonimmigrant aliens, because they are granted visas based on political considerations, including political or gender persecution in their native countries. Refugees and asylum seekers may adjust their temporary status to that of lawful permanent resident after one year. Refugee status refers to asylum seekers who have been recog- nized as refugees by the UN High Commissioner for Refugees and granted the right of settlement in the United States through a complex relocation system. Refugee resettlement in the United States reflects U.S. geopolitical interests across the world, with the majority of refugees fleeing the regions of Southeast Asia (e.g., Vietnam, Cambodia, and Lao), the Balkan region in Eastern Europe (e.g., Bosnia, Serbia, and Herzegovina), and the horn of Africa (e.g., Ethiopia, Somalia, and Eritrea). A smaller portion of asylum cases involve individuals who apply for asylum after entering the United States. Thus, throughout this chapter, the terms "immigration" or "immigrant" is used to refer to the broad meaning of foreign-born individuals who reside in the United States unless otherwise specified.

U.S. IMMIGRATION AGENCIES AND IMMIGRATION LAW ENFORCEMENT

In 2001 the Immigration and Naturalization Services (INS) was incorporated into the newly formed Department of Homeland Security (DHS). The DHS

TABLE 6.1 Immigrant Categories and Proportion of the U.S. Population

OFFICIAL U.S. IMMIGRANT CLASSIFICATION	DESCRIPTION	PERCENTAGE OF U.S. POPULATION IN 2005
U.S. Citizen	A foreign-born person who was granted U.S. citizenship through the naturalization process. Requires English literacy, "good moral character," and knowledge of civics. Must be at least eighteen years of age to naturalize or Naturalized Citizen.	32%
Lawful Permanent Resident	A foreign-born person with permission to reside permanently in the U.S. LPRs are permitted to work and may apply for naturalization after five years from the time they adjust to LPR status. LPRs who reside outside the United States must return every six months for a minimum of three days to retain their residency status. LPRs who are convicted of certain crimes may be deported.	29%
Conditional Resident	A noncitizen who applies for legal permanent resident as a spouse of a U.S. citizen or legal permanent resident is called a "conditional resident" if married for less than two years when making application for legal permanent residence. To keep their lawful permanent residence status, conditional residents must file a "joint" petition with their spouse. Conditional residents have all the rights of legal permanent residents (Pendelton and Kemp 2006).	
Refugee or Asylum Seeker	A foreign-born person granted permission to reside in the United States because of a well-founded fear of persecution in her or his country of origin. Refugee status is designated prior to entry to the United States Asylum is granted to persons who entered the United States by various means, and then applied for asylum within one year of entry. Refugees and asylum seekers may apply to adjust their status to LPR after one year.	7%
Nonimmigrant (visa holder)	A foreign-born person granted a visa to enter the United States on a temporary basis for a specific purpose and limited period of time. Includes visa holders who are diplomats, crewmen on ships, temporary workers, international students, company transfers, tourists, and other international visitors.	3%
Undocumented Immigrant	A foreign-born person who entered the United States without legal documentation or who entered the United States on a nonimmigrant visa but then violated the terms of entry. Also referred to as an "illegal alien."	29%

Source: For immigrant categories, see National Immigration Law Center 2002; for percentage of the population, see Passel 2005; for characteristics of undocumented immigrants, see Passel 2006.

is a cabinet department in the U.S. federal government, created under the National Strategy for Homeland Security and the Homeland Security Act of 2002. In addition to other responsibilities, the DHS is charged with ensuring safe and secure borders, regulating immigrants and visitors, and monitoring international trade and commerce (see Table 6.2 for details).

Immigrant survivors of abuse commonly do not know their immigration status, because abusers often try to use immigration documents and status as a mechanism of control (Salcido and Adelman 2004). Immigration law and immigration policy is constantly changing, and so advocates should always consult with a qualified immigration lawyer and foster working relationships with immigration lawyers who have experience with legal options for battered immigrants.

IMMIGRATION AND DOMESTIC VIOLENCE

Although studies have shown that domestic violence impacts women around the world (Heise 1998; WHO 2002) there are significant challenges to estimating the prevalence of domestic violence for immigrant populations in the United States, given their diverse ethnic and national origins. Many immigrants are underrepresented in national surveys because of language barriers that prevent them from participating. Immigrants are also underrepresented

TABLE 6.2 U.S. Immigration Agencies

U.S. AGENCIES WITHIN THE DEPARTMENT OF HOMELAND SECURITY (DHS)	DESCRIPTION
U.S. Citizenship and Immigration Services (USCIS or CIS)	Responsible for applications, petitions, and adjudications of different immigration-related statuses and permits.
U.S. Immigration and Customs Enforcement (USICE or ICE)	Responsible for immigration-related investigations, detentions, deportations, and SEVIS (Student and Exchange Visitor Information System)
U.S. Customs and Border Protection (USCPB or CPB)	In charge of border patrol control and inspections at the ports of entry and customs service.

in law enforcement records of crimes and victimization as a result of the small likelihood of reporting crimes in general (Davis and Erez 1998). Although research illustrates that domestic violence occurs across diverse ethnic groups (Krishnan et al. 1997; WHO 2005), specific acts of abuse recognized as domestic violence vary greatly by ethnic and cultural communities, as do responses to the violence. Definitions of domestic violence primarily have been formulated by European or American investigators who have paid little attention to cross-cultural manifestations of abuse. Further, perpetrators use different tools and tactics to assert power and control based on their own socio-cultural context. Lindhorst and Tajima (2008) have recently suggested five contextual dimensions to domestic violence against immigrants: the situational or relational context; the individualized social construction of meaning; the cultural and historical contexts; and the context of oppression. Cross-cultural research and research with specific ethnic or national populations has demonstrated that rates of reported abuse increase when culturally rooted forms of violence are added to survey questionnaires. For example, Yoshihama (2001) found that after adding a few items—throwing liquid, overturning a dining table, and forced sexual intercourse when concerned about other people nearby (e.g., in an adjoining room)—respondents' reported physical assault increased by 5 percent and reported sexual assault increased by 11 percent among a community-based sample of Japanese women. Research with Chinese American women found that personality traits, such as "men with hot-temper" or "frustrated men with stress," were seen by research participants as more salient terms when describing batterers versus other terminology circulating in the literature on "battering men" (Lee and Au 1998).

Sources of perpetration also vary across cultural groups and for immigrants whose social networks are transnational. Most domestic violence theories focus on the intimate partner or marital spouse as the primary perpetrator. This conceptualization does not reflect circumstances where the nuclear family is interconnected, even perhaps cohabitating with in-laws, siblings, and other relatives. For example, in extended families the perpetrators of abuse may include in-laws in addition to or instead of the spouse (Raj et al. 2006).

Despite the challenges in generating comparable data, it remains important to consider the increased risk of domestic violence among immigrant populations. Studies with immigrants in the United States indicate high rates of physical and sexual violence among immigrant women (Dutton, Orloff, and Hass 2000; Tjaden and Thoennes 2000). In a community sample of South Asian immigrant women, 40 percent reported intimate partner violence in their current relationships (Raj and Silverman 2003). A study with 292 Latina women indicate high lifetime abuse rates with over one-third of women reporting physical violence, 21 percent reporting sexual coercion, and 83 percent reporting psychological aggression (Hazen and Soriano 2007). The risks associated with domestic violence are potentially higher for undocumented women who lack basic social and political rights.

In addition to high levels of risk, immigrants face numerous obstacles both within their communities and from society at large in seeking help and getting support. General factors that prevent or impede survivors from resisting, mediating, or leaving abusive partners relate to women's economic dependence, fear of losing custody of children, and social isolation. For many immigrants, disclosing or seeking help depends on the survivors' English proficiency in addition to knowledge of policies, laws, and resources. Institutional racism and culturally insensitive professionals and organizations may also discourage immigrant survivors from seeking help.

At a structural level, immigration policies reinforce social norms for heteronormativity (i.e. nuclear families where the husband is head of household and has decision-making power over wife and children). For example, family reunification policies only apply to legal spouses and children. The Defense of Marriage Act of 1996 narrowly defines marriage to heterosexual couples; same-sex marriages are not recognized by U.S. immigration law, and thus same-sex partners do not have the option of sponsoring the immigration of their family members. Patriarchal social values also shape the practice of spousal migration. Immigration law historically relied on the legal principle of coverture, wherein the wife's existence is civilly merged, for many purposes, into that of her husband's; therefore, in general, she can make no contracts without his consent, express or implied. In common law, coverture operated to the extent that a husband had the legal right to "chastise" his wife, and even kill her. In immigration law, coverture linked women's citizenship to her husband. Between 1907 and 1922 a woman would lose her U.S. citizenship by marrying someone of a different nationality. In 1954 the Immigrant and Nationality Act changed the policy to make it gender-neutral, allowing male and female U.S. citizens or legal permanent residents to extend their status to their spouse upon marriage. However, immigration sponsorship still remains in the hands of the spouse who is a citizen or legal permanent resident. Women, who comprise the majority of marriage migrants, thus depend on their husbands for immigration status. In situations where domestic violence occurs, immigration sponsorship remains a powerful mechanism for control.

Immigration status does not only indicate the right to legal entry and legal presence in the United States, but it also determines the social and political rights for immigrants across many social institutions. Social rights regulated through federal, state, and local laws include eligibility for driver licenses, legal work authorization, eligibility for public assistance, eligibility for in-state tuition for higher education, access to social security benefits that are withdrawn from one's paycheck, and freedom to travel abroad and reenter the United States. Political rights include the right to vote, the right to representation in the political system, the right to due process in the law, and the right to reside in the United States even after living in the country for more than two decades.

SPECIAL CONSIDERATIONS FOR REFUGEE CONTEXT

The United States receives a small portion of refugees worldwide who are eligible for and seeking resettlement. Regions of the world where the United States has signed agreements to resettle refugees include countries with historically strong economic, political, or military ties. A significant portion of refugees that sought resettlement in the United States had been dislocated during the country's military involvement in Vietnam, Laos, and Cambodia. Refugees from El Salvador and Cuba also make up a sizable portion of refugees in the United States. More recent resettlement has stemmed from the conflict in Northeastern Africa from Somalia, Ethiopia, and Eritrea. Once in the United States, refugees are provided public assistance intended to facilitate their steady incorporation into society.

Refugees most often come from war-torn regions of the world. For these individuals, domestic violence has occurred against the backdrop of several waves of violence and trauma—the violence of war and civil strife, the trauma of fleeing their homes and living in a marginal existence in refugee camps, and the challenges of adjusting to life in the United States (Bhuyan and Senturia 2003).

LEGAL PROTECTIONS FOR BATTERED IMMIGRANTS

Legal provisions for "battered immigrants" were introduced with the Battered Spouse Waiver of 1990 and the Violence Against Women Act of 1994 (VAWA), and were expanded in the renewal of VAWA in both 2000 and 2005. These provisions seek to limit the ability of U.S. citizens and legal permanent residents to use the immigration system to assert power and control over a foreign-born spouse, fiancé, intimate partner, or child. This legislation offers five types of immigration relief to battered immigrants, each with different eligibility and evidentiary requirements: the battered spouse waiver; a VAWA self-petition; a VAWA cancellation of removal; the U-visa for crime victims including victims of domestic violence crimes; and the T-visa for victims of human trafficking. (For a comprehensive summary of VAWA, see Lin and Orloff 2005; and Wood 2004.) Noncitizens who are or have been married to their abusers, who are a U.S. citizen or lawful permanent resident, may apply for lawful permanent residency through a battered spouse waiver, a VAWA self-petition, or a VAWA cancellation of removal. Noncitizens who have never been married to their abusers or their abusers are not a U.S. citizen or lawful permanent resident are not eligible for residency under VAWA. Noncitizens who have been victims of crime, including crimes related to domestic violence and sexual assault, may be eligible for a U-visa. The U-visa does not require being married to the abuser, so this option is also open to persons in same-sex relationships or individuals whose abuser is not a U.S. citizen or lawful permanent resident. The U-visa does require proof that a crime has been committed (e.g., a police report) in addition to evidence that the victim is cooperating with law enforcement. Although the U-visa was created with VAWA reauthorization in 2000, the U.S. Citizenship and Immigration Services issued regulations as of September 17, 2007. Persons granted U-visas may remain in the United States for up to four years, receive work authorization, and after three years may attain lawful permanent residency.

Table 6.3 lists federal legislation including provisions for victims of crimes related to domestic violence, sexual assault, stalking, and human trafficking. Despite this significant legislation, there is still little support for groups of immigrants who are ineligible for immigration relief for several reasons: they have been abused by someone who is not a U.S. citizen or legal permanent resident; they lack knowledge of these provisions; they lack resources to obtain credible legal assistance; they do not have the financial and social resources to apply for legal provisions; or they are unable or fearful of engaging service providers or the criminal justice system.

ADVOCACY WITH IMMIGRANTS AND REFUGEES

Comprehensive domestic violence advocacy involves assisting a survivor in navigating multiple systems related to criminal justice, health care, and

TABLE 6.3 Laws Affecting Battered Immigrants

DATE	POPULAR NAME	LEGAL CODE
11/10/1986	Immigration Marriage Fraud Amendment of 1986	Public Law 99-639, Title VII, Sec. 701
11/29/1990	Battered Spouse or Child Waiver in the Immigration Act of 1990	Public Law 101-649, Title VII, Sec. 701
9/13/1994	Violence Against Women Act	Public Law 103-322, Title IV
8/22/1996	Personal Responsibility and Work Opportunity Reconciliation Act of 1996	Public Law 104-193
8/22/1996	Illegal Immigration Reform and Immigration Responsibility Act of 1996	Public Law 104-208, Div. C, 110, Stat. 3009-546
10/28/2000	Victims of Trafficking and Violence Protection Act of 2000	Public Law 106-386, Div. B
1/05/2006	Violence Against Women and Department of Justice Reauthorization Act of 2006	Public Law 109-162

social services (Allen, Bybee, and Sullivan 2004). However, advocates who work with immigrants find that many standard advocacy tools do not serve immigrants well. Temporary and undocumented immigrants are particularly vulnerable to domestic violence owing to their insecure immigration status and lack of legal and social rights. Noncitizens (including lawful permanent residents) are often ineligible for commonly available services that support survivors through times of crisis, including housing assistance, income assistance, or health insurance (Salcido and Adelman 2004). Immigrants are also wary of the criminal justice system and may avert police intervention for fear of deportation or the removal of themselves or their abuser (Raj and Silverman 2002).

The following case studies illustrate different factors that may arise for immigrant women contending with domestic violence. These case studies are fictional yet based on the practice experience of the three authors, in addition to valuable input from community-based advocates working with immigrant survivors of abuse. Following each case study, we discuss advocacy strategies and ethical dilemmas related to each scenario, using an intersectionality framework.

CASE STUDY 1: DOMESTIC VIOLENCE AS AN IMMIGRANT SPOUSE OF A U.S. CITIZEN

BACKGROUND: SPOUSAL IMMIGRATION FROM KOREA

Historically there have been many waves of immigration from Korea to the United States, reflecting in part the U.S. political and military interests in Korea. Although significant migration from Korea to Hawai'i took place in the early 1900s, the majority of Korean immigrants migrated after the Korean War and the Immigration and Nationality Act of 1965. Korean immigrants now make up the seventh largest group of foreign-born in the United States, with the majority originating in South Korea (Yau 2004). Koreans today migrate for various reasons including education, family reunification, political freedom, and economic opportunity. Although the educational background and socioeconomic status before and after their migration may vary, women who entered the United States through spousal migration are in a particularly vulnerable position because of their conditional permanent resident status.

Rooted in Confucianism, Korean values of strong kinship ties, obedience to the family, and protection of the family make it challenging for survivors to respond to domestic violence. Confucianism represents a traditional worldview in Korean culture, regardless of one's current religious or spiritual practices. Confucian traditions construct the individual primarily in relationship to significant others through a communal context (Chu 1985; Lee 2000). Thus, when individual well-being conflicts with the family's well-being, it is expected that an individual will defer for the collective good (Lee 2000).

KI-DAE

Ki-Dae is a 30-year-old Korean woman with a 6-month-old daughter. She was raised in South Korea, earned a master's degree in fine arts, and worked at an art institute in South Korea until she married a Korean-American businessman and moved to join him in New York City. Her husband, a U.S. citizen, sponsored her immigration to the United States through family reunification policies. Ki-Dae was granted conditional legal residence for two years. After the two-year period, Ki-Dae and her husband

"CONTINUED"

would be able to apply to adjust her status to lawful permanent resident and then to that of U.S. citizen.

After their marriage, Ki-Dae joined her husband in New York. Upon arrival he would not allow her to work or leave home. He held onto all her immigration papers, so she did not know her immigration status. He warned her that she was safer staying home; if she wandered around independently, she could be stopped by the police and deported because of her immigration status. Ki-Dae believed her husband, and was always nervous and anxious leaving home without him and would only leave home to visit her in-laws.

Ki-Dae's husband began abusing her physically soon after her arrival in the United States. The physical abuse included swinging a golf club at her, ultimately striking her head with the club on one occasion for talking back to him without his approval. After their daughter was born the physical abuse continued. When their two-month-old daughter had a colic crying spell, Ki-Dae's husband threatened to kill them both with a kitchen knife. Ki-Dae managed to run away with the baby to her parents-in-law's house, but they scolded her and sent her back home to her husband.

Ki-Dae had little contact with the outside world, other than with her husband, in-laws, and the Korean Church they attended each week. When Ki-Dae shared her marital problems with her pastor, he told her he was reluctant to speak out against her husband because her in-laws were important and well-respected senior members of the church. Ki-Dae grew to fear her husband, but she was also afraid that leaving her husband would mean losing her legal and social status and being deported to Korea. Ki-Dae also worried that, if she left, her husband would get custody of their daughter because she was born in the United States and was a citizen like him.

Ki-Dae ultimately sought help at a domestic violence counseling center serving Asian immigrants in New York. Advised by the center staff and a pro bono attorney, Ki-Dae filed for a VAWA self-petition as a victim of "battery and extreme cruelty." Ki-Dae found the process of documenting her experiences of abuse very difficult. She was counseled that in order for her application to be complete, she would need to document "extreme hardship" if she were to prevent a return to her country of origin. This required Ki-Dae to write a sworn statement that characterized Korean culture and traditions as the context for abuse. Ki-Dae completed her VAWA self-petition and secured permission to adjust her status to lawful permanent resident. However, she felt deeply ashamed at having to condemn her Korean cultural roots in order to be granted the legal right to stay in the United States. For Ki-Dae, the disgrace of dishonoring her country of origin equaled that of being beaten by her husband.

ADVOCACY STRATEGIES AND ETHICAL DILEMMAS WHEN WORKING WITH SPOUSAL IMMIGRANTS

As we saw in Ki-Dae's story, spousal immigration can be a controlling tactic for an abusive spouse. Often the sponsored immigrant is not knowledgeable about immigration laws and also lacks resources to survive without the sponsoring husband in part due to language barriers and the abuser's tactic of isolation. Although, legally, immigrants with conditional permanent resident status are allowed to work, their batterers may control their employment by driving them to and from work; others might call their wives at work and at home constantly to check up on them; or they might take care of all the household financial responsibility and withhold their earnings from their wives (Shim and Hwang 2005). When the in-laws and the community align themselves with the perpetrator, at times with the expectation that the wife needs to work harder to keep the family together, the victim is left with few options. In these cases, it is crucial for the service providers to have the cultural and linguistic sensitivity to provide meaningful support to immigrants.

In South Korea the concept of domestic violence has only recently been introduced and publicized by the passage of the Domestic Violence Prevention Act in December 1997. When working with immigrants from different ethnic or national origins, labeling survivors' experience as "domestic violence" may not be congruent with how women perceive their relationship to an abusive spouse or the problems for which they seek help. Advocates should adopt the descriptions used by survivors, while sharing information on state and federal laws that criminalize abusive behaviors in the United States. It is also important to consider social pressure among immigrants whose commitment to communal obligation surpasses their individual needs. This is particularly significant when immigrants fear losing ties to their ethnic or immigrant communities, while seeking relief from their abusive situations.

The Violence Against Women Act provides legal provisions for immigrants who can demonstrate that they suffered abuse by their spouse to self-petition to adjust their immigration status to that of legal permanent resident (Conyers 2007). Early versions of the VAWA self-petition required the applicant to document exposure to "battery and extreme cruelty" in the relationship, in addition to "extreme hardship" that the individual would experience if they had to return to their country of origin. This often meant characterizing their country of origin as disrespectful of women and women's rights. Although this requirement has been lifted, the practice of blaming the victim's culture and country of origin continues to concern advocates working with immigrant survivors.

Advocacy strategies for working with spousal immigrants are needed at micro-, mezzo-, and macro-levels. Micro-level advocacy would require helping survivors to find strengths within themselves but also within their own community of origin so that they do not feel rootless after separating from an abusive husband. Advocates can share information about the immigration system and immigrant rights, in addition to immigration options through the Violence Against Women Act that may be available based on the survivors' circumstances. Immigrant survivors vary in their desire or capacity to remain in the United States. Often survivors' first priority is to end the abuse. Thus discussion for safety-planning should include attention to immigration options, without assuming that this is the highest priority for an immigrant survivor of domestic violence.

At the mezzo-level, domestic violence advocates should develop working relationships with qualified immigration attorneys who can provide pro-bono or affordable legal assistance. Advocates can also work with local law enforcement to develop training on legal provisions for battered immigrants. Coordination with law enforcement for the U-visa for victims of crime is particularly important, since successful applications require a police report. Reaching out to secular and religious leaders in immigrant communities is also an important strategy for raising a general awareness of domestic violence as well as specific legal provisions for abused immigrants.

An example of macro-level practice would be strengthening and educating immigrant communities. This can only be achieved if trust has been established between the mainstream service providers and key community leaders. Immigrant communities are not unique in their wariness of having social problems within their community surfaced for public view. Advocates who approach immigrant communities to talk openly about domestic violence might not receive a warm welcome; we advise them to consider alternate approaches to develop relationships with community leaders. Educational forums and outreach on related issues including welfare benefits, information on immigration law and immigrant rights, and the impact of domestic violence on children can help initiate involvement among community members, which can then lead to more targeted outreach on domestic violence.

CASE STUDY 2: DOMESTIC VIOLENCE AS AN UNDOCUMENTED IMMIGRANT

BACKGROUND: UNDOCUMENTED IMMIGRATION FROM MEXICO

Mexicans make up the majority of undocumented immigrants at over 50 percent or 5.3 million, and another 23 percent or 2.2 million come from other countries in Central and South America in addition to the Caribbean. The remaining 25 percent of undocumented immigrants come from Asia, Europe, and Canada. A portion of undocumented immigrants have entered the United States on a temporary visa as students, tourists, and business travelers, and then remain beyond the terms of their visa. The majority of undocumented immigrants, particularly those who enter by foot, take significant risks to cross the physical border between the United States and Mexico. Because of increased surveillance, border crossings have become less frequent and more perilous, leading to more deaths every year. Immigrants seeking to enter the United States often rely on the expensive and dangerous services of "coyotes," individuals who arrange for escort over the border.

Migration from Mexico increased following the passage of the North America Free Trade Agreement (NAFTA), which severely restructured the Mexican economy and dislocated up to 2 million peasants from their lands. Migration patterns into the United States generally begin with a single male worker seeking employment, who then later sends for his wife, children, and other family members. Children who migrate before the age of 15 are often considered the 1.5 immigrant generation, because they have grown up both in their country of origin and in the United States. Although these children lack legal status, they may be socialized in the United States with high levels of incorporation into society. It is nearly impossible today for undocumented immigrants to obtain legal residency. Without comprehensive immigration reform at the federal level, millions of undocumented immigrants in the United States have little guarantee of social or political rights.

RAMONA

Ramona is a 25-year-old woman with two daughters 4 and 6 years of age. She has been living in the United States since she was eight years old, when her parents paid a "coyote" to escort her over the border to join them in the United States where they had been working for a few years. During most of her childhood, she and her family were migrant workers, moving with the seasonal jobs up and down the western United States. Despite the many disruptions, Ramona was a bright student and, with her parents' encouragement, graduated from high school. Ramona wanted to attend college, but her undocumented status meant she was not qualified for financial aide or in-state tuition. Her family could not afford the cost of out-of state tuition, so she took a job working as a housecleaner in a town nearby to her parents. When Ramona

"CONTINUED"

turned 20, she married her high school boyfriend, Manuel, who is also an undocumented immigrant from Mexico.

Although neither Ramona nor Manuel earned much money, they were able to save enough to buy a car to help with Manuel's business as a landscaper. The state where they lived required a valid Social Security number to obtain a driver's license, so neither Manuel nor Ramona had a license to drive. Manuel took extra precaution when driving. He was particularly afraid of getting into an accident and not being able to pay damages, since they were not eligible for car insurance. Manuel was also careful to avoid neighborhoods where police, in search of undocumented immigrants, were known to racially profile drivers. The tense climate made Manuel nervous and irritable. He often came home from work and took out his anger on Ramona, who did not experience the same stress around driving as she took the bus to work.

The situation grew worse when Ramona became pregnant a year after they were married, and within the year another child followed. Manuel blamed Ramona for getting pregnant. Their finances became tighter when Ramona stayed home to care for their two young children. It was then that Manuel started drinking more. One night he returned home drunk, and yelled at and cursed Ramona. He hit her and threatened the children. Ramona was scared, and so she left quickly with the girls and took a bus to her parents' house about an hour away. Her parents were worried about Ramona and let her and the children stay with them for a week, but they continued to encourage Ramona to go back to Manuel and be nice to him so he would not get so mad. The following week Ramona returned home, and their life together resumed as it had been.

Manuel's behavior became increasingly erratic with more intense outbursts. The abuse eventually became bad enough that Ramona feared he might hurt the children; she threatened to call the police. Manuel told her that, if she did, they would both be deported and their children, who are U.S. citizens, would be sent to a foster home. Ramona was terrified of losing her children.

One night while Ramona was being beaten, her oldest child, who was six at the time, called 911. When the police arrived they arrested Manuel and told Ramona that she should go to a battered women's shelter with her children. Ramona refused to give the police a statement, terrified that her husband would be deported if she told the police anything. Manuel was arrested anyway, and Ramona was taken to a local shelter.

While in the shelter, Ramona was afraid to tell the shelter staff that she was undocumented and was relieved when they did not pressure her. The shelter was a calm place for her and her children. One of the shelter workers was bilingual and a Mexican immigrant herself. This made it easier for Ramona to talk about her problems. At times, she wanted to leave the shelter, but she was not ready to return home. After thirty days the staff encouraged her to apply for transitional housing, so she could have more time to think through her situation. Ramona filled out the paper work for transitional housing with the staff's help. But two weeks later, housing officials called to say they had reported Ramona to Immigration and Customs Enforcement (ICE), because they learned that she was an unauthorized immigrant. Within a day, the ICE officers came to the shelter to pick up and detain Ramona. She was placed in an ICE

"CONTINUED"

detention center for one week and then put on a flight back to Mexico. When Ramona was detained she refused to disclose the name of her husband, fearing that he, too, would be deported. So her children, who, as noted, are U.S. citizens, were placed in the custody of Child Protective Services. Ramona, who was back in Mexico for the first time since she was eight years old, was in shock and did not know how to get back to her children and family in the United States.

ADVOCACY STRATEGIES AND ETHICAL DILEMMAS WHEN WORKING WITH UNDOCUMENTED IMMIGRANTS

Advocacy with undocumented immigrants is challenging and often frustrating. The general public, post-9/11, has an underlying fear of immigrants and foreign individuals, mainly fueled by racism and the fear of terrorism. The political and social climate remains tense, especially after highly visible workplace raids by ICE in 2006. Domestic violence service providers are not immune to this general fear. Some advocates might experience ethical dilemmas when trying to meet the best interests of their undocumented clients while at the same time upholding the law.

Given the specific role of social workers and advocates as mandated reporters of child abuse and neglect, it is important to clarify that this responsibility *does not* include the reporting of undocumented immigrants to the Department of Homeland Security. The primary role of the advocate and social worker is to ensure the rights and human dignity of the clients and communities with whom they work. Thus advocates should not involve or act as the Department of Homeland Security by alerting authorities to the presence of an unauthorized alien. Advocates who function as an extension of Immigration and Customs Enforcement can cause serious consequences for their undocumented clients.

Federal law defines unlawful entry into the United States as both a civil and criminal offense, and thus grounds for detention and removal. Unlawful presence in the United States is only a civil offense. Unauthorized aliens residing in the United States are subject to detention and removal (i.e., deportation) but are not automatically subject to criminal prosecution (Garcia 2006). The exception is in cases where the alien is present in the United States after having previously been removed.

In addition to federal law, some states are passing stringent laws penalizing those who employ undocumented workers (e.g., Arizona House Bill 2279 passed in 2006). In 2007 the Oklahoma legislature passed House Bill 1804, the most extensive law to date, making it a felony to harbor, transport, shelter, or conceal undocumented immigrants. Social workers and domestic violence advocates should defend their professional obligation to support people in times of crises, including people who reside in the United States unlawfully. Ironically this very tactic is used by batterers to exert their power over undocumented women. Domestic violence service providers who notify authorities of undocumented clients only reinforce the validity of a batterer's threats, which inadvertently encourages women to endure violent relationships in order to continue living in the United States with their children.

Because undocumented immigrants are generally afraid of members of the mainstream community and authority figures, they often exist in small, close-knit communities. As a result of the higher percentage of Spanish-speaking people now residing in the United States, Latino women are more likely to establish informal support systems from which they seek assistance when experiencing violence. Common forms of support might include finding a job, sharing housing with other immigrants, receiving support from religious communities, and getting assistance with basic needs from church or other community groups. Some women are supported and encouraged by their communities to leave the batterer and begin life away from abuse. A few landlords in a community might rent houses or apartments to women who are undocumented, with or without knowledge of their status. A few women's groups in religious institutions help battered women and children reestablish themselves away from the abuser by helping them find housing, employment, and other necessities. However, Mexican women are often discouraged by their support system from leaving the batterer because of social norms that focus on preserving the marriage and because of the cultural expectation that women are strong and should persevere in the face of adversity.

Many immigrants from Mexico are closely tied to their religious community. This can be a source of support and strength for survivors. However, in cases where the religious leaders minimize or discount domestic violence, women may be counseled to stay with their abuser and prioritize the sanctity of marriage over their own well-being. When working with survivors, it is important to honor their faith and trust in religion while also encouraging them to seek support from religious leaders who will not condone the domestic violence but support their right to live a life free from abuse.

Most of the undocumented immigrant population fears deportation and are reluctant to share their legal status with advocates, mainstream community members, or even peers. At the micro level, it is important for advocates to be mindful of this common fear when working with any group of immigrants and to be patient as they establish trust over time. Advocates may need to assure immigrants that the information shared in their interactions will not be disclosed to immigration officials. Some undocumented immigrants are highly functional in the mainstream community because of their English proficiency or other skills, which makes it difficult to presume their legal status. False assumptions and lack of knowledge around immigration laws pose a threat to members of this population if advocates direct them to apply for cash assistance, transitional housing, or any other type of public assistance, which inadvertently may lead to their detention and removal from the United States.

Mezzo-level advocacy across systems requires some investigation of how immigrants with different status might be treated or viewed within systems, given the constantly changing local, state, and federal laws. Although undocumented immigrants are ineligible for most federal and state forms of public assistance, undocumented women are often mothers to U.S. citizens, who are eligible. Thus, when supporting survivors who seek public assistance for their children, it is particularly important to ensure that the children attain proper access to benefits while not jeopardizing the status of the undocumented individual. Domestic violence service providers should consult with attorneys who specialize in immigration law for formal legal advice when unsure of the needed course of action.

Advocates should also consider the potential harm resulting from "don't ask, don't tell" practices. Many organizations adopt the practice of not soliciting information about immigration status and even discouraging some groups from disclosing their status. This can be one way to protect the client when the organization cannot guarantee that the information will remain confidential. However, this practice can lead to unintended consequences, as illustrated in Ramona's case. It is important for advocates to be mindful of the common fear of deportation among foreign-born survivors regardless of their documentation status. Advocates need to be patient, as clients establish trust with them before disclosing their status.

At the macro level, domestic violence advocates can engage in policy advocacy at the local, state, and federal level to expand social and political rights for immigrants. This includes the right to obtain a driver's license, the right to housing, access to public assistance, and comprehensive immigration reform that includes a legal path to citizenship.

CASE STUDY 3: DOMESTIC VIOLENCE AS A REFUGEE

BACKGROUND: SOMALI BANTU REFUGEE RESETTLEMENT IN THE UNITED STATES

The Somali Bantu make up a small portion of Somali refugees that have been resettled in the United States. Somalia is a country in the northeast corner of Africa, often referred to as the Horn of Africa. In 1991 civil war broke out in Somalia with armed forces ousting the president of Somalia and assuming control of the government. Since 1991 nearly one million Somali are thought to have died in the conflict, and thousands of others fled to refugee camps in neighboring Kenya (Stephen 2002). The Somali Bantu are an ethnic minority within Somalia, originally brought to Somalia as slaves by Arab colonialists in the nineteenth century. Somali Bantu typically have not had access to education and held unskilled or semi-skilled jobs in agriculture and labor. Owing to their low social status and separation from Somali clan systems, they have been particularly vulnerable to attacks during the civil strife and have been actively seeking third-country resettlement since 1993. In 1999 the United States agreed to resettle 12,000 of the remaining Somali Bantu refugees in Kenya, who had been seeking protection for more than ten years (Stephen 2002).

AZIZA

Aziza is a 40-year-old Bantu woman, originally from Somalia. She has five children between 6 and 14 years of age and has been living in the United States since she was granted resettlement in 2001. In 1993 Aziza, her husband, and their children fled to Ethiopia after their village had been raided and many of their friends and neighbors raped or murdered. Aziza herself had suffered a rape during this attack, but she was lucky to escape when a fire broke out in the village and her attackers fled for their own safety. Aziza was separated from her family for a few months and then was reunited with her husband, his two other wives, and their children, who had also sought safety in a refugee camp. Aziza was devastated when she learned that her youngest child, who was only a year, had not survived the journey and died before reaching the camp.

Aziza and her family remained in the refugee camp for more than eight years. The camp was well organized, but there was little for her and her husband to do and no regular schooling for the children. At times the food rations were limited, and for

CONTINUED

many months they would each have just one meal a day. When the war in Somalia ended, Aziza's husband refused to return, convinced that the status of Somalia Bantu would not improve. Rather than return to their country to live in hardship, they sought third-country resettlement.

In 2001 Aziza's husband was granted third-country resettlement in the United States. Because the United States does not recognize polygamous marriage, her husband chose Aziza to accompany him as she was his youngest wife, leaving the other two wives and their children behind. Aziza was relieved to go to the United States, but she was also scared at the prospect of starting a new life in a foreign land.

Adjustment to the United States was very hard for Aziza and her husband. Immediately they were each given work permits, and the local refugee resettlement organization found them jobs at a factory near their apartment. The children were enrolled in the nearby public school, while Aziza and her husband went to work. The days were very long and lonely. At home, Aziza struggled to feed and take care of the family with their limited income in an unfamiliar environment. Her husband was used to each of his three wives providing him with comfort and attention. He grew angry with Aziza and started beating her regularly soon after their arrival in the United States. Aziza was also suspicious that her husband was sexually abusing her oldest daughter who was nine years old. One afternoon, when Aziza returned home from shopping, she found her husband standing naked, with her daughter on her knees performing oral sex. Her husband immediately grew violent, attacking both Aziza and the girl with his belt and throwing things around their apartment. One of the older children ran to a neighbor who called the police. When the police arrived, they arrested Aziza's husband and sent Aziza and her children to a shelter for battered women. The police also notified Child Protective Services, which began an investigation into the child sexual abuse.

The shelter was a difficult place for Aziza and her children. Aziza's English was very limited, making it difficult for her to communicate with the shelter staff. Communication was even harder when Aziza refused to work with a Somali interpreter through the language line. She did not trust that the interpreter, who was Somali but not Bantu. She feared that the interpreter would tell the entire community about her problems. At times the staff would rely on the oldest child, her 14-year-old son to interpret. When asked about the sexual abuse, both the child and Aziza denied everything. The CPS worker, frustrated that the mother was noncompliant with the investigation, reported Aziza as a neglectful parent and threatened to take away her parental rights from all the children.

ADVOCACY STRATEGIES AND ETHICAL DILEMMAS WHEN WORKING WITH REFUGEES

Displaced refugee populations who have resettled in the United States generally face challenges in adjusting to the post-industrial context of the country. Refugees are eligible to adjust their status to lawful permanent resident within one year, such that legal status may not be a priority issue. However, many refugees experience persistent unemployment and financial hardship, partly because of their lack of experience in a post-industrial society and lack of transferable job skills suitable to the United States market.

Somali Bantu refugees often have multiple layers of trauma relating to war, violence, and life in the refugee camp. Layers of trauma are particularly prevalent in women because of the high rates of rape during wartime, when fleeing conflict, and while residing in refugee camps (Cole et al. 1992). During the civil war in Somalia, rape was a common weapon used to punish rival ethnic groups or clans. The Somali Bantu were particularly vulnerable, as they lacked clan affiliation and clan-based protection. Another serious obstacle when working with these clients is the unrecognized level of sexual abuse and child sexual abuse among Somali refugees. Providers working with Somali families may encounter resistance to acknowledging sexual abuse or efforts within families to minimize harm related to sexual abuse. Service providers need to be aware of the prevalence of posttraumatic stress disorder, depression, and other psychological effects within refugee populations.

Bantu customarily have multiple wives who each bear several children. A household with multiple children was congruous with the largely agriculturally based subsistence that characterized life prior to displacement from Somalia; this family structure is much harder to support in the United States. Upon immigrating to the United States, male immigrants are required to officially recognize only one wife. In many cases, a Somali Bantu man may immigrate with one wife, and support the wives and children who remain in Somalia or in the refugee camps to the extent possible. This may contribute to increased pressure and expectations on the wife in the United States, who must now juggle the responsibilities of a job in addition to caretaking roles she had shared with others.

Cultural and language barriers are problems for Bantu survivors of domestic violence in the United States. Interpreter services are harder to secure, as the Bantu dialect is different from the main language spoken in Somalia. In addition, existing tribal tensions within the refugee population and distrust among tribes persist in the United States. Because of these experiences with members of other clans, preferential treatment is often noticed for people in the same tribes. The Somali Bantu may also experience marginalization from other Somali groups in the United States. This creates challenges for advocates who are unable to find an interpreter with whom the survivor feels comfortable or who is willing to work. This isolation only becomes worse when women are no longer receiving support from extended families and kin networks, which is their traditional support system.

At the micro level, advocates should seek competent interpreters in collaboration with the immigrant survivors. For example, advocates should explore whether volunteer interpreters from the local immigrant community would risk the client's confidentiality. In such a case, utilizing a random language help-line may ensure anonymity in the initial assessment process. The challenge in utilizing language help-lines and working with random interpreters each time you work with a client is that the subtle nuances in a client's statement may be lost, as the interpreter will not have all the background knowledge of the case. Moreover, interpreters may or may not have training in domestic violence.

Thus mezzo-level advocacy should include working with local interpreter services in the community to develop training and build relationships with interpreter services to increase both cultural competence and sensitivity to the complex dynamics of domestic violence. Language access policies have received more serious attention by providers in many social service fields. However, it is critical to approach language access as needing ongoing development. As a first step toward becoming more culturally and linguistically competent, agencies should adopt a formal language access policy. This should include access to language lines, developing working relationships with interpreters, and training them on the dynamics of domestic violence. We also need to address the resource limitations to providing adequate interpretation. This may be dealt with by building alliances with the immigrant and refugee communities to identify and train community-based interpreters.

At the macro level, domestic violence service providers can advocate for implementation of Title VI of the Civil Rights Act of 1964 to ensure that language access is provided across systems (i.e., criminal justice, health care, and social services). For example, many police departments have language policies that prohibit using children as interpreters, but in practice they may rely on children to complete a police report. Advocates should hold systems accountable for upholding and implementing already existing policies.

CONCLUSION

This chapter addresses culturally competent advocacy with immigrants and refugees through critical analysis of the political and social position of immigrant groups within U.S. society. The changing demographics of immigrants in the United States requires domestic violence advocates to attend to complex cultural, social, and political dynamics when working with foreign-born survivors of domestic violence. Here we addressed intersecting oppressions and structural power dynamics impacting immigrant survivors of domestic violence. The information in this chapter is intended to introduce basic areas of knowledge for further exploration. Comprehensive analysis of specific cultural and social factors for different immigrant groups, is beyond the the scope of this chapter. Hence we encourage advocates to learn more about the social and cultural histories of each client group toward developing cultural competency specific to the immigrants with whom they work.

HOW TO BE AN EFFECTIVE ADVOCATE TO IMMIGRANT SURVIVORS

QUICK CHECKLIST

- Know the local resources that can help you offer comprehensive support
- Do not involve or function as the Department of Homeland Security
- Do not collude with batterers' tactics to control through immigration procedures
- Examine assumptions about culture and different immigrant groups
- Address the ethical issues and effectiveness of "don't ask, don't tell" policies
- Create and document language access policies
- Know the rights of noncitizens
- Know the rights in the immigration system
- Ensure access to accurate legal immigration advice

WEB RESOURCES

IMMIGRATION LAW AND IMMIGRANT RIGHTS RESOURCES

American Immigration Lawyers Association
This association provides a lawyer referral service to private immigration attorneys. It provides contact information for a lawyer, and the initial half-hour consultation

is no more than $100. During this consultation, ask the attorney what the rate is for further services. All lawyers participating in the service are licensed to practice law in a state or territory of the United States and are currently a member in good standing of a State Bar Association.
Web site: http://www.aila.org

National Immigration Law Center
Web site: http://www.nilc.org/

National Immigrant Justice Center
Web site: http://www.immigrantjustice.org/contactUs.asp

National Network for Immigrant and Refugee Rights
Web site: http://www.nnirr.org/

DOMESTIC VIOLENCE RESOURCES FOR ADVOCACY WITH IMMIGRANTS

ASISTA Immigration Technical Assistance Project
Web site: http://www.asistaonline.org

Catholic Charities
In most states, Catholic Charities provide legal representation and information for victims of domestic violence with immigration issues. Find the program closest to where you live.
Web site: http://www.catholiccharitiesinfo.org

Legal Momentum, Immigrant Women Program
Provides current policy updates, legal resources, and research on legal issues for battered immigrant women. Also provides training and support to advocates and lawyers who are representing battered women.
Web site: http://www.legalmomentum.org/legalmomentum/programs/iwp/

National Network to End Violence Against Immigrant Women
Web site: http://www.immigrantwomennetwork.org/index.htm

VAWnet. A National Online Resource on Violence Against Women
This link takes you to a repository of models for serving immigrant women and provides up-to-date information on immigration laws that impact immigrant

survivors of domestic violence. Web site: http://new.vawnet.org/category/index_pages
.php?category_id=607
Violence Against Women Office, U.S. Department of Justice
Provides information about relevant laws, including the Victim's of Trafficking Act
Phone: (212) 789–2830
Web site: http://www.usdoj.gov/ovw/

WomensLaw.org
Web site: http://www.womenslaw.org/immigrantsBasicQs.htm

REFERENCES

Allen, N. E., D. I. Bybee, and C. M. Sullivan. (2004). Battered women's multitude
    of needs: Evidence supporting the need for comprehensive advocacy. *Violence
    Against Women*, 10(9), 1015–1035.
Bhuyan, R., and K. Senturia. (2003). Understanding domestic violence service
    utilization and survivor solutions among immigrant and refugee women:
    Introduction to the special issue. *Journal of Interpersonal Violence* 20(8), 895–
    901.
Camarota, S. A. (2007). Immigrants in the United States 2007: A profile of America's
    foreign-born population: Center for Immigration Studies.
Chen, S. W. (2000). The immigrant women of the violence against women act: The
    role of the Asian American consciousness in the legislative process. *Georgetown
    Journal of Gender and the Law, 1,* 823–848.
Chu, G. (1985). The changing concept of self in contemporary China. In A. J. Mar-
    sella, G. DeVos, and F. L. K. Hsu (Eds.), *Culture and Self, Asian and Western
    Perspectives.* New York: Tavistock.
Cole, E., O. M. Espin, and E. D. Rothblum (Eds.). (1992). *Refugee Women and
    Their Mental Health.* Binghamton, N.Y.: Haworth.
Conyers, J. (2007). The 2005 reauthorization of the violence against women act:
    Why Congress acted to expand protections to immigrant victims. *The 2005, 13*(5),
    457–468.
Crenshaw, K. W. (1995). Mapping the margins: Intersectionality, identity politics,
    and violence against women of color. In K. Crenshaw, N. Gotanda, G. Peller,
    and K. Thomas (Eds.), *Critical Race Theory: The Key Writings That Formed the
    Movement* (pp. 357–383). New York: New Press.
Cross, T., B. Bazron, K. Dennis, and M. R. Isaacs. (1989). *Towards a Culturally
    Competent System of Care.* Vol. 1. Washington, DC: CAASP Technical Assis-
    tance Center, Georgetown University Child Development Center.

Davis, R. C., and E. Erez. (1998). *Immigrant Populations as Victims: Toward a Multicultural Criminal Justice Dystem: Research in Brief.* Washington, DC: National Institute of Justice.

Dinan, K. A. (2005). *Federal Policies Restrict Immigrant Children's Access to Key Public Benefits.* New York: National Center for Children in Poverty, Columbia University, Mailman School of Public Health.

Dutton, M. A., L. E. Orloff, and G. A. Hass. (2000). Characteristics of help-seeking behaviors, resources, and service needs of battered immigrant Latinas: Legal and policy implications. *Georgetown Journal on Poverty Law and Policy, 7,* 245–305.

Garcia, M. J. (2006). Criminalizing unlawful presence: Selected issues. Order Code RS22413. Retrieved February 22, 2008, from http://www.ilw.com/immigdaily/news/2006,0509-crs.pdf.

Hazen, A. L., and F. I. Soriano. (2007). Experiences with intimate partner violence among Latina women. *Violence Against Women, 13*(6), 562–582.

Heise, L. L. (1998). Violence against women: An integrated, ecological framework. *Violence Against Women, 4*(3), 262–290.

Kanuha, V. (1996). Domestic violence, racism, and the battered women's movement in the United States. In J. L. Edleson and Z. C. Eisikovits (Eds.), *Future Interventions with Battered Women and Their Families* (Vol. 3). Thousand Oaks, CA: Sage.

Krishnan, S. P., J. C. Hilbert, D. VanLeeuwen, and R. Kolia. (1997). Documenting domestic violence among ethnically diverse populations: Results from a preliminary study. *Family and Community Health 20*(3), 32–48.

Lee, M. Y. (2000). Understanding Chinese battered women in North America: A review of the literature and practice implications. *Journal of Multicultural Social Work, 8*(3/4), 215–241.

Lee, M., and P. Au. (1998). Chinese battered women in North America: Their experiences and treatment. In A. R. Roberts (Ed.), *Battered Women and Their Families: Intervention Strategies and Treatment Programs* (2nd ed., pp. 448–482). New York: Springer.

Lindhorst, T., and E. Tajima. (2008). Reconcenptualizing and operationalizing context in survey research on intimate partner violence. *Journal of Interpersonal Violence, 23*(3), 362–388.

National Immigration Law Center. (2002). *Guide to Immigrant Eligibility for Federal Programs.* National Immigration Law Center.

Passel, J. S. (2005). Unauthorized migrants: Numbers and characteristics. Retrieved February 20, 2008, from http://pewhispanic.org/files/reports/46.pdf.

——. (2006). The size and characteristics of the unauthorized migrant population in the U.S.: Estimates based on the March 2005 current population survey. Retrieved February 20, 2008, from http://pewhispanic.org/files/reports/61.pdf.

Pendelton, G., and E. Kemp. (2006). Realities for immigrant populations: How they experience the system. Retrieved February 13, 2008, from http://new.vawnet.org/category/index_pages.php?category_id=607.

Raj, A., and J. Silverman. (2002). Violence against immigrant women: The roles of culture, context, and legal immigrant status on intimate partner violence. *Violence Against Women*, 8(2), 367–398.

——. (2003). Immigrant South Asian women at greater risk for injury from intimate partner violence. *American Journal of Public Health*, 93(3), 435–437.

Raj, A., K. N. Livramento, and M. C. Santana. (2006). Victims of intimate partner violence more likely to report abuse from in-laws. *Violence Against Women*, 12(10), 936–949.

Salcido, O., and M. Adelman. (2004). "He has me tied with the blessed and damned papers": Undocumented-immigrant battered women in Phoenix, Arizona. *Human Organization*, 63(2), 162–172.

Stephen, P. (2002). *Somali Bantu Report*. Nairobi: International Organization for Migration.

Tjaden, P., and N. Thoennes. (2000). *Full Report of the Prevalence, Incidence, and Consequences of Violence Against Women* (No. NCJ 183781). Washington, DC: U.S. Department of Justice, Office of Justice Programs.

World Health Organization (WHO). (2002). *World Report on Violence and Health*. Retrieved July 25, 2003, from http://www.who.int/mediacentre/releases/pr73/en/.

——. (2005). *WHO Multi-Country Study on Women's Health and Domestic Violence Against Women: Summary Report of Initial Results on Prevalence, Health Outcomes and Women's Responses*. Geneva: World Health Organization.

Yau, J. (2004). The foreign born from Korea in the United States. Retrieved February 28, 2008, from http://www.migrationinformation.com/USFocus/display.cfm?ID=273.

Yoshihama, M. (2001). Immigrants-in-context framework: Understanding the interactive influence of socio-cultural contexts. *Evaluation and Program Planning*, 24(3), 307–318.

7

DOMESTIC ABUSE IN LATER LIFE

Ann Turner, Deb Spangler, and Bonnie Brandl

DOMESTIC VIOLENCE affects women of all ages. Older abused women are a hidden and invisible population. Some older women do not tell anyone about the abuse in their lives. Others give subtle hints or offer coded disclosures that generally go unrecognized or unaddressed by family, friends, or professionals. Often those working with survivors of domestic violence or older individuals fail to understand that abuse does occur in later life; therefore they ignore obvious indicators, fail to ask questions, and do not practice standard screening.

This chapter provides an overview of the dynamics of abuse in later life and addresses the many considerations when working with elder abuse victims. Since cases of abuse in later life often raise challenging ethical dilemmas and concerns, such as mandatory reporting and confidentiality, these topics are addressed. The chapter concludes with a discussion of culturally sensitive and effective services to older adults using a case example.

LATER LIFE: AGING ISSUES

The population is aging. In 2001 the U.S. Census Bureau reported that the three fastest-growing five-year age groups in the United States since the last census were 50–54 year olds at 55 percent, 45–49 year olds at 45 percent, and 90–94 year olds at 45 percent (U.S. Census Bureau 2001). In July 2003, 36 million people were aged 65 and older. The U.S. Census estimates a substantial increase in older adults, with the projected population doubling between 2000 and 2030—from 35 million to 72 million. Reports have determined that many Americans are living longer. Persons reaching age 65 have an average life expectancy of an additional 18.5 years; 19.8 years for females and 16.8 years for males (U.S. DHHS, AOA 2005 Profile of Older Americans). With this increasing population, it is imperative that service agencies prepare to address abuse of the elderly, including domestic abuse in later life.

Poverty is an issue for many older Americans. Significant disparities exist based on gender and race. The median income of older American men in 2004 was $21,102 compared to $12,080 for women. For one-third of the population over 65, Social Security benefits constitute 90 percent of their income. Reports have shown that almost 10 percent of the elderly population lived below the poverty level in 2004; another 6.4 percent were classified as "near poor." When looking at poverty rates by gender in 2004, 12 percent of older women lived in poverty compared to 7 percent of older men. Poverty rates are even more severe for people of color: 7.5 percent of white elders lived in poverty compared to 23.9 percent of African American elders, 13.6 percent of Asian American elders, and 18.7 percent of Hispanic elders (U.S. DHHS, AOA, 2005 Profile of Older Americans).

Defining "later life" can be complicated. Aging services programs often use the age 60+ years, 65+ years or 70+ years. This chapter focuses on the needs of women 50 years of age and older for several reasons. First, many domestic violence programs indicate that the numbers of women using their services declines significantly after age 50 when services tailored for the age group are not available (Vinton 1992). Second, the financial needs of women age 50 and older are often similar. Most are not parenting young children and therefore are ineligible for Temporary Assistance for Needy Families (TANF) or welfare type financial assistance. Those who are unemployed may have difficulty finding a job because of age discrimination or lack of marketable skills after many years of full-time parenting. To use the age of 65+ years or 70+ years would mean excluding these populations from the discussion.

One challenge in considering "later life" broadly is that older women are a diverse population. Historical perspectives, norms, and generational values for women in their fifties can be very different than for women in their seventies or nineties. These perspectives, values, and belief systems can greatly impact decisions made regarding the options individuals view as available when considering their situations. Key considerations include personal and cultural history, life experience, aging issues, beliefs, and values.

ISSUES TO EXPLORE

Older women have many more years of experience and history than younger clients. At the time of this writing, they may have lived through one or both world wars. They may have experienced the Great Depression. Some may have grown up long before major political and social movements changed societal values and practices, such as the civil rights movement, the women's movement and the gay and lesbian movements. Others may have been deeply engaged in the struggles, or at least experienced the events through television, radio, and newspapers. Their experiences with racism, sexism, classism, and homophobia will not only be very different from their younger cohorts but also within the population of those 50 and older.

Also shaping an older woman's viewpoints is where she lives and her work experience. Older women may have been born and raised in the United States or may have immigrated years ago or only recently. Some women have lived in rural communities, others in urban areas, and still others have experienced both environments. Other women in this generation have never worked outside the home or have been a farm wife their entire lives; some have held professional careers and are financially independent.

Functional capabilities and limitations often change as individuals grow older; however, many older adults experiencing abuse are not frail, medically compromised, or dependent on others for care. Some older adults are active and participate in vigorous activities such as running, biking, or swimming competitively. Still others may have or are beginning to experience decreased vision or hearing, loss of stamina, or illness and other limitations that might require accommodations when providing services.

Some older individuals experiencing abuse meet state statutory definitions for an adult-at-risk or a vulnerable adult. These are generally individuals who depend on others for care and have a limited ability to report abuse on their own. They may have physical or cognitive limitations or both. Often the adult protective service agency (APS) provides the primary response to these cases.

ELDER ABUSE AND DOMESTIC ABUSE IN LATER LIFE

There is no universally accepted definition of "elder abuse." The National Center on Elder Abuse (2006) defines it as follows: "Elder abuse is a term referring to any knowing, intentional, or negligent act by a caregiver or any other person that causes harm or a serious risk of harm to a vulnerable adult." Elder abuse can occur in private dwellings in the community and in facility settings, and can include physical, sexual, and emotional abuse, financial exploitation, neglect, and abandonment. Some state statutes include self-neglect as a form of elder abuse. Unlike other forms of elder abuse that involve a perpetrator harming an older individual, self-neglect occurs when elders are unable or unwilling to provide for their basic health and living needs.

Domestic abuse in later life is a subset of elder abuse. Domestic abuse in later life involves abuse, neglect, or exploitation of an older individual by an abuser who has an ongoing relationship with the person being abused, a relationship where there is an expectation of trust or love or both. Perpetrators can include intimate partners or spouses, adult children and other family members, and some caregivers. Domestic abuse in later life does not include self-neglect or stranger scams.

Abuse in later life usually follows a pattern of coercive tactics used by an abuser to achieve a specific goal. In many cases abusers want to gain and maintain power and control. Some perpetrators are more interested in financial exploitation and will use various tactics to steal money and resources. Abusers generally believe that they are entitled to use various methods to achieve their goal with little or no consideration for the feelings or wishes of their target. Many of the same tactics are used in abuse in later life as are seen with younger battered women. Abusers also target vulnerabilities, for example, they may hide eyeglasses, destroy dentures, move walkers, wheelchairs, or canes to make it difficult for the women to function independently. Abusers also target the survivors' strengths such as ridiculing their spiritual, personal, and cultural values or limiting access to important events, especially when survivors depend on their abusers for transportation. Relationships with children or grandchildren can also be threatened or poisoned, and job or volunteer opportunities can be sabotaged. Emotional abuse and psychological abuse are almost always present in abusive relationships. Emotional abuse involves tactics such as the silent treatment, belittling comments, name calling, and other demeaning behaviors. Psychological abuse involves manipulative strategies such as making survivors doubt their sanity and judgment by moving items so they cannot be found, changing versions of events and then blaming the confusion on the survivor, telling them they are losing their memory or that they have dementia.

RELATIONSHIPS

Older women who experience abuse have a relationship with an expectation of trust with their abuser, and that expectation of trust provides the environment for an abuser to use the power and control tactics to maintain control over the survivor. Physical violence may only happen once in a relationship or not at all, but the threat is often there; however, it is the many other coercive tactics such as emotional and psychological abuse that allow an abuser to manipulate the relationship.

Intimate partner abuse may have persisted throughout the long-term relationship, such as one lasting 50 or 60 years. Or an older woman may find herself single later in life because of divorce or the death of a spouse and enter a new relationship with a partner who is abusive, neglectful, or exploitive. Intimate partner abuse in later life may also be late onset abuse. In these situations, by all accounts the abusive behavior is recent and starts later in life. In some cases a medical condition, such as Alzheimer's disease, can manifest itself in aggressive or inappropriate behavior. In these cases medical professionals should be involved in case management. Keep in mind that abusers lie to justify their behavior and are masters at manipulating not only the person being abused but others around them as well. A professional assessment is necessary to assure that the medical condition is not being used as an excuse by the abuser to avoid legal and personal consequences for the abusive behavior.

Caregivers can also be abused by the person for whom they are providing care. An older woman may provide care for an abusive spouse who may continue to abuse even though he may now be ill or frail. For example, the abuser may use his wheelchair to run into his partner's legs while she is preparing food or otherwise distracted, causing significant pain and bruising.

Adult children, grandchildren, and other family members can also be abusers. Research indicates that often the abuser is living with the person who is being abused. Contrary to popular belief, generally the older adult is not dependent on the abuser. Often the abuser is emotionally or financially dependent on the older adult (Wolf and Pillemer 1997; Seaver 1996.; Pillemer and Finkelhor 1989). For example, a grandson and his family may move in with a grandparent under the guise of preventing relocation to a nursing home. It looks and sounds good, but the reality is that the grandson has a history of financial problems, possibly an alcohol or drug problem, and needs the older adult's income to support himself and his family.

CAUSES AND PREVALENCE

A number of factors can coexist with abuse in later life but have not been found to be primary causes. In the past, caregiver stress had been considered the primary cause of elder abuse, but current research does not support this contention (Reis 2000; Wolf 2000). By definition, caregiver stress occurs when a caregiver is overwhelmed by the demands of caring for another individual. Early research linked caregiver stress to elder abuse, because abusers told researchers that the reason they harmed or neglected an older adult was that they were doing the best they could but the job was stressful. Abusers often claimed that the abuse was an isolated incident. They portrayed themselves as the person needing help, because they were overwhelmed by the stress of providing care. Subsequent research and experience in the field has found the following:

1. Caregiving can be stressful, but it is not a primary cause of elder abuse (Godkin, Wolf, and Pillemer 1989; Phillips, de Ardon, and Brione 2000; Pillemer and Finkelhor 1988, 1989; Reis and Nahmiash 1997, 1998). Caregivers under stress are more likely to engage in behaviors that are harmful to themselves, such as overeating, substance abuse, or lack of exercise or sleep (International Longevity Center-USA (ILC-USA), with the Schmieding Center for Senior Health and Education [SCSHE] Taskforce 2006).
2. A primary cause of abuse in later life is power and control dynamics like those seen when working with younger abused women (Pillemer and Finkelhor 1988; Podnieks 1992).
3. Abusers lie, manipulate, blame the person being abused, and justify their behavior to both the person being abused and professionals who attempt to assist. They do not want to lose access to the person being abused or be held accountable for their actions; therefore they can be charming as well as manipulative with professionals (Salter 2003).
4. Stress is not an excuse for abusing, neglecting, or exploiting an older adult. Everyone experiences stress, but few of us abuse loved ones. Abusers choose who they will harm—those with less power than they themselves have. In most cases they are not violent with an employer or law enforcement. They are able to control their behavior, when and where the violence occurs, and often plan how and when to strike someone to assure that bruises are not obvious (Schechter 1987).

Currently there are no methodically sound national prevalence and incidence studies to document the frequency of abuse in later life. A study of 257 older women ages 50–59 found that one-third (32%) had experienced physical abuse or threats from their partners at some point in their lives (Mouton et al. 1999). Another study of 1,057 adults age 65 and older who used domestic violence program services reported that 71 percent had experienced physical abuse (Lundy and Grossman 2004). Given that the number of older individuals is increasing, cases of domestic abuse in later life will continue to rise.

BARRIERS FACED

Survivors of abuse in later life face many difficult choices when trying to protect themselves from the violence perpetrated by a family member, partner, or caregiver. Each woman will have different issues when making these difficult decisions, a unique blend of complicated factors including fear, finances, living arrangements, health concerns, religious and generational values, and family relationships.

Fear can be a significant barrier for some older victims. Similar to younger survivors, many fear being killed or seriously injured by the abuser if they attempt to end the relationship or do not comply with the abuser's demands. Older survivors may also fear being ostracized by their family or community for not fulfilling the expectations placed on them. Moreover, older survivors may already be experiencing the loss of friends and siblings to death and aging issues, creating additional fears of the loneliness that may result in ending the relationship. They may also fear being forced to move or live in poverty or being placed in a facility such as a nursing home.

Financial issues often play a role in a woman's decisions regarding her available options. If she was exploited financially, she may have lost her life savings with little or no hope that the funds will be returned. Women who were homemakers would have had no income, and thus would ultimately be eligible for limited Social Security in their later years or none at all.

Living arrangements and location can also be a significant issue. Many victims want to remain in their own home and have the abuser leave, but, for some, this is not safe or financially realistic, and finding safe, affordable housing can be difficult. Living in rural, isolated areas with little or no public transportation and long distances to travel to the nearest neighbor or small town can create additional barriers. In farming communities, families may have occupied the family farm for many generations, making it difficult to leave. Farmers would hesitate to leave crops or livestock or family pets. If the abuser is a friend or relative of a prominent town member such as the sheriff or judge, the situation becomes more difficult.

Health problems also create obstacles to living free from abuse. Older adults who have survived long-term abuse may experience numerous physical and mental health conditions as a direct result of the abuse. Many experience longer recovery periods from physical injuries that occur as a result of abuse. Research has shown that corroborated cases of elder mistreatment are associated with shorter survival (Lachs et al. 1998). Women who have not worked outside the home may be dependent on the abuser for health insurance, especially those who are not yet eligible for Medicaid nor for other services because they have no minor children in the home. Medical conditions may be severe enough to require ongoing care. Staying with an abuser may seem a more attractive option than asking strangers to provide care or moving to a nursing home.

An abuser's health problems also influence the decisions an abused person must make. For example, a woman who is seventy-five probably grew up learning that her role in life was to provide care for her husband and children, and so she may feel responsible to remain in the abusive situation in order to care for a husband or adult child in need (Brandl, 2002). This sense of obligation may cause survivors who are planning to leave or have already left to stay or return if the abuser acquires functional limitations or becomes critically ill. Whereas a similar belief structure may persist for a woman who is closer to age 50, it is likely that the women's movement and society's increasing acceptance of divorce and separation have lessened or removed this sense of responsibility.

Generational, religious, cultural, and personal values about what it means to be a wife or a parent influence the options seen as available for a woman being abused. Some older adults may believe that their religious teachings (either through written word or messages from faith leaders) mandate that they stay in a marriage. Relationships defined as abusive today may have been considered "normal" many years ago. Strict male and female roles were clearly defined for earlier generations, when women were expected to stay home and take care of the household and the family.

Relationships in the life of the person being abused can significantly impact an adult's perspective when living with abuse. Spouses or a life partners may have been together for many years, and the person being abused may value the longevity of the relationship. Adult children and grandchildren may want the couple to stay together and apply pressure on the person being abused to stay. Memories, shared friends, family, a familiar home, and fear of being alone are often contributing factors.

Parents face unique challenges if they are being abused by their adult children. Often the parent experiences guilt and shame, blaming their past parenting for their adult child's abusive behavior. They may feel that being a parent means always being available to your child and that parents are to do whatever they can to help a child in need. They may resist interventions that may result in their child being arrested, institutionalized, or living on the streets.

The barriers confronting a survivor of abuse may be seen from three different perspectives: from the survivor's point of view, from a perspective driven by the abuser's tactics, or from the perspective of societal attitudes and issues. An example of a survivor-driven barrier is when a survivor faces the choice of having her drug-addicted, abusive son move out and struggles with issues of guilt and shame regarding her adult child. She most likely still loves her son and may feel responsible for some of the problems he has as an adult. She may hope that he will change if she allows him to continue to live with her. An abuser-driven barrier is when the abusive son tells his mother that he is sick or threatens to harm himself or her if she makes him leave. The societal-driven barrier in this scenario would be the lack of health care or treatment options for her son, no affordable housing, and a societal expectation that a parent should take care of a child, no matter what.

ISSUES FOR DIVERSE COMMUNITIES

Issues for older adults who are being abused can be additionally complicated when working with diverse communities. Economic and health disparities for older persons are significant. On average, the total value of all assets held (including home value) for white older people is $181,000; for African Americans it is $13,000.[1] The average life expectancy for whites is 77 years compared to 71 years for African Americans; three-quarter of the older white population reported that they were in good heath compared to little more than half of African Americans (58%) and two-thirds of the Hispanic population (65%). Many chronic illnesses become evident at earlier ages for older people within minority populations, including obesity, diabetes, and hypertension (Henrichsen 2006). Many of the disparities result from societal oppression (i.e., segregation) experienced by older populations and years of unequal access to employment and health care (Henrichsen 2006; Whitfield and Brandon 2000).

Older victims from different racial and ethnic backgrounds may define abusive behavior in different ways. Studies have compared the perceptions of members of different racial and ethnic groups about behavior that constituted elder abuse, and they found significant differences in the definitions (Hudson 1999; Anetzberger 1998; Moon 1993). One potential reason for this is that different cultures have different expectations about the responsibility of adult children to provide care for their elders (Sanchez 1999). Cultural norms also vary about parents continuing to provide support (emotional or financial) to grown children (Sanchez 1999; Griffin; 1994; Brown 1989).

Both documented and undocumented immigrants experience additional obstacles when trying to seek help from abuse in their lives. Many fear deportation for themselves, their spouse or partner, or other family members. Many do not speak English. They may have difficulty getting a job or are ineligible for Social Security or pensions that would give them some financial independence. Some may have been sponsored by an abusive family member who now uses the threat of deportation to control the older adult (Brownell 1997).

Older lesbian, gay, bisexual, and transgender (LGBT) partners may fear ending a relationship for fear of loneliness because of limited contact with other LGBT individuals in their community. They may have kept their relationship a secret for many years and fear being "outed" at work or to family and friends. They may be afraid to talk with clergy, counselors, or others about their relationship and the abuse. Some may be unwilling to contact law enforcement because of past negative experiences. Many will encounter legal and financial barriers such as no rights to property, pension, or Social Security when trying to make decisions about staying or leaving an abusive relationship. Additional barriers may exist if the person who is being abused or the perpetrator needs ongoing medical care, especially for transgender individuals (Allen and Turner 2006).

TIPS FOR PRACTITIONERS

- Examine personal biases about age, race, ethnicity, and cultural values and traditions for the diverse communities.
- Learn about the ethnic or racial history of diverse communities. Older individuals who experienced segregation and racism as children may have difficulty trusting anyone who is not from their community. One advocate described how her father, who was 80+ years of age, would react with anger and disgust if anyone rubbed the top of his head. When he was a child it was considered good luck to rub the head of an African

American child, an event he was forced to tolerate or risk further harm and violence. It was also important to call him by his formal name, for example, Mr. Jones, until he gave you permission to be less formal. This type of respect can be crucial when working with the older population.

- Understand that some older survivors will want to involve the whole family in any intervention. The survivor-based focus of traditional domestic violence organizations, which often excludes addressing the needs of the perpetrator or the whole family, can be a barrier to some marginalized communities and to older adults who are being abused.

- Recognize that some older victims of color may not trust the criminal justice system. They may not want their adult child jailed, especially within communities where the justice system has historically treated marginalized communities unfairly or violently. Many communities of color have experienced disproportionate confinement within the current justice system and may be hesitant to cooperate with that system.

- Learn about immigration laws to assist adults in determining whether deportation is a real or unlikely threat.

- Consider creating culturally sensitive or, preferably, culturally based service programs. Older survivors may not respond to workers not from their own communities, and language barriers may also be a problem. Become familiar with elder services currently provided within the racial and ethnic communities by contacting existing services.

- Consider hiring older staff and volunteers. Some older adults may feel more comfortable talking with providers who are of the same age or generation, feeling that the younger worker will not understand their generational values.

- Think about hiring bilingual staff or have planned access to interpreters, a crucial matter for non-English-speaking adults who currently rely on potentially abusive family members as interpreters. Even if the interpreter is not the potential abuser, information might be shared with the abuser, creating additional risk factors for the individual being abused.

ETHICAL ISSUES

Mandatory reporting statutes require individuals to report some cases of abuse or neglect to law enforcement, social services, or a regulatory agency such as Adult Protective Services (APS). Depending on the state laws and statutes, domestic violence, elder abuse, or abuse against vulnerable adults may require reporting. Who is required to report also varies, based on state statutes. In some states everyone must report suspected abuse. In others, certain professional groups are mandated reporters, while others are encouraged to voluntarily report suspected abuse or neglect (American Prosecutors Research Institute 2003).

Mandatory reporting of elder abuse is a controversial and complex issue. Supporters of mandatory reporting believe that it affords safety for the person being abused, because, it is reasoned, many elders may not recognize that they are being abused, are unaware of services, or may be too afraid or physically unable to seek help on their own. Those who oppose mandatory reporting of elder abuse reason that adults should be afforded their right to decide if they want help and, if so, from whom. Some professionals argue that it is an ageist response to treat abused adults differently simply because they are age 60 or 65 and older (Faulkner 1982). Risks and consequences of mandatory reporting can include (1) risk of retaliation by the perpetrator; (2) reduced decision-making power for the person being abused; and (3) broken trust and confidentiality. Some authors argue that these individuals may be in greater danger because there is no guarantee that reporting will result in successful APS intervention (Capezuti et al. 1997). A perpetrator may retaliate because of the disclosure or may become more careful to avoid being "caught." The person being abused may become more isolated and have freedoms curtailed as a result of an investigation (Hyman 1994). Even a successful investigation does not mean, necessarily, that the perpetrator will be removed or that the person being abused will be safer. Some professionals fear that individuals who are experiencing abuse in their homes will not ask for help a second time if they know a report will be made to police or APS. Professionals also worry that breaking confidentiality will harm their relationship between the survivor and the worker. Unsubstantiated cases can fuel an abuser's abusive behavior. The abuser can manipulate the situation, telling the person being harmed that the abuse is not really happening: "I'm not really hurting you—the social worker doesn't even believe you or doesn't think what I am doing is wrong."

Some professionals argue that mandatory reporting assumes that supportive, culturally appropriate services are in place with qualified staff and necessary resources. Unfortunately the current trend in this economy is an increase in the numbers of older adults needing assistance with limited service providers and dwindling or eliminated resources. Without adequate services and resources, ineffective interventions can lead to re-victimization or no resolution

(Brandl 2005). For these reasons, if a report is made, it is crucial to be able to secure the safety of the person experiencing the abuse.

PRACTICE STRATEGIES FOR OLDER SURVIVORS OF ABUSE

Older adults who are being abused often face limited poor choices. Deciding to stay or leave a relationship is a life-altering decision, and older adults will need support and information to help make their decisions. In order to help them move forward in their lives, listen to their wants and needs.

Focus on the survivor's strengths and assets. When working with older individuals, beliefs and values can be driving forces guiding or limiting what a survivor views as available options. Questions about faith and spirituality can help a practitioner learn how those beliefs may guide in the decision making. A discussion about family can elicit information about how the older woman sees herself as a spouse or partner and a mother or grandmother, how she views her role as a woman both within her family and in her community, and the importance of cultural values and community in her life. Asking women questions about their personal history or life experience not only builds rapport but can also provide valuable information that can assist with case work. It will also help the worker understand the social network and identify the potential risks, strengths, fears, and values of the person who is abused, assisting the worker in understanding what choices may be available. Survivors of abuse in later life may have experienced years of abuse. They have learned how to keep themselves safe with a variety of personal strengths and creative coping strategies. Those strengths may include loyalty, creativity, tolerance, patience, resiliency, determination, and courage to seek help and face change, an understanding of life's difficulties and complexities, and the wisdom that often comes in our later years (Gondolf 1998). However, rather than identify and build on these strengths, sometimes professionals label survivors as difficult, clumsy, co-dependent, impaired, or passive. Too often society "infantilizes" the elderly, treating them like children rather than the adults they are. One advocate shared the story of a 92-year-old survivor of a brutal physical and sexual attack by her nephew. The woman's permanent injuries from the attack required her to move into a nursing home. On every holiday or when the season changed, cheery staff members would enter her room and put childlike pictures on the walls. They would talk to the survivor in a cheery voice, telling her how pretty her wall looked. After they left, the survivor looked at her advocate and quietly said, "Why do they do that . . . I am not a child." The survivor's generational values made her believe it would be impolite to confront the staff regarding the issue, so she quietly tolerated what she felt was disrespectful behavior.

Take the additional time necessary to completely explore the possibility of abuse with older adults. Professionals who do not fully explore the possibility of elder abuse leave the person being abused in harm's way. If one form of abuse is occurring, such as financial abuse, it is important to explore other forms of abuse as well. Workers should look for physical evidence and behavioral cues that abuse may be occurring. Some medical and physical conditions in aging may mirror abuse injuries, for example, an older adult may bruise easily as a result of certain medications, have balance issues and experience frequent falls, or may have osteoporosis causing bones to become frail and break. Even though these conditions may exist, it is crucial to ask questions about abuse. Persons being abused may also display behavior that could cue workers to the presence of abuse, such as withdrawing from normal activities and isolating themselves, displaying evidence of fear, or giving coded disclosures of abuse such as "my son has a temper." Practitioners should explore any allegation of abuse by an older adult or someone else, even if the person being abused is not able to verbalize what is occurring in their life.

Recognize the right to self-determination for older individuals with capacity. Professionals may criticize someone who decides to maintain contact with an abuser and label the behavior "poor judgment." For older adults, poor judgment can be used as criteria for determining capacity. Post-traumatic symptoms may be recognized in a younger person who is abused but may be identified as dementia or age-related memory problems in an older person. Some may have their decision-making power removed by well-meaning workers who misunderstand trauma and the difficult choices faced by older adults when ending an abusive situation (Gondolf 1998). For example, an older woman who lives in the home she has occupied for many years with her abusive husband is now experiencing age-related health issues and is receiving daily assistance for her care from the abusive spouse. A well-meaning worker decides to remove the woman from her home for "her own good" and place her in a nursing home. The assumption is that moving the woman to the nursing home has made her safer, but, in reality, the abusive spouse continues to have access to her. There is also the potential for additional abuse perpetrated by staff or other residents. These issues underscore the challenge of providing services to older individuals experiencing abuse.

Respect confidentiality. Assuring confidentiality with older survivors of abuse is as important as it is with younger survivors, but it may present additional challenges with the elderly. In a mandatory reporting state, inform the survivor of what information needs to be reported and under what circumstances. Discuss with the survivor what the ramifications such a report may have in his or her life and plan for the survivor's safety after the report is made. Inquiries about suspected abuse should be made in private, with only the person who is experiencing the abuse present; family members or others should not be within earshot. When working with someone who has language barriers or speech or cognitive disabilities, workers can mistakenly direct conversation to the family member or helper that is assisting rather than directly to the survivor. When working with a survivor with language or speech difficulties, use an outside interpreter, if necessary; never ask friends or family members to interpret.

Use an empowerment and survivor-centered approach. Effective interventions generally focus (to the degree possible) on restoring the survivors' control over their lives. A survivor-centered approach focuses on the older individual's strengths and safety needs, recognizing that individuals can best judge their own safety and risk. The person being abused is the primary client, not the entire family. Professionals work with the survivor to create a plan that focuses on the older adult's goals and safety needs (Hightower et al. 2006). Survivors should neither be encouraged nor discouraged to maintain a relationship with the abuser. This approach promotes anchoring the power with survivors for making decisions. Information about the dynamics of abuse and available resources should be provided to support the person in making an informed choice.

When a victim wants to maintain contact with her abuser, focus on safety planning and breaking her isolation. Ask her what a successful intervention would be for her situation. Many older adults who are being abused want to continue to have a relationship with their abuser; they simply want the abuse to end (Hightower et al. 2006; Vinton 1992). This is particularly true if she is being abused by an adult child. Many older women were raised to believe that their most important role in life was to be a wife and mother. They feel that they are in some way responsible for their child's abusive behavior. For older women who choose to maintain contact with or live with their abuser, strategies to interrupt the isolation and to ensure safety are important. Women who choose to end the relationship may need financial resources, housing assistance, and ongoing support.

Offer various options by being familiar with community resources. Clients may benefit from referrals to a number of specific services. Support groups for older women or survivors of domestic violence can be very helpful (Hightower et al. 2006; Vinton 1992). The domestic violence or sexual assault hotline—available 24 hours a day—provides support and information by phone. Legal advocacy can include protective orders, information on immigration laws, and accompaniment through the court process. In cases where the older individual has significant physical or cognitive limitations, adult protective services or elder abuse agencies may be helpful. The aging network, the faith community, and culturally specific groups also offer a number of programs that can break isolation and provide social contacts. To find information about these programs, contact a state unit on aging, a local area agency on aging, the National State Units on Aging, or the National Association of Area Agencies on Aging (Spangler and Brandl 2007). For specific information on contacting these resources, see the list of resources at the end of the chapter.

CASE STUDY

MARTA GARCIA

When Marta Garcia reached out for services, she was a 66-year-old widow. She and her husband had moved from Mexico five years earlier to a small, rural community in Colorado to live closer to their adult daughter, who had moved to the United States years earlier to find a job. Marta spoke some English and had a part-time job at a local, family-operated Mexican restaurant. Her husband had been physically and sexually abusive throughout their 40-year marriage. Marta was an active Catholic who did not believe in divorce. She stayed with her husband until his death nine months earlier.

Marta lived in a small apartment. Four months ago, her daughter and daughter's boyfriend moved in with her after having been evicted from their residence. The boyfriend stole Marta's money and threatened her. He had a large snake and a gun that he used to taunt and intimidate her. Marta was so frightened for her safety that she moved out and spent several days and nights living in her car. Cold, tired, and hungry, she went to the local senior center to meet with a counselor for help.

CONSIDERATIONS

BUILDING A RELATIONSHIP

Take the time necessary to build rapport when talking with a survivor of abuse in later life. Inquire about the victim's family, grandchildren, other family members, and friends. In the case described above, the worker could immediately begin building rapport by addressing her client as Mrs. Garcia rather than using her first name until Marta requested it. That Marta was active in the Catholic Church indicates that her faith and religious practices were important to her.

It is also important to discover the outcome the survivor hopes for in the situation. Find out the fears a survivor has about making changes in her current living situation. Discussing a survivor's fears and wishes can later help to identify the obstacles the survivor may face when trying to make the changes they she wants to make. In the above situation, Marta's role as a mother was a key factor in her life, and she had no interest in changing that.

When working with older adults experiencing abuse, focus on the safety of the survivors. Explore the options available to improve their safety. Although no plan is foolproof, and some abusers continue to stalk and do harm, safety planning is a vital component of an effective intervention. Discuss the dynamics of family violence with the survivor and stay alert to potential risks that are identified, even inadvertently.

In Marta's case, a number of safety aspects had to be considered. She had been threatened with a gun and a snake. She had been living in her car without adequate food, water, heat, or access to her medications. Having been widowed and living alone, her relationship with her daughter was important to her and she wanted it to continue even though the daughter's boyfriend was abusive.

Initial conversations with Marta should focus on where she could live safely, both short and long term, and should also address the threats made by the daughter's boyfriend. For example, could a local domestic abuse program provide emergency housing for Marta? Were emergency housing funds available in her area? Could she identify other family members or friends with whom she could stay for the short term? Long-term solutions required a discussion on how to remove her daughter and her daughter's boyfriend from Marta's apartment or, alternatively, how to seek other long-term housing. If Marta had decided she wanted her daughter to remain with her, safety planning would have become more difficult but not impossible. The worker would need to focus on removing the gun and the snake from the premises; the possibility of any emergency notifying device she could use such as a call help pendant or necklace; neighbors or church members who could be alerted to the problem; working out a code word to inform a caller that a potential victim is in danger; and instructions on calling for help or creating the opportunity for others to visit regularly. Workers would have to be creative and remember to focus on safety planning no matter what decision Marta made.

USING AN EMPOWERMENT MODEL

In cases of abuse in later life, the abuser systematically removes choices and options from the person being abused. Restoring decision-making power to the individual being harmed is often an effective strategy to help someone who has experienced abuse regain confidence and control over her life again. A survivor-centered empowerment model requires that the worker assist the older adult in identifying what she would like to have happen and creating a successful plan. It builds on the strengths and strategies that a person who has lived with abuse has relied upon to stay safe.

In Marta's case, a worker pointed out some of Marta's strengths. Many of these were discovered while talking with Marta while building rapport. As noted, she was active in the Catholic Church and her faith was important to her. She was loyal to her religious beliefs regarding her marriage vows to her husband. It took great courage for Marta to reach out for help and face the changes that may be required for her to protect herself. She was maintaining her own apartment and had a job that she enjoyed.

Marta wanted to move back into her apartment and have her daughter and the boyfriend move out. She wanted to be free from harassment by the boyfriend, but she wanted to maintain a relationship with her daughter. She wanted to keep her job. She also said that she wanted to talk to someone who spoke her language.

DEVELOPING AND IMPLEMENTING A PLAN

Marta and the worker put the following plan in place:

1. Marta stayed at the local domestic abuse shelter where she received legal advocacy to assist her in getting a protective order so she could move back into her own home.

2. Arrangements were made for Marta to meet with her daughter (without the daughter's boyfriend present) and a Spanish-speaking counselor. During these meetings, Marta expressed concern for her daughter's safety. They were able to talk freely and begin to rebuild their relationship. The daughter decided that she and her boyfriend would move out. She initially pressured Marta to pay their expenses or let them move back in. With support from friends, the domestic violence program, her counselor, and the senior center staff, Marta was able to learn strategies to set boundaries with her daughter.

3. Marta joined a support group at the senior center, tailored to meet the needs of older survivors of abuse. This group was co-sponsored by the local domestic abuse agency and provided an ongoing support network of other survivors experiencing some of the same issues.

ADDRESSING ADDITIONAL ISSUES

1. *Mandatory report to APS.* Colorado does not have a mandatory reporting statute for elder abuse, so a report was not required. In many states Marta would not have met the statutory definition of an at-risk or vulnerable adult and would not have been eligible for APS services. In states with an age-based definition, a mandatory report may have been necessary, and the worker would have told Marta of the requirement immediately. She may also have been eligible for some support, referrals, and APS services.

2. *Immigration status.* The local Domestic Violence program and senior center did not ask Marta about her immigration status. Though initially fearful to talk to professionals because they could contact immigration authorities, she was relieved to find that this was not an issue with these professionals.

3. *Health.* Marta's health status was relatively good. As she worked more with the senior center, the staff discovered that Marta needed glasses and had not seen a doctor for some time. She was given information to help her address these needs.

4. *Family and religious values.* Because of Marta's religious values and beliefs about divorce, she stayed with her husband until his death. Because of her family values and view of what it meant to be a parent, Marta wanted to continue to have a relationship with her daughter, despite the daughter's abusive boyfriend and attempts to manipulate Marta for money and resources. Marta gave her daughter money and continued to see her, but only in supervised settings so that the boyfriend could not join them.

5. *Generational values.* Marta was concerned about her maternal role and forcing her daughter to move out of her house. She believed her duty as a mother was to care for her daughter and share whatever resources the family had. Marta received support from her church community, friends, and the domestic abuse program to take care of herself, and she learned other ways to fulfill her role as a mother to her child.

6. *English not the primary language.* Because Marta spoke limited English, communication was a significant issue. Although a Spanish-speaking counselor was available in Marta's case, this is not true for many non–English-speaking survivors.

7. *Rural community and confidentiality.* Marta was worried that because she lived in a small community, others would come to know about the treatment at the hands of her daughter and boyfriend. On the other hand, she had benefited from the various systems working together and professionals who knew one another and also available resources.

8. *Involvement of law enforcement or APS.* Marta was fearful that if law enforcement or APS were contacted, her immigration status would be questioned. Marta also did not want her daughter to go to jail. In Mexico Marta had experienced problems with law enforcement and the system's response when she sought help from the abuse by her husband.

In Marta's case, professionals worked closely together to provide an array of options and services to enhance her safety, decrease her isolation, and support her. A collaborative response is often crucial to the success of abuse in later life cases.

COLLABORATION

Collaboration can be an effective tool to better meet the needs of older adults suffering abuse. Working with persons from different systems and cultures creates challenges and issues around defining abuse, agency philosophy, historical tensions, and different work styles. It requires a willingness to have frank discussions with all members present, as well as the effort to encourage key players to attend meetings. If collaborators can agree that the goal is survivor safety and ending abuse, workers can save time and resources recognizing how they can learn from one another rather than working in isolation. Cross-training between disciplines can be useful for understanding what services each agency offers and how the different programs can compliment one another.

Because abuse in later life crosses all racial, ethnic, religious, economic, and cultural groups, coalitions on abuse in later life must address the needs of diverse groups in a community. To create a truly effective coalition, the needs and issues for the entire community must be addressed. This requires individuals to make a conscious decision to take steps to connect with marginalized communities in their area (National Clearinghouse on Abuse in Later Life and AARP National Training Project 2004).

CONCLUSION

When examining abuse in later life, many similarities to younger battered women emerge. Working with the aging population adds additional challenges and unique situations as professionals assist survivors in creating a peaceful place in their personal world, whether or not they choose to maintain a relationship with their abuser. Options can become increasingly complicated by additional fears and risks for the survivor. Living with the memories and consequences of societal oppression in the United States and the current ageism, racism, and homophobia that continues in society today, older adults from marginalized communities experiencing abuse face additional challenges. Workers must be diligent to learn all they can about these populations, be vigilant to use respectful terms, and keep an open mind when working with the older adults to determine what a successful outcome may look like to the survivor.

RESOURCES

Adult Protective Services
Web site: http://www.napsa.org

American Association of Retired Persons (AARP)
601 E Street, NW
Washington, DC 20049
Phone: 1 (888) 687–2277
Web site: http://www.aarp.org

American Bar Association—Commission on Law and Aging
740 15th Street NW, 9th floor

Washington, DC 20005
Phone: 202–662–8690
Web site: http://www.abanet.org/aging

American Society on Aging
833 Market Street, Suite 511
San Francisco, California 94103
Phone: (415) 974–9641
Web site: http://www.asaging.org

Lesbian and Gay Aging Issues Network (LGAIN)
See information, above, for the American Society on Aging

National Association of Area Agencies on Aging
Web site: http://www.N4A.org

National Center on Elder Abuse (NCEA)
1201 15th Street NW, Suite 350
Washington, DC 20005
Phone: (202) 898–2586
Web site: http://www.elderabusecenter.org
E-mail: ncea@nasua.org

National Clearinghouse on Abuse in Later Life (NCALL)
307 S. Paterson Street, Suite 1
Madison, Wisconsin 53703
Phone: (608) 255–0539
Web site: http://www.ncall.us
E-mail: ncall@wcadv.org

National Domestic Violence Hotline
Phone: 1–800–799-SAFE (for information about local programs)
Phone: 1–800–858-HOPE (for local sexual assault services)

National State Units on Aging
Web site: http://www.nasua.org
Senior Action in a Gay Environment (SAGE)
305 Seventh Avenue, 16th Floor
New York, New York 10001
Phone: (212) 741–2247

REFERENCES

Allen, M., and A. Turner. (2006). Abuse in later life in LGBT communities. *Wisconsin Coalition Against Domestic Violence*, 25(2), 8–11.

American Prosecutors Research Institute. 2003. *Fifty-one Experiments in Combating Elder Abuse: A Survey of State Criminal Laws Relating to Elder Abuse and Mandatory Reporting.* Alexandria, VA: National District Attorney's Association, American Prosecutors Research Institute, National District Attorneys Association.

Anetzberger, G. (1998). Psychological abuse and neglect: A cross-cultural concern to older Americans. In Archstone Foundation (Ed.), *Understanding and Combating Elder Abuse in Minority Communities* (pp. 141–151). Long Beach, CA: Archstone Foundation.

Brandl, B. (2002) *From a Web of Fear and Isolation to a Community Safety Net: Cross-training on Abuse in Later Life, Participant Manual.* Madison, WI: National Clearinghouse on Abuse in Later Life, a project of the Wisconsin Coalition Against Domestic Violence, Pennsylvania Coalition Against Domestic Violence, and the Pennsylvania Department of Aging.

——. Brandl, B. (2005). *Mandatory Reporting of Elder Abuse: Implications for Domestic Violence Advocates.* Madison, WI: National Clearinghouse on Abuse in Later Life/Wisconsin Coalition Against Domestic Violence.

Brown, A. (1989). A survey on elder abuse at one Native American tribe. *Journal of Elder Abuse and Neglect*, 1(2), 17 – 37.

Brownell, P. (1997). The application of the culturagram in cross-cultural practice with elder abuse victims. *Journal of Elder Abuse and Neglect*, 2, 19–33.

Brownell, P., et al. (1999). Mental health and criminal justice issues among perpetrators of elder abuse. *Journal of Elder Abuse and Neglect*, 11(4), 81–94.

Capezuti, E., et al. (1997). Reporting elder mistreatment. *Journal of Gerontological Nursing*, July, 24–32.

Faulkner, L. (1982). Mandating the reporting of suspected cases of elder abuse: An inappropriate, ineffective and ageist response to the abuse of older adults. *Family Law Quarterly*, 16(1), 69–91.

Godkin, M., R. Wolf, and K. Pillemer. (1989). A case-comparison of elder abuse and neglect. *International Journal of Aging and Human Development*, 28(3), 207–225.

Gondolf, E. (1998). *Assessing Woman Battering in Mental Health Services.* Thousand Oaks, CA: Sage.

Griffin, L. (1994). Elder maltreatment among rural African-Americans. *Journal of Elder Abuse and Neglect*, 6(1), 1– 27.

Henrichsen, Gregory A. (2006). Why multicultural issues matter for practitioners working with older adults. *Professional Psychology: Research and Practice*, 37(1), 29–35.

Hightower, J., M. J. Smith, and H. Hightower. (2006). Hearing voices of abused older women. *Journal of Gerontological Social Work*, 46(3/4), 205–227.

Hudson, M., and J. Carlson. (1999). Elder abuse: Its meaning to Caucasians, African Americans, and Native Americans. In T. Tatara (Ed.), *Understanding Elder Abuse in Minority Populations* (pp. 187–204). Philadelphia: Brunner/ Mazel.

Hyman, A. (1994). Mandatory reporting of domestic violence by health care providers: A misguided approach. Paper by the Family Violence Prevention Fund, *Women's Health Issues* (winter 1995), 5(4), 208–213. Available at http://www.ncbi. nlm.nih.gov/pubmed/PMID: 8574117 [PubMed—indexed for MEDLINE].

International Longevity Center-USA (ILC-USA), with the Schmieding Center for Senior Health and Education (SCSHE) Task Force. (2006). *Caregiving in America*. Available at http://www.ilcusa.org/media/pdfs/Caregiving%20in%20America-%20Final.pdf (accessed April 1, 2009).

Lachs, M. S., C. S. Williams, S. O'Brien, K. A. Pillemer, and M. E. Charlson. (1998). The mortality of elder mistreatment. *Journal of the American Medical Association 208*, 428–432.

Lundy, M., and S. Grossman. (2004). Elder abuse: Spouse/intimate partner abuse and family violence among elders. *Journal of Elder Abuse and Neglect*, 16(1), 85–102.

Mellor, M. J., and P. Brownell (Eds.). (2006). *Elder Abuse and Mistreatment: Policy, Practice, and Research*. Binghamton, NY: Haworth.

Moon, A., and O. Williams. (1993). Perceptions of elder abuse and help-seeking patterns among African-American, Caucasian American and Korean-American Elderly Women. *Gerontologist*, 33, 386–395.

Mouton, C., S. Rovi, K. Furniss, and N. Lasser. (1999). The associations between health and domestic violence in older women: Results of a pilot study. *Journal of Women's Health and Gender-Based Medicine*, 8(9), 1173–1179.

National Center on Elder Abuse et al. (2006). The 2004 survey of state Adult Protective Services: Abuse of adults 60 years of age and older. Funded by the Administration on Aging, U.S. Department of Health and Human Services. Available at http://www.ncea.aoa.gov/NCEAroot/Main_Site/Library/Statistics_Research/ Abuse_Statistics/National_Statistics.aspx (accessed April 1, 2009).

National Clearinghouse on Abuse in Later Life, AARP National Training Project. (2004). Building a Coalition to Address Domestic Abuse in Later Life. Available at: http://www.ncall.us (accessed April 1, 2009).

Otiniano, M., et al. (1998). Hispanic elder abuse. In Archstone Foundation (Ed.), *Understanding and Combating Elder Abuse in Minority Communities*. Long Beach, CA: Archstone Foundation.

Phillips, L., E. de Ardon, and G. Briones. (2000). Abuse of female caregivers by care recipients: Another form of elder abuse. *Journal of Elder Abuse and Neglect*, 12(3/4), 123–144.

Pillemer, K., and D. Finkelhor. (1989). Causes of elder abuse: Caregiver stress versus problem relatives. *American Journal of Orthopsychiatry*, 59(2), 179–187.

——. (1988). The prevalence of elder abuse: A random sample survey. *Gerontologist*, 28(1), 51–57.

Podnieks, E. (1992). National survey on abuse of the elderly in Canada. *Journal of Elder Abuse and Neglect*, 4(1/2), 5–58.

Reis, M. (2000). The IOA Screen: An abuse-alert measure that dispels myths. *Generations*, 24(11), 13–16.

Reis, M., and D. Nahmiash. (1998). Validation of the Indicators of Abuse (IOA) Screen. *Gerontologist*, 38(4), 471–480.

——. (1997). Abuse of seniors: Personality, stress, and other indicators. *Journal of Mental Health and Aging*, 3(3), 337–356.

Salter, A. (2003). *Predators, Pedophiles, Rapists, and Other Sex Offenders: Who They Are, How They Operate, and How We Can Protect Ourselves and Our Children*. New York: Basic Books.

Sanchez, Y. (1999). Elder mistreatment in Mexican American communities: The Nevada and Michigan experiences. In T. Tatara (Ed.), *Understanding Elder Abuse in Minority Populations* (pp. 67–77). Philadelphia: Brunner/Mazel.

Schechter, S. (1987). *Guidelines for Mental Health Practitioners in Domestic Violence Cases*. Denver: National Coalition Against Domestic Violence.

Seaver, C. (1996). Muted lives: Older battered women. *Journal of Elder Abuse and Neglect*, 8(2), 3–21.

Spangler, D., and B. Brandl. (2007). Abuse in later life: Power and control dynamics and a victim-centered response. *Journal of the American Psychiatric Nurses Association*, 12(6), 322–331.

U.S. Census Bureau. (2005). 65+ in the United States. Available at http://www.census.gov/prod/1/pop/p23-190/p23-190.html (accessed April 1, 2009).

——. (2001). Age: 2000, Census 2000 Brief. Available at http://www.census.gov/prod/2001pubs/c2kbr01-12.pdf (accessed April 1, 2009).

U.S. Department of Health and Human Services, Administration on Aging. (2005). Profile of Older Americans: 2005. Available at http://www.aarp.org/research/reference/statistics/aresearch-import-519.html (accessed April 1, 2009).

Vinton, L. (1992). The status of older battered women. AARP Women's Initiative,

Forum on Older Battered Women. Washington, DC: American Association of Retired Persons.

Whitfield, K. E., and D. Brandon. (2000). Individual differences, ethnicity, and aging: What can gero-genetic studies contribute? *African American Research Perspectives*, 6(2), 115–121.

Wolf, R. (2000) The nature and scope of elder abuse. *Generations- Journal of the American Society on Aging.* 24(2), 6–12.

Wolf, R., and K. Pillemer. (1997). Older battered women: Wives and mothers compared. *Journal of Mental Health and Aging*, 3(3), 325–336.

8

CULTURALLY COMPETENT PRACTICE WITH LATINAS

Blanca M. Ramos, Bonnie E. Carlson, and Shanti Kulkarni

AT THE turn of the twenty-first century, Latinos represent the largest, fastest growing ethnic/racial minority in the United States. There are approximately 44 million Latinos, of which 17 million (52%) are women (U.S. Census Bureau 2007). The dramatic growth of the Latina subpopulation has important ethical implications for social workers who must be culturally competent in practice with diverse clients (National Association of Social Workers [NASW] 2001). "Latinas" is the umbrella term for women with Latin American roots, whose identifiable characteristics differentiate them from women of other ethnicities. Latinas trace their ancestry to several different countries, including Mexico and others located in the Caribbean and Central and South America (Parrillo 2000). Yet, despite their substantial cultural uniqueness and individuality, some generalizations can be made drawing upon their shared Latino values, traditions, sentiments, and cultural networks. These similarities provide the sociocultural context for this chapter.

This chapter provides a working knowledge on intimate partner violence (IPV) toward Latinas and explores strategies for cultural competent practice with victims. We begin with a brief portrayal of Latinas, focusing on the ecological contexts in which Latinas are embedded. An overview of the incidence of IPV toward Latinas and of risk and protective factors follows. We then review strengths and limitations of traditional and cultural-specific domestic violence approaches. A case study illustrates the application of culturally competent strategies in generalist practice with abused Latinas. The ecological perspective provides an organizing framework throughout the discussion.

CULTURAL DIMENSIONS

This section provides a glimpse into the cultural influences that define and structure some aspects of Latinas' collective group life. Latino culture reflects the language and the overarching cultural values, beliefs, and norms of its legacy of Spanish colonial, African, and indigenous culture. Latino culture blended these cultural traits, speech patterns, food, and music. Western culture also has affected Latin American societies through industrialization and modernization. A discussion of the key core values of familism, collectivism, *simpatia*, and respect can help in understanding the sociocultural realities of Latinas. This collective narrative is constructed loosely so that generalizations offered here still acknowledge cultural borderlands and Latinas' individuality (Falicov 1998).

Familism is perhaps the single most salient cultural influence grounding Latina women's experience; it lies at the center of gender socialization and supports the social construction of womanhood (Flores-Ortiz 1993). Its system of attitudes, beliefs, and norms sanctions and legitimizes a patriarchal, hierarchical structure. For example, *machismo* and *marianismo* prescribe appropriate hierarchical female and male domains, as well as the roles, both individually and collectively, that must be assumed in the community and at home. Men are the breadwinners and protectors of the family, and women are the kin keepers, nurturers, and caregivers. Inaccurate interpretations have resulted at times in unidimensional, negative stereotypes of *machismo* and *marianismo*, wherein men are depicted as authoritarian and domineering and women as submissive and powerless (Ramos 1997). As defined in Latino societies, *machismo* also directs men to behave with honor and courage, and *marianismo* prescribes women to be strong, flexible, perseverant, and able to survive (Comas-Diaz 1993). Familism underscores the centrality of the family, promoting close ties to nuclear and extended family, including non-kin members, as well as interdependence, loyalty, affiliation, and reciprocity (Marin and Marin 1991).

Collectivism contrasts with mainstream values of individualism, emphasizing the group as the central locus for behavior and prioritizing the needs of the group over those of the individual (Marin and Marin 1991). *Simpatia* promotes positive, amiable social interactions, and *respeto* commands adherence to authority, determining appropriate differential behaviors based on a complex set of rules according to gender, age, and socioeconomic and authority status (Comas-Diaz 1993). For example, respect has been traditionally accorded to a family's adult males, who are to be treated with deference and obedience, reinforcing the power differential ascribed to men through patriarchy.

Although certain elements of familism, collectivism, *simpatia*, and *respeto* still persist among Latinas (especially as newly transitioned immigrants), current practices reflect adaptations to continuous person-environment interactions in the United States. For example, Latinas' increased participation in the workforce challenges cultural norms prescribing men to be the sole economic provider and also diminishing women's availability to fulfill familism expectations. Traditional gender roles are transformed and replaced with less clear-cut, more fluid, flexible roles. Nonetheless, familial roles and a patriarchal structure continue to influence Latinas gender identities and daily experiences (Ramos 1997).

One must understand Latino cultural practices within the environmental complexities and geographic setting in which they originated in order to have an accurate perspective of the culture. When practiced outside their original environmental contexts or in extreme, static, or rigid ways, traditional cultural traits can sometimes become maladaptive and dysfunctional, adversely affecting the fit between the individual and the environment. Further, the interaction of culture with social structures that perpetuate inequality and oppression can be conducive to harmful, even destructive behaviors. IPV toward women provides a prime example of this predicament.

THE SOCIOHISTORICAL CONTEXT

The sociopolitical history of Latinos greatly affects the lives of contemporary Latinas. This includes the historical circumstances under which each subgroup has come into contact with mainstream society—through the relocation of borders for Mexican Americans and Puerto Ricans in the nineteenth century or immigration for all other subgroups from the early twentieth century until now. These events initiated the ongoing experiences of prejudice, inequality, and racism. Mexican or Puerto Rican older Latinas heard firsthand accounts of the traumatic experiences of ancestors who suddenly were deemed inferior and encompassed by a different cultural value system (Ramos, Jones, and Toseland 2005). Cubans from the second major wave of exiles in the 1980s, who were mostly urban working class of dark skin and lower socioeconomic status, encountered a negative national reception fueled

by racism, growing economic troubles, and media accounts that sensational-
ized the felons and mentally ill whom Castro sent among these refugees (Parrillo 2000). For some clusters of Central Americans in the 1990s who sought
political refuge, the government's aid and welcoming has not been favorable,
and most have not been granted political asylum and remain in this country
with undocumented status (McGoldrick, Giordano, and Pearce 2005).

For more than a century, Latina immigrants have endured a social system
wherein continuous anti-immigrant sentiments have hindered, challenged, or
deterred their successful integration into the larger society. Further, in a race-
conscious society, discrimination and racial prejudice is more pronounced
against Latinas, whose darker skin color and physical features more closely
resemble people of Native American or African ancestry.

Through time, Latinas have experienced oppression as a result both of
racism and sexism. Latinas have endured a subordinate status because of
the presumption of male superiority predicated on the ideology of sexism,
as has occurred for centuries with women in patriarchal societies. The persistent, negative effects of sexism continue to shape the lives of Latinas
today. The social inequalities Latinas face as women overlay racial discrimination and ethnic prejudice. This double oppression is clearly illustrated
by the exploitation suffered by Latinas in the labor force. Latinas have
made substantial contributions to the U.S. economy as domestic, factory,
sweatshop, and migrant workers, enduring deplorable working conditions
that require long, physically demanding hours for very low pay and few or
no benefits (Hesse-Biber and Carter 2004). Today the patterns remain of
disempowerment, marginality, and social disadvantage resulting from his-
toric unequal distribution of resources, social exclusion, and differential
treatment. Latinas are among the poorest, most vulnerable, and exploited
groups in U.S. society. Current labor force participation among Latinas
without legal status closely mirrors that of a century ago and indicates the
lack of progress made.

Historically, members of oppressed groups have drawn upon their own
communities and culture for survival and continuity, relying on their racial
and ethnic identities as sources of strength, pride, and support. For Latinas,
distinct non-Western cultural elements, some of which have been practiced
for generations, have often offered the means to cope, adapt, or resist oppressive environments. These include, for example, reliance on large kinship networks for resources and support, fatalistic beliefs for coping, and resilience in
the face of hardship and distress. Some of these remain and are continuously

readapted and revitalized as a result of back-and-forth migration, continued immigration, and globalization. As such, Latinas' current sociopolitical realities are intertwined with their cultural contexts.

SOCIODEMOGRAPHIC CHARACTERISTICS

Among Latinas, Mexicans (59%) and Puerto Ricans (10%) comprise the largest segment. Latinas are geographically dispersed throughout the United States and can be found in every state, both in rural and urban areas. They tend to be young—the median age is 27 years—with 56 percent under 30 and 37 percent under 20. More than half are married (55%), 58 percent have children under the age of 18, and 83 percent have a spouse living in the household. Latinas head 12 percent of Latino families with the highest rate among Puerto Ricans (48%). Many Latinas were born outside the continental United States (38%) (Giachello 2001; U.S. Census Bureau 2007). Although they all speak Spanish, distinct dialects and other cultural nuances, depending on the country of origin, distinguish these groups of Latinas.

Latinas exhibit a vulnerable socioeconomic profile. Only 54 percent of those 25 years of age and older, largely those born in the U.S., have finished high school, and only 10 percent have some college education. Their unemployment rate is twice that of white non-Latinas (11%). Most hold low-paying jobs and few have professional-managerial positions. The median income among full-time workers hovers between $15,000 and $20,000. Over 24 percent live in poverty, especially families headed by single women. The poverty rates for Latinas are as follows: Dominicans, 49 percent; Puerto Ricans, 39 percent; Mexicans, 38 percent; Central and South Americans, 27 percent; and Cubans, 15 percent. Myriad socioeconomic disadvantages negatively affect Latinas' well-being and severely curtail health-care access and utilization (Giachello 2001; U.S. Census Bureau 2007).

DOMESTIC VIOLENCE AGAINST LATINAS

Available data on the prevalence rates of IPV against Latinas show substantial variability. As with most domestic violence statistics, wide variations in prevalence reflect methodological differences in definitions of domestic violence, sampling, and data collection. Estimates for past-year prevalence range from a high of 35 percent to a low of 2.3 percent (Kantor, Jasinski, and Aldarondo 1994; Plichta 1996; Straus and Smith 1995). In a recent national study, 55 percent of the Latina sample reported violent victimization (National Women's Law Center 2000). In a study of 309 mostly immigrant Latinas from Mexico in the Southeast, 70 percent reported violent victimization in the previous year (Murdaugh et al. 2004).

Comparative data are also inconsistent. For example, Straus and Smith (1995) found that past-year marital violence rates were 23 percent for Latino couples compared to 15 percent for white couples. Other studies found lower IPV (15%) among Latinas than non-Latinas (18%); specifically, a rate of 7 percent for Latinas compared to white (9%) and black (12%) women (Tjaden and Thoennes 1998). Research also indicates similar IPV rates for Latinas compared to other racial and ethnic groups (Kantor et al. 1994). Although the findings on prevalence rates are inconclusive, IPV still appears to be a serious problem for Latinas, and certain socioeconomic, ethnic, and cultural factors may place many at high risk (Ramos and Carlson 2004).

RISK FACTORS FOR IPV TOWARD LATINAS

IPV risk factors may relate to characteristics of the perpetrator, the victim, or both. Latina victims tend to be young, live in urban settings, and are of low socioeconomic status and education, variables known to increase the risk for IPV for women in general (Cunradi, Caetano, and Schafer 2000; Klevens 2007; Lown and Vega 2001). Other risk factors include psychosocial stress (Perilla, Bakerman, and Norris 1994), witnessing IPV as a child (Perilla 1999), use of alcohol by the perpetrator, and childhood victimization (Caetano et al. 2000). Victims have described jealousy and a need for control as factors contributing to Latinos' tendency to engage in IPV (Torres 1991).

Other factors implicated in IPV, such as unemployment of the male partner (Kaufman et al. 1994) and occupational stress (Jasinski, Asdigian, and Kantor 1997) may also increase Latinas' vulnerability to victimization. Gender role reversal, particularly when the male partner is unable to fulfill the role of sole breadwinner, can be a significant risk factor. While women's homemaking skills are more readily transferable, making them highly sought after for low-wage jobs, men find it particularly challenging to gain employment (Vega 1995). This is not uncommon among Latino immigrant families when the gender-specific skills they bring, limited education, and lack of language proficiency interface with oppression, prejudice, and discrimination. A woman's newfound economic power may threaten the male partner, who may then channel his frustration through unhealthy behaviors including IPV. Research indicates that the more a woman contributes to family income, the greater the risk for abuse (Perilla et al. 1994).

Other risks of victimization include being married (Caetano et al. 2000) and having children in the home (Lown and Vega 2001). Social isolation or lack of social support, which may be particularly acute for undocumented Latinas, has been linked to IPV (Lie and Lowery 2003). Also, placing Latinas at high risk is adherence to and deviation from traditional cultural norms that contribute to women's disempowerment, such as the expectation that they are submissive and accord men respect. For instance, a woman's inability to fulfill gender role prescriptions in the home because of outside employment can contribute to IPV. Another factor is the perceived reluctance of Latinas to leave abusive relationships. The reasons behind this reluctance are complex; some decide that they are not ready to leave because of a lack of viable alternatives or economic, immigration, and child-related concerns. Latina immigrants often decide to remain in the relationship as a survival strategy, given the dangers involved in leaving the abuser (Dutton 2000). Cultural prescriptions that reify women's roles as kin keepers and mothers can also contribute. Torres (1991) found that Latinas reported a narrower range of behaviors as IPV and were "more tolerant" of wife abuse than non-Latinas.

Immigration and acculturation may heighten a Latina's vulnerability to IPV by generating multiple life stressors that disrupt the fit between the person and the environment. Immigration brings losses, uncertainties, and daily demands associated with uprooting and resettlement. Undocumented status can add strains stemming from fears of deportation; it severely curtails employment, housing, education, and access to health care. These stressors can elicit IPV from male partners who lack healthy coping strategies. For undocumented Latinas, male partners with legal immigration status can threaten deportation as a way to exert power through abuse and oppressive behavior and to perpetuate the cycle of violence; higher IPV has been found among Latinas with uncertain immigration status (Anderson 1993). Research on the impact on IPV risk of acculturation or the length of time spent in the United States has been inconclusive (Caetano et al. 2000; Ingram 2007).

COMMUNITY REACTIONS TO DOMESTIC VIOLENCE AGAINST LATINAS

Latina victims often first disclose their situation to trusted community members. How confidants react can be critical in setting the course for a successful or unsuccessful resolution of the abuse (Dutton 2000). Community opinions about domestic violence influence whether IPV is recognized as a social problem, ignored, condoned, or rejected, and whether a victim is excluded or supported (Kelly 1996). These beliefs, attitudes, and cultural norms vary across ethnic groups and genders (Locke and Richman 1999). In a recent qualitative study of California-based Mexican immigrants of both genders and including young, middle-aged, and elderly individuals, some participants believed that the family should support victims, although most thought that the family would not want to become involved (Klevens et al. 2007). Participants also suggested that victims should get divorced or leave the abuser. For victims, friends had been the most supportive, and neighbors ignored or minimized the situation. Some participants thought that the victim or her family and friends should call the police, whereas others were reluctant to involve the police because of language barriers and potential problems for the Latino community. In response to an IPV vignette that guided the study discussion, many—both men and women—faulted the woman. They also mentioned "a change in culture" as the cause for IPV, suggesting that marital conflicts result from disparities between the rights and independence that mainstream American culture accords women, not traditionally available in Latin America (Klevens et al. 2007). Klevens and her colleagues concluded that, in the Latino community they studied, domestic violence is recognized as a problem and the community is aware of its potential causes and consequences. Although more research is needed that would permit broader generalizations, this finding is encouraging, for apparently some Latinos may be responding positively to public education about IPV, such as posters in Spanish in community settings and educational messages interwoven into the plots of popular soap operas and discussed on talk programs on Spanish TV. Yet some deeply rooted traditional Latino attitudes may continue to work against community efforts to support victims. Prescriptions to keep family problems behind closed doors run counter to views of IPV as a community rather than a private problem, a cornerstone of the antiviolence movement. Similarly public attitudes that blame the victim and condone IPV may be difficult to eradicate, particularly among Latinos socialized in more rigid patriarchal societies.

A few mostly grassroots movements aimed at mobilizing Latinas and their communities to participate collectively in efforts to end IPV, and to generate resources for victims, are slowly emerging. These initiatives offer linguistic and cultural sensitive services for Latina victims and their families but often are limited to major metropolitan areas, leaving women in nonmetropolitan and rural areas without services. Much remains to be learned to effectively challenge traditional Latino opinions that may lead to harmful responses and to ensure resources to support victims in their communities. Although crucial for IPV victims, these may be even more critical for Latinas, who historically have had limited contact with formal institutions, relying primarily on their own communities for continuation and survival.

CULTURALLY SENSITIVE PRACTICE WITH BATTERED LATINAS

TRADITIONAL AND CULTURALLY SPECIFIC DOMESTIC VIOLENCE SERVICES

A most significant advance of the battered women's movement is the development of multiple interventions and preventive strategies for victims, which are drawn from various theoretical approaches and reflect an interactionist, multi-disciplinary perspective. For example, feminist and grassroots activists, scholars, legal experts, and service professionals have been the driving force behind the surge of shelters, specialized assistance programs and services, community education, and legislation reform and advocacy in the criminal justice system (Kanuha 1994). These strategies, originally based on the needs and experiences of mostly mainstream white, heterosexual, middle-class women, must be viewed with caution by social workers working with Latinas. Although the theoretical underpinnings, particularly feminism, recognize sociocultural factors as essential determinants in IPV, for both its causation and necessary intervention, the focus has been almost exclusively on gender (Espin 1994). Unaddressed is the impact of gender inequality as it intersects with other forms of individual and structural inequalities and the marginalization in the lives of battered Latinas.

To increase their effectiveness and appeal to Latina victims, traditional IPV services must be relevant to their distinct environmental contexts. Recent approaches call for culturally specific services challenging the primacy of gender and underscoring the simultaneous, interlocking nature of gender with race, ethnicity, class, age, immigration status, geographical location, and varying levels of emotional, physical, and mental abilities in understanding IPV and society's response (Sokoloff and Dupont 2005). Culturally sensitive practice with Latina victims should take into account their multiple, complex ecological contexts, which extend beyond gender, including their own and mainstream cultures, immigration, and ethnic minority status. Consistent with a basic tenet of feminist practice, personal changes must accompany social change through social action and empowerment. However, culturally specific models of IPV are still not widespread, and social workers must be ready to address ensuing barriers emerging from the micro, mezzo, and macro levels of practice that can seriously interfere with appropriate and effective practice with battered Latinas.

BARRIERS TO LATINAS UTILIZING TRADITIONAL DOMESTIC ABUSE SERVICES

The benefits of traditional IPV services seldom reach Latina victims. Data consistently indicate that Latinas underutilize traditional IPV services primarily owing to barriers that derive from cultural differences and shortcomings inherent in traditional IPV services (Ingram 2007).

CULTURE-BOUND VALUES AND LINGUISTIC BARRIERS Latinas want to escape, avoid, and stop their victimization and actively engage in efforts to prevent, confront, endure, and end domestic abuse (Dutton 2000). Although formal services can facilitate these efforts, cultural values influence a woman's perception of the problem, her preferred ways to resolve it, and how she seeks help. Furthermore, as discussed above, certain cultural values may dissuade Latinas directly or indirectly from using traditional IPV services. The extent to which cultural values can constitute a barrier can vary significantly as a function of a victim's acculturation level and sociodemographic characteristics.

First, some Latinas may have difficulty recognizing that the abusive situation is a violation of basic human rights and that they are entitled to receive help. Victims may not recognize IPV as a problem, may deny or ignore their own needs, and may choose not to seek outside support, reflecting the values of collectivism and familism that expect women to keep the peace in the family and prioritize its needs above their own (Vazquez 1994).

Second, a victim who is ready to disclose the abuse, perhaps out of concern for the safety of her children or because of increased public awareness or acculturation, may wish to do so in harmony with cultural norms that define the type of problems for which a woman can seek assistance and from whom it is acceptable to receive it. She may prefer to utilize an informal network where family and non-kin members of her social network provide mutual advice and support. An abused Latina may fear that seeking help from someone outside this network would reflect her family unit's inability to meet its own needs, which threatens the cherished values of pride and dignity. A victim may be concerned about losing face and its consequent stigma that extends to the nuclear family and broader Latino community. Because of deep-rooted internalized beliefs, she may blame herself for the abuse and feel ashamed and guilty, which would lead to further isolation.

Third, for Latina victims who opt to use traditional services, linguistic and cultural dissonance and value conflicts may not only jeopardize effectiveness but may also discourage continued participation. For example, the Western value of individualism, in contrast to Latino collectivism, promotes independence, autonomy, and an ability to become one's own person (Sue 2006). Victims may find it troubling to accept individual-centered services geared to benefit the individual first and foremost, often even to the exclusion of the family. Individualism also runs counter to familism's prescriptions of reciprocity and interdependence. Its emphasis on the nuclear family as a basic principle of social organization overshadows the important role that family and social networks play in the lives of Latina victims. Overall, culture can exert a powerful influence on a Latina victim's decision to use formal services to strengthen her efforts to manage the situation. Despite its crucial role, culture does not function in a vacuum. In the lives of Latina victims it is mediated through structural forms of oppression.

SHORTCOMINGS OF TRADITIONAL DOMESTIC ABUSE SERVICES Based on her work with battered African American women, Vann (2003) identifies structural barriers common to traditional services. The following sections discuss these structural barriers as they relate to Latina victims.

Failure to Address the Larger Cultural Context Typically, traditional services do not address the multiple ecological contexts of Latina victims' cultural milieus. Their focus on gender inequality tends to ignore other forms of inequality, including those associated with Latinas' place within the dominant culture; such inequality exerts a powerful impact on the daily experiences of Latinas and their communities, which leads to further disempowerment and oppression. Historical forces linked to ethno-cultural translocation, immigration, migration, and colonialism are also integral to understanding the nature and sources of Latinas oppressive environments. Workers should be aware of immigration laws as well as acculturation and resettlement issues as they intertwine with mainstream cultural patterns, social institutions, and political structures. Ethnocentric beliefs inherent to traditional services must be recognized and addressed at the micro, mezzo, and macro levels of practice. For example, attending to linguistic and cultural differences is an important first step to overcome barriers to services for Latinas; they can aid in effective communication and help victims feel comfortable expressing themselves and shed concerns about being misunderstood or judged. Particularly when in crisis, some victims find it easier to share the intense emotions in their first language. Even bilingual Latinas tend to switch back and forth between English and Spanish when experiencing emotional distress (Ramos and Carlson 2004).

Given the multiple forms of oppression that Latinas experience, it is imperative that domestic violence services concurrently address both the dangers of the abusive situation and the dangers of their social positions. Further, the impact of institutional racism on a victim's decision to report and use traditional services must be clearly understood. For example, a decision not to report abuse or seek services in order to protect one's family and community from further stereotyping and stigma may be misconstrued and viewed as denial and acceptance of the woman's victimization, rather than distrust rooted in oppressive institutional practices, particularly by the police and criminal justice system (Kanuha 1994). Thus, as a result of decades of marginalization by the mainstream, Latinas may be reluctant to turn to traditional services for support and remain skeptical about whether these can be beneficial given their ethno-cultural realities.

Victim-Based Focus Since their inception, and consistent with their feminist roots, traditional domestic violence services have attended almost exclusively to the victim's needs, paying limited attention to the needs of affected family members, such as children and the perpetrator. Although this approach originally worked to underscore the unique plight of victimized women in a male-dominated society, its narrow perspective does not accommodate the ethno-cultural realities of abused Latinas. A more culturally appropriate, family-centered approach that recognizes the salience of the family and other Latino cultural values would expand services and resources beyond the victim to her loved ones (including extended family members).

Perhaps the most significant barrier deterring Latinas from using traditional services is its emphasis on encouraging women to leave their abusive partners or to pursue incarceration. Although this emphasis has been intended to ensure the safety and well-being of the victims and end the abuse, it can alienate Latinas from using IPV services. Historically, oppression by the criminal justice system and racist police brutality toward Latinos have exacerbated the magnitude of this barrier; Latina victims often choose to conceal and endure the abuse rather than risk their batterers being injured and maltreated. Taking action against the abuser with these drastic measures for the well-being of individual members, and which may result in the breakup of the family, is incongruent with Latino cultural values of family preservation and unity (familism and collectivism). Services that include culturally sensitive couple therapy and treatment for offenders to reduce further violence may be viable options as long as the focus remains on victim safety and offender accountability.

Limited Comprehensive Services Consistent with their victim-based focus, traditional services attend almost exclusively to the abuse itself. IPV does not occur in a vacuum, however, and Latina victims grapple with a host of life situations concurrently. Services for Latina victims must also address their multiple needs stemming from the adverse conditions of their lives. For example, a woman's efforts to escape the abuse usually requires tangible assistance to find employment, housing, schools for her children, and support to ameliorate the accompanying financial and psychological distress. Some victims may use alcohol or drugs in order to cope with the effects of the abuse, presenting for services with co-occurring health and mental health conditions. Latina immigrants have even more specialized needs for resources and may encounter additional barriers in navigating a disconnected and complicated service delivery system. When Latinas do report their abuse to authorities, legal advocacy is essential to assist them in understanding the intricacies and mechanisms of the judicial process, especially their rights as victims and the implications of immigrant status for both the victim and the perpetrator. Latinas may also need civil legal services to negotiate divorce and custody arrangements.

Advocates have promoted a coordinated community response to IPV with a more comprehensive service delivery system. Culturally sensitive systemic approaches that offer social, health, mental health, and legal services can help close gaps in traditional services. This comprehensive approach should include outreach and treatment for the batterer to prevent continued abuse. Services should also provide victims with tools that help them reduce their economic and social powerlessness and vulnerability. Optimally, these multilevel services should all be offered in one accessible setting with multiple pathways into these services through information and referral networks.

Lack of Access to Services in Latino Communities Although domestic violence services, as traditionally organized, have not had a strong presence in Latino communities, relocating services in geographic proximity to the communities where victims reside can increase access and utilization among Latinos. Latina victims who lack access to transportation may feel apprehensive when venturing outside their familiar surroundings for help, adding to the many challenges they already face. Culturally sensitive services that incorporate the victim's community in the delivery process integrate community members, leaders, and activists into policy development and create linkages with grassroots ethnic organizations, churches, and service professional groups. Given the sensitive nature of IPV, it is essential to ensure that the community, individuals, and institutions involved do not represent a risk to the victims' safety, privacy, and confidentiality, do not endorse victim-blaming ideologies, and are genuinely interested in the well-being of the victims.

Differential Application of Policy Responses It is critical that social workers acquire knowledge of the laws that protect victims and understand how policy is differentially implemented as a function of race and ethnicity, immigrant status, age, sexual orientation, and English-language proficiency.

Ethical Dilemmas and Concerns Social workers continually face ethical dilemmas in their practice and must decide between conflicting and alternative courses of action. Common ethical dilemmas at play when working with Latina victims include mandatory reporting of domestic abuse, confidentiality when a client threatens to harm another person, involving police in communities of color, and assisting undocumented immigrants. Workers must consider the potential unintended consequences of decisions to these dilemmas that may be incongruent with Latina victims' ethno-cultural realities. Confidentiality will especially be an issue in communities where the Latino community is small. Social workers should engage in ethical practice when using interpreters. Ideally an interpreter will be a trained professional with deep cultural knowledge about the Latina for whom she is translating.

Social workers should refrain from using the victim's children to translate, particularly when making sensitive inquiries. Social workers, when deciding on any course of action, must continually weigh the benefits and potential damages to the client.

CULTURALLY COMPETENT INTERVENTIONS WITH BATTERED LATINAS

THE CASE OF ANA

Ana, a 23-year-old immigrant from Mexico, has been married to Juan for six years, and she speaks some English. They have two children, Paulo is 5 years old and Elena is 3. The family has been living in a U.S. border city for five years. Neither Ana nor Juan graduated from high school. Ana is a skillful seamstress, and Juan is a carpenter. Life has been difficult for them in the United States. Juan has not been able to find a regular job and works temporarily in landscaping. Paulo is in kindergarten, and Ana works part-time cleaning homes and brings Elena along. They have difficulty making ends meet and feel scared, disempowered, and alone, knowing that many people in the city openly dislike Hispanics, deny them jobs and services, and constantly persecute them. They are sad and miss the loved ones they left behind. Paulo has asthma and the family has no health insurance, and so Ana and Juan worry about paying for doctor's visits and the medicine their son needs to breathe.

Juan has hit Ana in the past but never often or seriously enough to require medical attention. Lately they argue all the time, particularly about Juan's sporadic jobs, the cost of Paulo's medicine, and Ana's working, which Juan does not like but accepts because they desperately need the money. After work, Juan is spending more time with other men, mostly undocumented landscape workers, who often drink beer and talk about how difficult their lives are in this country and how much they miss their families back home. At first, Ana thought it was good for Juan to have friends with whom he could let off steam. But lately the drinking is lasting long into the night. Sometimes he is so hung over that he is late for work, getting in trouble with his employer. For two weeks Ana has worked very little because her employers are away. She expressed concern to Juan about his drinking, fearful that he will lose his job, and has asked him for money for Paulo's medicine. Juan exploded and hit her in front of the children, who started to cry and scream. The next day she went to work for Ms. Lin with a split lip and a black eye.

Ms. Lin, whom Ana had begun to trust, asked what happened, and she burst into tears. Ana reluctantly told her what Juan had done and how frightened she was that Paulo would get sick if she could not give him his medicine. Ms. Lin told Ana that what Juan did to her was domestic abuse and against the law. Ana initially disagreed

CONTINUED

and defended him, saying he was a good man who was doing the best he could, and that it was stressful for both not to have their families close for support. Ana said that her own father beat her mother quite severely and that what was happening to her was not nearly as bad as what her mother had endured. After a long discussion, Ana acknowledged that Juan had abused her. Ms. Lin tried to persuade her to take the children and leave Juan but Ana refused, saying that they all had to live together as a family. In the end, Ms. Lin persuaded Ana to seek help at a local community agency and agreed to go with her.

When Ana arrives at the agency, she notices that the posters and magazines in the waiting area are all in English. Ms. Ross, a social worker experienced in practice with Latino families, greets her and invites Ana into her office, leaving the children to play with Ms. Lin. Although Ms. Ross speaks Spanish, she requests Ms. Perez, the agency's interpreter, to be available for support. She begins with a friendly conversation about neutral, everyday pleasant topics, encouraging Ana to participate fully. To help offset Ana's apprehension at disclosing intimate details with a stranger, Ms. Ross offers personal information she normally does not share with clients such as her children's ages, ethnic heritage, and where she grew up. In an effort to set an egalitarian tone to the interactions and establish a sense of connectedness, she tells Ana, with empathy, "It must be difficult to be in a country with a different culture and language and so far from your family."

When asked, "What brings you to the agency?" Ana replies that she has some "trouble at home" and is worried about her son's health. The remnants of the black eye are still visible, but since Ana does not mention the IPV right away, Ms. Ross does not ask about it and instead engages Ana around the issue of Paulo's asthma and her worries about him. Ms. Ross makes a mental note to follow up on the "trouble at home" and black eye after rapport has been established. She agrees to help Ana find medicine and secure doctor visits for her son at a free clinic for immigrants. Together they identify Ana's multiple strengths, including her love for her children, her good parenting, and her work ethic. Here the themes of strength and empowerment are crucial, given Ana's sense of powerlessness because of the abuse and her minority and undocumented statuses.

Ms. Ross identifies similarities and differences in the values, attitudes, and assumptions they have about each other and about the abuse, and tries to handle them with respect and sensitivity. Ms. Ross asks Ana about her values, identity, and involvement in mainstream culture, as her acculturation level can influence her perceptions of the abuse and the helping process. These include questions about Ana's language preference, her views about gender roles, and her help-seeking behaviors.

Using a respectful, nonjudgmental approach, Ms. Ross recognizes and validates Ana's strengths and experience. She continuously reminds herself of Ana's right to self-determination, particularly because her choices conflict with what she thinks is in Ana's best interest. When she catches herself becoming judgmental or overly protective, she makes a mental note to talk about it during peer supervision. The worker gathers information about Ana's situation, needs, and resources using a collaborative, strengths-oriented approach.

Open-ended questions encourage Ana to tell her story. Here Ana relates her experience and is prompted to fill in the details as she feels comfortable doing so. She speaks of how lonely she feels away from her family, how she worries about her children, and how she should be more patient with Juan who is such a good husband and father. As her story unfolds, she becomes increasingly distressed and unable to continue, sobbing and repeating how ashamed she feels about her situation and about being there seeking help for something that was not a really big deal. Ms. Ross acknowledges how difficult it is to talk about these matters and how much courage and strength it takes to do so. She recognizes Ana's desire to make life better for her entire family. Ms. Ross labels Ana's experiences as abuse and notes that Juan's actions are against the law, emphasizing that Ana has a choice to take legal action or not. She further reassures Ana that she does not deserve to be abused and that the abuse is not her fault. Ana emphatically states that she could never call the police because she is afraid the officers would hurt Juan. Using an alternative strategy, Ms. Ross asks Ana about the times when the violence occurred, including the most recent, the first, and the worst incidents, to assess the severity of the abuse—physical, sexual, and emotional. Ana is not forthcoming in her responses, denying and minimizing the harm inflicted upon her, perhaps because of traditional Latino values that expect women to be strong and stoical.

Ms. Ross evaluates Ana's affect and finds that she is moderately depressed. She evaluates Ana's self-esteem and self-concept, openly recognizing the negative impact of the oppression and injustices she has seen, heard, and experienced. Other concerns are the family's limited income and undocumented status. Ana's and her children's specific material needs are also identified.

Jointly they evaluate Ana's assets such as her problem-solving and coping skills, especially in relation to past abuse, and they explore Ana's natural supports and her social isolation. The worker points out Ms. Lin's supportive role in recognizing the abuse and accompanying Ana to the agency. Ms. Ross asks about Ana's experiences with the church, neighborhood associations, and mainstream and Latino-focused agencies, including their sensitivity to her immigration and cultural issues, ability to meet her needs, and the type of services provided.

Ms. Ross encourages Ana to take an active role in setting achievable concrete and realistic goals that she perceives and asks her opinion about what she thinks might be done to improve the situation, seeking clues congruent with her ethnic reality and individual and cultural preferences. Initially Ana appears uncomfortable and resistant to actively participating in the decision-making process, which may be because of cultural norms that discourage assertiveness among women and promote less egalitarian protocols.

Ms. Ross helps Ana evaluate her options, and she informs her that the law provides protection for IPV victims. Ana responds that all she wants is for her family to be together and knows that Juan needs help to stop drinking and hurting her. Clearly Ana is not ready to leave Juan, and so the worker does not discuss this as an option. She does not pressure Ana to leave, convey the notion that leaving is the best option, or say that a commitment to leave the relationship is required in order to receive services. They develop a safety plan in case Juan again uses violence against her, exploring short- or long-term options for where she could escape with her children or, alternatively, leave the abusive relationship. Ana is encouraged to keep important papers, keys, and money where she can readily access them. Ms. Ross offers information about a local domestic violence shelter that has bilingual staff, but Ana states that she is not likely to use or need one. Concerned about Ana's social isolation, she mentions the domestic violence program's free, confidential support groups for women which are conducted in Spanish. She also gives her the phone number for the National Domestic Violence Hotline (1–800–799-SAFE), which has Spanish-speaking advocates on call 24 hours a day, 7 days a week.

Ana asks about a prevention-oriented group for Latino men that Ms. Lin had mentioned. Ms. Ross responds that she is not aware of this option but offers to find more information. She uses supportive and cognitive strategies to address Ana's depression. Future plans include following up on Juan' drinking problem and referring him to an Alcoholics Anonymous group where Spanish is the language spoken, and locating a group therapy program for

Latino men. In an effort to contribute to broader systemic changes, Ms. Ross joins a taskforce of grassroots advocacy groups and social service agencies to develop cultural competent IPV services for Latina immigrants. She will also seek opportunities to advocate for services that attend to the myriad social needs of Latina victims.

CONCLUSION

Increasingly more often social workers are being called upon to provide services to Latinos, their families, and their communities. An appropriate, effective social work response requires a commitment to understanding, respecting, and negotiating cultural differences. Indeed, cultural differences are perhaps nowhere more starkly drawn than between mainstream and Latino values, norms, and attitudes about the family. In order to engage and assist Latinas who are experiencing domestic violence, we must seek practice frameworks and adopt skills that accommodate these cultural differences and empower Latinas within their own ethno-cultural contexts. This chapter offers social workers an opportunity to take a step forward in this direction. The authors hope this discussion sparks readers' enthusiasm and commitment to deepen the knowledge and practice strategies that will enhance their ability to provide culturally competent services.

RESOURCES

Break the Cycle
5200 W. Century Boulevard
Los Angeles, CA 90045
Phone: (310) 286–3383
E-mail: info@breakthecycle.org
Web site: http://www.breakthecycle.org

Casa de Esperanza
P.O. Box 75177
St. Paul, MN 55175
Phone: (651) 646–5553
E-mail: info@casadeesperanza.org
Web site: http://www.casadeesperanza.org

Family Violence Prevention Fund
383 Rhode Island Street
San Francisco, CA 94103
Phone: (415) 252–8900
E-mail: fvpf@netcampaign.com
Web site: http://www.endabuse.org

Information Center
1515 E. Lake Street, Suite 131
Minneapolis, MN 55407
Phone: (612) 728–5438
Crisis Hotline: (651) 772–1611

National Compadres Network
P.O. Box 2007
Santa Ana, CA 92707
Phone: (714) 745–8718
E-mail: info@nationalcompadresnetwork.com

National Latino Alliance for the Elimination of Domestic Violence
P.O. Box 672, Triborough Station
New York, NY 10035
Phone: (646) 672–1404 or 1 (800) 342–9908
E-mail: inquiry@dvalianza.org
Web site: http://www.dvalianza.org

National Latino Fatherhood and Family Institute
5252 E. Beverly Boulevard
East LA, CA 90022
Phone: (323) 728–7770
E-mail: admin@nlffi.org
Web site: http://www.nlffi.org

National Network to End Domestic Violence
2001 S Street, NW
Washington, DC 20009
Phone: (202) 543–5566
Web site: http://www.nnedv.org

Office on Violence Against Women
800 K Street, NW, Suite 920

Washington, DC 20530
Phone: (202) 307–6026
Web site: http://www.usdoj.gov/ovw

Violence Against Women Resource Center
E-mail: endvaw@jhuccp.org
Web site: http://www.endvaw.org

REFERENCES

Anderson, M. (1993). A license to abuse: The impact of conditional status on female immigrants. *Yale Law Review*, 102(6), 1401–1430.

Caetano, R., J. Schafer, C. Clark, C. Cunradi, and K. Raspberry. (2000). Intimate partner violence, acculturation, and alcohol consumption among Hispanic couples in the U.S. *Journal of Interpersonal Violence*, 15(1), 30–45.

Comas-Diaz, L. (1993). Hispanic communities: Psychological implications. In D. Atkinson, J. Morton, and D. Sue (Eds.), *Counseling American Minorities* (pp. 241–296). Iowa: Brown & Benchmark.

Cunradi, C., R. Caetano, C. Clark, and J. Schafer. (2000). Neighborhood poverty as a predictor of intimate partner violence among white, black, and Hispanic couples in the United States: A multilevel analysis. *Annals of Epidemiology*, 10(5): 297–308.

Dutton, M. (2000). Characteristics of help-seeking behaviors, resources, and service needs of battered immigrant Latinas. *Georgetown Journal on Poverty Law and Policy*, 7(2), 245–305.Espin, O. (1994). Feminist Approaches. In L. Comas-Diaz and B. Greene (Eds.), *Women of Color: Integrating Ethnic and Gender Identities in Psychotherapy* (pp. 428–454). New York: Guilford.

Falicov, C. (1998). *Latino Families in Therapy*. New York: Guillford.

Flores-Ortiz, Y. (1993). La mujer y la violencia: A culturally based model for the understanding and treatment of domestic violence in Chicana/Latina communities. In N. Alarcon (Ed.), *Chicano Critical Issues* (pp. 169–182). Berkeley, CA: Third Woman Press.

Giachello, A. L. (2001). The health of elderly Latinas. In M. Aguirre-Molina, C. Mollilna, and R. Zambrana (Eds.), *Health Issues in the Latino Community* (pp. 157–178). San Francisco: Jossey-Bass.

Hesse-Biber, S., and G. Carter. (2004). *Working Women in America: Split Dreams* (2nd Ed.). New York: Oxford University Press.

Ingram, E. (2007). A Comparison of help seeking between Latino and non-Latino victims of intimate partner violence. *Violence Against Women*, 13(2), 111–122.

Jasinski, J., N. Asdigian, and G. Kantor. (1997). Ethnic adaptations to occupational strain. *Journal of Interpersonal Violence, 12*(6), 814–831.

Kanuha, V. (1994). Women of color in battering relationships. In L. Comas-Diaz and B. Greene (Eds.), *Women of Color: Integrating Ethnic and Gender Identities in Psychotherapy* (pp. 428–454). New York: Guilford.

Kaufman, G., J. Jasinski, and E. Aldarondo. (1994). Sociocultural status and incidence of marital violence in Hispanic families. *Violence and Victims, 9*(3): 207–222.

Kelly, L. (1996). Tensions and possibilities: Enhancing informal responses to domestic violence. In J. Edelson and Z. Eiskovits (Eds.), *Future Interventions with Battered Women and Their Families* (pp. 67–86). Thousand Oaks, CA: Sage.

Klevens, J., G. Shelley, et al. (2007). Latinos' perspectives and experiences with intimate partner violence. *Violence Against Women, 13*(2), 111–122.

Lie, G., and C. Lowry. (2003). Cultural competence with women of color. In D. Lum (Ed.), *Culturally Competent Practice* (pp. 282–309). Pacific Grove, CA: Brooks/Cole.

Locke, L., and C. Richman. (1999). Attitudes toward domestic violence: Race and gender issues. *Sex Roles, 40*, 3–4.

Lown, E., and W. Vega. (2001). Intimate partner violence and health: Self-assessed health, chronic health and somatic symptoms among Mexican American women. *Psychosomatic Medicine, 63*(3), 353–360.

Marin, G., and B. Van Oss Marin. (1991). *Research with Hispanic Populations.* Newbury Park, CA: Sage.

McGoldrick, M., J. Giordano, and J. Pearce. (2005). *Ethnicity and Family Therapy* (3rd Ed). New York: Guilford.

Murdaugh, C., Hunt, S., Sowell, R., and Santana, I. (2004). Domestic Violence in Hispanics in the Southeastern United States: A Survey and Needs Analysis. *Journal of Family Violence, 19*(2), 107–115.

National Association of Social Workers (NASW). (2001). *Standards for Cultural Competence in Social Work Practice.* Silver Springs, MD. NASW Press.

National Women's Law Center (2000). *Making the Grade on Women's Health: A National and State-By-State Report Card.* Washington, DC: National Women's Law Center.

Parrillo, V. (2000). *Strangers to These Shores: Race and Ethnic Relations in the United States.* Boston: Allyn and Bacon.

Perilla, J. (1999). Domestic violence as a human rights issue: The case of immigrant Latinos. *Hispanic Journal of Behavioral Sciences, 21*(2), 107–133.

Perilla, J., R. Bakerman, and F. Norris. (1994). Culture and domestic violence: The ecology of abused Latinas. *Violence and Victims, 9*(4): 325–339.

Plichta, S. (1996). Violence and abuse: Implications for women's health. In M. Falik and K. Collins (Eds.), *Women's Health: The Commonwealth Fund Study* (pp. 237–272). Baltimore, MD: John Hopkins University Press.

Ramos, B. (1997). Acculturation and depression among Puerto Ricans and Puerto Rican veterans in the continental U.S. Ph.D. dissertation, State University of New York, Albany.

——. (2001). Parenting, caregiving stress, and child abuse and neglect. In A. Sallee, H. Lawson, and K. Briar-Lawson (Eds.), *Innovative Practice with Vulnerable Children and Families* (pp. 209–228). Dubuque, Iowa: Eddie Bowers.

——. (2004). Culture, ethnicity, and caregiver stress among Puerto Ricans. *Journal of Applied Gerontology*, 23(4), 469–486.

Ramos, B., and B. Carlson. (2004). Lifetime abuse and mental health distress among English-speaking Latinas. *AFFILIA*, 19(3), 239–256.

Ramos, B., L. Jones, and R. Toseland. (2005). Practicing with elderly of color. In D. Lum (Ed.), *Cultural Competence, Practice Stages, and Client Systems: A Case Study Approach* (pp. 320–358). Pacific Grove, CA: Brooks/Cole.

Sue, D. (2006). *Multicultural Social Work Practice*. Hoboken, NJ: Wiley.

Sokoloff, N., and I. Dupont. (2005). Domestic violence at the intersections of race, class and gender. *Violence Against Women*, 11(1), 38–64.

Straus, M., and C. Smith (1995). Violence in Hispanic families in the United States: Incidence rates and structural interpretations. In M. Straus and R. Gelles (Eds.), *Physical Violence in American Families: Risk Factors and Adaptations to Violence in 8,145 Families* (pp. 341–367). New Brunswick, NJ: Transaction Books.

Tjaden, P., and N. Thoennes. (1998). *Prevalence, Incidence and Consequences of Violence against Women: Findings from the National Violence Against Women Survey*. Washington, DC: U.S. Department of Justice, Office of Justice Programs, National Institute of Justice and the Centers for Disease Control and Prevention.

Torres, S. (1991). A comparison of wife abuse between two cultures: Perceptions, attitudes, nature, and extent. *Issues in Mental Health Nursing*, 12(1), 113–131.

US Bureau of the Census. (2004). Hispanic population in the United States. Census 2000 Brief. Washington, DC: U.S. Government Printing Office.

——. (2007). *American Community Survey Reports*. Washington, DC: U.S. Government Printing Office.

Vann, A. (2003). *Developing Culturally Relevant Responses to Domestic Abuse: Asha Family Services, Inc*. Harrisburg, PA: National Resource Center on Domestic Violence.

Vega, W. (1995). The study of Latino families: A point of departure. In R. Zambrana (Ed.), *Understanding Latino Families* (pp. 3–17). Thousand Oaks, CA: Sage.

Vega, W. (1995). The study of Latino families: A point of departure. In R. Zambrana (Ed.), Understanding Latino Families (pp. 3–17). Thousand Oaks, CA: Sage.

9

OUTING THE ABUSE

Considerations for Effective Practice with Lesbian,
Gay, Bisexual, and Transgender Survivors of Intimate
Partner Violence

Taryn Lindhorst, Gita Mehrotra, and Shawn L. Mincer

MALE OR female, gay or straight, victim or perpetrator—these dichotomies permeate both theory and practice related to intimate partner violence (IPV).[1] For members of the lesbian, gay, bisexual, and transgender (LGBT)[2] communities, these binaries, along with the larger social context of homophobia and heterosexism, are implicated in how IPV is defined, in what abuse looks like in LGBT relationships, and in the barriers LGBT people face for receiving support and help when experiencing violence in their relationships. Violence in LGBT relationships is often dismissed as mutual, or not as violence at all (i.e., a "cat fight" if two women are involved) (Ristock 2002). Outside large urban areas, few domestic violence service systems have specialized programs providing assistance to LGBT persons experiencing IPV. Even within urban areas, assistance for all LGBT survivors is difficult to find, especially for gay men and transgender persons. As social workers and community advocates dedicated to providing effective support and services in a range of settings, it is critical for us to better understand the unique experiences, issues, and challenges facing LGBT survivors of IPV.

Our discussion in this chapter focuses primarily on educating heterosexual social workers, domestic violence advocates, and students who may or may not consider themselves allies to members of the LGBT community. Our rationale for this approach rests on our belief that, whereas LGBT communities within large metropolitan regions may be able to develop specialized services for members of LGBT communities (see the listing of resources at the end of the chapter), the majority of LGBT people struggling with abuse will interact with hospitals, police, and domestic violence service providers or other social service agencies, most of which have had little experience responding to abuse in LGBT relationships. At the same time, we acknowledge that practitioners from within LGBT communities, or who are working within LGBT-specific organizations, may have distinct perspectives and challenges in working within their own communities on partner abuse issues. We recognize the importance of educating people within LGBT communities and organizations about dynamics related to IPV. However, given the scope of this chapter, our primary goal is to provide basic information to orient service providers to the unique barriers encountered by LGBT survivors of IPV, and to highlight practice considerations when working with this population, in a range of settings and across system levels.

To accomplish this goal, we focus our discussion on four areas. First, we describe the role of heterosexism and homophobia in creating a climate of risk for LGBT people, and the unique manifestations of power and control stemming from individual and systemic homophobia and heterosexism. Second, we explain considerations for practice with individuals, organizations, and community or policy levels of practice specific to the LGBT community; at each of these levels, we explore barriers facing LGBT persons and communities, and suggest strategies to increase competent social work practice. Third, we present three case studies illustrating some of the distinctive issues for LGBT persons who are experiencing IPV, along with reflection questions for practitioners. Finally, we provide a listing of resources related to LGBT communities, and specific resources on LGBT IPV.

TABLE 9.1 Basic Terms Related to Sexual Orientation and Gender Identity

TERM	DEFINITION
Gender	Set of meanings a culture assigns to someone based on the person's perceived biological sex. Gender is composed of roles and expressions (clothing, career choices, and body language) and identity (one's internal view of one's gender).
Sexual Orientation	Set of meanings a culture assigns to describe a person's sexual attractions. Sexual orientation includes attraction (the gender one is drawn to), behavior (sexual acts), and identity (how one describes oneself). People can have sex with a person of the same gender but not see themselves attracted to the same gender, or identify as gay or lesbian.

"CONTINUED"

TABLE 9.1 Basic Terms Related to Sexual Orientation and Gender Identity (*continued*)

TERM	DEFINITION
Lesbian	Women whose primary romantic and sexual attractions are to other women. Some women prefer the term "gay woman" instead of "lesbian."
Bisexual	A person who is attracted to more than one gender.
Gay Men	Men whose primary romantic and sexual attractions are to other men.
Transgender	A person with a gender identity that is different from their birth sex or who expresses their gender in ways that contravene societal expectations of the range of possibilities for men and women. This umbrella term may include cross-dressers, drag kings/queens, transsexuals, people who are androgynous, Two-Spirit people, and people who are bi-gendered or multi-gendered, as well as people who do not identify with any labels. Some people prefer the terms "trans," "genderqueer" or "gender nonconforming" instead of "transgender." (*Note on pronouns: All transgender folks should be referred to by their preferred name and with pronouns of the gender they see themselves as being. If in doubt, ask the individual.)
Queer	A term reclaimed from its derogatory use, particularly by younger or political LGBT people. Some LGBT people find the term "queer" offensive.
Heterosexism	Set of institutionalized practices through which heterosexual people receive benefits and through which LGBT persons are excluded or oppressed (e.g., marriage laws, actions of the criminal justice system, and media portrayals of heterosexual and LGBT persons).
Homophobia	Irrational fear, discomfort, and sometimes hatred toward persons who are attracted to others of the same gender, or who appear to be gay or lesbian because of their gender expression.
Biphobia	Irrational fear, discomfort, and sometimes hatred toward persons who have romantic attractions to more than one gender.
Transphobia	Irrational fear, discomfort, and sometimes hatred toward transgender persons or persons who differ from traditional gender expression or are gender ambiguous.
Coming Out	The process of internally identifying one's gender or sexual identity and then voluntarily telling other people.
Outing	Having one's sexual or gender identity disclosed against one's will or without one's consent.

CONTEXT OF HETEROSEXISM AND HOMOPHOBIA

Building a foundation for understanding IPV among LGBT persons requires an examination of the role heterosexism plays in shaping personal and social values as well as societal institutions and resources. For our purposes here, we assume two key aspects about heterosexism. First, it represents a set of beliefs about the "natural" superiority or rightness of traditional gender definitions and their expression through heterosexual relationships and marriage (Morrow and Messinger 2006; Pharr 1988; Sears 1997). These prejudices are sometimes specified as homophobia, transphobia, and biphobia (for definitions, see Table 9.1). Second, heterosexism is a set of institutionalized power relations that overtly favors heterosexuality and conformity to masculine and feminine gender regimes. Examples of these institutionalized relations include legislative policies such as those governing marriage (i.e., Defense of Marriage Acts) and adoption, which overtly exclude lesbian and gay couples (Cahill 2004); legal practices like the use of "gay panic" defenses in which crimes are justified based on the attacker's fear of LGBT persons (Chen 2000); denial of child custody to gay, lesbian or transgender parents (Dudley 2002); the invisibility and frequent negative portrayals of LGBT persons in most media (Nardi 1997); and the use of mental health diagnoses to pathologize non-normative sexual and gender identity expression. Until 1973 homosexuality was listed as a mental disorder in the *Diagnostic and Statistical Manual of Mental Disorders* (Drescher 2002); "Gender Identity Disorder" continues to be listed as a disorder today (American Psychiatric Association 1994; Tarver 2002.) As a consequence of personal prejudices and institutional relations, many LGBT persons face routine discrimination in a variety of settings, including the workplace, public accommodations, health-care settings, and within their families.

As a result of heterosexism, LGBT persons have had to fight for the legitimacy of their relationships. This stance within LGBT communities against the larger society's discriminatory practices has made it difficult to recognize that violence exists *within* LGBT relationships (McLaughlin and Rozee 2001). For instance, in one of the first books to discuss the issue of abuse in lesbian relationships, Kerry Lobel states:

> Many lesbians are understandably reluctant to air issues related to lesbian battering, for fear of triggering homophobic attacks on our communities. In a society where there has been no acceptance of lesbian relationships, the fears

are legitimate. By discussing these issues openly we risk further repression. Yet our alternative is one of silence, a silence that traps battered lesbians into believing that they are alone and that there are no resources available to them. (Lobel 1986, p. 7)

Although this passage was written more than 20 years ago, it reflects a concern that reverberates through more recent research among lesbians and domestic violence service providers, reported in Ristock (2002). Anxieties persist about whether information about IPV among LGBT persons will be used against the LGBT community by those who view LGBT relationships as inherently sinful or wrong. As occurs in many marginalized communities, LGBT survivors of abuse may feel particularly protective of their intimate relationships and fearful of exposing unhealthy or abusive dynamics. They may feel concern that "airing dirty laundry" beyond the community will fuel anti-gay sentiments (Balsam 2001).

Lobel's passage raises other critical issues related to understanding IPV within LGBT relationships. First, the majority of published work available on issues of abuse in LGBT communities has been undertaken with lesbian and bisexual women (for early examples, see Lobel 1986; Renzetti 1992). Island and Letellier (1991) published a book describing issues related to abuse among gay men; to date, no similar works are available for experiences among transgender persons. Second, most research on IPV in LGBT communities has been conducted with white women, with the result that the experiences of lesbian, gay, bisexual, and transgender persons of color have been invisible and marginalized (Kanuha 1994). More work is needed to strengthen our understanding of the intersections between LGBT concerns and those who endure other forms of oppression, such as those based on race, class, ability, and age.

IPV IN LGBT RELATIONSHIPS

When facing IPV, LGBT persons are subjected to abusive tactics of power and control, including verbal abuse, physical violence, social isolation, sexual abuse, economic control, and threats against their children and family. In addition, because of the larger social context of homophobia and heterosexism, an abusive partner can exploit the victim's identity as transgender, lesbian, gay, or bisexual to leverage power and control (Allen and Leventhal

1999). (See Figure 9.1 for an example of a "power and control wheel" that focuses on some of the effects of heterosexism for lesbian and gay survivors of IPV.)

An example of how heterosexism can be used to control a partner is related to "coming out" – the process of internally identifying and socially disclosing one's status as a transgender, bisexual, lesbian, or gay man. Coming out is an ongoing, iterative process, because social identity is negotiated daily in the context of other relationships and experiences (Barrett and Logan 2002; Fisher and Akman 2002). Depending on a person's circumstances—geographic location, age, race, religion, class, and other factors—each individual's coming out process is unique and involves different risks. For example, coming out in rural areas has a different trajectory and consequences than revealing one's sexual or gender identity in an urban metropolis (Leedy and Connolly 1998; Whittier 1997). As a result of heterosexism, an abusive partner can threaten to disclose the person's sexual orientation or gender identity status without permission—"outing" the survivor—to maintain control. For instance, LGBT persons with children from a heterosexual relationship may not have disclosed their sexual orientation to the former partner; the threat of disclosure by an abusive partner could result in the potential loss of children in locales where family law judges rule against LGBT parents in custody proceedings (Richman 2002). Conversely, an abusive partner may isolate a person from the LGBT community by refusing to allow them to interact with other LGBT persons as a pattern of controlling the person's access to social support, and information about LGBT relationships.

Although heterosexism can be used against LGBT persons, there are also differences between the experiences of these individuals that are important to recognize. For example, some gay men who are in abusive relationships with other men may hesitate to disclose abuse because society's message about masculinity assumes that a man should be able to defend himself against abuse (Ristock and Timbang 2005). Gay and bisexual men have been greatly affected by HIV/AIDS, although the population contracting HIV at the fastest rate today is low-income women of color infected by male partners (Hanson and Maroney 1999). Issues related to HIV can play into dynamics of IPV, such as when an HIV-positive man relies on his violent partner for care and support or when an HIV-positive abuser pressures a partner to have unprotected sex as proof of love and loyalty.

Because IPV services have been constructed based on gender, women, whether gay, bisexual, or transgender, may have more access to help than

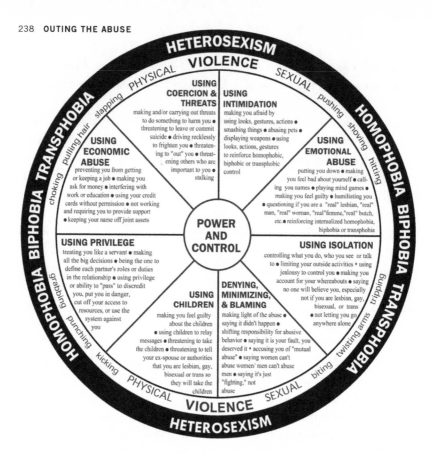

FIGURE 9.1. Power and Control Wheel for Lesbian, Gay, Bisexual and Trans Relationships. Developed by Roe & Jagodinsky. Adapted from the Power & Control Wheel Developed by Domestic Abuse Intervention Project.

men do, although these services are limited compared to those available for heterosexual women. Bisexual individuals report struggles with accessing support from either heterosexual or LGBT communities because they are not seen as belonging to either community. As Sulis notes, "The batterer may threaten to out her [or his] partner as a lesbian [or gay man] to family and coworkers, yet also threaten to out her as bisexual within the lesbian community. Such threats reinforce the isolation bisexual women already experience within both the lesbian community and society as a whole" (1999, p. 175). As a result, abusive partners may be able to threaten their bisexual partner with revealing their sexual identity to either heterosexual friends or family, or to LGBT community members who may have ambivalent feelings regarding bisexual women or men (Sulis 1999).

The vulnerability of transgender persons experiencing abuse from a partner is also pronounced. A transgender person's gender identity may or may
not closely match their gender presentation; some transgender people are
better at "passing" as the gender with which they identify. Also, a transgender
person's legal documentation—such as a driver's license or birth certificate—
may not match their present gender identity (i.e., they are still considered
legally to be male but live as a woman). Many laws and government policies and programs depend on gender identification. Consequently, the access
of transgender persons to institutions such as marriage, adoption, and community services is tenuous and can be disputed (Burdge 2007). Although 20
states prohibit discrimination against lesbian and gay men, only 13 states and
the District of Columbia extend this same protection to transgender persons
(National Gay and Lesbian Task Force 2007). As a result, transgender persons have fewer legal protections if their status becomes known by persons
hostile to them. When LGBT persons are also disabled, older, people of
color, immigrants, or have limited English-speaking skills, other issues such
as racism, ageism, or poverty can make accessing resources for help even
more complex.

EMPIRICAL RESEARCH ON IPV IN LGBT POPULATIONS

Since the early 1970s, researchers have conducted population-based studies
about IPV among heterosexuals, and are now able to estimate the prevalence
of violence and risk factors associated with partner violence for heterosexual women and men (see Straus, Gelles, and Steinmetz 1980; Tjaden and
Thoennes 2000). A similar body of research is not yet available to guide practice with the LGBT community, related in part to the challenges involved
in conducting research with LGBT persons. For instance, only since 2000
has the U.S. Census provided information on same-sex households. Problems with the U.S. Census data illustrate the difficulties in researching LGBT
populations. The Census asked about the gender of the "main householder"
and his or her relationship to the person completing the Census form, which
allowed identification of same-sex households but did not allow identification
of a host of other permutations: persons whose sexual orientation is lesbian
or gay but who are not currently partnered; people who may be in a same-sex
relationship but not report it as such; and bisexual or transgender persons.

Research that uses strategies similar to those of the U.S. Census seriously undercounts the LGBT population (Smith and Gates 2001).

As a result of this difficulty in conducting population-based research on LGBT experiences, most studies on IPV with LGBT persons use nonrepresentative samples of persons recruited through LGBT events, organizations, or Web sites. This approach excludes LGBT persons not already connected to the social networks used for recruitment. Persons of color, persons with fewer financial resources, older and younger persons, and people who have not adopted an LGBT identity remain underrepresented in research. Survey studies using these nonrandom sampling techniques have found rates of IPV in gay/lesbian relationships ranging from 17 to 52 percent (Waldner-Haugrud, Gratch, and Magruder 1997). Only a handful of these studies have explored issues among bisexual men and women (see Balsam, Robthblum, and Beauchaine 2005, for one of the few studies to compare rates of violence among gay, lesbian, and bisexual men and women); only one study is available that used a random sample, but this study likely underreported the number of same-sex partners (Tjaden, Thoennes, and Allison 1999; Tjaden and Thoennes 2000).

At this time, we have insufficient information to know how rates of IPV in LGBT communities compare to IPV rates in heterosexual relationships. It is also noteworthy that most violence that occurs in LGBT communities is not reported to the police or to organizations that may collect statistics on IPV. Not in question is whether IPV occurs in lesbian, gay, bisexual, and transgender relationships. Future research is needed to better understand the prevalence, context, risk factors, and experiences of IPV in LGBT communities.

WORKING AT MULTIPLE SYSTEM LEVELS TO ADDRESS IPV IN LGBT COMMUNITIES

Culturally competent practice with LGBT communities requires that community advocates and social workers gain knowledge that informs their work at levels of self, survivor, organization, community, and policy systems. Entering into this work requires the skill of being critically self-aware about our own biases, social identities, and position as practitioners. Workers across a variety of practice settings need to become knowledgeable and familiar with assessment and intervention with survivors of IPV. Likewise, service providers need to develop organizational responses and policies that address both IPV and the rights and resources available to LGBT persons. Finally, practitioners must enhance their general knowledge about LGBT communities in order to address systemic barriers and inequalities at the community and policy level. Each of these practice levels are discussed in the following sections.

LGBT COMPETENT PRACTICE WITH INDIVIDUALS

Working effectively with LGBT persons who are experiencing IPV requires four basic skills: an understanding of one's own beliefs and knowledge about LGBT persons; the ability to establish an empathetic, nonjudgmental relationship with a presenting client; skills for assessing dynamics related to IPV in LGBT relationships; and the development of realistic safety plans relevant to a survivor's context and situation.

Social work practice teaching stresses the need for critical self-awareness as the starting point in learning to work with persons experiencing oppression and marginalization. In relation to LGBT persons, strong cultural biases often promote a view of gender or sexual diversity as deviant, immoral, or a sign of mental illness. Within this environment, all community advocates and social workers must work to understand their own identities, personal biases, and cultural experiences, and the effects these may have on their practice. Social workers who have religious or other beliefs contradicting the values of the profession must be particularly careful to consider if they can work effectively with LGBT clients. The National Association of Social Workers (NASW) notes that "same gender orientation should be afforded the same respect and rights as other gender orientation . . . [and] NASW is committed to working towards the elimination of prejudice and discrimination based on sexual orientation, both inside and outside of the profession" (NASW 2006). Efforts continue to incorporate gender identity into the profession's statements related to nondiscrimination (Burdge 2007). One step in confronting these biases is to examine issues of heterosexual privilege (e.g., see Unpacking the Knapsack II, n.d.) or to understand our own unconscious associations with sexuality (see Project Implicit, n.d.). Additional questions to stimulate critical self-reflection are provided in Table 9.2.

TABLE 9.2 General Questions for Reflection: LGBT Cultural Competency

LEVEL OF PRACTICE	QUESTIONS TO CONSIDER
Self-reflection (for practitioner)	How do I define my own sexual orientation? How do I define my gender identity?
	What are my values and beliefs regarding LGBT people and communities?
	What do I anticipate as personal challenges in working with LGBT survivors of IPV? What kind of support and resources can I access to overcome these challenges?
Micro	What is similar to other victims of IPV in this situation? What is different that is related to the person's status as an LGBT person?
	What issues would you need to consider (in yourself and in the survivor) in attempting to build a relationship with this person?
	What do you see as the key assessment issues with this person?
	What other concerns or risks might the person experiencing IPV be trying to balance or consider?
	What are the particular safety concerns and barriers to safety facing the person you are serving?
	What strengths and resources does this person have?
	What would you do to help this person plan for safety?
Mezzo	What issues within your practice setting/organization are related to competence in working with LGBT persons? How would you help your organization become more competent in its work with LGBT communities?
	What agencies are serving LGBT communities in your area? What agencies are addressing IPV? Are any organizations specifically addressing IPV in LGBT communities?
	What do you know about your community's funding streams for LGBT-related IPV programs and resources?
Macro	What are the policy-level issues highlighted by this case? What possible current laws and policies may affect LGBT survivors of IPV (e.g., restraining order eligibility, antidiscrimination protections, domestic partnership, and immigration)?
	How would you organize in your community to address these issues?
	What other organizations or groups might you work with to further these efforts?

BUILDING RELATIONSHIPS WITH LGBT CLIENTS

An empathetic, nonjudgmental relationship provides the necessary foundation to encourage voluntary disclosure of abuse, particularly for LGBT persons. For example, research with battered women has found that when professionals appear uninterested or uncaring, abused women perceive them as untrustworthy and are unlikely to disclose the abuse (Ambuel, Hamberger, and Lahti 1997; Davies and Lyons 1998; Saunders et al. 2005). For LGBT survivors of IPV, fears of homophobia and of being judged are triggered by both the abuse and by the larger community or societal responses to the person's sexual or gender identity. Given the legitimate safety concerns of LGBT persons within the larger context of heterosexism and other potential simultaneously occurring oppressions, trust in the social worker or advocate is especially crucial.

Service providers can enhance trust with LGBT clients in several concrete ways. Since most LGBT persons experience a devaluation of their relationship in the larger society, workers must affirm the relationship as valid, seeing the LGBT client as part of a "real" couple, not as simply roommates, friends, or in a relationship that can easily be ended. LGBT persons draw upon the language used by practitioners to interpret a worker's underlying values. For instance, workers that use the word "homosexual" to refer to LGBT communities are likely to be distrusted; this word has negative connotations for many LGBT persons. Referring to clients and their partners with the terms used by the client (including the pronouns clients use to refer to themselves and their partners) also signals the level of comfort a worker has in working with LGBT persons. Finally, asking about or referencing some of the unique issues related to confidentiality for LGBT persons can also increase the client's trust in the service provider. Because many LGBT communities are small, survivors may need additional reassurance about the confidentiality of their disclosure. This need for confidentiality governs interactions with other systems, such as immigration or the courts, since systemic heterosexism interferes with immigration processes and can result in the removal of children from LGBT families.

ASSESSING DYNAMICS RELATED TO IPV
IN LGBT RELATIONSHIPS

Although many issues are similar between heterosexual and LGBT relationships when assessing IPV (see Lindhorst, Nurius, and Macy 2005 for an overview of general contextualized assessment strategies), two areas present unique challenges: identifying the abusive partner and understanding the environmental context that exists for LGBT persons. To accurately assess for abuse in an LGBT relationship, workers must carefully identify the dynamics in the relationship, since gendered visual, linguistic, and social cues that typically differentiate the abuser and survivor are intensely complicated. Practitioners have to remain aware of their own biases and assumptions based on the ways they use gender cues (i.e., women are victims) as short-cuts to determine the principal victim of abuse in an intimate relationship. For instance, service providers who rely on external characteristics—size, strength, or masculine presentation—to differentiate the perpetrator from the victim may make the incorrect assumption that the bigger or stronger partner is perpetrating the abuse. Assessment issues are complex and cannot easily be simplified, as Ristock notes in the following example of the issues confronting service providers for lesbian survivors:

> Two service providers who run support groups for survivors of same-sex abuse reported that . . . they accept only women who have never used violence (not even in self defense) . . . an unintended consequence of this "nonviolent victim" approach is that the "real victim" is constructed as the one who never responds or defends herself . . . [other] organizations that are confronted with both members of a lesbian couple may define the initiator of the violence as the abuser . . . [so that] "victim" gets reconstructed from "the one who is abused" to "the one who did not start it." (2002, pp. 152–153)

As Ristock and these service providers indicate, social workers face a difficult task in understanding the dynamics in the relationship, and defining who may be primarily responsible for the violence in LGBT relationships. For instance, understanding the motivation for the violence is important. If the violence is used as a tactic of control over the partner, rather than in self-defense, this may help identify a survivor. In addition, survivors often have higher levels of self-doubt and low self-esteem that may lead them to blame themselves for problems in the relationship or to wonder if they are an abuser. In contrast, people who are abusive tend to blame others (including the survivor) for the violence, and may use tactics such as threatening suicide to control the partner. It is also useful to assess the violence happening in a relationship over time and to remember that IPV is about a pattern of power and control, not just a one-time use of violence in a particular situation (Osthoff 2002).

In assessing intimate partner violence in LGBT communities, it is critical to consider how larger environmental contexts, including those of family, community, culture, and policy, affect individuals' experience of abuse and create unique barriers to accessing support, services, and safety. Specifically macro-level forces, such as discriminatory social policies, homophobic community norms, and institutionalized heterosexism, may affect how LGBT individuals define their experiences of abuse and should be assessed by practitioners. Homophobic community norms can significantly influence whether an LGBT person recognizes the nature of an abusive relationship because homophobic others do not recognize the legitimacy of such relationships and may invalidate claims of abuse. Because heterosexism is also institutionalized via discriminatory social policies and laws, LGBT persons may be reluctant to discuss the violence they are experiencing because acknowledging their sexual or gender identity or the abuse may negatively affect them in other arenas, such as in pursuit of adoption or legal immigration. It is incumbent upon social workers and community advocates who are assessing for IPV to remain aware of these larger social influences that may affect the assessment and safety-planning process.

DEVELOPING REALISTIC SAFETY PLANS WITH LGBT SURVIVORS

Once abuse has been identified, the next step is to work with survivors to develop a safety plan that builds on their strengths and those of LGBT communities in general (see Davies and Lyon 1998 for general information on safety planning). As noted above, negotiating safety in an abusive LGBT relationship is difficult within a larger social context that demeans these relationships. The context of heterosexism complicates safety planning for LGBT persons in four important ways: it may reduce access to traditional sources of support within families of origin; it complicates the recognition of abuse by members of LGBT communities; common institutional resources (such as the police) may be unresponsive or unavailable; and services within the domestic violence system may be inaccessible.

Because of heterosexism and homophobia, social networks of family and heterosexual friends may be difficult to access for support. For instance, many LGBT persons become estranged from family members at various points in their coming out process; this estrangement may persist for many years and, in some cases, for the duration of those people's lives. If not estranged from family members, being LGBT may still strain family relationships, which could be further compounded by IPV. Heterosexual community members or friends may not know of a person's gender or sexual identity, or, if they do and are supportive, they may not know that IPV occurs in LGBT relationships and consequently they may be unable to help. If a person does not have support in their immediate nuclear family, it is important to assess with the survivor whether extended family members may be more accepting of the person's sexual or gender identity than the survivor's parents or siblings. As LGBT persons negotiate the coming out process, they sometimes find a family member who advocates for them within the family. Extended family members who have been supportive may also be able to assist when planning for safety; service providers should assess for such family members.

A defining characteristic of LGBT communities is an emphasis on creating families of choice, often motivated because their original family rejected them or they desire empowerment through social support and shared identities and experiences. In the context of IPV, however, social networks in LGBT communities may have difficulty responding appropriately to an abusive situation. LGBT community members may be unaware of IPV or believe that IPV is only a "heterosexual" problem. In lesbian communities, for example, people perceive that IPV is only about male violence against women, with the corollary that within women's communities a "lesbian utopia" exists free from violence in relationships. In many circumstances, LGBT communities are small, as noted, particularly in rural areas, similar to communities formed by differences in physical abilities (such as Deaf and hard of hearing communities), and communities of color. Identifying one member of a couple as abusive may have rippling effects across the social network. Even in larger urban areas, social circles overlap between partners who must draw support from the same networks. Within marginalized communities, a survivor of violence may want the abuse to stop but may fear that disclosing the violence may result in either partner being ostracized from the community. Given the context of homophobia and other forms of oppression, survivors may not want to inflict further isolation on themselves or the abusive partner from the support network they both share.

When discussing the risks and benefits of police intervention with LGBT survivors, practitioners need to provide information about the possible consequences of this decision. Traditional institutional resources—police or civil restraining orders—may be unavailable or may pose even greater risks than the abuse for an LGBT person, who may face harassment, arrest, or violence from police officers acting upon homophobic or transphobic feelings (Amnesty International 2006). Typically, in IPV safety planning, survivors are encouraged to call the police and file a police report if they are abused. When the police are called in a case of LGBT IPV, they may be unable to discern the abusive partner and, consequently, arrest the wrong person. Given these dynamics, practitioners must carefully assess IPV dynamics for clients with arrest records.

Similarly, civil protection order policies may explicitly exclude same-sex couples or couples who do not cohabit, which is currently the case in several states (National Coalition of Anti-Violence Projects 2001). As states pass referendums and laws, such as the Defense of Marriage Act, which limit the rights associated with marriage to heterosexual partners, it is unclear whether protection orders will be viewed as a universal legal right. Practitioners need to be cognizant that resources typically called upon to assist battered heterosexual women—restraining orders or support groups—may be unavailable or may further harm battered LGBT persons. In those communities where this is the case, it is important to plan strategies with the survivor to secure other resources within LGBT communities, and to work with police and legal processes to make these more accessible and safe for LGBT persons.

Finally, services from domestic violence providers may be inaccessible to LGBT persons. Only a handful of large urban areas have developed specialized resources for LGBT survivors of IPV (see listing at the end of the chapter). Even many of these resources may have been tailored to meet the needs of certain members of the LGBT community, such as lesbians, and thus may not respond adequately to other groups such as transgender communities, non–English-speaking people, or youth. In most communities, because few LGBT-specific or knowledgeable resources are available, survivors rely on traditional domestic violence resources that may or may not serve them. In the case of gay or bisexual males or transgender persons, few emergency resources, such as shelters, exist. Although lesbians and bisexual women may have some limited access to services, many women are reluctant to expose themselves to the potentially homophobic attitudes and behavior of staff or other shelter or support group participants. The ability of transgender women to access resources may depend on their ability to pass as a woman or on the program's definition of a woman. Some organizations may define transgender women as eligible for services only if they have had surgical alterations to conform to their gender identity, or if they are living 24/7 as a woman (i.e., dressing as a woman, using a female name, etc.). For all these reasons, safety planning with LGBT persons may be more complicated and require greater creativity and commitment on the part of social workers and other service providers working with members of this community.

LGBT COMPETENT PRACTICE WITH ORGANIZATIONS

Similar to micro-level practice concerns, LGBT persons face barriers to service generated at the organizational level of social work practice. Organizational practice that is sensitive to members of oppressed communities requires that workers assess the policies and practices of the agency; consider the ways in which the organization presents itself to potential clients; and participate in ongoing training of staff and community members in IPV and LGBT concerns.

The history of oppression and discrimination embedded in organizational policies and practices can make LGBT individuals affected by IPV feel unwelcome or excluded. At the organizational level, community advocates and social workers need skills in understanding how agencies and organizations may inadvertently mirror the greater culture's prejudice against LGBT individuals. There is no current research outlining steps to enhance LGBT cultural competency at the organizational level, but efforts that foster cultural competence in agencies for other groups (such as those working with racially and ethnically diverse clientele) provide important insights (see, for example, Betancourt, Green, and Carillio 2002; Dana and Matheson 1992). Oliver Williams and the staff of the Institute on Domestic Violence and the African American Community, for instance, have written on organizational issues and cultural competence (Williams 1993; Williams and Becker 1994).

The first step for an organization to develop culturally competent services requires critical assessment of the experiences of LGBT clients, including the ways in which agency policies and practices may create barriers. Goode, Jones, and Mason (2002) from the National Center for Cultural Competence provide framing principles for organizational assessment that are relevant: these principles include focusing on strengths, creating a non-judgmental space for assessment, and incorporating the meaningful involvement of relevant communities. Examples of questions that might be asked in an organizational assessment include: Does the agency provide services to LGBT persons? Given the social contexts of heterosexism, unless the agency affirmatively states that it serves LGBT clients in its written materials, potential clients may assume that the organization only serves heterosexuals. Does the organization include openly LGBT members on its board or as members of the staff? Does the agency provide ongoing training for staff on LGBT concerns? We provided further ideas for organizational assessment in Table 9.2.

Many clients' first contact with an agency is through the written organizational materials—including those available through the Internet—designed for those seeking assistance. Agencies frequently use heteronormative language and images in brochures, forms, and agency screening practices, with unintended consequences. For instance, some agencies may automatically assume the gender of the abuser or may only use images that represent heterosexual women or couples. Language and images used in brochures, on outreach posters and fliers, and agency forms should be inclusive of the experiences of LGBT clients. Many of the LGBT organizations listed at the end of the chapter, as well as some statewide and local domestic violence agencies, provide examples of brochures that can be used as models for local organizations. An agency can also enlist the LGBT community to help them assess and develop competent organizational practice.

Another commonly overlooked area for critical analysis is the physical space that clients encounter at the agency. A space review can start with the types of images presented through posters and artwork in the offices and the messages these images may subtly, or not so subtly, convey. For example, the message that the organization is supportive of and open to LGBT people could be conveyed by hanging a rainbow flag, displaying posters or artwork presenting same-sex couples or transgender issues, and seeking out representations that reflect an understanding of the lives and experiences of LGBT clients. Concerned practitioners can assess agency materials to determine whether the images and wording used are inclusive and inviting to LGBT people.

Another area where social workers and community advocates can help increase the cultural competency of agencies is by institutionalizing staff trainings for working effectively with LGBT survivors of IPV. In most areas, various LGBT-knowledgeable organizations and practitioners are available to work with staff, boards of directors, and policymakers in social service organizations, institutions, and within the domestic violence service network. Domestic violence agencies, as well as first-responder organizations such as hospitals and law enforcement, need training on specific issues affecting the LGBT community, including the social context of homophobia and heterosexism, LGBT terminology, LGBT history and social norms, and LGBT-specific practice skills and resources. Agencies working with IPV survivors should consult with LGBT community members to provide cultural sensitivity training. In exchange, LGBT service-provider organizations and agencies need training about the specific needs of IPV survivors. Anecdotal reports suggest that survivors reach out to their local or regional LGBT service-provider agencies for assistance with IPV. These LGBT organizations may not have the necessary knowledge about IPV to address survivors' specific needs. Mainstream domestic violence agencies and other community service providers need to obtain specific training to address the needs of LGBT clients, agencies, and organizations that have historically provided services to the LGBT community and must strive to be fully trained in relation to the special needs of IPV in their clients' lives. Social workers and advocates who practice in or with these systems can take an active role in advocating for training programs and policies to increase the cultural competency of service providers.

LGBT COMPETENT POLICY AND COMMUNITY PRACTICE

According to Mullaly (2002), anti-oppressive social work practice at the structural level changes institutions, systems, laws, and norms that have served to benefit the dominant social group at the expense of subordinate groups. Macro-level social work practice can span many areas, including community practice (e.g., community organizing and community development), policy advocacy and analysis, and social action. As illustrated in the above discussion, heterosexism and homophobia negatively impact LGBT communities. To enhance cultural competency and effective practice with LGBT communities, social work practitioners must gain knowledge about macro-level policies and social norms that limit this group's rights and access to resources. Abusers use the inequalities faced by LGBT people to gain power and control over their partners and also to perpetuate obstacles people face when seeking support, services, and safety. Therefore, as advocates and social workers committed to addressing IPV in diverse communities, it is important to consider macro-level practice strategies that more broadly promote justice and equality for LGBT people. Addressing IPV in LGBT communities could include some of the following types of macro-level social work practice:

POLICY ADVOCACY

Many local, state, and national organizations around the country focus on policy advocacy within and for the LGBT community (see the resources listed at the end of this chapter). There are also many groups, particularly state domestic violence coalitions, that engage in legislative advocacy on issues of domestic violence and other social justice concerns affecting survivors of IPV. For practitioners supporting LGBT persons and addressing IPV within diverse communities, staying current with and advocating for policy issues that affect LGBT people and domestic violence survivors is an important ongoing activity (see Table 9.2 for reflection questions on macro-practice issues affecting LGBT survivors of IPV).

Policy work that specifically supports LGBT people involves advocating for policies that recognize the benefits of healthy relationships via marriage equality, domestic partnership, or civil unions, including sexual orientation and gender identity protections in antidiscrimination policies; supporting second-parent adoption laws; and encouraging progressive immigration laws that recognize bi-national same-gender relationships. At the local or state level, initiatives that could significantly affect LGBT survivors of IPV include restraining order eligibility for same-sex partners, protections against gender identity discrimination, issues concerning state or county domestic violence funding, or health-care access issues.

Social work settings and domestic violence service agencies primarily focus on crisis intervention, referrals, counseling, and other direct practice to individuals, families, and groups. Often these organizations do not have the resources or time to focus on macro-level practice in addition to the demands of service provision. Service providers can, however, connect with other groups such as national LGBT policy groups, state domestic violence coalitions, or social service networks within local communities to build effective collaborations to further policy practice goals. Building partnerships and coalitions between domestic violence service organizations and agencies working within LGBT communities is also important in addressing IPV within LGBT communities. For example, local-level domestic violence programs might work with LGBT groups to participate in LGBT or IPV-focused lobby days, cross-training efforts, or exploring collaborative programming and funding to address LGBT IPV.

Many funding streams that support IPV prevention and intervention programs come from government sources—city, county, and federal. Currently, federal funding sources (such as the Violence Against Women Act) do not specifically support programs in LGBT communities. Given the challenges of obtaining governmental as well as nongovernment funding for IPV programs, it is important to be aware of how the sociopolitical climate may impact possible funding for IPV, particularly in LGBT and other historically marginalized communities. For example, more conservative government funders may be reluctant to support efforts in LGBT communities. At the same time, it is critical to be creative in advocacy efforts to gain financial support for IPV work in LGBT communities. Some groups have leveraged grant monies through funding streams focused on supporting antiviolence efforts in traditionally underserved and underrepresented communities or through funding sources focused on LGBT commun-ity projects.

COMMUNITY PRACTICE

Much work needs to be done to educate mainstream communities about LGBT and IPV issues as well as to educate within LGBT communities about IPV. Several community-based organizations around the country have created innovative approaches to engaging and organizing LGBT people around issues of IPV and healthy relationships. For example, some domestic violence and LGBT organizations have implemented creative outreach campaigns about IPV in lesbian/gay community spaces such as bars by distributing resource information and basic IPV facts on matchbooks, nail files, and small business cards. Several groups have also created and implemented workshops or classes focused on building healthy intimate relationships within LGBT communities.

Survivors of IPV are more likely to seek support from their friends and social networks before seeking help from formal systems or agencies (Tolman 2003). Given the importance and strength of peer networks and alternative family structures within LGBT communities, several groups around the country have focused their IPV prevention and intervention efforts on building knowledge and resources to respond to IPV within LGBT communities (Lee and Utarti 2003). For example, the "Peer Resource Model Project" of the Asian Women's Shelter in San Francisco brings together small groups of friends at dinner parties to discuss healthy relationships, how to recognize abusive relationship dynamics, and how to respond to someone experiencing violence within a relationship. The FAR OUT ("Friends Are Reaching Out") project of the Northwest Network in Seattle also supports peer networks to be more aware of IPV and to help friends make agreements with one another about how to have healthy, safe relationships (Lee and Utarti 2003). In addition to creating and supporting innovative strategies, continuing to invest in building sustainable partnerships and coalitions between domestic violence service organizations and agencies working within LGBT communities is also useful in addressing IPV within LGBT communities.

CASE STUDIES ILLUSTRATING MULTILEVEL PRACTICE WITH LGBT PERSONS

The following three case studies describe situations that a social worker might encounter when working with LGBT people experiencing intimate partner abuse. These cases represent composites of people, agencies, and circumstances that the authors have worked with as social workers, and focus specifically on the experiences of a gay man, a male-to-female transgender woman, and a lesbian/bisexual couple. The case studies start at the level of the survivor, but each is designed also to reflect organizational, community and policy levels of practice. They are written in different styles (interview transcript, and case summaries) to provide differing viewpoints in the transactions between social workers, advocates, and LGBT IPV victims. As you read through the case studies, please consider the questions listed in Table 9.2. Brief reflections on issues that emerged in the three case studies are presented at the end of this section.

GAY MALE INTIMATE PARTNER VIOLENCE

ALAN

A local agency provides various services in the community related to IPV, including crisis intervention services and a shelter for those at immediate risk of harm. During a typical day at intake and assessment, a young man who appears to be in his late twenties arrives. He walks around the entry waiting area, looking at the literature and posters of women talking about abuse. The agency has a policy that workers and volunteers should be on heightened alert when unknown men appear because of the potential for violence when a female survivor's batterer attempts to locate her; the policy is to monitor the situation and buzz for assistance if there is a perceived threat or risk. After a short time the young man approaches the intake desk.

He seems nervous and asks if there is anyone with whom he can talk, in private. He says he is having problems at home and does not have any support. The intake staff member is unsure about how to handle this request. There are no existing policy protocols for serving men. The intake worker asks the Assistant Director for advice about how to handle the situation. The Assistant Director agrees to speak with the man in a quiet corner of the waiting area so as not to violate internal policies that restrict unknown men to the main staff and shelter areas.

Alan tells of how his male partner of four years has become increasingly threatening over the past 18 months. Things started out fine between them, but his partner has become verbally abusive and derogatory toward Alan. Over the past three to four months his partner has also been hitting Alan and throwing things at him when the partner is upset. Alan, who is HIV positive, explains that he deeply fears ending the relationship with his partner because of his HIV status. Alan has not told anyone that he has HIV. His partner's health-care benefits have provided him with health-care coverage. Because Alan has a limited income he cannot afford to buy health insurance should he lose his partner's coverage. Alan feels isolated from his family because they do not know that he is gay, and he does not feel connected to the local gay community because he has not "come out" to many people. Alan's partner has threatened to tell other people about Alan's HIV status.

Alan feels threatened and fears that his partner could and would physically harm him if he tried to leave. Yet, he also appreciates the fact that his partner could seriously injure him if he stays—the violent episodes are getting progressively worse and also more frequent. He does not know what to do or where to turn for help. He is uncertain whether this local domestic violence agency and women's shelter can help him. Nothing he has seen or heard leads him to believe that the agency provides services to gay or bisexual men.

TRANSGENDER ISSUES IN INTIMATE PARTNER VIOLENCE

MONIQUE

You are an emergency department (ED) social worker in a public metropolitan hospital. You have received a referral from another staff member to assess Michael (40 years old) for violence exposure after he presented to the ED with a broken arm and a bruised face. The nurse has told you that he got into a fight with his boyfriend and that he is now afraid to go home.

J: Hi, Michael. My name is Jo. I'm a social worker here at the hospital. The nurse asked me to come and talk with you about how you're doing and if there are any concerns you have about going home that I could help you with.

M: My name is Monique.

J: I am so sorry! The nurse told me your name was Michael.

M: That's what my driver's license says, but that's not my name.

J: I see. Names are very important and I'm sorry I got yours wrong. Can we try again?

M: OK. (seems discouraged)

J: Monique, can you tell me a little about what brought you here to the emergency room?

M: (pause) My boyfriend got a little wild tonight and broke my arm.

J: A little wild?

M: Mmm hmm. He was drinking. He got upset with me.

J: He got upset and broke your arm. (M nods.) What was he upset about?

M: He gets upset sometimes when I go out with my friends. He gets jealous and when he drinks . . .

J: When he drinks, he gets upset and gets physical with you?

M: Yes. Sometimes.

J: How long have you two been together?

M: Three years, off and on. Mostly he treats me really good. He takes me out to dinner, pays the rent, and tells me he loves me.

J: Has he hurt you before?

M: A few times. Never this bad. Not ever like tonight.

J: Do you have any idea what made tonight different?

M: No. He has been more stressed out lately, having a hard time at his job.

J: How are you feeling about going home tonight?

M: (pause) I don't know.

J: Are you feeling afraid?

M: (long pause) I don't want to, but I've never seen him like this! He looked crazy. I was really scared that he was going to kill me. (Monique gets teary-eyed.)

J: Monique, it is normal to feel afraid after someone has hurt you like this. No one should ever be hurt by another person like you have been tonight.

M: (crying) It's just that I love him, but I'm scared, too. I don't want to go home. I'm sure he'll be waiting there. I don't know what he'll do. He has a gun. I don't want to go home.

J: OK. It sounds like it wouldn't be safe for you to go home tonight and that you're feeling pretty worried. Do you have somewhere else you could go while you sort things out?

M: I don't know. I don't know.

J: Monique, you've told me that you are afraid to go home, that your boyfriend has hurt you in the past, that he gets jealous of other people in your life, and tonight he has broken your arm and given you a black eye. These are all signs that you might be in an abusive relationship.

M: (Monique nods silently through her tears)

J: It is important for you to know that you're not alone, that you didn't cause this. The most important thing we can concentrate on right now is helping you to find somewhere safe to stay. I am concerned that your boyfriend has a gun—we know that women who are domestic violence victims are more likely to be seriously injured if their abuser has access to a weapon. Once we figure out where you can stay, then we can talk more about what else you might do to keep yourself safe.

M: All right.

J: We have two shelters in town for women who need a safe place when they have an abusive partner, but I don't know if they'd take a transgender woman.

M: I don't think they'd take me. I was homeless a few years ago when I first started to transition. They would only let me stay at the men's shelter. I've been taking hormones for over five years now.

J: I see. I'm sorry to hear that happened to you. I know that many people are not aware of the needs of transgender women. (Monique nods.) Do you have other people who you could call for help?

M: Not really. My mother has refused to talk to me since I started transitioning. She is ashamed of me. My brother lives in another state, and he's not really thrilled about me either. My friends are mainly other transgender women I've met.

J: Do you think any of them would be willing to help you right now?

M: I don't know. (Monique pauses.) I have a friend in the north end. Maybe I could call her. She knows that Dave gets out of hand sometimes.

J: I'd be happy to help you call her and see if you could stay there. But before we do that, would Dave know where she lives? Would this be a safe place for you?

M: Dave only knows her first name, and he doesn't know where she lives or how to contact her.

J: OK. That sounds like a good first step. I think the other thing we should talk about is whether you need a Protection Order. Do you know what that is?

M: No.

J: A Protection Order is given by the court and, depending on the circumstances, it tells a person that he cannot have contact with you, that he has to stay away from you physically. If he disobeys the order, you can call the police and have him arrested.

M: I can't call the police. I know I can't get a Protection Order.

J: Why not?

"CONTINUED"

M: Do you have any idea what the police do to transgender people like me? No. That's not going to help me.

J: Hmm. It sounds like you've had some bad experiences with the police. (Monique nods.) Monique, what if I gave you some information about Protection Orders for you to take and read? (Monique shrugs and nods.) For right now, I think we should try calling your friend, and I have some other information about domestic violence. Would you be interested in seeing it?

M: I suppose so.

J: OK, let's see if you can get in touch with your friend.

LESBIAN/BISEXUAL INTIMATE PARTNER VIOLENCE

ELISA AND KATRINA

You are a social worker in a community mental health agency and have just started to see a new client, Elisa, for counseling. She is experiencing depression and is coming to you with concerns about her current relationship. From her initial assessment, you know the following information.

Elisa is a 30-year-old Mexican American woman who has been with her girlfriend Katrina, a 37-year-old Filipina woman, for almost three years. They met through a mutual friend and have been living together for the past year. Prior to dating Katrina, Elisa has primarily been in relationships with men and identifies herself as bisexual. Katrina has been out as a lesbian for many years and is well known in the local LGBT community. Elisa and Katrina share many mutual friends who are primarily other Asian lesbians and other lesbians of color. They are also close to Katrina's family who lives nearby. Elisa has not told her parents that she is in a relationship with a woman and is afraid that they will disown her if it becomes known. Before meeting Katrina, Elisa was also very involved with a local Catholic Church but has since stopped attending because of her concern that the church would not accept her sexuality.

Early on in the relationship, Katrina began to criticize Elisa in front of their mutual friends, would accuse Elisa of having crushes on other women, and would check Elisa's cell phone to see who was calling and texting her. Katrina would get upset with Elisa for speaking Spanish with her friends and would insist that Elisa neglected her. Elisa gradually drifted away from her own friends and began to spend most of her time with Katrina. Over time, their arguments became more frequent. Katrina accused Elisa of sleeping with men, saying that she was not a "real" lesbian since she had not been in a relationship with a woman before and identified herself as bisexual.

In the past year Katrina has been pressuring Elisa to "come out" to her family, claiming that if Elisa really loved her that she would be honest with her family about

"CONTINUED"

their relationship. Katrina recently told Elisa that she was a bad person for lying to her family and that if she did not tell her parents soon, Katrina would find them in Mexico and tell them herself. Elisa is fearful of what will happen if Katrina "outs" her to her family. Recently, in the midst of an argument, Katrina threw a glass against the wall in a rage, blaming Elisa for making her so angry. Katrina has threatened to kill herself, saying that Elisa was making her feel like her life wasn't worth living. When Elisa tried to leave the room recently, Katrina blocked the door, and Elisa pushed Katrina, causing her to fall and injure herself. Elisa was mortified that she had done this and is worried that she is becoming abusive, a fear that Katrina has repeated to others.

Elisa is confused, unsure, and overwhelmed with what is going on with Katrina and is hesitant to talk to anyone. When she tried to tell a friend about Katrina's behavior, the friend said that she did not believe that Katrina could possibly act that way. Since Katrina is well respected in the local lesbian community and their friends are a small and close-knit group, Elisa feels that there is no one she can safely go to for support. She also feels protective of Katrina's reputation and does not want to isolate Katrina from the community. Elisa would like to stay in her relationship with Katrina and wants her to get counseling for her anger and controlling behavior. She is also possibly interested in couples counseling with Katrina.

REFLECTIONS ON THE CASE STUDIES

These cases contain issues that confront clients at each level of practice. Establishing a relationship with a client is a critical first step in working with individuals, and in the case of Monique, we see a social worker who excels at recognizing the need to respect Monique's gender identity; she refers to Monique with her preferred name, treats her relationship as real, and signals her openness to working with Monique as a transgender woman. In Katrina and Elisa's case, we see some of the complexity of assessing for IPV in LGBT relationships. In this situation, it is important to attend to the patterns of behavior each partner displays. Katrina is using several tactics of control in her relationship with Elisa. She is using emotional abuse, isolating Elisa, threatening to "out" her to her family, disallowing her from speaking Spanish with her peers, and throwing objects at her. During an argument where Katrina was blocking her escape, Elisa pushed Katrina which caused Katrina to be injured. Elisa is not attempting to restrict Katrina's social network, and she is not contesting her identity as a lesbian. In this case, the patterns of behavior indicate that Elisa is more likely a victim of abuse and not the abuser.

Safety planning is challenging in each of these cases because of the context of heterosexism and homophobia. For example, Alan feels isolated from his family and the community at because they do not know he is gay. He has not come out to many people, so he has a limited support network to draw upon for help with his relationship. In addition to the issues created by not being out to her family, Elisa also faces the challenge of being part of a small community of lesbians of color that faces multiple oppressions. She is part of a social network of support that both partners share, and within this network, her partner is well known and well respected, making it difficult for Elisa to access support. The emergency department social worker discovers barriers to obtaining help for Monique because of her transgender status. In the past, other shelters have refused to recognize Monique's gender identity and have insisted that she be treated as a man. In this context of limited resources (including a lack of family assistance related to the client's transgender status), the social worker helped Monique to identify a potential safe place to stay with another transgender person in Monique's social network.

Several organizational issues are revealed in these case studies. For example, hospital staff demonstrated insensitivity to transgender issues, as the referral to the social worker ignored Monique's gender identity, relying instead on the driver's license that stated she was male. In this situation, the social worker could ask for a review of hospital policy related to how clients' transgender status will be identified and respected. In Alan's case, the domestic violence service agency implicitly appears to subscribe to a model in which IPV only happens between men and women, with men as the abusive partner. As a result the agency has not developed policies, protocols, or materials for a gay male audience. Each of these agencies would benefit from assessing their current policies and practices in relation to LGBT survivors of abuse, and developing community-based programs to address barriers to safety for these clients.

These cases also illustrate community and policy concerns. For instance, Katrina and Elisa's social networks of family, friends, and community members may not be knowledgeable or supportive in helping Elisa address the abuse. At a policy level, we see an example in which the hospital social worker has proposed that her transgender client obtain a Protection Order. In this situation, the social worker needs more information about the larger policy context, including whether civil protection orders are actually available for transgender persons, and how safe a transgender woman would be in calling on the police to implement an order, were it available. Clearly further work would be needed to help Monique determine other available options, something that may be beyond the role of an emergency department social worker. In this case, it will be important for the social worker to know whether local LGBT services or domestic violence providers would be available to continue working with Monique. These are some of the issues that would arise when seeing clients in the situations described, and we invite readers to identify others.

CONCLUSION

Intimate partner violence among LGBT persons is a problem that needs to be addressed in our work with individual clients, in the ways we structure and provide services through organizations, and through our efforts at the community and policy levels to create lasting change. Social workers, domestic violence advocates, and other concerned community members have to examine their stance toward LGBT persons and question the overt and subtle ways in which they have used gender assumptions to define abuse in relationships. We must maintain an awareness of the ways in which heterosexism and homophobia contribute to IPV and create unique barriers for LGBT survivors who may be seeking support and safety. Even within the difficult context created by heterosexism, LGBT community members and survivors of abuse have created resources, challenged the domestic violence service system and the larger society to recognize LGBT relationships, and partnered in efforts to prevent violence in relationships. In our continuing work, we can draw on the legacy of strengths, resources, and coping strategies that have been developed by previous generations of lesbian, gay, bisexual, and transgender persons in our efforts to end abuse in all intimate relationships.

RESOURCES

IPV-SPECIFIC RESOURCES

Communities United Against Violence (CUAV)
170 A Capp Street
San Francisco, CA 94110
Phone: (415) 777-5500
E-mail: info@cuav.org
Web site: http://www.cuav.org

Fenway Community Health
7 Haviland Street
Boston, MA 02115
Phone: (617) 267–0900
Toll Free: 1 (888) 242–0900
Web site: http://www.fenwayhealth.org

Gay Men's Domestic Violence Project
Cambridge, MA 12139
Hotline: 1 (800) 832–1901
Phone: (617) 354–6056
E-mail: education@gmdvp.org
Web site: http://www.gmdvp.org

National Coalition of Anti-Violence Programs
(for LGBT violence, mainly related to hate crimes)
240 West 35th Street, Suite 200
New York, NY 10001
Phone: (212) 714–1184
E-mail: info@ncavp.org
Web site: http://www.ncavp.org/about/default.aspx
Web site: http://www.ncavp.org/AVPs/default.aspx (for a list of local anti-violence
programs serving LGBT communities throughout the U.S.)

The Network/La Red
(lesbian, bisexual women, and transgender domestic violence)
P.O. Box 6011
Boston, MA 02114
Phone: (617) 695–0897
Hotline : (617) 742–4911
Web site: http://www.networklared.org

Northwest Network of Bi, Trans, Lesbian, and Gay Survivors of Abuse
PO Box 20398
Seattle, WA 98102
Phone: (206) 568.7777
TTY: (206) 517.9670
E-mail: info@nwnetwork.org
Web site: http://www.nwnetwork.org

Queer Asian Women's Services (QAWS)
(a project of Asian Women's Shelter)
3543 18th St., #19
San Francisco, CA 94110
Phone: (415) 751.7110
Web site: http://www.sfaws.org

Survivor Project (for transgender survivors of IPV)
Phone: (503) 288–3191
E-mail: info@survivorproject.org
Web site: http://www.survivorproject.org/index.html

LGBT LEGAL AND POLICY-RELATED RESOURCES

Lamda Legal (National Office)
120 Wall Street
Suite 1500
New York, NY 10005–3904
Phone: (212) 809–8585
Web site: http://www.lambdalegal.org

National Center for Lesbian Rights (NCLR) (National Office)
870 Market Street Suite 370
San Francisco CA 94102
Phone: (415) 392–6257
E-mail: info@nclrights.org
Web site: http://www.nclrights.org

National Gay and Lesbian Task Force
1325 Massachusetts Ave. NW, Suite 600
Washington, DC 20005
Phone: (202) 393–5177
Web site: http://www.thetaskforce.org

Transgender Law Center
870 Market Street, Room 823
San Francisco, CA 94102
Phone: (415) 865–0176
E-mail: info@transgenderlawcenter.org

Queer Immigrant Rights Project
c/o American Friends Service Committee
15 Rutherford Place
New York, NY 10003
E-mail: info@quir.org
Web site: http://www.quir.org

INTERNET RESOURCES

An Abuse, Rape and Domestic Violence Aid and Resource Collection
(Web-based information)
Web site: http://www.aardvarc.org/dv/gay.shtml

National Center for State Courts
(Web page of LGBT domestic violence resources and links)
Web site: http://ncsconline.org/wc/CourTopics/ResourceGuide.
asp?topic=FamVioandguide=5

REFERENCES

Allen, C., and B. Leventhal. (1999). History, culture and identity: What makes GLBT battering different. In B. Leventhal and S. E. Lundy (Eds.), *Same-Sex Domestic Violence: Strategies for Change* (pp. 73–82). Thousand Oaks, CA: Sage.

Ambuel, B., L. K. Hamberger, and J. L. Lahti. (1997). The family peace project: A model for training health care professionals to identify, treat and prevent partner violence. In L. K. Hamberger, S. Burge, A. Graham, and A. Costa (Eds.), *Violence Issues for Health Care Educators and Providers* (pp. 55–81). Binghamton, NY: Haworth.

American Psychiatric Association. (1994). Sexual and gender identity disorders. In *Diagnostic and Statistical Manual of Mental Disorders* (4th Ed.) (pp.493–538). Washington, DC: American Psychiatric Association.

Amnesty International. (2006). Stonewalled — Still demanding respect. Police abuses against lesbian, gay, bisexual and transgender people in the USA. Retrieved February 13, 2008, from http://www.amnesty.org/en/library/info/AMR51/001/2006.

Balsam, K. F. (2001). Nowhere to hide: Lesbian battering, homophobia and minority stress. *Women and Therapy*, 23(3), 25–37.

Balsam, K. F., E. D. Rothblum, and T. P. Beauchaine. (2005). Victimization over the life span: A comparison of lesbian, gay, bisexual and heterosexual siblings. *Journal of Consulting and Clinical Psychology*, 73(3), 477–487.

Barrett, B., and C. Logan. (2002). *Counseling Gay Men and Lesbians*. Pacific Grove, CA: Brooks/Cole.

Betancourt, J. R., A. R. Green, and J. E Carrillo. (2002). *Cultural Competence in Health Care: Emerging Frameworks and Practical Approaches*. New York: Commonwealth Fund.

Burdge, B. J. (2007). Bending gender, ending gender: Theoretical foundations for social work practice with the transgender community. *Social Work*, 52(3), 243–250.

Cahill, S. (2004). *Same Sex Marriage in the United States: Focus on the Facts*. Lanham, MD: Lexington Books.

Chen, C. P. (2000). Provocation's privileged desire: The provocation doctrine, "homosexual panic," and the non-violent unwanted sexual advance defense. *Cornell Journal of Law and Public Policy*, 10, 195–235.

Dana, R. H., and L. Matheson. (1992). An application of the agency cultural competence checklist to a program serving small and diverse ethnic communities. *Psychological Rehabilitation Journal*, 15(1), 101–105.

Davies, J., and E. Lyons. (1998). *Safety Planning with Battered Women: Complex Lives/Difficult Choices*. Thousand Oaks, CA: Sage.

Drescher, J. (2002). Sexual conversion ("reparative") therapies: History and update. In B. E. Jones and M J. Hill (Eds.), *Mental Health Issues in Lesbian, Gay, Bisexual and Transgender Communities* (pp. 71–91). Washington, DC: American Psychiatric Publishing.

Dudley, R. G. (2002). Offering psychiatric opinion in legal proceedings when lesbian or gay sexual orientation is an issue. In B. E. Jones and M J. Hill (Eds.), *Mental Health Issues in Lesbian, Gay, Bisexual and Transgender Communities* (pp. 37–70). Washington, DC: American Psychiatric Publishing.

Fisher, B., and J. S. Akman. (2002). Normal development in sexual minority youth. In B. E. Jones and M. J. Hill (Eds.), *Mental Health Issues in Lesbian, Gay, Bisexual and Transgender Communities* (pp. 1–16). Washington, DC: American Psychiatric Publishing.

Goode, T. D., W. Jones, and J. Mason. (2002). *A Guide to Planning and Implementing Cultural Competence: Organizational Self-assessment*. Washington, DC: National Center for Cultural Competence.

Hanson, B., and T. Maroney. (1999). HIV and same-sex domestic violence. In B. Leventhal and S. E. Lundy (Eds.), *Same-Sex Domestic Violence: Strategies for Change* (pp. 97–110). Thousand Oaks, CA: Sage.

Island, D., and P. Letellier. (1991). *Men Who Beat the Men Who Love Them*. New York: Harrington Park.

Kanuha, V. (1994). Women of color in battering relationships. In L. Comez-Dias and B. Greene (Eds.), *Women of Color: Integrating Ethnic and Gender Identities in Psychotherapy* (pp. 428–454). New York: Guilford.

Lee, S., and H. Utarti. (2003). *Creating Community, Hope, and Change.* San Francisco, CA.: Family Violence Prevention Fund.

Leedy, G., and C. Connolly. (2008). Out in the cowboy state: A look at lesbian and gay lives in Wyoming. *Journal of Gay and Lesbian Social Services* 19(1), 17–34.

Lindhorst, T., P. Nurius, and R. Macy. (2005). Contextualized assessment with battered women: Strategic safety planning to cope with multiple harms. *Journal of Social Work Education,* 41(2), 371–393.

Lobel, K. (1986). *Naming the Violence: Speaking Out against Lesbian Battering.* Seattle, WA: Seal.

McLaughlin, E. M., and P. D. Rozee. (2001). Knowledge about heterosexual versus lesbian battering among lesbians. *Women and Therapy,* 23(3), 39–58.

Morrow, D. F., and L. Messinger. (2006). *Sexual Orientation and Gender Expression in Social Work Practice: Working with Gay, Lesbian, Bisexual, and Transgender People.* New York: Columbia University Press.

Mullaly, B. (2002). *Challenging Oppression: A Critical Social Work Approach.* Don Mills, Ontario: Oxford University Press.

Nardi, P. M. (1997). Changing gay and lesbian images in the media. In J. T. Sears and W. L. Williams (Eds.), *Overcoming Heterosexism and Homophobia* (pp. 427–432). New York: Columbia University Press.

National Association of Social Workers (NASW). (2006). *Social Work Speaks* (7th Ed.). Washington, DC: NASW Press

National Coalition of Anti-Violence Projects. (2001). Protection order availability chart. Retrieved September 15, 2007, from http://www.ncavp.org/backup/document_files/Order%20of%20Protection%20Availability%20Chart.pdf.

National Gay and Lesbian Task Force. (2007). Jurisdictions with explicitly transgender-inclusive nondiscrimination laws. Retrieved January 29, 2008, from http://the taskforce.org/downloads/reports/fact_sheets/all_jurisdictions_w_pop_12_07 .pdf.

Osthoff, S. (2002). But, Gertrude, I beg to differ, a hit is not a hit is not a hit: When battered women are arrested for assaulting their partners. *Violence Against Women,* 8(12), 1521–1544.

Pharr, S. (1988). *Homophobia: A Weapon of Sexism.* Little Rock, AR: Chardon.

Project Implicit. (n.d.). Implicit association demonstration tests. Retrieved October 12, 2007, from: https://implicit.harvard.edu/implicit/demo/selectatest.html.

Renzetti, C. (1992). *Violent Betrayal: Partner Abuse in Lesbian Relationships.* Newbury Park, CA: Sage.

Richman, K. (2002). Lovers, legal strangers and parents: Negotiating parental and sexual identity in family law. *Law and Society Review,* 36(2), 285–324.

Ristock, J. (2002). *No More Secrets: Violence in Lesbian Relationships*. New York: Routledge.

Ristock, J., and N. Timbang. (2005). Relationship violence in lesbian/gay/bisexual/transgender/queer (LGBTQ) communities: Moving beyond a gender-based framework. *Violence Against Women Online Resources*. Retrieved November 1, 2007, from http://www.mincava.edu/documents/lgbtqviolence/lgbtqviolence.html.

Saunders, D. G., M. C. Holter, L. C. Pahl, R. M. Tolman, and C. E. Kenna. (2005). TANF workers' responses to battered women and the impact of brief worker training. *Violence Against Women*, 11(2): 227–254.

Sears, J. T. (1997). Thinking critically/intervening effectively about homophobia and heterosexism. In J. T. Sears and W. L. Williams (Eds.), *Overcoming Heterosexism and Homophobia* (pp. 13–48). New York: Columbia University Press.

Smith, D. M., and G. J. Gates. (2001). *Gay and Lesbian Families in the United States: Same Sex Unmarried Partner Households*. Washington, DC: Human Rights Campaign Fund.

Straus, M. A., R. J. Gelles, and S. K. Steinmetz. (1980). *Behind Closed Doors: Violence in the American Family*. Garden City, NY: Anchor Press/Doubleday.

Sulis, S. (1999). Battered bisexual women. In B. Leventhal and S. E. Lundy (Eds.), *Same-Sex Domestic Violence: Strategies for Change* (pp. 173–180). Thousand Oaks, CA: Sage.

Tarver, D. E. (2002). Transgender mental health: The intersection of race, sexual orientation and gender identity. In B. E. Jones and M J. Hill (Eds.), *Mental Health Issues in Lesbian, Gay, Bisexual and Transgender Communities* (pp. 93–108). Washington, DC: American Psychiatric Publishing.

Tjaden, P., N. Thoennes, and C. J. Allison. (1999). Comparing violence over the life span in samples of same-sex and opposite cohabitants. *Violence and Victims*, 14(4), 413–425.

Tjaden, P., and N. Thoennes. (2000). *Extent, Nature and Consequences of Intimate Partner Violence: Findings from the National Violence Against Women Survey*, NCJ 181867. Washington, DC: National Institute of Justice and Centers for Disease Control.

Tolman, R. (2003). Help-seeking by battered women receiving welfare benefits. Paper presented at the Trapped by Poverty/Trapped by Abuse Conference, Austin, TX, October.

Unpacking the invisible knapsack II: Daily effects of straight privilege. (n.d.). Retrieved October 12, 2007, from http://www.cs.earlham.edu/~hyrax/personal/files/student_res/straightprivilege.htm.

Waldner-Hangrud, L. K., L. V. Gratch, and B. Magruder. (1997). Victimization and perpetration rates of violence in gay and lesbian relationships: Gender issues explored. *Violence and Victims*, 12, 173–184.

Whittier, D. K. (1997). Social conflict among "gay" men in a small(er) southern town. In J. D. Smith and R. J. Mancoske (Eds.), *Rural Gays and Lesbians: Building on the Strengths of Communities* (pp. 53–72). New York: Haworth.

Williams, O. J. (1993). *Are Partner Abuse Programs Prepared to Work with African American Men Who Batter?* Minneapolis, MN: University of Minnesota School of Social Work.

Williams, O. J., and L. R. Becker. (1994). Partner abuse programs and cultural competence: The results of a national study. *Violence and Victims*, 9(3), 287–296.

10

IN SERVICE TO OUR COUNTRY

Military Responses to Domestic Violence

Delores F. Johnson and Deborah D. Tucker

THIS CHAPTER provides an overview of domestic violence issues for women whose partners are members of the military as well as for women serving in the military. The dynamics of domestic violence are often the same in both civilian and military communities, and the military's response to domestic violence mirrors the development of appropriate community strategies that have been instituted around the country. For example, just as many communities have adopted mandatory arrest policies, the military has adopted a "zero tolerance" policy toward domestic violence. However, the military has its own culture, including its own rules, protocols, customs, cultural norms, and legal system.

This chapter discusses the unique characteristics of military life and how these may contribute to the risks for domestic violence, the availability of service options within the military, and the need for collaboration between military and civilian service providers and responders. The military's Family Advocacy Program provides services to women and their children who are or have been impacted by domestic violence. However, given that many military personnel and their families live off military installations and in the general community, civilian social workers and domestic violence advocates may encounter families connected to the military as part of their caseloads. It is important, therefore, that civilian service providers understand military culture, and how to access services and support on military facilities and within military organizations.

OVERVIEW OF THE MILITARY

The mission of the military is to defend U.S. territories and occupied areas and to overcome any aggressor that imperils our nation's peace and security.

To meet this mission, the military has five primary branches: the Army, Navy, Air Force, and Marines who all report to the U. S. Department of Defense (DoD) headquartered in the Pentagon, and the Coast Guard, which reports to the Office of Homeland Security. In 2007 almost 1.5 million active duty military personal were in the Army, comprising the largest number (522,388), followed by the Navy (336,214), Air Force (332,663), Marines (186,209), and finally, the Coast Guard (41,738) (U.S. DoD 2007). Although the total number of military personnel has decreased from a high of 3.07 million in 1970, the number of women in the military has steadily increased up to the late eighties, early nineties. In recent years the number of enlisted women and officers appears to have slightly declined in the Army, Navy, and Air force but has remained steady in the U.S. Marine Corps (U.S. Census Bureau 2007). In 2007 more than two hundred thousand women comprised about 14 percent of the total military personnel (U.S. DoD 2007).

According to the Military HOMEFRONT Web site, nearly 80 percent of the active duty personnel are 35 years old or younger, and 50 percent of those are 25 years of age or younger. Slightly more than half the active duty personnel are married (52.9%) and 6.8 percent of service members have partners who also serve in the military. Women married to active duty service members earn less and are less likely to be employed than their civilian counterparts (Hosek et al. 2002). One-third of those who are married have children. Close to 900,000 children live with military parents, 55 percent of whom are 5 years old and younger (U.S. DoD Military HOMEFRONT 2006).

Approximately 70 percent of all military personnel are stationed in the United States at any given time, and 56 percent of service members stationed in the United States will live in the civilian community because of a limited supply of military installation housing (U.S. DoD Military HOMEFRONT 2006). The states with the most military personnel in descending order are California, Virginia, Texas, North Carolina, Georgia, Florida, Washington, Hawaii, South Carolina, and Kentucky (Military HOMEFRONT 2006).

Based on these demographics, service members apparently share some of the domestic violence risk factors common among civilian populations, including economic dependency on an abuser and the prevalence of young children impacting women's decisions to stay or leave. Aspects of military life may exacerbate domestic violence risks for women and their children. These include separation and isolation from support networks of family and friends because of continually changing locations, more youthful populations than their civilian counterparts, and a complex culture that often facilitates the very behaviors it seeks to eradicate.

PREVALENCE AND INCIDENCE OF DOMESTIC VIOLENCE IN THE MILITARY

As in the civilian population, efforts to capture exact incidents and prevalence of domestic violence are difficult and inconclusive. Because of the concentration of youthful age groups within the military, it is not possible to say whether those within the armed forces are more likely to be abusers than those in the general public. And because service members live in surrounding civilian communities, surveillance and detection efforts do not always capture the full extent of the problem within the military.

The prevalence of domestic violence among women serving in the military is also important to consider. In a sample of active-duty women, lifetime prevalence of domestic violence was reported at approximately 30 percent, which is comparable to the civilian population, and the prevalence of intimate partner violence (IPV) during the time of military service was 21.6 percent. Although enlisted women were more likely to be abused, women officers (14.5%) also reported abuse during their military service. Women were most likely to be abused by their active duty partners (43%), followed by retired military partners (38%). Also, women with three or more children were more likely to be abused than women with fewer children (Campbell et al. 2003).

The military's Family Advocacy Program keeps data on reported incidents of domestic violence. In fiscal year 2005, approximately 16,000 incidents were reported. In the majority (63%) of cases, the abusers were reported to be active-duty members. In 37 percent of cases, the abuser was identified as the civilian partner of an active-duty member (U.S. DoD 2005). In 2005, 11 fatalities occurred. The risks of domestic violence at army installations were underscored by four homicides in 2002 involving active-duty soldiers and their spouses at Fort Bragg, North Carolina. Those cases led to an extensive Army review, which concluded that the Army could do more to support soldiers and their families (Hickman and Davis 2003).

Information from the Army about whether the prevalence of domestic assaults increases among personnel returning from combat is currently not available. However, the Department of Veterans Affairs acknowledges the increased risk for domestic violence for service members suffering from Post

Traumatic Stress Disorder (PTSD) (National Center for Post Traumatic Stress Disorder 2007).

UNDERSTANDING MILITARY CULTURE

Civilian social workers and community-based advocates must be aware of several unique characteristics of military life. These include an understanding of the "chain of command," standards of discipline, mental and physical conditioning, ethos of loyalty and self-sacrifice, the multidisciplinary support system, and the military's ceremonies and etiquette.

"CHAIN OF COMMAND"

Military personnel are accorded responsibility and authority depending on their rank. Commanding Officers are responsible for following and enforcing regulations and sustaining mission readiness. Unlike executives and supervisors in corporations, military commanders have a great deal of power over their subordinates both at work and at home. Not only do they have authority over work assignments, they also can discipline members of their units for unacceptable work performance or other behaviors (e.g., intimate partner violence) that may have a negative influence on that member's mission readiness. In this way, they have powers much like those of civilian judges. Consequently, work and home life of military personnel are not separated as distinctively for military families as for civilian employees.

Commanding Officers need to know virtually every aspect of their members' lives. There is no right to privacy or confidentiality. There are no institutional boundaries between one's employer, doctor, judge, social worker, or advocate. Commanding Officers are entitled to know whether a service member sought treatment for an abscess tooth, a lump on the breast, or depression.

The chain of command is necessary to maintain good order and discipline in peace and war; it exerts a powerful control over the individuals in the command. Because the commander is primarily responsible for successful outcomes related to actions of their subordinates, he/she has a pivotal role in ensuring that the system responds appropriately to every reported or suspected incidence of abuse. However, the commander's role also is impacted by overall Army culture. The military policy of zero tolerance of domestic violence may contribute to an environment where both soldiers and leaders are reluctant to come forward for fear of discharge or other negative consequences.

STANDARDS OF DISCIPLINE

High standards of discipline, mental and physical conditioning, and an ethos of loyalty and self-sacrifice are key elements to achieving order on the battlefield and in the unit. These characteristics may contribute to reluctance by personnel to admit weakness by seeking help. Personnel who are concerned about a member within their unit may also be reluctant to reach out to the abused person or to report any acts or suspicion of domestic violence to superiors. Reporting suspected abuse that affects a member of your unit may be seen as a disloyal act, especially with military policies stating that there is a zero tolerance toward abuse.

THE MULTIDISCIPLINARY SUPPORT SYSTEM

The military system of support, which incorporates a multidisciplinary approach, is seamless but can appear daunting to those not involved. The military system multidisciplinary approach includes its own police force and legal system. The overlapping jurisdiction between military installations and civilian communities creates the potential for confusion regarding the entity responsible for responding to domestic violence. The majority of domestic violence among military families occurs behind closed doors; these doors, however, most likely will be on local community/civilian land because housing on military installations across the country is limited.

Because both civilian and military communities are likely to have contact with abusive and abused partners, it is important that these overlapping entities have good working relationships and coordinate their services to enhance safety for victims and accountability for abusers. Civilian social workers and advocates must recognize that the complexity of the military requires additional attention to developing and establishing professional rapport. It is important not to assume how things are organized but to ask respectful questions to allow military personnel to explain how they address certain situations.

MILITARY CEREMONIES AND RITUALS

Finally, the military culture has its own ceremonies and etiquette that include shared rituals emphasizing group behavior and esprit d'corps. These practices differ between the branches of services and various communities in the same way that one county's practices differ from another. It is important to understand how this strong sense of belonging and individualism can influence the reporting behavior of unit members. For example, a strong sense of esprit d'corps may influence a member's desire to "cover" for their brothers or resist reporting offenses to the chain of command for fear of negative consequences, such as reprisals for themselves or their friends. The military's emphasis on individual values underscores the need to ensure that military members do the right thing on an individual basis to strengthen the overall community. Thus the contradiction between being responsible for one's own behavior and being responsible to the group may be a barrier to reporting to a commander or voicing concern about domestic violence to unit members for fear it will negatively impact the unit as a whole.

REASSIGNMENTS AND DEPLOYMENTS

The frequent reassignment of service member families from place to place, often with unfamiliar cultures and values, isolates many victims from familiar support systems and strengthens an abuser's isolation tactics. The primary support system for military families becomes other military families, thus potentially increasing the need to keep abuse secret.

Deployments to combat areas also contribute to family separations and reunifications. The partner left at home, usually the wife, must assume roles and responsibilities that her husband had fulfilled. Upon his return, issues may arise related to his resuming those same roles without renegotiating around current circumstances or acknowledging that the family has developed new ways of working together. Abusive partners are often insensitive to the feelings of other family members and may interpret any changes as "violations" of their family rules. Long separations can foster distrust between the couple and uncertainty about their future.

Service members returning from active combat duty may also be suffering from PTSD. Symptoms such as hyper-arousal, difficulty concentrating, aggressive behavior, sleep disturbances, depression, drinking, and substance abuse may also increase the risk factors for domestic abuse (Veterans Administration 2007). Keep in mind that service members may not want their commanding officer to know that they are experiencing PTSD and may delay seeking help.

Civilian practitioners must be familiar with the idiosyncratic culture of the military in order to frame effective intervention approaches that support victim safety and well-being while encouraging offenders to rethink attitudes, beliefs, and behaviors contributing to their use of intimidation or violence. Practitioners must at least be able to speak in the language of that culture if they are to effect positive change and secure victims' safety.

IMPACT ON MILITARY FAMILIES

The cultural norms of concentrated power, blending of home and work, separations and deployments, and emphasis on group behavior and esprit d'corps can profoundly influence military families and may exacerbate the dynamics of power and control common in domestic abuse. Keeping the violence behind closed doors has even stronger primacy; service members have a strong desire to keep confidential information that might negatively impact how they are viewed by their commanding officers. Many batterers justify their abuse as the need to "correct bad behavior" demonstrated by their partners. The notion that service members are responsible for the behavior of their wives and children may serve as additional justification for those inclined to abuse.

For the abused woman, fear of career consequences to her partner is also a strong deterrent to reporting domestic violence. Although few service members are actually discharged as a result of domestic violence, the numbers who face other adverse career consequences (e.g., loss of assignment or promotion) is unknown. For certain service members, conviction of a domestic violence offense (in either a civilian or military court) means that they will (or should) be discharged, reassigned, or otherwise separated from the service.

Economic dependency of the abused partner is also a significant deterrent to reporting abuse. Not only does the military issue a paycheck, but the other benefits of military service such as housing assistance, day care, health care, and formal support services are highly valued benefits for many young families. The potential of losing these services contributes to the life-generated risks women may consider in their decision to stay or leave an abusive partner.

MILITARY RESPONSE: POLICY AND INTERVENTION

Each service branch has its own specific policies and procedures that implement congressional, presidential, and DoD directives, which are announced in written memorandums. Common to all branches are benefit entitlements, applicability of federal laws, and the existence of the Family Advocacy Program (FAP) and its Victim Advocacy Services. Differences between services may include standardized protocols and operating procedures, types of services provided to families and victims, housing policies and procedures, and types of outreach and prevention programs (Beals and Erwin 2007).

The Family Advocacy Program is the internal military department with primary responsibility for family violence prevention, identification, assessment, victim support, and abuser intervention programs (U.S. DoD 2007). The FAP, which is present on every military installation in the world, is responsible for addressing both child and domestic abuse in military families. Military regulations require military and DoD officials to report any suspicion of family violence to the FAP. In most cases the commander or first sergeant will order the military member to reside in the barracks away from the family until a safety assessment can be conducted or the investigation is completed. On the installation, military police investigate the incident and notify Family Advocacy personnel and the service member's commander.

If the abuser is a civilian-connected military person, the investigation is turned over to the civilian law enforcement personnel. If the incident occurs off the installation, the civilian police will likely be the first responders. Upon learning of the case, Family Advocacy staff assigns a victim advocate, typically a social worker, to assess the victim's safety, develop a safety plan, interview the offender, and develop a recommended treatment strategy to present to the multidisciplinary case management team. The team, consisting of social workers, lawyers, criminal investigators, drug and alcohol personnel, and chaplains, decides whether the evidence indicates that abuse occurred. Based on the team's recommendation, the commander determines what actions to take regarding the abuser, including sanctions, disciplinary actions, or military discharge. This process is undergoing changes based on the recommendations from the 2001–2003 congressional-appointed Task Force on Domestic Violence convened by the DoD.

The Task Force was comprised of civilian experts on domestic violence as well as military officials who have a role in addressing domestic violence such as command, personnel officers, attorneys, and law enforcement. The membership of the task force mirrored a civilian coordinated community response. The Task Force reviewed policies and procedures; visited installations; talked to victims, perpetrators, interveners, local officials, and domestic violence agency staff to understand the challenges and barriers to effective intervention; and made recommendations for changes, by both the military services and local interveners. Three annual reports describe the work of the task force, its findings, and recommendations (see http://www .ncdsv. org/ncd_militaryresponse.html). As a result of the Task Force, the Department of Defense issued several directives emphasizing that domestic violence will not be tolerated in the military.

The DoD also adopted a different and more comprehensive definition of domestic violence. The new definition includes assault, battery, threat to injure or kill, other acts of force or violence, and emotional maltreatment inflicted on a partner in a lawful marriage when one or more partners is a military member or employed by the DoD and is eligible for treatment in a medical treatment facility. A spouse under the age of eighteen is included in this definition. A standardized definition of domestic violence helps to provide consistent implementation of DoD policies.

Other recommendations that have been enacted include standardized Military Protective Orders, the Armed Forces Domestic Security Act (PL 107–311), options for confidentiality, increased victim services at Family Advocacy Programs, standardized safety plans, and formal collaborations between military installations and the civilian communities where they are located.

MILITARY PROTECTIVE ORDERS

Military Protective Orders (MPOs) are similar to civilian protective orders and are issued by Commanding Officers. MPOs prohibit contact and communication between service members and protected persons, requires them to stay a certain distance away from the residence or workplace of the abused individual, and requires them to vacate the shared residence, attend counseling, and surrender their weapons. When a commanding officer issues an MPO it is automatically sent to FAP and to military law enforcement. An MPO has full force and effect anywhere in the world but can only be enforced by military police intervention.

THE ARMED FORCES DOMESTIC SECURITY ACT

The Armed Forces Domestic Security Act addresses confusion over military and civilian jurisdictions for protective orders. Because many active duty service members live off the installation, an abused partner may seek a Protective Order (PO) from a civilian jurisdiction. Prior to this new law, an abusive service member could avoid being served or avoid accountability for a violation of a civilian PO by staying on the military installation. This new law allows for civilian POs to have the same force and effect on a DoD installation. However, military POs have not been granted full faith and credit beyond the boundaries of the military installation. If an MPO is in effect, civilian law enforcement can hold someone until military police arrive, at which time there is a Memorandum of Understanding (MOU) between the installation and civilian law enforcement. It is also important to note that DoD civilian employees who violate a civilian PO while on a military installation are also subject to disciplinary action (Chu 2003).

RESTRICTED AND UNRESTRICTED CONFIDENTIALITY OPTIONS

One of the barriers abused women face when seeking help has been the lack of confidentiality within the military. Because a commanding officer is notified about the nature of counseling sessions, many women are reluctant to seek services on the installation. In response to this barrier, the DoD issued a policy allowing victims to obtain basic information and guidance without having to file a formal complaint with military law enforcement or command (U.S. DoD 2006). This is called a Restricted Report.

Abused persons seeking help from a military victim advocate now chooses whether to make a restricted or an unrestricted report. In the former, a victim can confidentially receive medical treatment, advocacy services, support, and counseling, and any evidence collected is destroyed after one year. Neither law enforcement nor command is notified, and no action is taken against the offender. However, concerns about child abuse or serious and imminent threat to the health and safety of the victim or another person are exceptions to confidentiality in a restricted report.

In an unrestricted report, military law enforcement, the offender's commanding officer, and the victim's commanding officer (if applicable) are notified of the report. A law enforcement investigation will occur. The victim can also receive an MPO and be encouraged to obtain a civilian PO through local courts. With an unrestricted report, the victim is entitled to medical treatment, advocacy services, support, and counseling. The advantage of the unrestricted report is the potential for swift intervention: Commanding Officers may order MPOs and mandate offenders to attend intervention programs. Service members are subject to command orders 24 hours a day, 7 days a week; even without a formal military protective order, violation of a direct order from one's Commanding Officer may be grounds for disciplinary action. Some abused partners may want to test the waters by using a restricted report first, which allows the victim to learn about what might happen and what support is available before making an unrestricted report later on when the victim is aware of the steps that will follow (see Table 10.1).

VICTIM ADVOCACY PROGRAM

The establishment of a victim advocacy program within FAP ensures access to support and information for victims of domestic violence. Victim advocates are responsible for providing information about military response options; conducting risk assessments; safety planning; assisting in obtaining military and civilian protective orders; discussing confidentiality options;

TABLE 10.1 Differences Between Restricted and Unrestricted Reports

RESTRICTED REPORT	UNRESTRICTED REPORT
1. Report to victim advocate, supervisor of victim advocate, or health care provider	1. Report to commander, Family Advocacy Program, or law enforcement
2. No law enforcement investigation	2. Law enforcement investigation
3. Eligible for victim advocacy services	3. Receives family advocacy services
4. Safety is addressed through safety planning	4. Commander focuses on immediate safety; can order active-duty member abuser into quarters on the installation
5. Eligible for medical care	5. Eligible for medical care
6. No Military Protective Order; can obtain a civilian PO but, if enforced, will trigger a military investigation	6. Commander can issue a Military Protective Order; encourage civilian PO
7. Allows more time to make informed decisions about future reports to command or law enforcement	7. Immediately sets a military response in motion.
	8. Case Review Committee Meeting held to coordinate treatment plan
	9. Can order individual or group treatment for the abuser; FAP updates abuser's progress and changes in family circumstances
	10. Counseling for the victim, stress management classes
	11. Couples counseling never ordered

and offering referrals for military and civilian services. Victim advocates use standardized military safety plans that include information for contacting military police, commanding officers, family advocacy program, and military chaplains.

Victim services personnel also provide training about domestic violence to other personnel on an installation and participate in military and civilian coordinated community response programs. FAP is also responsible for coordinating and implementing prevention programs that include public awareness and education, and participating in screening programs available through family centers, medical clinics, and chaplains. Some installations offer stress management and couples counseling, and have batterer intervention programs available.

One of the military services available to families is the Transitional Compensation Program, which provides financial, health, and dental care, and commissary and exchange benefits for abused partners and their children for 12 to 36 months. Household goods can also be shipped to a new residence should the abused partner relocate.

COLLABORATION BETWEEN INSTALLATIONS AND CIVILIAN COMMUNITIES

A Memorandum of Understanding between local courts, law enforcement, local domestic violence programs, and the military installation can help identify specific and joint roles and responsibilities, service availability, and referral protocols. The Commanding Officer of the installation is responsible for initiating and signing an MOU on behalf of the installation and all its personnel. Civilian social workers and advocates involved in domestic violence programs may also want to contact installation commanders to develop an MOU if one does not already exist. (See Hickman and Davis 2003, for more information about establishing MOUs between military installations and civilian communities.)

Involving military personnel in civilian coordinated community response task forces and coordinating councils is critical to developing and implementing policies and procedures that insure that victims do not fall through bureaucratic cracks, whether civilian or military. With the victim's permission, case reviews to coordinate services should be conducted either regularly or as needed.

CASE STUDY

Kate had been married for 13 years and has three minor children ages 3, 8, and 12. The older children attend community schools. Kate's husband had been in the Army for 15 years. The couple lived off the installation. The local police responded to a domestic violence call and observed that the victim's clothing was torn, her right eye was swollen, and two fingers were severely swollen and reddened. Kate stated that her husband had dragged her out of bed by her hair, strangled her, broke her fingers, and punched her in the eye. She reported that her husband has a drinking problem and had threatened suicide. Her husband denied having hit her. The police arrested him. During the follow-up investigation, Kate denied that her husband had caused her injuries. She stated that she and her husband had had a verbal argument which started when she carelessly tripped and fell down the stairs, hitting her eye on the corner of the newel post at the stair base. Her husband had been upset because she had almost crashed into their three-year-old child and had been afraid her clumsiness would endanger the child. Kate expressed concern that he might lose rank or lose pay. She also expressed concerned that he might be discharged from the Army. There was no other household income. All three children had been present in the house at the time of the incident. The older son was having behavioral problems at school.

The local police provided Kate with the phone number of the National Domestic Violence Hotline. She called and was referred to a local domestic violence community program. The advocate from the local program listened to Kate, who revealed that the abuse had been going on for several years and was apparently happening more frequently. She expressed feelings of guilt for her wish that the husband would be sent to some combat zone to get him out of the house. Kate also told the advocate about her worries that her son was developing some of his father's behaviors and was becoming increasingly unmanageable at home and at school. The advocate reassured Kate that she was not alone. Their program received many requests for help from military wives each month. She explained the various options for women who are married to a military service member and those who are not. The local community advocate then offered to refer Kate to a military social worker who was a victim advocate at the Army's Family Advocacy Program.

Kate contacted the FAP. Before she could tell her story, the social worker or victim advocate explained options regarding confidentiality and its limitations. At this point Kate pursued a restricted report to prevent jeopardizing her husband's career as well as retaliation should he discover that she reported the abuse. The victim advocate helped Kate develop a safety plan. Kate also decided to attend a confidential counseling group with other military wives, knowing that other military spouses would understand the problems she was facing.

Before Kate attended her first group, she was severely assaulted by her husband. He had not received the promotion he expected and blamed her for having called the civilian police the week before. Somehow word spread that he had lost his temper with her, and now he had lost his promotion. Kate saw something in him that she had

"CONTINUED"

not seen before. Whereas his abuse had been primarily emotional and sometimes physical in the past, this time he had assaulted her sexually. He threatened that she would pay for his losing his promotion. Kate was raped and became more fearful of her husband than ever before.

The next day, after her husband returned to work, Kate contacted the FAP victim advocate. This time she was certain that she needed to secure distance from her husband, take the children, and stay with her family back home. With promises of a safe place to stay, Kate made an unrestricted report to FAP. She understood that her husband's Commanding Officer would be notified, and that FAP and the military police would conduct an investigation to substantiate a claim that domestic violence had occurred. The investigation might include interviewing children, neighbors, or other witnesses, and also a medical referral to document her injuries. If the family advocacy substantiated the case, then FAP would recommend an intervention strategy that would increase Kate's safety as well as secure access to the various programs that could assist her. FAP could also recommend that her husband be mandated to a Batterer Intervention Program and would help Kate get a Military Protective Order. Kate also thought he should get help for his drinking problem.

Kate saw this as her best option at this time and felt more certain that the case would be substantiated when her medical records revealed her broken finger and bruises. She needed help from the FAP in arranging for relocation expenses; the Transitional Compensation Program would provide some income and health insurance for Kate and the children. Kate was not sure she wanted her marriage to end, but she was sure that she wanted distance from her husband until he obtained help. She also understood that if the domestic violence case was not substantiated, she would still be offered services and would have the right to take out a Protective Order in the local community that would be honored on the installation.

CONCLUSION

Military service adds additional levels of complexity to the lives of service members and their families. Unique military characteristics present additional challenges for how support is provided for women married to active-duty members. Frequent relocation adds to isolation from family and friend support networks; deployments to combat areas may increase the risk factors for abuse. Many military families live off the installation in local civilian communities, and this creates jurisdictional challenges in providing services and holding abusers accountable.

The military has developed unique programs to address domestic violence, including Military Protective Orders, the recognition of civilian Protective Orders on military installations, restricted reporting options, transitional compensation, and relocation help. The role of the FAP's military social workers and victim advocates is key to assisting women in understanding and negotiating the complexity of military options. Civilian social workers and domestic violence advocates located in communities near military installations need to reach out and work with Commanding Officers and their designees to develop MOUs between professionals on the installation and local responders, as well as to ensure participation of social workers, law enforcement, and others in local coordinated community response efforts.

RESOURCES

Active Duty Members and Family Members
Military One Source 1 (800) 342–9647 (User name: military; Password: one source)

American Domestic Violence Crisis Line
Phone: 1 (866) US WOMEN (866–879–6636)
International support 10–6 Pacific Time

Department of Defense Family Advocacy Program
1745 Jefferson Davis Highway
Crystal Square 4, Suite 302
Arlington, VA 22202
Phone: (703) 602–4990
DSN: 332–4990

Department of Defense Task Force on Care for Victims of Sexual Assault
Hotline: 1 (800) 497–6261

Military Family Resource Center
4040 North Fairfax Drive, Room 420
Arlington, VA 22203–1635
Phone: (703) 696–9053
DSN: 426–9053

National Center on Domestic and Sexual Violence
Web site: http://www.ncdsv.org.

Sexual Assault Prevention and Response Office
Web site: http://www.sapr.mil.

U.S. Air Force Family Advocacy Program
AFMOA/SGZF
2664 Flight Nurse, Building 801
Brooks AFB, Texas 78235–5135
Phone: (210) 536–2031/32
DSN: 240–2031/32

U.S. Army Family Advocacy Program
Family and MWR Command
Department of the Army
4700 King Street, 4th Floor
Alexandria, VA 22302–4418
Phone: (703) 681–7396/93

U.S. Marine Corps
HQMC MandRA (MRO)
3280 Russell Road
Quantico, VA 22134–5009
Phone: (703) 784–9546
DSN: 278–9546

U.S. Navy Family Advocacy Program
Naval Personnel Command P661
Department of the Navy
5720 Integrity Drive
Millington, TN 38055–6610
Phone: (901) 874–4355
DSN: 882–4355
Service-Specific Information
Air Force: 1 (800) 435–9941
Army: 1 (800) 833–6622
Marines: 1 (800) 847–1597
National Guard Bureau: 1 (888) 777–7731
Navy: 1 (877) 414–5358
Department of Veterans Affairs: 1 (800) 827–1000

Red Cross/Emergency Messages
Active-duty service members and family members may contact the Red Cross
Armed Forces Emergency Service Centers at 1 (877) 272–7337. The following
information is helpful in sending an emergency message: full name, rank/rating,

branch of service, social security number, and military address or information about the deployed unit and home installation unit.

REFERENCES

Beals, J. E., and P. E. Erwin. (2007). Understanding the military responses to domestic violence: Tools for civilian advocates, Battered Women's Justice Project, Minneapolis, MN. Retrieved January 21, 2008, from httw://www.bwjp.org.

Campbell, J. C., M. A. Garza, A. C. Gielen, P. O'Campo, J. Kub, J. Dienemann, A. S. Jones, and E. Jafar. (2003). Intimate partner violence and abuse among active duty military women. *Violence Against Women*, 9, 1072–1092.

Campbell, J. C., and A. D. Wolf. (2002). *Intimate Partner Violence and Physical and Mental Health Consequences among Active Duty Military Women*. Retrieved February 16, 2008, from http://www.endabuse.org/resources/facts/Military.pdf.

Chu, D. S. C. (2003). Under Secretary of Defense, Memorandum re: Implementation of Armed Forces Domestic Security Act, Armed Forces Domestic Security Act (PL 107–311).

Deputy Secretary of Defense (2006). Restricted reporting policy for incidents of domestic abuse. Retrieved January 21, 2008, from http://www.ncdsv.org/images/RestrictedReportingPolicyIncidentDA.pdf.

Hickman, L. J., and L. M. Davis. (2003). Formalizing Collaboration: Establishing domestic violence memorandums of understanding between military installations and civilian communities, RAND Issue Paper. Retrieved from http://www.rand.org/pubs/issue_papers/IP254–1/ on January 28 2008.

Hosek, J., B. Asch, C. C. Fair, C. Martin, and M. Mattock. (2002). *Married to the Military: The Employment and Earnings of Military Wives, Compared with Those of Civilian Wives*. Washington, DC: RAND Corporation.

Lloyd, D. W. (2005). Information paper: Spouse abuse reported to the Family Advocacy Program from Fiscal Years 1998 through 2004. U.S. Department of Defense. Retrieved December 20, 2007, from http://www.ncdsv.org/images/SpouseAbuseReportedFAP1998–2004.pdf.

National Center for Post Traumatic Stress Disorder (2007). Veterans and their families. United States Department of Veterans Affairs. Retrieved January 27, 2008, from http://www.ncptsd.va.gov/ncmain/veterans/.

U.S. Census Bureau (2007). Statistical Abstract of the United States National Defense and Veterans Affairs Section, Department of Defense Personnel: 1960–2005. Retrieved January 27, 2008, from http://www.census.gov/prod/2006pubs/07statab/defense.pdf.

U.S. Department of Defense (DoD) (n.d.) Military HOMEFRONT, child care overview. Retrieved February 25, 2008, from http://www.militaryhomefront.dod .mil/portal/page/mhf/MHF/MHF_HOMEPAGE.

——. (2006). Restricted reporting policy for incidents of domestic abuse. Retrieved January, 27, 2008 from http://www.ncdsv.org/images/RestrictedReportingPolicy-IncidentDA.pdf.

——. (2007). Department of Defense Personnel Reports. Retrieved December 20, 2007, from http://siadupp.dmdc.osd.mil/personnel/MILITARY/MSO.pdf.

U.S. Department of Defense Task Force on Domestic Violence. (2001–2003). Retrieved December 20, 2007, from http://www.ncdsv.org/ncd_military_dtfdvwork.html.

11

WEAVING THE PAST INTO THE PRESENT

Understanding the Context of Domestic Violence Against Native American Women

Brenda Bussey and J. B. Whipple

DOMESTIC VIOLENCE has reached epidemic proportions against Native women. In December 2006 the Bureau of Justice Statistics reported that Native American and Alaskan Native women's rate of intimate partner violence (victimization per 1,000 females aged 12 years and older) was highest in the nation, at 18.2. Compared to other ethnic groups, their rate was double that of African Americans (18.2 vs. 8.2), exceeded by three times the rate for whites (18.2 vs. 6.3) and 12 times the rate for Asians (18.2 vs. 1.5). Many advocates, scholars, and practitioners working with Native women believe the rates to be even higher than that reported (Deer 2005). What accounts for the disproportionate victimization of Native women?

Racism, oppression, and the lasting legacy of colonization all contribute to and intersect with the domestic and sexual violence experienced by Native women. In the 500 years since Europeans arrived in the North American hemisphere, Native Americans have experienced a variety of targeted violence, including attempted genocide, physical and sexual violence targeting women and children, and efforts to destroy Native culture and communities (Gover 2000).

This chapter examines the political and legal status of Native women, the historical context through which violence entered their society, cultural norms shared by Native Americans, current realities for Native women who are being sexually assaulted and battered, and considerations for providing culturally competent social work practice. We dedicate this chapter to our grandmothers, mothers, aunties, sisters, daughters, and friends whose hearts, stories, and lives are woven throughout these pages.

DIVERSITY AMONG TRIBES

There are roughly 562 federally recognized tribes in the United States, with a total current membership of about 4.4 million, or 1.7 percent of the total U.S. population. Sixty percent of Native American people live in urban areas, with the remaining living on reservation or trust land (U.S. Census Bureau 2000). A "federally recognized" tribe is a group, band, nation, or other organized indigenous group of Americans (including any Alaska Native village) recognized by the federal government as constituting a distinct and historically continuous political entity; individual states recognize more than 60 additional tribes residing in their boundaries that go unrecognized by the federal government. An additional 100 tribes currently seek federal recognition, a process that often takes decades (U.S. Census Bureau 2000).

Among the more than 500 federally recognized Native Nations living in the U.S., approximately 300 exist within the continental United States; the remaining reside in Alaska. Tribal lands may be referred to as reservations, rancherias, villages, or pueblos. Collectively tribal lands are often referred to as "Indian Country." Native people exhibit tremendous diversity; no Native language, social or community structure, religion, or form of government predominates (Weaver 1997).

Native people in the United States are referred to in several different ways. Some prefer Native American, Native, Indian, or American Indian. The authors use the terms "Native" or "Native American" interchangeably throughout the chapter. Further, indigenous peoples in Alaska are often referred to as "Alaska Native." Paying attention to how Native people identify themselves has been a key aspect of providing culturally competent services. For example, a Native woman may identify herself as "Indian," "Native American," or as a member of her nation, such as Navajo or Apache. It is helpful for social workers to be aware of the personal distinctions made by those with whom they are working.

There are many degrees of acculturation among Native people, varying from being raised traditionally to living in urban areas with little or no connection to a traditional culture. Any attempt to generalize specific "Native" characteristics or traits would further the stereotypes that already exist for Native people (Weaver 1997). Social workers' understanding of the diversity that exists among tribal nations is essential in providing culturally competent social work practice. Social workers must continuously acknowledge and reflect on their own beliefs and biases, and examine what they know and what they do not know about Native people, individual tribes, culture, and history (Weaver 1997). Social workers, such as Hillary Weaver and Yellow Horse Brave Heart, have written extensively about culturally competent practice with Native people; their work should be referenced as an additional resource for social workers and other advocates (see Weaver 1997; Yellow Horse Brave Heart 1999).

SOVEREIGNTY

Native Americans are not simply another ethnic or racial minority in this country. Native American tribes exist as sovereign nations with rights to self-governance and with distinct and separate criminal justice systems within the boundaries of the United States. Tribes are sovereign entities whose existence predates the ratification of the U.S. Constitution (Jones 1995). Tribal sovereignty was not granted, given, or negotiated. At the time America was discovered by Europeans, Indian tribes were recognized as individual sovereign nations and treated as such by other nations during the treaty-making process. The plethora of distinct cultural and legal issues complicates consideration of domestic violence in Indian Country.

It is commonly misunderstood that treaties somehow "granted" Native American tribes sovereignty or land. This is entirely erroneous. Instead, treaties established agreements between sovereign nations granting trade (commerce) and land rights to the newcomers on this continent. Treaties did not grant rights *to* Native nations; they granted rights *to* the newcomers *from* Indian nations in exchange for certain types of payments, goods, or services. The U.S. government has violated all treaties it established with tribal nations (Weaver 2005, p. 89). The treaties remain, however, as the legal foundation for the relationship between the federal government and individual tribal nations. State governments have no power to limit or affect the sovereign status of Indian nations.

It is true that American Indians have been treated as an ethnic group for statistical purposes, such as the U.S. Census and crime victim surveys. However, in these instances, racial designations are based on how people identify themselves. The U.S. Supreme Court considers laws that single out American Indians and Alaska Natives to indicate a classification based on the sovereign status of tribal nations rather than as racial classifications (See *Morton v. Manacari,* 417 U.S. 535 [1974]). The sovereign status of tribes has been explained through congressional acts and Supreme Court case law in three cases known as the "Marshall Trilogy" (American Indian Policy Center 2002). These cases form the foundation of federal Indian law, which is the cornerstone of today's tribal/federal relationship.

HISTORICAL ROOTS OF VIOLENCE AGAINST NATIVE WOMEN

To understand the present reality of Native women, one must recognize how colonization led to the destruction of Native cultures and families, and began a sustained epidemic of violence against Native Women. Prior to European contact, violence against women was not a tradition in Native cultures. Many scholars and advocates have concluded that physical and sexual violence against Native women occurred rarely before European contact (Deer 2004; Valencia-Weber and Zuni 1995). It was not tolerated on the rare occasion that it did occur.

> A man who battered his wife was considered irrational and thus could no longer lead a war party, a hunt, or participate in either. He could not be trusted to behave properly . . . He was thought of as contrary to Lakota Law and lost many privileges of life and many roles in Lakota society and the societies within the society (White Plume 1991, p. 67).

Native Americans lived in a way that reflected a belief system that supersedes individualism—the health and well-being of the whole community and nation (Jones 1995). Women were seen and treated as sacred because of their life-giving powers; they were valued for their contributions to their families, communities, and clans (Wolk 1982). Women's responsibilities in bearing and raising children brought Native women authority within the community itself. Native children were raised by their families but also within the context of their extended families, kinship systems, and clans, where all children were seen as belonging to each specific clan (Jones 1995). Long-standing beliefs and traditions shaped the roles of every person involved in a child's life. The responsibilities of raising children were often divided between family members and community members (Cross, Earle, and Simmons 2000). Though specific practices varied from tribe to tribe, these were common realities in precolonial tribal life.

COLONIZATION AND THE RAPE OF NATIVE WOMEN:
PAST AND PRESENT

Upon European contact, the way of life among Native Americans was immediately and profoundly disrupted. The rape of Native women commonly occurred during the conquest of the land that became the United States. In 1492 the first documentation of a sexual act between a European man and a Native woman clearly describes rape:

> While I was in the boat I captured a very beautiful Carib woman the Lord Admiral gave to me, and with whom, having taken her into my cabin, she being naked according to their custom, I conceived desire to take pleasure. I wanted to put my desire into execution but she did not want it and treated me with her fingernails in such a manner that I wished I had never begun. But seeing that (to tell you the end of it all), I took a rope and thrashed her well, for which she raised such unheard of screams that you would not have believed your ears. Finally we came to an agreement in such manner that I can tell you that she seemed to have been brought up in a school of harlots (Sale 1990, p. 69).

Violence against Indian women, including battering and rape, was used in the colonization process as a weapon to dominate and dehumanize Indian peoples (Abbott 2003). Native women were systematically raped, sexually abused, and forced into prostitution throughout the colonization process (Gould 1998). This was not an uncommon occurrence; sexual assault and rape has long been used as a tool by colonizers against indigenous people (Deer 2005). An eyewitness account from the Sand Creek Massacre on November 29, 1864, vividly illustrates the degradation and humiliation that Native women and their families endured:

> I heard one man say that he had cut a woman's private parts out and had them for exhibition on a stick. I heard another man say that he had cut the fingers off an Indian, to get the rings off his hand. I also heard of numerous instances in which men had cut out the private parts of females, and stretched them over their saddle-bows and some of them over their hats (Vasicek n.d.).

■ The effect of this legacy, along with other colonizing influences, disrupted the balanced gender roles of Native communities (Abbott 2003;

Deer 2004). Today studies indicate that rape among Native women occurs at 2.5 to 3.5 times the rate of all other women (Perry 2004; Tjadden and Thoennes 2000). Native women are also more likely to be sexually assaulted by a man of another race (nearly four in five American Indian victims of rape and sexual assault describe the offender as white); to be sexually assaulted with a weapon used in the commission of the crime; and to suffer injuries as a result of the sexual assault (Perry 2004).

Sexual assault is a tool of an abusive partner; it also exists as historical legacy for every Native American woman. Whereas the dynamics of domestic violence assert power and control of one partner by another, the dynamics of colonization asserts the domination of one race and culture by another. Native American women are at the receiving end of both types of domination, and the experiences of these multiple forms of violence are intertwined. It is critical that social workers and other domestic violence advocates understand that the dynamics of oppression are the root *cause of the violence*. Separating the different forms of violence (i.e., "domestic violence" or "sexual assault") or defining the violence by who does it (husband, partner, acquaintance, etc.) will simplify, or overlook, the nature of Native women's experience of violence. As McEachern, Van Winkle, and Steiner (1998) aptly state, working with Native Americans "requires the ability to collapse the past and present into a current reality (p. 34)."

THE LOSS OF CHILDREN: BOARDING SCHOOLS, FOSTER CARE, AND ADOPTION

Many Native American and Alaska Native people believe that the cause of Indian-on-Indian domestic and sexual violence that exists today is rooted in the forced removal of Native children from their families and communities into government or religious-run boarding schools (Cohen 2005). Beginning in 1878 and continuing into the 1950s, the boarding school era created a lasting legacy of inexplicable grief and loss of Native identity (Fleming 1992). Based on the assumption that Indian families and culture were inferior to those of the "mainstream" culture and family systems, authorities involuntarily removed Native children from their families, homes, and communities and placed them in boarding schools. The acting Commissioner of Indian affairs at that time stated:

When a white youth goes away to school, his moral character and habits are already formed and well defined. With the Indian youth it is quite different. Born a savage and raised in an atmosphere of superstition and ignorance, he lacks at the outset those advantages that are inherited by his white brother and enjoyed from the cradle (Prucha 1990, p. 201).

Richard Henry Pratt, who founded the Carlisle Indian School, stated that the intent of his school was to "kill the Indian and save the man" (Iverson 1998, p. 21). The atrocities that Native children endured during the boarding school era cannot be overstated. Native children lost their families, communities, languages, cultures, spirituality, and anything else that could identify them as a part of Indian society. Physical, emotional, and sexual abuse were also common (Weaver 2005). The policy of taking children from their nations, communities, and families deliberately attempted to destroy Native people and thus Native nations. Since family existed as the heart of the culture, the loss of children equated to the loss of a future (Weaver 2005). The policy nearly destroyed the interconnectedness between extended Native families and the nuclear family system as the central core for Native life (Redhorse et al. 2000).

Although the boarding school era ended in the mid-1950s, the Indian Adoption Project, which placed Indian children into non-Indian foster and adoptive homes, continued to profoundly disrupt Native families until the enactment of the Indian Child Welfare Act (ICWA) in 1978. By the mid-1970s the "success" of the Indian Adoption Project was apparent: in 1974 approximately 25 to 35 percent of all Indian children were separated from their families, either through adoption or foster care. In Minnesota almost one in four Indian children under the age of one was placed for adoption (George 1992, p. 12).

The ICWA reaffirms tribal sovereignty and gives tribes the inherent right to oversee foster care and adoption proceedings involving their children (Weaver 2005). Social workers in the child welfare field are encouraged to learn more about ICWA. When working with abused Native women, it is important to note that the federal and state government's legacy of forced removal of Indian children contributes to a deep distrust of the current child welfare system and in itself is a major barrier to women seeking help for domestic violence.

SOUL WOUND: THE EFFECT OF TRAUMA

Because of the systematic damage meted out to Indian children, families, and nations, some have suggested that a clinical type of trauma response has taken root within Indian communities, passing from generation to generation, similar to the historical trauma response commonly attributed to the experience of Jewish people during the Holocaust (Felson 1998). This phenomenon in Indian communities has been characterized by Duran and Duran (1995) as the "soul wound," which theorizes that past oppression experienced in Indian families is passed onto future generations. Yellow Horse Brave Heart (1999) speaks of the collective response to historical trauma by Indian people:

> An important element of the theory of the historical trauma response is its intergenerational transmission. The psychological transfer of a trauma response across generations has been explained by theories of (a) transposition where descendants not only identify with ancestral history but emotionally live in the past and the present, (b) loyalty to the deceased and identification with their suffering which necessitates perpetuation in one's own life, and (c) memorial candles where descendants assume a family role of identifying with ancestral trauma (pp. 111–112).

Duran and Duran (1995) also mentioned that Indian Country acknowledges the negative effects of cumulative federal policy. Within the context of historical trauma response and the soul wound, those examining some Indian communities will observe a collective "depression and self-destructive behavior, substance abuse, identification with the ancestral pain, fixation to trauma, somatic symptoms, anxiety, guilt, and chronic bereavement" (Brave Heart 1999, p. 111). Duran and Duran (1995) stated that, for Native Americans,

> Suicide rates have been the highest of any ethnic group for decades. In order for the anger to be held in some sort of abeyance, the individual requires an anesthesia. The incidence of alcoholism among Native Americans over the last two hundred years shows the extent to which alcohol has served as a medicine that keeps this rage within some type of boundary (p. 37).

Native Americans also suffer from economic and health disparities. Overall, close to half (45%) of Native persons live at or below the poverty level; three-quarters of the Native workforce earns less than $7,000 per year; almost half the Native population is unemployed (45%); and on some reservations the unemployment rate exceeds 90 percent (Russell 2004). Income from tribal casinos and gaming establishments has not significantly lowered the poverty level of Native people nationwide (*Indian Gaming and Indian Poverty*

1997). Despite the gaming boom, poverty among Indians has actually risen (Ewen and Wollock 1996). Among American Indians living on reservations, more than half exist below the poverty level, a rate four times the national average (Russell 2004). As discussed in other chapters in this book, economic dependency is a principal reason for women staying in abusive relationships. Also, Native women are not always able to call for help. According to reports from the U.S. Department of Commerce (1995), one in four rural Native American households did not have access to telephones, the lowest rate of all racial groups, and only 28.3 percent of rural Native households had access to the Internet through a computer and a modem.

Because of a diet often dependent on surplus government commodities—foods high in fat and carbohydrates and low in protein—the diabetes rate for Native Americans is 6.8 times greater than the rate among other populations (Carlson 1997; Russell 2004). Native Americans also have higher rates of infectious diseases—tuberculosis, pneumonia, and influenza, for example—and die, on average, six years earlier than other Americans (Russell 2004). These disparities may also contribute to the barriers that abused native women experience when seeking help for domestic violence, as health status may take precedence. A native woman who is being battered may have health issues that drastically affect her life on a daily basis, in addition to the violence she is experiencing. Depending on what those health issues are, she may or may not be able to focus on getting help that addresses domestic violence, or she may necessarily be more focused on her health issues.

HELP-SEEKING BARRIERS FACED BY NATIVE WOMEN WHO HAVE BEEN ABUSED

Limited research exists on the individual and systemic barriers for Native women reporting domestic violence or sexual assault. One can safely assume, however, that many of the reasons cited by victims in the general population would apply. These include wanting to keep the abuse a private family matter, fear of reprisal, and desire to protect the offender. They may also not report abuse because of perceived bias on the part of law enforcement; geographic isolation; lack of information about victim services; self-blame or imagined culpability as a result of alcohol or drug consumption or other risk-taking behavior; fear of their families learning about the assault; parents' reprisal; and fear of re-victimization by the criminal justice system. As a result of these barriers, victims/survivors may choose not to report domestic violence offenses or may wait to report it until the violence has escalated to dangerous levels.

Some factors are unique to Indian Country. Native women distrust the dominant culture's societal norms that support male superiority and sexual entitlement while maintaining women's inferiority and sexual submissiveness. They are acutely attuned to victim blaming, racist responses, attempts to impose Western belief systems, values, and treatment methods, and lack of respect for their own self-determination. Also, the English language and the languages of the Native American cultures lack linguistic parallels for the concept of domestic violence (Hamby 2004).

Perhaps the most critical obstacle experienced by Native women when reporting violence is the fear that their children will be removed and placed in foster care because of the violence in the home. Whereas certainly this is also a concern for non-Native women, social workers must remember the historical context of the boarding school and foster care eras. Subsequently many Native women fear being formally charged with failure to protect their children from witnessing domestic violence. This policy fails to recognize the strength and fortitude of women who try to safeguard themselves and their children, and ignores the limited resources available to support battered women who do leave their abuser. When children are placed in foster care as a result of a "failure to protect" allegation, children lose the support of their mother at a time when they need it the most (White, White, and Barrington 2005).

System factors unique to Indian Country include the widespread shortage of tribal law-enforcement officers, 911 systems, and tribal jails; the need to patrol large geographic areas; the complex maze of criminal jurisdiction in Indian Country; and the lack of response by the state and federal criminal justice systems. The complexities inherent in these jurisdictional issues are so complex that they cannot possibly be addressed briefly. However, it would be most helpful for social workers who work with Native clients to receive training about the governing tribal, federal, and state laws as it pertains to domestic violence and sexual assault. Native owned and operated organizations (The Tribal Law and Policy Institute, for example) provide extensive training to those who work with Native populations. These training programs are often free of charge and facilitated by specialists in the field of law as it relates to Native nations.

RECOMMENDATIONS FOR CULTURALLY SENSITIVE PRACTICE

There are a number of key points regarding culturally competent practice when working with Native women who have been battered. Non-native social workers and other domestic violence advocates need to remember that cultural competence is an aspect of professional development that needs constant attention during a career (Cross 1988). For those working with Native families and children, the goal and focus of cultural competency practice should not be on receiving training pertaining to these issues; rather, it should be on positive outcomes for people who have *already been harmed* by racism and other forms of oppression (Redhorse 2000).

Mainstream clinical social work and psychology practice do not always recognize the differences between Native worldview perspectives and non-Native Americans. For example, many Western belief systems focus on the aspect of the mind being separate from the body or spirit, which directly contradicts many fundamental Native beliefs. Duran and Duran (1995) said:

> In Western experience it is common to separate the mind from the body and spirit and the spirit from mind and body. Within the Native American worldview this is a foreign idea . . . thus the Native American worldview is one in which the individual is a part of all creation, living life as one system and not in separate units that are objectively relating with each other. The idea of the world or creation existing for the purpose of a human domination and exploitation—the core of most Western ideology—is a notion that is absent in Native American thinking (p. 15).

Just as the mind cannot truly be separated from the spirit in Native American thinking, the individual cannot be separated from the community. The relationship between the individual, the family, and the community is a vital aspect of understanding a woman's sense of well-being, both personally and as a member of her community and nation. In the words of Redhorse (1997, p. 218): "Extended kin systems, clan membership, tribe, and the land base represent cornerstones to an Indian sense of self." This is directly connected to a woman's ability to move through what she is experiencing and also to seek the help she needs.

To respond most effectively to domestic and other forms of violence against Native women, it is vital to work toward an integrated, coordinated effort among practitioners across differing systems (i.e., tribal leaders, child welfare and social services, advocates, probation and parole officers, attorneys, and law enforcement officers). Since domestic and sexual violence is a cross-cutting issue that could bring any or all of the above-mentioned professionals into a woman's life, the more communication and coordination undertaken, the better outcomes for Native women and their children. It is essential that social workers understand that they are only one aspect of many systems that come into a Native woman's life when she has been battered. It is also advisable for social workers to be mindful that each system has its own lens through which a battered Native woman will be viewed. Although these lenses can be helpful when assessing the situation, there is still a much larger context to the Native woman's life that may not be "seen" by that particular lens, which is why collaboration and cooperation is so important.

Every person involved in responding to domestic violence should build relationships and trust with other practitioners in the service area, attend cross-training to assist with understanding one another's roles and job duties, and participate in domestic violence and sexual assault training. Training might include basic information about domestic violence and sexual assault, team building and communication skills, victim services and advocacy, and working toward cultural competency. Ideally, trainers should be Native American. However, if non-Native, trainers should have a demonstrated history and knowledge of working effectively in Native communities. Some tribal communities have domestic violence and sexual assault programs or tribal coalitions that actively collaborate with other agencies in their community. Native American resources are provided at the end of the chapter.

Another recommendation for working with Native women is to actively learn about the culture and traditions of the tribe or tribes in your service area. There is often a protocol or expected code of conduct involved when asking for information or assistance, such as giving tobacco. Tribes vary considerably, and what is acceptable to one may be disrespectful to another. Social workers must take care not to risk alienating a client and losing credibility. Thus it is best to respectfully ask. It is advisable to actively look for Native agencies in the area and ask how *they* see possibilities for fostering beneficial relationships in the service area or community. Answers to community and family issues are most effective and long-lasting when they come from within the community, not from without. This requires humility and a willingness to listen. It is not advisable for social workers or practitioners to assume that it is acceptable to ask about or learn about customs from their clients, which puts an undue burden on a woman who is already shouldering sufficient burden.

CULTURALLY RELEVANT STRATEGIES FOR NATIVE AMERICAN WOMEN

CASE STUDY, BASED ON ACTUAL EVENTS

Winona is a Native American victim of domestic violence who reported the domestic abuse for the first time. You are the social worker on duty at the hospital and you meet her at the emergency room where she awaited facial X-rays. While waiting, you observe the medical staff treating her as if she were drunk. You see no indication that she has been drinking. You watch several other people come in and receive medical treatment, while Winona continues to wait. When you begin to advocate for her by asking for assistance on her behalf, you are tersely told by a nurse that she "will have to wait," and you overhear her say under her breath as she turns around, "Just another drunk Indian."

After Winona has received the treatment she needs, you take her to the local shelter. There Winona seems frightened at the surroundings. At the shelter, there are no other Native women. You notice that other shelter residents stopped talking and stared at Winona when you entered the room. While she is in the intake interview, you notice Winona inching away from the advocate who pats her back throughout the intake process. After the intake is complete, you witness another advocate send Winona to the shower with fresh clothes and a bottle of shampoo designed to kill lice. When she is assigned a place to sleep, you say good-night and tell her you will check with her in a day or two.

The next afternoon, you arrive at the shelter and learn that Winona has disappeared. When people got up for breakfast that morning, she wasn't in her room, and her sheets were in the laundry. She left without saying anything to anyone. The shelter had done no follow-up. The staff tells you that Native women "take off from the shelter all the time."

In a few weeks you learn that Winona has been taken to the hospital again in critical condition, having been left for dead from an attempted strangulation.

THE WORKING RELATIONSHIP

The first step in initiating a working relationship with Winona is to establish trust. Meeting a client "where she is at" involves validating her experiences as a victim of the crime of domestic violence, including the institutionalized racism she must now navigate through as a result of being battered. Refrain from falling victim to stereotypes, as well as from making assumptions about a client's spirituality, level of assimilation, similarities (or lack thereof) to members of other tribal nations. Other pitfalls to avoid are attempting to show how much you know about Native American culture by talking about powwows you may have been to or any other customs you may have heard about.

The best ways to establish trust with a Native American client is to listen, validate, and be mindful of the power differential that exists in this context. Recognize her strengths and point them out. Think back to what you witnessed in the shelter and how you might have been able to advocate for Winona. Follow up on the visual cues you saw during her intake process. You might say, "I noticed you were uncomfortable during the interview; what was that like for you? Was something said or done that was upsetting for you?" At this point you may learn from Winona that touching is not something that is done freely in her culture; that being touched by someone she did not know made her very uncomfortable.

Regarding the overt racism you witnessed at the shelter, there are avenues you may want to take, such as asking to speak to the shelter supervisor to report what you saw and actively looking for Native resources to which you could refer Winona.

ASSESSMENT STRATEGIES

The most effective assessment strategy for a case involving a Native victim of domestic violence is to listen to the victim. Listen to her story about what happened and validate her experience. Listen for clues to her cultural beliefs and worldview, and respectfully ask questions about whatever you do not understand. Listen to your client's account of her experience with providers such as hospitals, shelters, law enforcement, or other social service agencies that may not have indigenous staff available to assist.

Social workers and others who are in helping professions must remember to see the big picture when dealing with Native women and their families. Social workers must keep in mind that a history and legacy intertwines with the experience of every Native woman or family they work with. That multilayered legacy is directly connected to the present experience of Native women who are being battered. Social workers must remember, therefore, to look past the current situation and grasp its historical context if they are to be truly helpful to Native clients. For example, if Winona appears to have issues related to parenting, it is important that the social worker sees that situation in context. What is Winona's family history? Where was she raised? Were her parents ever in boarding schools? If so, how would that impact their parenting of her? Culturally sensitive practice must include the capability to ask these kinds of questions and the willingness to seek out the big picture of Winona's life situation.

A common misunderstanding is that these injustices and issues took place against Native people so long ago that they should not matter now. The authors have observed many who asked, "This happened so long ago, so why do we need to learn about this now?" or "I didn't do this so I'm not responsible." These comments are critically hurtful to Native clients and their families. The present and the past cannot and should not be separated when working with Native clients.

Successful empowerment-based solutions are possible if the client is allowed to frame the situation in her own way. Does she have children? Is she concerned that the ICWA laws will not be followed? What could have caused Winona to flee from the shelter and put herself at risk by returning to her abusive partner? What safety issues is she currently facing?

As noted above, it is highly recommended to look immediately within the service area for culturally based resources to which you might refer Winona. It is also recommended that practitioners actively build working relationships with Native agencies and resources within and outside the service area. There may be a tribally based domestic violence program, sexual assault program, tribal domestic violence or sexual assault coalition, or other Native organizations. Also explore whether Native social service agencies are located in or near your service area. Take this a step further and actively seek out a good working relationship with these agencies and organizations by calling the agency, asking to speak with an advocate or case worker, and introducing yourself as someone who wants to learn how you can best serve the Native women with whom you are working. If cross-training is available between local agencies, attend them and further develop your working relationships.

In real-life situations, non-Native women are not automatically treated for lice upon entering a shelter, whereas Native women are subjected to this treatment. Moreover, whereas many non-Native women can practice their religion by saying grace before eating, for example, many Native women have told us that they are not allowed to engage in spiritual practices that are meaningful to them, such as burning sage or cedar, or other practices. An empowerment-based practice model might include support in spiritual areas if the client expresses that need. It is just as important to be mindful that some of the Native clients you work with are also Christian. It is best not to assume how the client practices her spirituality but to ask if she has any religious or spiritual practices that she would like to follow while at the shelter.

GOAL SETTING AND CONTRACTING

Setting goals can be daunting for any client who has experienced trauma such as domestic violence. The layers of issues are often overwhelming. Since domestic violence does not happen in a vacuum, the unraveling that is done in the assessment provides a basis from which to set goals. Several short-term attainable goals should be established without losing sight of the long-term goal of ending violence in the relationship. Using a marathon as a metaphor, breaking up the goals into, say, 26 individual milestones may be useful. The ultimate goal may seem far out of reach, but running just a mile or two becomes much more attainable.

Short-term safety, of course, is always one of the mile markers. Other needed services may be culturally appropriate child care, medical care and follow-up, disability services owing to injuries or other long-term disabilities, transportation, and communication with support systems. Mainstream services may not be appropriate, because they may re-victimize the client by being culturally insensitive. Preference may be given to housing with a relative in the community or in a nearby Native community, rather than a geographically closer non-Native program.

Taking the time and space truly to listen is especially helpful when setting goals. The client knows what spiritual or traditional practices would be helpful to her and her children. She may need help in accessing these, even though she may not wish to discuss them in depth. Both you and your client may need assistance wading through the myriad of legal jurisdictions and law-enforcement responses. Even Native advocates find these jurisdictional minefields overwhelming, and it is a fair assumption that you, too, will need coaching in this area. As mentioned, it is best to seek assistance from Native organizations specializing in these areas.

ALTERNATIVE INTERVENTIONS

Sometimes circumstances arise in which your client may be unwilling or unable to make a safety decision on her own. Many, but certainly not all, Native societies are organized in such a way that the elders must be consulted before certain decisions can be made. Going against the wishes of her elders may result in being ostracized or other unintended consequences. Alternatively, different societies and even individuals within those societies practice different levels of interdependence. Sometimes this depends on your client's level of assimilation, and sometimes other factors are involved. Each client must be evaluated individually to identify the best possible intervention.

A counselor who is from the same culture as the client will not only be familiar with these nuances but will probably be familiar with a client's beliefs, values, and worldview. If there is a Native counselor or social worker available, the client should be given the option of a referral. The worker who is familiar with the client's culture and community will be aware of resources unknown to an outsider. There are also some aspects to culture that simply cannot be effectively explained to someone from outside that culture.

RESOLVING ETHICAL DILEMMAS

There is one highly conspicuous value conflict between the worldview of most social workers and the general Native American worldview, namely, individualism versus interdependence. The importance of making one's own decisions is reflected in the social work value of self-determination. Within an individualistic worldview, social workers are often taught that it is against the code of ethics to make a life decision for a client. So how does one reconcile the independent and the interdependent worldviews in the face of a society whose people routinely and willingly relinquish their power to others for making decisions for themselves and their family?

In this case, there is a way of looking at the issue that reconciles the two worldviews. Many factors are involved when an Indian woman makes a decision. She may need to consult a plethora of individuals, and the definitive decision may not be what she would choose for herself. However, it is ultimately her decision to take or reject the advice of her community members.

There are many other worldviews, such as nuclear versus extended family, harmony with nature versus dominance and control of it, and others that may result in ethical dilemmas for the social worker. Many times the worker will feel that the decision made is not in the client's best interest. To maintain a trusting relationship, however, the worker must respect the decision and the decision-making process even though the worker may neither agree nor understand. Above all else, practitioners should be mindful that they are likely operating from a different worldview than that of their clients.

SELECTING APPROPRIATE INTERVENTIONS

Whereas models of best practices certainly exist—and they are becoming ever more refined—no model fits with the Native experience. Just as others have found that a model that works best for the dominant society does not necessarily benefit other minority populations, it is exponentially true for Native societies. Therefore, it is highly advisable to treat each case individually, making no assumptions whatsoever.

MONITORING AND EVALUATING A SYSTEM'S IMPACT AND OUTCOMES

With trust and consistent support, progress can be achieved and evaluated one milestone at a time. For instance, one success might be that your client hangs a garment out the window to signal for help, indicating her willingness to seek help and to follow through on a safety plan.

Services for Native American victims of domestic violence must also be monitored for the delivery of culturally appropriate services. One incident of racism and re-traumatization of a victim could deter her and others from using the service in the future.

ENDINGS

Worker should follow their clients' lead when it becomes apparent that the client no longer desires the worker's assistance. The ideal situation would be that the client has achieved the desired level of safety and freedom from violence in her life. Other reasons for the client's desire to terminate the relationship may be that she has found culturally appropriate services within her own community. With the continuation and expansion of funding through The Violence Against Women Act (VAWA), culturally appropriate services for Indian victims of sexual and domestic violence are becoming more available.

The client's reason for terminating services, and the method of doing so, should be the client's decision. Owing to variations in cultural and individual needs, it is not possible to forecast the number of visits between social worker and client or how the closing session should unfold, as long as the client feels closure and knows that the door is open should she be in need of further services.

CONCLUSION

This chapter has attempted to interface the historical context of violence that Native women experience, how that history continues to impact and interplay with contemporary life, and what culturally competent practice would look like when working with Native women and their families. Above all, practitioners should be aware of the strengths that exist within Native communities, despite what has occurred in the context of colonization. Despite all that was done in an attempt to destroy Indian communities, Native American nations and people have maintained languages, along with value systems, extended family and kin systems, and spiritual practices. Acknowledging and respecting these strengths and building relationships and collaborations across multiple systems is essential to laying the foundation necessary for healing among Native women, their families, and their communities.

RESOURCES

DOMESTIC VIOLENCE SHELTERS AND PROGRAMS SERVING NATIVE WOMEN

ALEUTIAN ISLANDS
Unalaskans Against Sexual Assault and Family Violence (USAFV)
P.O. Box 36
Unalaska, AK 99685
Phone: 1 (800) 478–7238

Fax: (907) 581–4568
E-mail: usafved@arctic.net

ANCHORAGE, AK
Alaska Native (Willa's Way)
Safe Housing Program
Anchorage, AK 99508
Phone: (907) 729–2500
Web site: http://www.scf.cc/willa.cfm

APACHE TRIBE OF OKLAHOMA
Violence Free Living Center
P.O. Box 1220
Anadarko, OK 73005
Phone: (405) 247–9495
E-mail: violencefree@apachetribeofoklahoma.org

BIG LAGOON RANCHERIA
Two Feathers Native American Family Services
2355 Central Avenue, Suite C
McKinleyville, CA 95519
Phone: (707) 839–1933
Toll Free: 1 (800) 341–9454
Web site: http://www.twofeathers-nafs.org

BRISTOL BAY NATIVE ASSOCIATION
Safe and Fear-Free Environment (SAFE)
P.O. Box 94
Dillingham, AK 99576
Phone 1 (800) 478–2316 (SAFE)
Fax: (907) 842–2198
E-mail: avbaim@besafeandfree.org

CHEYENNE RIVER SIOUX
Sacred Heart Center Women's Shelter
P.O. Box 2000
Eagle Butte, SD 57625
Phone 1 (800) 390–9298
E-mail: SHC@Rapid.Net.com

COEUR D'ALENE
Coeur d'Alene Women's Center
2201 North Government Way, Suite E
Coeur d'Alene, ID 83814
Phone: (208) 663–9303
DV Hotline/Crisis: (208) 664–1443
Rape Hotline/Crisis: (208) 661–2522
E-mail: wcgen@adelphia.net
Web site: http://www.cdawomenscenter.org

Stop Violence Against Indian Women
160 11th Street
Plummer, ID 83851
Phone: (208) 686–0900
Fax: (208) 686–6501
Web site: http://www.cdatribe-nsn.gov/stop.shtml

CROW CREEK
Project SAFE and the Children's Safe Place
Wiconi Wawokiya, Inc.
P.O. Box 49
Fort Thompson, SD 57339
Phone: (605) 245–2471
Fax: (605) 245–2737

EIGHT NORTHERN PUEBLOS
Peacekeepers Domestic Violence Program
706 A-1 Lahoya Street
Espanola, NM 87532
P.O. Box 969
San Juan, NM 87566
Phone: (505) 753–4790
Toll Free: 1 (800) 400–8694
Fax: (505) 753–5233

EMMONAK VILLAGE, AK
Emmonak Women's Shelter (EWS)
P.O. Box 207
Emmonak, AK 99581
Phone: (907) 949–1443

Fax: (907) 949–1718
E-mail: ammonakws@aol.com

FOND DU LAC BAND OF LAKE SUPERIOR CHIPPEWA
Min no wii jii win House
927 Trettel Lane
Cloquet, MN 55720
Phone: (218) 879–1989
24-hour line: (218) 348–1817

HOULTON BAND OF MALISEET INDIANS
Domestic Violence Response Program
88 Bell Road, Suite 2
Littelton, ME 04730
Phone: (207) 532–6401
After Hours Phone: (207) 694–1353
Web site: http://www.maliseets.com/domestic_vilence.htm

JUNEAU
Aiding Women from Abuse and Rape Emergencies (AWARE)
P.O. Box 20809
Juneau, AK 99802
Crisis Line: (907) 586–1090
Web site: http://www.juneau.com/aware

SUN'AQ TRIBE OF KODIAK
Stop Violence Against Native Women
312 West Marine Way
Kodiak, Alaska 99615
Phone: (907) 486–4449
Fax: (907) 486–3361

NAVAJO NATION
The Navajo Nation Victim Assistance Program
Contact: Christine J. Butler
P.O. Box 1168
Tuba City, AZ 86045
Phone: (405) 247–5579
Fax: (405) 247–5579

PUEBLO OF LAGUNA
Laguna Family Shelter Program
Laguna, NM 87206
Phone: (505) 552–9701

RED LAKE BAND OF CHIPPEWA
Family Advocacy Center of Northern Minnesota (FACNM)
North Country Health Services
1300 Anne Street NW
Bemidji, MN 56601
Main Desk: (218) 751–5430
Phone: (218) 333–6011

Equay Wiigamig (Red Lake Women's Shelter)
Red Lake, MN 56671
Phone: (218) 679–3443
Hotline: 1 (800) 943–8997

ROSEBUD SIOUX TRIBE
White Buffalo Calf Woman's Society
North Main Street
Mission, SD 57555
Phone: (605) 856–2317
Fax: (605) 856–2994
Web site: http://calthunderhawk.tripod.com/wbcws/wbcws_index.html

SOUTHERN UTE RESERVATION
Alternative Horizons
P.O. Box 503
Durango, CO 81302
Hotline: (970) 247–9619
Fax: (970) 247–8408
E-mail: info@alternativehorizons.org
Web site: http://www.alternativehorizons.org

ZUNI PUEBLO
New Beginnings
Zuni, NM 87327
Phone: (505) 782–4600 or (505) 782–4881

URBAN AREA PROGRAMS AND SHELTERS

NEW MEXICO
Morning Star House (Native American Women and Children)
6001 Marble Avenue NE., Suite 15
Albuquerque, NM 87110
Phone: (505) 232–8299
Toll Free: 1 (800) 658–6967
Fax: (505) 268–0622
E-mail: morningstarwomen@uswest.net

MINNESOTA
Dabinoo'Igan
Native American Shelter
Duluth, MN
Phone: (218) 722–2247

Women of Nations
P.O. Box 40309
St. Paul, MN 55014
Phone: (651) 222–5830
Fax: (651) 222–1207
Crisis line: (651) 222–5836
Toll-free: 1 (877) 209–1266
Web site: http://www.women-of-nations.org

TRIBAL DOMESTIC VIOLENCE AND SEXUAL ASSAULT COALITIONS

The following organizations are excellent resources for information about domestic violence and sexual assault against Native women and available community/regional resources:

Alaska Native Women's Coalition
Tammy Young, Director
P.O. Box 30
Anvik, AK 99558
Phone: (907) 663–6331

American Indians Against Abuse
Sharon Paulson-Tainter

P.O. Box 1617
Hayward, WI 54843
Phone: (715) 634–9980; (715) 634–9981
Fax: (715) 634–9982

Arizona Native American Coalition Against Family Violence
Joyce Lopez, Director
Rt. 2, Box 730-B
Laveen, AZ 85339
Phone: (520) 550–2648
Fax: (520) 550–1062

Coalition to Stop Violence Against Native Women
Evone Martinez and Amber Corrillo, Co-Coordinators
2401 12th Street NW, Suite 210N
Albuquerque, NM 87104
Phone: (505) 243–9199
Fax: (505) 243–9966

Native Women's Society of the Great Plains Reclaiming Our Sacredness
Karen Artichoker, Director
P.O. Box 638
Kyle, SD 57752
Phone: (605) 455–2244
Fax: (605) 455–1245

Community Resource Alliance
Lisa Brunner, Director
P.O. Box 28
Callaway, MN 56521
Phone: (218) 375–2762
Fax: (218) 375–2763

Minnesota Indian Women's Sexual Assault Coalition
Nicole Matthews, Executive Director
1619 Dayton Avenue, Suite 303
St. Paul, MN 55104
Phone: (651) 646–4800
Fax: (651) 646–4798

Web site: http://www.miwsac.org

Nin gikenoo Amaadamin (We Teach Each Other)
Sacred Hoop Coalition
Tina Olson, Project Coordinator
Rebecca St. George, Coalition Coordinator
202 E Superior Street
Duluth, MN 55802
Phone: (218) 722–2781
Fax: (218) 722–5775

Niwhongh xw E:na:wh Stop the Violence Coalition, Inc.
Jolanda Ingram-Marshall, Director
P.O. Box 309
150 Mille Creek Road
Hoopa, CA 95546
Phone: (530) 625–1662
Fax: (530) 625–1677

Spirits of Hope
3701 SE 15th Street
Del City, OK 73115
Phone: (405) 619–9707
Fax: (405) 619–9715
Web site: http://www.onadvc.com

Southwest Indigenous Women's Coalition
Leanne Guy, Director
P.O. Box 1279
Chinle, AZ 86503
Phone: (480) 766–2201
Fax: (928) 674–8218

Strong Hearted Women's Coalition
Germaine Omish-Guachena, Executive Director
P.O. Box 2488
Valley Center, CA 92082
Phone: (760) 749–1410 x5322
Fax: (760) 644–4781

The Healing Tree, Inc.
Shirl A. Robinson, Director
P.O. Box 541
Lame Deer, MT 59043
Phone: (406) 477–6749

We Asdzani Coalition
Gloria Champion, Executive Director
P.O. Box 547
Cronwpoint, NM 87313
Phone: (505) 368–5124
Fax: (505) 368–5129

Sicangu Coalition Against Sexual and Domestic Violence
Tillie Black Bear, Executive Director
P.O. Box 227
Mission, SD 57555
Phone: (605) 856–1217
Fax: (605) 856–2494

WomenSpirit Coalition
Dee Koster, Executive Director
P.O. Box 13260
Olympia, WA 98508
Phone: (360) 352–3120
Fax: (360) 357–3858

NATIVE ORGANIZATIONS AND TECHNICAL ASSISTANCE PROVIDERS

American Indian Policy Center (AIPC)
1463 Hewitt Avenue
St. Paul, MN 55104
Phone (651) 644–1728
Fax: (651) 644–0740
E-mail: aipc@epinternet.com
Web site: http://www.airpi.org

Clan Star, Inc.
P.O. Box 1835
Cherokee, NC 28719

Phone: (828) 497–5507
Fax: (828) 497–5688
Web site; http://www.clanstar.org

Cangleska, Inc.
P.O. Box 638
Kyle, SD 57752
Phone: (605) 455–2244
Fax: (605) 455–1245
Web site: http://www.cangleska.org

Mending the Sacred Hoop Technical Assistance Project
202 E Superior Street
Duluth, MN 55802
Phone: (218) 722–2781
Fax: (218) 722–5775
Web site: http://www.msh-ta.org

Minnesota Indian Women's Resource Center (MIWRC)
2300 15 Avenue
Minneapolis, MN 55404
Phone: (612) 728–2000
Fax: (612)-728–2039
E-mail: information@miwrc.org
Web site: http://www.miwrc.org

National Congress of American Indians (NCAI)
1301 Connecticut Avenue NW, Suite 200
Washington, DC 20036
Phone: (202) 466–7767
Fax: (202) 466–7797
Web site: http://www.ncai.org

National Indian Child Welfare Association (NICWA)
5100 SW Macadam Avenue, Suite 300
Portland, OR 97239
Phone (503) 222–4044
Fax: (503) 222–4007
E-mail: info@nicwa.org

Sacred Circle National Resource Center
722 St. Joseph Street
Rapid City, SD 57701
Phone: (605) 341–2050
Toll-free: 1 (877) 733–7623 (RED ROAD)
Fax: (605) 341–2472
E-mail: ssircle@sacred-circle.com
Web site: http://www.sacred-circle.com

Southwest Center for Law and Policy
4055 E. 5th Street
Tucson, AZ 85711
Phone: (520) 623–8192
Fax: (520) 623–8246
E-mail: info@swclap.org
Web site: http://www.swclap.org

Tribal Law and Policy Institute
1619 Dayton Avenue, Suite 305
Saint Paul, MN 55104
Phone (651) 644–1125
Fax: (651) 644–1157
Web site: http://www.tribal-institute.org

REFERENCES

Abbott, M. D. (2003). *Indigenous American Women: Decolonization, Empowerment, Activism*. Lincoln: University of Nebraska Press.

American Indian Policy Center (2002). *Fundamental Principles of Tribal Sovereignty*. Retrieved January 24, 2008, from http://www.airpi.org/research/st98fund.html.

Amnesty International. (2007). *Maze of Injustice: The Failure to Protect Indigenous Women from Sexual Violence in the USA*. Retrieved May 10, 2007, from http://web.amnesty.org/library/Index/ENGAMR510352007.

Catalano, S. M. (2006). *Criminal Victimization*. Washington DC: U.S. Departmentof Justice, Bureau of Justice Statistics.

Child, B. J. (1998). *Boarding School Seasons: American Indian Families, 1900–1940*. Lincoln: University of Nebraska Press.

Cohen, F. S. (2005). *Handbook of Federal Indian Law*. Charlottesville, VA: Michie Publishing.

Cross, T. (1988). Services to minority populations. Cultural competence continuum. *Focal Point* 3, pp. 1–9.

Deer, S. (2004). Toward an indigenous jurisprudence of rape. *Kansas Journal of Law and Public Policy*, 14, 121–143.

———. (2005). Sovereignty of the soul: Exploring the intersection of rape law reform and federal Indian law. 38 *Suffolk University Law Review* 455.

Duran, B., and Duran, E. (1995). *Native American Postcolonial Psychology*. Albany: State University of New York Press.

Evans-Campbell, T., T. Lindhorst, B. Huang, and K. Walters. (2006). Interpersonal violence in the lives of urban American Indian and Alaska Native women: Implications for heath, mental health, and help-seeking. *American Journal of Public Health*, 96(8), 1416–1422.

Ewen, A., and J. Wollock. (1996). *Survey of Grant Giving by American Indian Foundations and Organizations*. Native Americans in Philanthropy.

Felsen, I. (1998). The North American research perspective. In Y. Daniele (Ed.), *International Handbook of Multigenerational Legacies of Trauma* (pp. 43–68). New York: Plenum.

Fleming, C. M. (1992). American Indians and Alaska Natives: Changing societies past and present. In M. A. Orlandi, R. Weston, and L. G. Epstein (Eds.), *Cultural Competence for Evaluators: A Guide for Alcohol and other Drug Abuse with Ethnic/Racial Communities* (pp. 147–171). Rockville, MD: Office of Substance Abuse Prevention, U.S. Department of Health and Human Services.

George, L. J. (1997). Why the Need for the Indian Child Welfare Act? *Journal of Multicultural Social Work*, 5, 165–175.

Getches, D. H, C. F. Wilkinson, and R. A. Williams Jr. (1993). *Federal Indian Law: Cases and Materials* (3rd Ed.). St. Paul, MN. West.

Gonzales, J. (1999). Native American survivors. In *Support for Survivors Manual* (pp. 257–259). Sacramento: California Coalition Against Sexual Assault.

Gould, J. (1998). Native American women: West Coast. In Wilma Mankiller et al. (Eds.), *A Reader's Companion to U.S. History*. Boston: Houghton Mifflin.

Gover, K. (2000). Assistant Secretary of Indian Affairs, Department of Interior, at the Ceremony Acknowledging the 175th Anniversary of the Establishment of the Bureau of Indian Affairs, September 8, 2000. Retrieved December 20, 2006, from http://www.tribal-institute.org/lists/kevin-gover.htm.

Indian Gaming and Indian Poverty. (1997). Native Americas Magazine 18. Ithaca, NY: Cornell University.

Iverson, P. (1998). *We Are Still Here: American Indians in the Twentieth Century*. Wheeling, IL: Harlan Davidson.

Jones, B. J. (1995). *The Indian Child Welfare Act Handbook: A Legal Guide to the Custody and Adoption of Native American Children*. American Bar Association, May 25.

LaFramboise, T. D., S. B. Choney, A. James, and P. R. Running Wolf. (1995). American Indianwomen and psychology. In H. Landrine (Ed.), *Bringing Cultural Diversity to Feminist Psychology: Theory, Research, and Practice* (pp. 197–239). Washington, DC: American Psychological Association.

Lisak, D., and P. M. Miller. (2002). Repeat rape and multiple offending among undetected rapists. *Violence and Victims*, 17(1), 73–84.

McEachern, D., M. Van Winkle, and S. Steiner. (1998). Domestic violence among the Navajo: A legacy of colonization." In E. A. Segal and K. M. Kilty (Eds.), *Pressing Issues of Inequality and American Indian Communities*. Philadelphia, PA: Haworth.

National Congress of American Indians. *Fact Sheet: Violence against Women in Indian Country*. Retrieved January 30, 2007, from http://www.ncai.org/ncai/advocacy/hr/docs/dv-fact_sheet.pdf.

National Sexual Violence Resource Center. (2000). Sexual Assault in Indian Country: Confronting Sexual Violence.

Ogunwole, S. U. (2006). *American Indians and Alaska Natives in the United States. Census 2000 Special Reports*. U.S. Department of Commerce Economics and Statistics Administration. Washington, DC: U.S. Census Bureau.

Perry, S. (2002). *American Indians and Crime: A BJS Statistical Profile 1992–2002*. U.S. Department of Justice, Office of Justice Programs. Retrieved February 18, 2008, from http://www.ojp.usdoj.gov/bjs/pub/pdf/aic02.pdf.

Prucha, F. P. (Ed.). (1990). *Documents of United States Indian Policy* (2nd Exp. Ed.). Lincoln: University of Nebraska Press.

Redhorse, J., et al. (2000). *Family Preservation: Concepts in American Indian Communities*. Seattle, WA: Casey Family Programs.

Redhorse, J. (1997). Traditional American Indian family systems. *Families, Systems, and Health*, 3, 242–250.

Sale, K. (1990). *Conquest of Paradise: Christopher Columbus and the Columbian Legacy*. New York: Knopf.

Tjaden P., and N. Thoennes. (2000). *Full Report of the Prevalence, Incidence, and Consequences of Violence against Women: Findings from the National Violence Against Women Survey*. Washington, DC: U.S. Department of Justice, National Institute of Justice.

U.S. Census Bureau. (1994). *Phoneless in America*, Statistical Brief, Washington, DC, U.S. Department of Commerce, Economics and Statistical Administration. Retrieved March 14, 2008, from http://www.census.gov/aspd/www/statbrief/sb94_16.pdf.

——. (2001). *2000 Census Counts of American Indians, Eskimos, Aleuts, and American Indian and Alaska Native Areas*. Washington, DC: Racial Statistics Branch, Population Division.

U.S. Department of Commerce. (1995). *Falling through the Net: A Survey of the "Have Nots" in Rural and Urban America*. Retrieved March 14, 2008, from http://www.ntia.doc.gov/ntiahome/fallingthru.html.

Valencia-Weber, G., and C. Zuni. 69 *St. John's Law Review*. Retrieved October 5, 2005, from http://www.law-lib.utoronto.ca/Diana/fulltext/zuni.htm.

Vasicek, D. L. (Producer, Director, Writer). 2006. *The Sand Creek Massacre* [Motion Picture]. United States Olympus Films+, LLC.

Wakeling, S., M. Jorgensen, S. Michaleson, and M. Begay. (2001). *Policing on American Indian Reservations*. Washington, DC: U.S. Department of Justice.

Weaver, H. (1997). Training culturally competent social workers: What students should know about Native people. *Journal of Teaching in Social Work*, 15(1/2), 217-225.

——. (2005). *Explorations in Cultural Competence: Journeys to the Four Directions*. Pacific Grove, CA: Brooks/Cole.

White, J. G., H. B. White, and J. M. Larrington. (2005). *Criminal Prosecution of Native Battered Women for Failure to Protect*. Southwest Center for Law and Policy. Retrieved March 18, 2007, from http://www.swclap.org/FAILURETO PROTECT.pdf.

White Plume, D. L. (1991). The Work of Sina Waken Win Okolakiciye—Sacred Shawl Women's Society. In *Cante Ohitika Win (Brave Hearted Women): Images of Lakota Women from the Pine Ridge Indian Reservation*. Vermillion: University of South Dakota Press.

Williams, R.A., Jr. (1990). *The American Indian in Western Legal Thought: The Discourses of Conquest*. New York: Oxford University Press.

Wolk, L. E. (1982). Minnesota's American Indian battered women: The cycle of oppression. In *A Cultural Awareness Training Manual for Non-Indian Professionals*. Battered Women's Project, St. Paul American Indian Center.

Yellow Horse Brave Heart, M. (1999). Oyate Ptayela: Rebuilding the Lakota Nation through addressing historical trauma among Lakota parents. In H. Weaver (Ed.), *Voices of First Nations People* (pp. 109–126). New York: Hawthorne.

12

A COMMENTARY ON RELIGION AND DOMESTIC VIOLENCE

Marie M. Fortune, Salma Elkadi Abugideiri,
and Mark Dratch

RELIGION IS a fact of life in the United States for the vast majority of people. Whether in childhood or adulthood, most people have had some association with a faith tradition. For some it has been positive; for others, negative. But many retain and rely on values and doctrines that they received within a faith community. Because of the extraordinary diversity within the United States, many different traditions exist among us: Jews, Muslims, Buddhists, Hindus, Native Americans, plus many varieties of Christians including Roman Catholics, Evangelicals, Mainline Protestants, Pentecostals, and so on.[1] One chapter cannot do justice to the richness of these many traditions. Therefore we provide in this chapter a discussion of only the basic understanding of the place of religion in addressing domestic violence, illustrated through three Western religious traditions: Christianity, Judaism, and Islam.

THE IMPORTANCE OF RELIGION: ROADBLOCKS OR RESOURCES?

The crisis of domestic violence affects people physically, psychologically, and spiritually. Each of these dimensions must be addressed both for victims and those in the family who abuse them. Certain needs and issues tend to be disregarded when the issue is approached from either a secular or religious perspective alone. This reflects a serious lack of understanding of the nature of domestic violence and its impact on people's lives. Thus the importance of developing a shared understanding and cooperation between secular and religious helpers for addressing domestic violence cannot be emphasized strongly enough.

Religious traditions, teachings, and practices represent a fundamental aspect of culture for the vast majority of Americans. The intertwining of religiosity and culture are common and complex. For example, secular Jews may not participate in a synagogue but still identify themselves as Jewish and honor Jewish values. Many Korean immigrants are closely affiliated with Korean Christian churches, so issues related to Christian teaching and practice will be common. For many people, their racial/ethnic heritage is bound to their faith history, such as with African American Baptists, Irish Catholics, Russian Jews, and Sudanese Muslims. This is one of the reasons that cultural competency in addressing domestic violence must include an awareness and appreciation of religion and faith traditions.

Occasionally, a social worker, psychotherapist, or other secular service provider will wonder, "Why bother with religious concerns at all?" The answer is a practical one: religious issues or concerns that surface for people in the midst of a crisis are primary issues. If not addressed in some way, at some point, they will inevitably become roadblocks to the client's efforts to resolve the crisis. In addition, a person's religious beliefs and community of faith (church, mosque, or synagogue) can provide a primary support system for individuals and their families in the midst of an experience of domestic violence.

For a pastor, priest, rabbi, imam, and others approaching domestic violence from a religious perspective, there is little question about the relevance of religious concerns, which are paramount for them. They may, however, doubt the importance of dealing with concerns for shelter, safety, intervention, and so forth. "These people just need to get right with God and everything will be fine." This perspective overlooks the importance of practical issues. Domestic violence is complex and potentially lethal. Consequently seemingly mundane concerns represent immediate and critical needs.

When confronted personally by domestic violence, most people also experience a crisis of meaning in their lives, as occurs with all other crises, whether chronic or unexpected. Basic life questions arise, often expressed in religious or philosophical terms. Questions such as "Why is this happening to me and my family?" or "Why did God let this happen?" or "What meaning does this have for my life?" all indicate people's efforts to make sense of their experiences of suffering and place the experiences in a context of meaning for their lives. We recognize these questions to signal health, because they represent an effort to comprehend and contextualize the experience of domestic violence, allowing individuals to regain some control over their lives in the midst of crisis.

Many individuals and families in crisis express the questions of meaning in religious terms and, more specifically, in terms of Judaism, Islam, or Christianity, since the vast majority of people in the United States today grew up with some association with these traditions. Many continue their involvement with a church, mosque, or synagogue into adulthood. Further, religious values overlap with many American cultural values. (Most Americans maintain cultural values, consciously or not, that are primarily religious in nature.)

Religious concerns can become roadblocks or resources for those dealing with experiences of domestic violence, because these concerns are central to many people's lives. The outcome depends on how they are handled. Misinterpretation and misuse of religious texts and traditions have often had a detrimental effect on individuals and families dealing with domestic violence. Misinterpretation or misuse can contribute substantially to guilt, self-blame, and suffering among victims. They can also contribute to rationalizations used by those who abuse. For example, "But the Bible says" is frequently used to explain, excuse, or justify abuse that one family member inflicts on another. This need not be the case. Reexamining and analyzing those sacred texts can result in reclaiming the traditions in ways that support victims and abusers, while confronting and challenging abuse in the family.

A careful study of sacred texts makes it clear that although it is possible to misuse texts to justify the abuse of family members, these texts do not in fact justify the abuse. Misuse is a frequent practice (more on this below). Teaching people simple answers to the complex issues faced by many is another potential obstacle within contemporary teachings of some faith groups. Thus religious groups often have not adequately prepared people for the traumas they will face at some point in their lives: illness, death, abuse, divorce, and so on.

The following simple formulas, although perhaps fundamental to many religious faiths, are inadequate by themselves to deal with the complex human suffering of domestic violence:

- "Keep the commandments and everything will be fine."
- "Keep praying."
- "Just accept Jesus Christ as your Lord and Savior and you will be healthy, prosperous, popular, and happy."
- "Get closer to God."
- "Be patient, and you will be rewarded."
- "Go to services each week."
- "Pray harder."

When these teachings are offered as complete answers to life's questions, they create simple illusions that leave adherents vulnerable to becoming overwhelmed by their suffering. Moreover, these claims may set up a dynamic that blames the victims for their suffering.

The following formulas which make a theological assumption that God's unconditional love is in fact conditional imply that suffering is actually a punishment or abandonment by God.

- "If you are a good Christian, a good Jew, or a good Muslim, God will treat you kindly or take care of you or make you prosper as a reward for your goodness."
- "If you suffer, it is a sign that you must not be a good Muslim, a good Christian, or a good Jew, and that God is displeased with you."

Simple answers alone cannot explain significant personal or familial suffering. When such answers prove insufficient, people feel that their faith has failed them or that God has abandoned them. Jewish, Muslim, and Christian religious teachings have the depth to address the experiences of contemporary persons, but only when these teachings acknowledge the complexity, the paradox, and sometimes the incomprehensible nature of suffering. The synagogue, the church, and the mosque are vital resources of support for those who are suffering; they are a sign of God's presence and are there to struggle with questions that crises may raise. By offering sweet words of advice to "solve" life's problems, these religious institutions reduce the experience of the one who suffers to a mere slogan, and denies the depth of the pain and the potential for healing and new life.

One's faith tradition can offer spiritual resources as well as material resources to survivors and their children and also to repentant perpetrators. Whether it is the Psalms from the Hebrew Bible or teachings from the Qur'an or the life of Muhammad or the Christian Gospels, religious teachings can comfort, reassure, and strengthen. Congregations also can provide material support in times of crisis.

COOPERATIVE ROLES FOR THE SECULAR ADVOCATE OR COUNSELOR AND THE MINISTER OR RABBI OR IMAM

Both the secular advocate counselor and the religious leader have important roles to play when confronting domestic violence. Families experiencing abuse need their support and expertise in times of crisis. Sometimes their respective efforts will come into conflict, as illustrated by the following situation:

We received a call from a local shelter for abused women. The shelter worker indicated that she had a badly beaten woman there whose minister had told her to go back home to her husband. The worker asked us to call the minister and "straighten him out." Ten minutes later we received a call from the minister. He said that the shelter had one of his parishioners there and the shelter worker had told her to get a divorce. He asked us to call the shelter and "straighten them out."

In this situation, both the shelter worker and the minister had the victim's best interests in mind. Yet they were clearly at odds because neither understood the other's concerns for the victim's needs. The shelter worker did not understand the minister's concern for maintaining the family, and the minister did not understand that the woman's life was in danger. We arranged for the minister and the shelter worker to talk directly with each other, the victim, and one of our staff to share their concerns in order to seek a solution in the best interests of the victim. This was accomplished successfully. The need for cooperation and communication between advocates or counselors and imams, ministers, or rabbis is clear so that the needs of parishioners/congregants/clients are best served and the resources of both religious and secular helpers are utilized effectively.

ROLE OF THE SECULAR ADVOCATE OR COUNSELOR

In the secular setting, an advocate, social worker, or mental health provider may encounter a victim or abuser who raises religious questions or concerns. When this occurs, the following guidelines may be helpful:

- Pay attention to religious questions, comments, or references.
- Affirm these concerns as appropriate and determine their importance for the client.

Having identified and affirmed this area of concern, pursue it if you are comfortable doing so. Emphasize the ways in which the client's religious tradition can be a helpful resource and in no way can be used to justify or allow abuse or violence to continue in the family. If you are uncomfortable with these religious concerns or feel unqualified to pursue them, refer the client to a pastor, priest, rabbi, or imam who is trained to help and whom you know and trust.

ROLE OF THE CLERGY

The minister or rabbi or imam can most effectively help domestic violence victims and offenders by referring to and cooperating with secular resources. When combined, both provide a balanced approach dealing with specific external, physical, and emotional needs while addressing the larger religious, ethical, and philosophical issues.

When approached about domestic violence, the religious leader can use the following guidelines:

- Be aware of the dynamics of domestic violence and utilize this understanding for evaluating the situation.
- Use your expertise as a religious authority and spiritual leader to illuminate the positive value of religious traditions, while clarifying that they do not justify or condone domestic violence.
- Identify the parishioner or congregant's immediate needs and *refer* the individual to a secular resource (if available) to deal with the specifics of abuse, advocacy, intervention, and treatment.

If you are comfortable pursuing the matter, provide additional pastoral support and encouragement to help family members take full advantage of available resources.

The other important role that clergy and religious leaders can play is at the point of pre-marriage.[2] If a couple is planning a religious ceremony for their wedding, they will meet with their religious leader for reflection and counsel before taking this important step. This is an opportunity for the religious leader to inquire about any history of abuse in the partners' families, teach about the religious values that support a healthy marriage, and correct erroneous understandings that either partner may have. A couple needs to be able to share their family histories with each other and consider the impact these histories may have on the couple. The pre-marriage meeting also gives the religious leader the chance to be attuned to the dynamics of the couple's current relationship: if it seems that one partner is trying to control the other or there is the possibility of violence, the leader should meet separately with each partner to assess the situation.

SCRIPTURAL AND THEOLOGICAL ISSUES

SUFFERING

The experience of physical or psychological pain or deprivation is generally referred to as "suffering." When a person experiences suffering, often the first question asked is, "Why am I suffering?" This is really two questions: "Why is there suffering?" and "Why me?" Unfortunately there are no truly satisfactory answers to these classical theological questions.

Sometimes a person will answer these questions in terms of specific cause-and-effect relationships; for example, "I am being abused by my husband as punishment from God because 20 years ago, when I was 17, I had sexual relations with a guy I wasn't married to." Here the victim of abuse sees her suffering as just punishment for an event that happened long ago and for which she still feels guilty. This explanation has an almost superstitious quality. It reflects an effort on the part of the woman to make sense out of her experience of abuse by her husband. Her explanation takes the "effect" (the abuse), looks for a probable "cause" (her teenage "sin"), and directly connects the two. This conclusion is based on theological assumptions that support her view: God is a stern judge who seeks retribution, and God causes suffering to be inflicted as punishment.

However, the woman's explanation neither focuses on the real nature of her suffering (i.e., the abuse by her husband) nor places responsibility for her suffering where it lies: on an abusive husband. Sometimes people try to explain suffering by saying it is "God's will" or "part of God's plan for my life" or "God's way of teaching me a lesson." These explanations assume that God is stern, harsh, even cruel and arbitrary. This image of God runs counter to the biblical and Qur'anic images of a kind, merciful, and loving God. The God of this biblical teaching does not single out anyone to suffer for the sake of suffering, because suffering is not pleasing to God.

A distinction between voluntary and involuntary suffering is useful at this point. Someone may choose to suffer abuse or indignity in order to accomplish a greater good. For example, Martin Luther King Jr. suffered greatly in order to change what he believed to be unjust, racist laws. Although the abuse he experienced was not justifiable, he voluntarily chose suffering as a means to an end.

Involuntary suffering, which occurs when a person is beaten, raped, or abused, especially in a family relationship, can neither be justified nor is ever chosen. Involuntary suffering may be *endured* by a victim for any number of reasons including the belief that putting up with the suffering will eventually "change" the abuser's nature. This is unrealistic, however, and generally only reinforces the abuse.

THE NATURE OF SUFFERING

Christian Perspective Christian tradition teaches that suffering occurs because of the evil and sinfulness in the world. Unfortunately, when someone behaves in a hurtful way, someone else usually bears the brunt of that act and suffers as a result. Striving to live a righteous life does not guarantee protection from another's sinfulness. Individuals may find that they suffer from having made a poor decision (e.g., marrying a spouse who is abusive). But this in no way means that the person either wants to suffer or deserves the abuse.

In Christian teaching, at no point does God promise that we will not suffer. In the Scriptures, God *does* promise to be present with us during our suffering. This is especially evident in the Psalms, which give vivid testimony to people experiencing God's faithfulness during suffering (see Psalms 22 and 55).

A person's fear of abandonment by God is often strong in the midst of suffering and abuse, most often among victims of abuse who feel abandoned by everyone else—friends, other family members, clergy, doctors, police, lawyers, and counselors. Perhaps none of these people believed the victim's disclosures of abuse or were simply ill-prepared to help. For Christians, God's promise to victims is that even though all others might abandon them, God will be faithful. This message is in Romans 8:38–39 (RSV): "For I am sure that neither death, nor life, nor angels, nor principalities, nor things present, nor anything else in all creation, will be able to separate us from the love of God in Christ Jesus our Lord." This reassurance can be helpful to Christian victims of violence as well as to those who abuse them. Both victim and abuser should be reminded that God walks with them, seeking healing for victims and repentance for abusers.

Some people who regard suffering as God's will believe that God is teaching them a lesson or that hardship builds character. Experiences of suffering can, in fact, be occasions for growth. People who suffer may realize, in retrospect, that they learned a great deal from the experience and gained maturity as a result. This may often be the case, but only when the person who is suffering receives support and affirmation throughout the experience. With the support of others, people who are confronted with violence in their family can end the abuse, possibly leave the situation, make major changes in their lives, and grow as mature adults. They will probably learn difficult lessons: increased self-reliance; how to express anger; that they can survive better outside than inside abusive relationships; that they can be a whole person without being married; that they can exercise control over their actions with others; and that family relationships need not be abusive and violent.

This awareness of suffering as the occasion for growth, however, must come from the individuals themselves, and is recognized only at a time when they are well on their way to healing and renewal. It is never appropriate, when someone is feeling great pain, to point out that things really are not so bad and that someday the person will be glad that all this happened. These words of "comfort and reassurance" usually benefit the spiritual leader or the counselor, not the congregant or the client. At a later time it may be useful to share a perspective that new growth has taken place, and simply affirm the reality that this person has survived an extremely difficult situation. Suffering may present an occasion for growth; whether this potential is actualized depends on how the individual manages the experience of suffering.

Jewish Perspective Jewish approaches to the meaning and purpose of suffering reflect many of the themes that emerge from the Christian perspective. Biblical and rabbinic sources understand suffering to be divine punishment for sin and wrongdoing. This theme often appears in the liturgy, most notably in the prayers made during the High Holidays, Rosh Hoshana and Yom Kippur, when an inscription is made in the Book of Life depending on a person's repentance, prayer, and charity. Many Jewish teachings maintain, however, that divine punishment is not meted out in this world but is left for the World to Come.[3] All agree, however, that it is not for us humans to exact divine punishment or, for that matter, any punishment outside the judicial process. Acts of physical, sexual, or emotional abuse clearly are not understood to be instruments of divine justice or of proper legal proceedings. It is the divine gift of free will, so vital to human dignity, spirituality, and growth, that sadly allows some individuals to act in hurtful and sinful ways. The abusers, not God, are recognized as the source of suffering.

Judaism maintains that suffering may be a catalyst for personal and spiritual growth, and may serve a redemptive purpose. But, as stated, this is a lesson that must be accepted, contemplated, and internalized by the one who is suffering. It should never be imposed by others. Further, those who suffer are to find comfort in the help and support of family, friends, and community, and from God. Jews have a religious obligation to lessen another's burden and not to stand by callously or indifferently when another suffers.[4] Judaism maintains that humans reach their fullest human and spiritual potential through their acts of *chesed*—kindness and compassion.[5] Comfort is found with God through prayer and study, and also because God not only empathizes with those who suffer but identifies with them as well. For that reason, according to a rabbinic tradition expounding on the verse, "I am with him in trouble" (Psalm 91:15), that the burning bush in which God appeared to Moses was a thorn bush: "just as they are suffering in Egypt, so too [God] appeared in a place of travail, a bush of thorns."[6]

Muslim Perspective   The Qur'an teaches that this life is a test and that the way an individual responds to this test determines the type of life he or she will have in the hereafter.[7] Tests can come in a wide variety of forms, including illness, poverty, wealth, health, difficult relationships, and even oppression. Blessings like health and wealth are tests in the sense that believers must find a way to use these blessings in God's service and must be continuously conscious and grateful for them. A Muslim's goal is to respond to hardships by persevering and continuing to turn to God for guidance and help. When a person does not lose his or her faith and strives to worship God despite the difficulties life presents, then God promises rewards both in this lifetime and the next. A person who turns away from God in disbelief, or who seeks help from some other deity will be punished in the hereafter.

Patience (*sabr*) is one of the important qualities of a believer that can help a person make it through difficult times. The Qur'an refers to this quality as an active stance that is often linked with striving or struggling for a cause. Sometimes Muslims confuse the concept of patience and perseverance (sabr) with acceptance. In cases of domestic violence, a victim might mistakenly believe that by passively enduring the abuse, she is fulfilling her duty to be patient. However, the Qur'an is clear that those who are experiencing a hardship should strive to end that hardship. In the case of an illness, one should seek treatment. In the case of injustice and oppression, one is obligated to do whatever is in one's power to stop the injustice from continuing, including moving to another location where there is freedom from oppression.

Because all believers will be tested, the notion that a test is God's way of punishing someone for past deeds has no merit. On the contrary, a test is God's way of offering His servants opportunity to prove themselves worthy of His mercy and reward. In fact, Islam teaches that God tests the most those whom He most loves. Evidence for this teaching is abundant in the lives of the prophets and righteous people throughout history.

That people will be tested does not in any way relieve an abuser of being accountable for the violence imposed on others. The Qur'an emphasizes that each person is solely responsible for his or her actions, and that no one can blame another person (e.g., "She provoked me") as a way to justify their abusive behavior. In fact, the Qur'an describes oppressors as people who have wronged their own souls because their behavior will lead them to be punished in the hereafter.

The Qur'an also teaches that believers can avail themselves of God's mercy and compassion while they are experiencing tests and tribulations. God says that He is closer to a person than the jugular vein, and that He responds to His servant when called upon. Because of God's mercy, He provides ease in the midst of hardship. This ease might be in the form of an advocate providing resources to a victim, an imam providing guidance and inspiration, or a community providing financial assistance.

There are several relevant concepts that often provide comfort and assurance to victims of domestic violence. Islam teaches that God witnesses all and rewards efforts; this belief can motivate individuals to continue in the face of criticism or lack of support from others. The belief that God holds each person accountable and gives each person his or her due provides some consolation for victims unable to satisfactorily hold the abuser accountable or enforce consequences. Finally, awareness of God's infinite mercy and understanding in the face of community resistance or denial can prevent a feeling of being alone and unsupported.

NATURE OF THE MARRIAGE RELATIONSHIP

CHRISTIAN PERSPECTIVE

Christian teaching about the model marriage relationship has traditionally focused heavily on Paul's letters to the Ephesians, Corinthians, and Colossians. Misinterpretations and misplaced emphasis on these texts create substantial problems for many heterosexual married couples. Directives on marriage, based on the Scriptures, are most commonly given to women by clergy but not so often to men and state that wives must "submit" to their husbands, a directive intended to elevate the husband and father as the absolute head of the household whom the wife and children must obey without question. Unfortunately this idea has also been misinterpreted to mean that wives and children must submit to abuse from husbands and fathers as well. Those who abuse their families rationalize their misdeeds through these interpretations, as do counselors, clergy, and the victims of the abuse themselves.

A closer look at the actual scriptural references reveals a different picture. For example, Ephesians 5:21: "Be subject to one another *out of reverence for Christ*" (RSV; emphasis added). This is the first and most important verse in the Ephesians passage on marriage and also the one most often overlooked. It clearly indicates that all Christians—husbands and wives—are to be mutually subject to each other. The word translated as "be subject to" can more appropriately be translated as "defer" or "accommodate": "Wives accommodate to your husbands, as to the Lord" (Ephesians 5:22). This teaching implies sensitivity, flexibility, and responsiveness to the husband. In no way can this verse be taken to mean that a wife must submit to abuse from her husband.

The model suggested in the following Scriptural reference to the relationship between husband and wife is based on that between Christ and the Church: "For the husband is the head of the wife as Christ is the head of the Church, his body, and is Himself its savior. As the Church is subject to Christ, so let wives also be subject in everything to their husbands" (Ephesians 5:23–24, RSV). It is clear from the teachings and ministry of Jesus that his relationship to his followers was not one of dominance or authoritarianism but rather one of servanthood. For example, Jesus washed his disciples' feet in an act of serving. He taught them that those who would be first must in fact be last. Therefore, a good husband would not seek to dominate or control his wife but would serve and care for her, according to Ephesians.

"Even so husbands should love their wives as their own bodies. He who loves his wife loves himself. For no man ever hates his own flesh, but nourishes it and cherishes it, as Christ does the Church, because we are members of his body" (Ephesians 5:28–29, RSV). This instruction to husbands is clear and concrete. A husband is to nourish and cherish his own body and that of his wife. Physically battering one's spouse is probably the most blatant violation of this teaching and a clear reflection of the self-hatred within the abuser.

It is notable that these passages from Ephesians (5:21–29), which are commonly used as instructions for marriage, are intended primarily for husbands. Nine of the verses address husbands' responsibilities in marriage; three of the verses refer to wives' responsibilities, and only one addresses both parties. Contemporary interpretation, however, often focuses solely on the wives, misusing passages to justify abuse of the wife. Although spousal abuse may be a common pattern in a number of Christian marriages, it certainly cannot be legitimated by scripture.

In terms of sexuality in marriage, again this passage from Ephesians (see also Colossians 3:18–21) has been used to establish a relationship in which the husband has conjugal rights and the wife has conjugal duties. In fact, other scriptural passages are explicit on this issue: "The husband should give to his wife her conjugal rights, and likewise the wife to the husband. For the wife does not rule over her own body, but the husband does; likewise, the husband does not rule over his own body, but the wife does" (I Corinthians 7:3–4, RSV).

The rights and expectations between husband and wife regarding sexual matters are explicitly equal and parallel, and include the right to refuse sexual contact. The expectation of equality of conjugal rights and sexual access and the need for mutual consideration in sexual activity is clear. The suggestion that both wife and husband "rule over" the other's body and not their own refers to the need for joint, mutual decisions about sexual activity rather than arbitrary, independent decisions. A husband does not have the right to act out of his own sexual needs without the wife agreeing, and the same holds true for the wife. This passage directly challenges incidents of sexual abuse (rape) in marriage that physically abused wives frequently report.

JEWISH PERSPECTIVE

The Jewish marriage ceremony is known as "Kiddushin" or sanctification; through this ritual a couple's relationship is made holy and dedicated to God. This sanctification reminds Jews to strive to express their holiness through marriage and the home in a covenantal relationship based on mutual love and respect.

Judaism views marriage as necessary for personal fulfillment[8] and is the fundamental unit of community life. Marriage is part of God's plan. In the early account of creation God observes that "it is not good for man to be alone" (Gen. 2:18).

One of the fundamental values of Jewish family life is "Shalom Bayit," peace in the home. "Shalom," which is translated as "peace," also signifies wholeness, completeness, and fulfillment. Domestic harmony encompasses the welfare of all the inhabitants in a home.

The rabbis consider domestic tranquility as one of the most important ideals because it fulfills the biblical mandate to "love your friend as you love yourself," an obligation which speaks first and foremost to marital partners.[9] It is also the essential forerunner to peace on earth. "Peace will remain a distant vision until we ourselves do the work of peace. If peace is to be brought into the world, then we must first bring it to our families and communities."[10] The concept of Shalom Bayit should not be invoked to place the onus of domestic harmony solely on the shoulders of a wife, nor should it be used to encourage maintaining an abusive marriage. When domestic harmony is impossible because of physical abuse, the only way to achieve peace may be to dissolve the marriage. Although marriage is a sacred institution, divorce is always an option according to the Jewish tradition.

In Judaism, conjugal rights are obligatory upon the husband who must be available for his wife. "A wife may restrict her husband in his business journey to nearby places only, so that he would not otherwise deprive her of her conjugal rights. Hence he may not set out without her permission."[11] Just as a husband is responsible for his wife's sexual fulfillment, a wife, in return, is expected to have sexual relations with her husband. Jewish law, however, grants discretion in this area and requires consent on her part to every act of intimacy. If she refuses sexual relations with her husband "she should be questioned as to the reason . . . If she says, 'I have come to loathe him, and I cannot willingly submit to his intercourse,' he must be compelled to divorce her immediately for she is not like a captive woman who must submit to a man that is hateful to her."[12] This suggests that no wife is expected to submit to sexual activity with a husband she fears or hates. The arena of sexual sharing for Jewish couples is one of mutual responsibility and choice.

MUSLIM PERSPECTIVE

The first verse in a chapter of the Qur'an titled "The Women" establishes the equal nature of men and women, and reminds each gender that God is a witness to their fulfillment of their mutual rights: "O mankind! Reverence your Guardian-Lord, who created you from a single soul, created of like nature its mate, and from them both scattered (like seeds) countless men and women— Fear God through Whom you demand your mutual rights. And (reverence) the wombs (that bore you) for God ever watches over you."[13]

The Qur'an provides guidance for male-female relations, and describes men and women as "friends and protectors" of each other. Needless to say, this relationship is expected to carry into the marriage. Marriage is described in the Qur'an as a "solemn covenant,"[14] a contract witnessed by God between two consenting adults who agree to live together in accordance with His laws.

The Qur'an says: "He created for you mates from among yourselves that you may dwell in tranquility with them, and He has put love and mercy between your (hearts)" (30:21).

The mutuality of the marital relationship is described in many teachings. One example is the Qur'anic reference to spouses as garments for each other.[15] This verse specifically refers to the sexual relationship between spouses, highlighting the accommodation that each spouse should make for the other, and the comfort each should find in the other.

The Qur'anic teachings are exemplified and reinforced by the teachings of the Prophet Muhammad, who said, "The best among you is the one who is best to his family, and I am the best to my family." According to Muhammad's example, husbands and wives are partners; they should encourage each other to live in accordance with divine laws, consult each other when making decisions, support each other emotionally, and accommodate each other's needs.

Within this partnership, Islam recognizes that each partner may be better suited to particular areas in the relationship. For example, men have been given a leadership role, with the responsibility of providing financially for their families. Women, by virtue of their biological design, are obviously the only partner who can bear and nurse children. The roles of husband and wife are interdependent and complementary, perfectly manifesting the Arabic word for spouse (zawj), which means pair.

In his role as leader, a husband must remember his accountability to God and his responsibility to lead his family in accordance with Islamic values, which include justice, compassion, and equity. A wife should accept her husband's leadership as long as he is living according to God's teachings. She should never obey him or follow his lead in any matter that is contrary to these teachings.

In the case of domestic violence, abusers often distort or manipulate teachings to rationalize or justify their behavior. The same verse that holds men responsible for protecting and maintaining women financially also prescribes a process for men to use with a wife who has behaved in an immoral manner that compromises the integrity of the relationship (nushuz).[16] In a situation where there has been a serious breach, he is advised to talk to her first, then to sleep separately from her, and finally to chastise her if she does not change her behavior. This chastisement has been the subject of great controversy, with interpretations about its execution that range from a symbolic beating (using a handkerchief or something similar that would not cause injury) to abandonment. The goal of this verse is to preserve the marriage by bringing a wife back to the right path, not to give the husband permission to be violent or abusive. In fact, a parallel verse addresses how a woman may respond if her husband is guilty of unacceptable behavior (nushuz).[17]

Most important when considering the Islamic perspective on marriage is that teachings cannot be taken in isolation; rather, the Islamic paradigm must be considered as a whole. Using a holistic approach, the teachings provide a model for healthy relationships, with guidance that prevents any kind of abuse or oppression. An important juristic maxim that guides legal rulings is this: "Do not commit harm or allow reciprocation of harm." In addition, the teachings that reference equitable and just relations, mutuality, love, and compassion and tranquility between spouses all lead to the conclusion that violence has no place in a relationship between two God-fearing partners.

Although marriage is highly encouraged, and the preservation of a marriage is extremely important, the Qur'an also recognizes that not all marriages are sustainable. Couples are encouraged either to live together in kindness or separate in kindness if they are unable to live according to God's teachings. Divorce is an option of last resort to protect individuals from experiencing harm or from finding themselves in a situation where they may commit sins against the other out of their own misery. Unfortunately, in many cultures that are predominantly Muslim, divorce is surrounded by so much stigma that women may not even know it exists as an option. However, both the Qur'an and the teachings of Prophet Muhammad provide detailed instruction on the process of divorce, which can be initiated by either the husband or the wife.

THE MARRIAGE COVENANT AND DIVORCE: SHARED PERSPECTIVES

Strongly held beliefs in the permanency of marriage and sanctity of its vows may prevent an abused spouse from considering separation or divorce as options. For the Christian, the promise of faithfulness "for better or for worse . . . 'til death do us part'" is commonly taken to mean "stay in the marriage no matter what," even though death of one or more family members may be a real possibility when there is abuse. Jews view marriage as permanent, but the phrase "til death do us part" is not part of the ceremony. The Jewish attitude embodies a delicate balance. Marriage is taken very seriously; it is a primary religious obligation and should not be entered into or discarded casually. Nevertheless, since the days of Deuteronomy, Jewish tradition has recognized the unfortunate reality that some couples are hopelessly incompatible and divorce may be necessary. Similarly, Islam emphasizes the importance of keeping a marriage and doing whatever is possible to maintain it. However, it also provides for divorce as a peaceful solution for couples who are unable to live together in peace and tranquility or who simply are unhappy together.

For some Christians, a strong doctrinal position against divorce may inhibit them from exercising this means of dealing with domestic violence. For others, a position against divorce is a personally held belief often supported by family and church. In either case, a common assumption is that any marriage is better than no marriage at all and therefore should be maintained at any cost. This assumption arises from a superficial view of marriage as concerned only with appearances and not with substance. In other words, as long as marriage and family relationships maintain a facade of normalcy, there may be a refusal by church and community to look any closer for fear of seeing abuse or violence in the home.

Many cultural values and attitudes prevent Muslims from seeking divorce as a solution. Divorced women often face criticism from families and communities who hold them responsible for the success or failure of the marriage. There is also a belief that having two parents, regardless of what they are like, is better than a single parent. This belief often keeps abused women in their relationships, unaware of the damage children who witness abuse incur. Marriage also provides a social status that many are unwilling to lose, preferring instead to remain in an unhealthy relationship.

The covenant of Christian marriage is a lifelong, sacred commitment made between two persons and witnessed by other persons and by God. Jews also regard marriage as sacred and intend that it be permanent. Muslims enter into marriage as a covenant witnessed by God, and by at least two other people. It is a relationship that is to be used as a vehicle for worshiping God. For Jews, Christians, and Muslims, a covenant between marriage partners has the following elements:

- It is made in full knowledge of the relationship.
- It involves a mutual giving of oneself to the other.
- It is assumed to be lasting.
- It values mutuality, respect, and equality between persons.

A marriage covenant can be violated by one or both partners. A common belief in Jewish, Christian, and Muslim traditions is that adultery violates the marriage covenant and destroys the relationship. Likewise, violence or abuse in a marriage violates the covenant and fractures a relationship. In both cases the trust assumed between partners is shattered. Neither partner should be expected to remain in an abusive situation. Often one marriage partner feels a heavy obligation to remain in the relationship and do everything possible to make it work. This is most often true for women. A covenant relationship only works if both partners are able and willing to work on it. In all three traditions, it is clear that God does not expect anyone to stay in a situation that is abusive. In the Christian tradition, just as Jesus did not expect his disciples to remain in a village that did not respect and care for them (Luke 9:1–6), neither does he expect persons to remain in a family relationship where they are abused and violated.

Similarly the Qur'an reminds those who are oppressed that "God's earth is spacious enough to move away from evil" (4:97), and that believers who are oppressed "(are not cowed but) help and defend themselves" (42:39). These verses make clear that God would not want anyone to stay in an abusive or violent relationship.

In the Jewish literature the expectation is also apparent: "if a man was found to be a wife beater, he had to pay damages and provide her with separate maintenance. Failing that, the wife had valid grounds for compelling a divorce."[18]

If the abuser makes a genuine effort to change, the marriage covenant may be renewed but only by including a clear commitment to nonviolence. With counseling of family members, it may be possible to salvage the relationship. If the one who is being abusive is unwilling or unable to change, then the question of divorce arises. At this point in the marriage, divorce is only a matter of public statement: "Shall we make public the fact that our relationship has been broken by abuse?" The other option, of course, is to continue to pretend that the marriage is intact. (One woman reported that she divorced only a month ago but that her marriage ended ten years ago when the abuse began.)

In a home where one partner is abusive, divorce does not break up the family. It is the perpetrator's violence and abuse that breaks up the family. Divorce is often the painful, public acknowledgement of an already accomplished fact. Although divorce is never easy, in the case of domestic violence it is the lesser evil. In many cases divorce may be a necessary intervention to generate healing and new life from a devastating and deadly situation.

PARENTS AND CHILDREN: SHARED PERSPECTIVES

"Honor your father and your mother" is one of the Ten Commandments taught to all Jewish and Christian children. Muslim children learn the same commandment in the Qur'an. Some parents, however, misuse this teaching in order to demand unquestioning obedience from their children. In a hierarchical, authoritarian household, a father may misuse his parental authority to coerce a child into abusive sexual activity (incest). Parents may use this commandment to rationalize their physical abuse of a child in retaliation for a child's lack of obedience.

For Christians, the meaning of the Third Commandment is made clear in Ephesians:

> Children, obey your parents *in the Lord*, for this is right. "Honor your father and mother" (this is the first commandment with a promise) "that it may be well with you and that you may live long on the earth." Fathers, do not provoke your children to anger, but bring them up in the discipline and instruction *of the Lord*." (Ephesians 6:1–4, RSV; emphasis added)

Children's obedience to their parents is to be "in the Lord"; it is not to be blind and unquestioning. Parents receive instructions to guide and instruct their children in Christian values such as love, mercy, compassion, and justice. Disciplining a child must be in the child's best interest. The caution to the father not to provoke the child to anger is most appropriate. If anything will provoke a child to anger, it is certainly physical or sexual abuse by a parent.

Jewish tradition deals with the same concern explaining the juxtaposition of the two parts of the verse that speaks about the obligation to have reverence for one's parents: "A person shall revere his mother and his father, and shall observe My Sabbaths" (Lev. 19:3). Both parents and children share an obligation to fulfill the divine law; the divine will has priority over parental desires and all are duty-bound to submit to its strictures.[19] Furthermore, parents must be careful not to provoke their children unnecessarily.

> One is forbidden to beat his grown-up child, the word "grown-up" in this regard refers not to age but to maturity. If there is reason to believe that the child will rebel, and express that resentment by word or deed, even though children have not yet reached the age of maturity (12 for a girl, 13 for a boy), it

is forbidden to beat them. Instead, a parent should reason with them. Anyone who beats his grown-up children is to be excommunicated, because he transgresses the Divine Command (Lev. 19:14) "Thou shalt not put a stumbling block before the blind" (for they are apt to bring sin and punishment upon their children).[20]

Even though Jewish law gives great authority to parents in relationship to their children, the requirement for restraint is clearly indicated. Again, the priority is the child's welfare.

The other biblical injunction commonly used to justify abusive discipline of children is the Proverb generally summarized as "Spare the rod and spoil the child." "He who spares the rod hates his son, but he who loves him is diligent to discipline him" (Proverbs 13:24). This Proverb is commonly interpreted to mean that if a parent does not use corporal punishment on a child, the child will become spoiled. This is a good example of a misinterpretation based on a contemporary understanding. In fact, the image referred to in this Proverb is probably that of shepherd and the rod is the shepherd's staff (see Psalm 23.4: "thy rod and thy staff shall comfort me"). A shepherd uses his staff to guide the sheep where they should go. The staff is not used as a cudgel.

This image of the shepherd guiding the sheep certainly points to children's need for guidance and discipline from parents and other caring adults if they are to mature in a healthy way. Children do not need to be physically beaten to receive guidance or discipline. Beating children as discipline teaches them early on that it is all right to hit the people you love for their own good. This kind of lesson fosters early training for persons who grow up and later physically abuse their spouses and children.

For Muslims, the emphasis on obedience to parents is contingent on the parents not asking for anything that would be displeasing to God. Although obedience to parents is second only to obedience to God, parents also have obligations to their children. Prophet Muhammad identified six basic rights that parents owe their children: the right to live, the right to belong to a family, the right to a good name, the right to an education, the right to be provided for, and the right to be brought up according to Islamic teachings. The Prophet instructed parents to respect their children and teach them good behavior. Regarding the disciplining of children, the Prophet Muhammad was known never to have hit a child, and he always spoke to children in a gentle and respectful manner.

When parents obey God in raising their children in the best possible manner, without question they deserve to be held in the highest esteem. Children, including adult children, are instructed to be kind to parents, avoid words that are disrespectful, and "out of kindness, lower to them the wing of humility, and say: 'My Lord! Bestow on them your mercy even as they cherished me in childhood'" (17:24).

CONFESSION AND FORGIVENESS

When a person who is an abuser of a family member admits to wrongdoing, then that is a healthy sign that he or she is no longer denying the problem but may be ready and willing to face it. The offender may seek out a minister, an imam, or a rabbi for the purpose of confessing. Sometimes an abusive father confesses, asks forgiveness, and promises never to approach his daughter sexually again, or a mother swears never to hit her child in anger again. The religious leader is then put in a position of assuring forgiveness and evaluating the strength of the person's promise. Although the abuser may be genuinely contrite, it is rare that the person will be able to end the abuse without assistance and intervention.

The religious leader needs to assure the person of God's forgiveness along with the expectation of repentance and a change of behavior. Abusers must be confronted with the reality that they need additional help in order to stop the abuse. For some, a strong word from a minister, an imam, or a rabbi at this point is an effective deterrent. A strong directive such as "the abuse must stop now" can provide an external framework for beginning to change the abusive behavior.

For Jews, the Hebrew term *teshuvah* is the word for repentance. *Teshuvah* literally means "return," denoting a return to God and to a state of being sinless. The repentance process requires a number of steps: contrition, admission of wrongdoing, confession, acceptance never to repeat the offense, and confession. Repentance and reconciliation can only be accomplished with corresponding changes in behavior. This is true both for violations of ritual as well as interpersonal sins. However, before one can be forgiven for sins committed against another, one must first make amends by repairing any damage, appeasing and mollifying the victim for any hurt that was caused, and asking that person for forgiveness. Judaism teaches that God cannot and will not forgive those who repent until the ones they have harmed have themselves forgiven the perpetrators.[21] Simply put, forgiveness needs to be earned.[22]

Similarly, for Christians, Jesus provides a process in Luke's Gospel: "Take heed to yourselves; if your brother sins, rebuke him, and if he repents, forgive him; and if he sins against you seven times in the day and turns to you seven times, and says, 'I repent,' you must forgive him." (Luke 17:3–4). This process turns on repentance which means a change in behavior. Repentance is possible when one is called to account. "Rebuke" means to call to account. This is the responsibility of the community when domestic violence is disclosed.

The issue of forgiveness often arises for victims of abuse. A friend or family member may pressure the victim: "You should forgive him. He said he was sorry." Or it may arise internally: "I wish I could forgive him." In either case, the victim feels guilty for not being able to "forgive" the abuser. But the transgressed know that somehow forgiveness is linked to healing. Forgiveness often is misinterpreted as forgetting or pretending that the abuse never happened. Neither forgetting nor pretending is possible. Abuse is never forgotten; it becomes a part of the victim's history. Forgiveness involves the ability of victims to say that the experience will no longer dominate their lives; the individual can let go of the pain and move on. This usually requires some form of justice, whether legally or informally. A victim's forgiveness usually requires the abuser's repentance. Real repentance is reflected in profound changes in an abuser's behavior. This also assumes that the victim/survivor is safe and on the way to healing.

Another issue is timing. Too often the religious leader or counselor prematurely pushes the victim to forgive the abuser, in a misguided effort to assist the victim to finally resolve the abusive experience. They try to use "forgiveness" as a means to hurry the victim's healing process. All victims, however, move to forgive at their own pace and cannot be pushed by others' expectations. Their timing needs to be respected. It may take years before they are ready to forgive; they will forgive when they are ready. When forgiveness arrives, it becomes the final stage of letting go, enabling a victim to move forward in life.

The Qur'an strongly encourages Muslims to forgive one another, but it also takes into account the need people have for justice. The Jewish teaching of an eye for an eye is included in the Qur'an followed by, "but if anyone remits the retaliation by way of charity, it is an act of atonement for himself.[23] The ability to forgive is a quality held by believers who strive to model themselves after God's forgiving nature. But there is no specific time limit as to how soon forgiveness must occur. Forgiveness is a process that happens over time, as healing occurs. It cannot be rushed or imposed by others; it comes from within one's own spirit.

CONCLUSION

This chapter addressed some common religious concerns raised by people dealing with domestic violence within Judaism, Islam, and Christianity. We attempted to help the reader begin to see ways of converting potential roadblocks into valuable resources for those dealing with domestic violence.

Personal faith for the religious person can provide much needed strength and courage when facing a painful situation and making changes within. Churches, mosques, and synagogues can provide a much needed network of community support for victims, abusers, and their children.

Clearly those involved in religious congregations and institutions need to address these concerns directly. Ignorance and oversight can cause much harm. By being aware and taking action, however, we can contribute a critical element to the efforts to respond to domestic violence in our communities.

RESOURCES

FaithTrust Institute
2400 N. 45th Street
Suite 10
Seattle, WA 98103
Phone: 1 (877) 860–2255; or, outside the U.S.: (206) 634–0055
Fax: (206) 634–0115 (24 hours)
Web site: http://www.faithtrustinstitute.org

The Episcopal Church
Office of Women's Ministries
815 Second Avenue
New York, NY 10017
Phone: 1 (800) 334–7626 x 5346
Web site: http://www.episcopalchurch.org/

Evangelical Lutheran Church
8765 W. Higgins Road
Chicago, IL 60631
Phone: 1 (800) 638–3522 or (773) 380–2700
Web site: http://www.elca.org/churchinsociety/

Family, Laity, Women, and Youth U.S. Conference of Catholic Bishops
3211 4th Street, N.E.
Washington DC 20017–1194
Phone: (202) 541–3000
Web site: http://www.usccb.org/laity/women/violence.shtml

Islamic Society of North America
P.O. Box 38
Plainfield, IN 46168
Phone: (317) 839–1840
Web site: http://www.isna.net/services/dv/

Jewish Women International
2000 M Street
NW Suite 720
Washington, DC 20036
Phone: 1 (800) 343-2823 or (202) 857-1300
Web site: http://www.jwi.org

The Peaceful Families Project
P.O. Box 771
Great Falls, VA 22066
Phone: (703) 474-6870
Web site: http://www.peacefulfamilies.org/

Presbyterians Against Domestic Violence
100 Witherspoon Street
Louisville, KY 40202
Phone: 1 (888) 728–7228
Web site: http://www.pcusa.org/phewa/padvn

Union for Reform Judaism
633 Third Avenue
New York, NY 10017–6778

Phone: (212) 650-4000
Web site: http://urj.org/jfc/resilience/domestic/

Unitarian Universalist Association of Congregations
25 Beacon Street
Boston, MA 02108
Phone ; (617) 742-2100
Web site: http://www.uua.org/socialjustice/socialjustice/

PASCH—Peace and Safety in the Christian Home
Web site: http://www.peaceandsafety.com/

The Black Church and Domestic Violence Institute
Web site: http://www.bcdvi.org/

REFERENCES

Alkhateeb, M. B., and S. E. Abugideiri (Eds.). (2007). *Change from Within: Diverse Perspectives on Domestic Violence in Muslim Communities.* Herndon, VA: Peaceful Families Project.

Alwani, Z., and S. Abugideiri. (2003). *What Islam Says about Domestic Violence: A Guide for Helping Muslim Families.* Herndon, VA: Foundation for Appropriate and Immediate Temporary Help.

Anton, J. (Ed.). (2005). *Walking Together: Working with Women from Diverse Religious and Spiritual Traditions.* Seattle: FaithTrust Institute.

Fortune, M. M. (1995). *Keeping the Faith: Questions and Answers for Christian Women Facing Abuse.* In English, Spanish, and Korean. San Francisco: Harper-Collins. Available at http://www.faithtrustinstitute.org.

Lamm, M. (1991). *The Jewish Way in Love and Marriage.* New York: Harper and Row.

Landesman, T. (2004). *You Are Not Alone: Solace and Inspiration for Domestic Violence Survivors, Based on Jewish Wisdom.* Seattle: FaithTrust Institute.

Miles, A. (2000). *Domestic Violence: What Every Pastor Needs to Know.* Minneapolis, MN: Augsburg Fortress.

Murphy, N. (2007). *God's Reconciling Love: A Pastor's Handbook on Domestic Violence.* Seattle: FaithTrust Institute.

Twerski, Abraham J. (1996). *The Shame Borne in Silence: Spouse Abuse in the Jewish Community.* Pittsburgh, Pa: Mirkov.

13

APPALACHIA

Addressing Domestic Violence in the Rural Environment

Elizabeth J. Randall and Leslie E. Tower

DOMESTIC VIOLENCE is a tragic phenomenon that erodes the quality of life for everyone affected, wherever it occurs. It may, however, be particularly destructive and difficult to manage in rural areas because of the common characteristics of rural life and values. This chapter examines some of the unique manifestations and attributes of this insidious problem in rural areas, as well as systems of response.

In the social sciences, the term "rural" is often equated with the term "non-metropolitan area," as defined by the U.S. Bureau of the Census. This usage distinguishes "metropolitan area" from rural areas. Metropolitan areas (MAs), or large population centers, include the surrounding communities that share significant, reciprocal economic and social influences; these comprise a "metropolitan statistical area" (MSA). Areas outside an MA or MSA are "nonmetropolitan" areas (Blakely and Locke 2005), or "rural."

Although many lament the decline of rural America, this decline is one of proportion rather than sheer numbers. In 1900, 60 percent of the population lived in rural areas; by 2000, the proportion had diminished to 21 percent. During the same interval, however, the actual census of rural residents grew by about 13 million (Lohmann and Lohmann 2005).

Poverty and limited economic opportunity persist as problems for rural Americans. Because of a disproportionate number of low-wage industries, workers are more than twice as likely to earn minimum wages (Blakely and Locke 2005); rates of unemployment and underemployment are also higher in rural areas (Whitener, Weber, and Duncan 2001). More than 500 nonmetropolitan counties are classified as experiencing persistent poverty, meaning poverty rates consistently exceed 20 percent for a span of decades (Whitener, Duncan, and Weber 2002).

RURAL APPALACHIA

Just as the term "minority population" must take into account great diversity of cultural experience, depending on the particular minority population to which one refers, so the term "rural population" may mean many different things to many different peoples, depending on the unique rural region under consideration. "Rurality" is often inextricably intertwined with other ethnic, climate, and geographic variables. To create a framework that allows a more in-depth exploration of domestic violence in rural America, we have taken a case study approach focusing on one particular region, rural Appalachia. The 410 Appalachian counties are located in 13 states: Alabama, Georgia, Kentucky, Maryland, Mississippi, New York, North Carolina, Ohio, Pennsylvania, South Carolina, Tennessee, Virginia, and West Virginia (Appalachian Regional Commission [ARC] 2006). Of the 23 million people who live in Appalachia, 42 percent are rural, compared to 21 percent of the national population (ARC 2006).

The majority of rural Appalachians cannot be distinguished by outward appearance. In some areas, however, there is a distinct regional dialect, accompanied by unique vocabulary and syntax, which may lead to communication difficulties with outsiders (Purnell 2003).

A higher percentage of Appalachian residents are white (89%) compared to the national population (75%). Within Appalachia, the largest minority group is African Americans (8.4%), followed by Latino Americans, who constitute 2 percent of Appalachian people (Hayden 2004). Minority populations tend to be heavily concentrated within 26 of the 410 Appalachian counties (Hayden 2004).

Higher poverty rates are the norm in Appalachia, as they are for rural regions in general. Unemployment and underemployment rates exceed national averages, with 40 Appalachian counties having unemployment rates steadily above 10 percent (Pollard 2003). The residents of Appalachia also tend to have less education compared to national percentages. For instance, college graduates comprise 24.4 percent of the national population, but only 17.7 percent among Appalachians.

Some locales continue to lack basic water and sewer systems. Roads are often narrow; some homes can only be reached along an unpaved track off the nearest public road. The relatively depressed business and economic climate in portions of Appalachia depresses the tax base, creating difficulties for local governments that wish to invest in necessary infrastructure. These restricted tax bases affect funding for civic institutions and social services, particularly by inhibiting federal match grants (Shoaf 2004).

HISTORICAL ISSUES

Historically business and industry have exploited the Appalachian region for its natural resources, especially coal and timber (ARC 2006), as well as for its workforce. Corporations tended to be owned and managed from elsewhere (Miewald and O'Quinn 2006), draining away wealth and investment. Managerial whim dictated employees' lives, contributing to family stress; few jobs were available to women, which reinforced patriarchal control of the family and community (Burns, Scott, and Thompson 2006). Still today, women's participation in the paid labor force, or higher education, stimulates conflict between "modern" aspirations and traditional gender role expectations. Women's wages often remain insufficient to support a family (Miewald and O'Quinn 2006). The socioeconomic vulnerability among rural women, some of whom might yearn to leave an abusive partnership, can be extreme.

DOMESTIC VIOLENCE IN RURAL SETTINGS

Studies of the prevalence of domestic violence in rural regions in comparison with more populous regions have produced mixed results. Some studies assert higher rates of spousal abuse (Shannon et al. 2006), whereas others have found marginally less domestic violence, or have concluded that no significant differences exist (Sudderth 2003). Most authors agree, however, that domestic violence poses a dangerous threat, for several reasons. Websdale (1995), for instance, attributes the heightened danger rural victims face to intense isolation, which he separates into three components: (1) physical isolation owing to the great distances between dwellings and towns, which enables batterers to use control strategies that "would either be more visible or less effective in urban areas" (p. 104); (2) socio-cultural isolation, which traps women in violence in a particularly implacable way because of the prevalence of patriarchy and rigid gender roles; and (3) isolation from potentially helpful sources of aid and social services. Websdale (1995) points out that rural isolation increases dependency. To support his assertion, he cites a study by Kalmuss and Strauss (1982), which found that the more dependent the victim, the greater the likelihood that the victim will endure extreme violence.

Geographic isolation has many manifestations. Much of Appalachia, for instance, is hilly or mountainous, with winding roads often in poor condition that may be impassable for days at a time in severe weather (Adler 1996). Additional circumstances limit women's ability to leave the area, such as having only one vehicle, or having a partner disable a vehicle or withhold keys, and lack of public transportation (Grama 2000). Most rural communities have no taxi services.

Not only does geographic isolation make it more difficult to leave a violent home, it also makes it harder to receive help. Rural battered women are often geographically isolated from police attempting to respond to a 911 call. Some rural areas may lack a local police department, forcing citizens to rely on an overextended county sheriff's office for protection, resulting in lengthy response times.

The telephone plays a critical role in rural areas, particularly in emergencies; physical distance may preclude a neighbor's ability to hear screams for help. Lack of telephones or telephone service may prevent rural women from receiving support from family or friends or service providers. Cell phone service often is spotty or unavailable because of insufficient economic incentive for service providers to construct and maintain towers in areas of low demand.

Rural women further report that isolation is compounded by few resources (Davis, Taylor, and Furniss 2001). Based on a sample of 48 domestic violence victims in rural New Mexico, Hilbert and Krishman (2000) pointed to another form of isolation: social exclusion that leads to a profound sense of hopelessness and high levels of suicidal ideation. Shannon et al. (2006) also found that rural women use significantly fewer help-seeking resources compared to urban women.

Thus the plight of abused rural women who face serious obstacles as a result of seclusion and distance, lack of transportation, severe cultural inhibitions regarding disclosure, and greatly curtailed options for economic self-sufficiency because of limited employment opportunities and formidable structural barriers may often be particularly desperate.

DOMESTIC VIOLENCE IN APPALACHIA

Cultural values can play an inadvertent role in helping to perpetuate attitudes and behaviors that may often contribute to the problem. Some of these cultural values, common to rural areas, include family-centeredness, religious worldview, patriarchy, a powerful spirit of place, "rugged individualism" and self-reliance, and relative sociopolitical conservatism (Gross 2005; Jones 2006; Keefe 2001). Other cultural values, thought to be particularly Appalachian, include egalitarianism, personalism, and avoidance of conflict (Fiene 1991; Keefe 2000). Egalitarianism refers to the rejection of social status differences and disapproval of conspicuous consumption; personalism is evident in the preference for face-to-face interactions; and avoidance of conflict is seen in distinct notions of interpersonal etiquette that result in Appalachians tending not to get involved in the affairs of others unless directly asked (Keefe 2001). Although not universal, the influences of these traditional values linger throughout the region and may, inadvertently, promote cultural tolerance of family violence in the following ways:

- *Family-centeredness* can trigger strong inhibitions against asking for or accepting help from outsiders, and may also contribute to placing a higher priority on family honor (and hence secrecy) rather than safety.
- *Religious worldview* may support a belief that marital vows are sacred and must be upheld, no matter what happens and regardless of the quality (or potential danger) of the relationship.
- *Patriarchy* fuels the belief that women are subordinate, bearing the status of chattel.
- *Spirit of place* contributes to deep-seated feelings of rootedness, limiting the geographical flexibility of victims who might otherwise wish to distance themselves from harm.
- *Self-reliance* encourages the belief "I got myself into this, so it's up to me, alone, either to cope with it or get myself out of it."
- *Conservatism* may result in a tendency to disdain governmental institutions and social services.
- *Personalism* can lead to the relative mistrust of anyone one does not know personally or is not vouchsafed by a third trusted party.
- *Egalitarianism* can add to the mistrust of professionals and of persons with higher education or "paper credentials."

■ *Avoidance* of conflict yields a strong preference for "minding one's own business" and tends to promote a mind-set of secrecy.

Thus, at times, Appalachian culture may lend support to interpreting domestic violence as a private matter rather than a crime (Shoaf 2004).

POLICY AND COMMUNITY RESPONSE

Rural and Appalachian communities tend to have limited services for battered women. Rural regions generally support a small professional community, necessitating frequent contacts between advocates, law enforcement, private and prosecuting attorneys, magistrates or judges, and others involved in domestic violence intervention. As a result, battered women may suspect the professional relationships between these individuals. Paradoxically, however, it is the frequent contacts among the professionals that actually may enhance systemic responses. Based on the victim's association with a domestic violence advocate, victims and claims of abuse often are afforded increased credibility and recognition.

Laws affecting the societal response to domestic violence vary by state, but policies are slowly improving as the result of gradual awareness of the problem and by dedicated efforts on the part of the advocacy community. In one Appalachian state, new legislation has been passed almost every year, since 1989, that incrementally has contributed to improved victims' rights and to legally establishing domestic violence as a criminal rather than a private matter (Smith and Randall 2007b). Some within the state's professional advocacy community propose that hiring a staff attorney or a full-time political action specialist would significantly help, but present funding levels do not support this step (S. Julian, personal communication, October 19, 2006).

The importance and centricity of personal relationships often seen in rural areas can interfere with justice for battered women, such as when a perpetrator has a kinship connection or close tie to a law officer or other key person within the response system. In these situations, the cultural value of personalism may lead a friend or kinsman to place undue faith in his own experience of the accused ("he's a great fellah, I've knowed [sic] him all my life") and, accordingly, to discount the victim's dissonant narratives. Women may not be believed, particularly when the perpetrator is respected in the community (Cox et al. 2001). The value of family centricity may also encourage minimization or dismissal of testimony from a misplaced desire to protect a family's reputation or privacy. The prohibition against perpetrators possessing firearms has been known to trigger shudders of sympathetic dismay among friends and associates of batterers in West Virginia, where owning guns and hunting are centuries-old traditions of rural culture, symbolizing family heritage and independence as well as sport and an important means of supplementing food supplies (Goeckermann et al. 1994). Consequently reports may be minimized when criminal justice personnel know the abuser and try to protect him from losing his guns.

The lack of anonymity in rural life, where "everyone knows everyone," may also hamper systems of response and care from operating as intended. The preponderance of police scanners in homes, and the publication of arrests in small-town papers, may deter women from calling the police for help (Adler 1996; Grama 2000). Rural traditions of self-reliance may also reduce the odds that a woman will ever have interacted with institutional authorities, contributing to diminished faith in assurances about honoring confidentiality, thereby contributing to an unwillingness to disclose fully in emergency situations (Goeckermann, Hamberger, and Barber 1994).

CULTURALLY SENSITIVE PRACTICE WITH ABUSED APPALACHIAN WOMEN

Several of the cultural values described above have important implications for social workers in rural areas such as Appalachia. For instance, the spirit of place among Appalachian peoples often generates intense loyalty to communities and to the land, which non-natives may have difficulty fully understanding. Appalachian peoples not only want to make their land productive, but they also want to protect and preserve it (Eller, cited in Keefe 2001). This spirit of place is often an important if inexpressible source of strength and sustainment for rural people, yet it may also dramatically restrict the geographical flexibility when abused women consider their options. Rural women may also resist travel because of their ties to the land and caring for the animals on the farm (Grama 2000).

In order to be effective, social workers must strive to remain respectful of and sensitive to the centrality of these issues when working in Appalachia (Carlson and Choi 2001). For instance, a social worker may be inclined to encourage a rural woman to accept an offer of refuge with an out-of-state, urban family member as a way to escape a threatening partner. The client, however, may never have traveled and may be highly fearful or mired in anticipatory grief over the thought of leaving her home place and entering a fast-paced, alien environment. In order for this encouragement to succeed, the worker must first acknowledge and validate these feelings and next, perhaps, help the client explore potential benefits of exposure to novel experiences. The worker possibly could help the client identify an ally or traveling companion. If all else fails, however, and the client states that she would rather die than leave the place of her birth, then the worker must accept the client's self-determination and try to help the client within the parameters established by her choice.

Another significant consideration when working with this population is the cultural value of personalism, which places faith in personal connections and narratives. To the extent possible, social workers should craft assessment and service planning procedures that minimize the perception of being excessively data driven or impersonal. In the era of managed care, for example, utilization review coordinators often "front load" assessment procedures with compartmentalized information, some of which may be relevant to a given client but which also may serve primarily to increase the size and statistical power of proprietary data bases (Randall and Aldred-Crouch 2006). Social workers may feel forced to collect all this information immediately or risk the managed care gatekeeper denying the client's service eligibility. Understanding none of this, a client from whom all this detailed information is demanded immediately upon contact with the social worker may feel deeply alienated and will be considerably more likely to drop out (Gross 2005; Randall and Vance 2005). Instead, the social worker should first allow time for some relatively unstructured dialogue, thereby giving the client the opportunity to describe the situation using narrative rather than answers to closed-ended questions. The worker should also show a willingness to engage in a moderate amount of appropriate self-disclosure to allow the client to develop a feeling that she is interacting with a person rather than a bureaucracy. Further, a skilled social worker will find that categorical information can be deduced with great accuracy after concluding the dialogue simply by being attentive and discreetly making notes of pertinent information as disclosed by the client. If additional brief information is needed, explain the necessity for this and request the client's indulgence in a courteous tone.

A third cultural value that may often be significant is self-reliance among regional residents. This cultural trait suggests that extensive effort should be invested in exploring clients' personal strengths and resiliency, as well as supporting clients in the discovery or creation of their own uniquely personal answers to the challenges they face. In this way, clients may draw satisfaction and "quiet" pride from having been the primary agent of their own changes and success (Fiene 1991; Hall 1999). We advise social workers to work with victims of domestic violence according to the strengths perspective of social work practice (Saleeby 2005) or the principles of solution-focused treatment which emphasizes clients' strengths (De Jong and Berg 2007). These resources offer a wealth of additional information from a theoretical and a technical perspective. Additional comments on the importance of a strengths perspective and the significance of individualism and self-reliance for abused Appalachian women are offered in the following section.

APPALACHIAN NARRATIVES OF SURVIVAL AND RECOVERY

To gain a richer and more experiential sense of the journey of escape and healing from domestic violence among rural Appalachian women, we reviewed transcripts of 15 audio-taped interviews originally conducted by Smith (2003) as part of an ongoing phenomenological research project on the experiences of domestic abuse survivors. In the original study, 15 women described their experiences of recovering from intimate partner abuse, the factors that helped them along the way and those that did not. Our secondary analysis sought patterns of response that might prove helpful for social workers interested in providing appropriate and effective services for this population. Although qualitative methodology does not permit inferences to be drawn with statistical confidence, nevertheless some notable similarities and consistencies can be seen within the interviews that yield several useful insights despite this being a small, non-probability sample.

Four interviewees reported having participated in counseling or therapy during their recovery, and found that this to be very helpful or even pivotal in their healing. They particularly appreciated how the counseling elevated their self-esteem, sense of personal empowerment, and self-efficacy, and found the relationship with the counselor to be an important source of support and encouragement. Two others participated in Al-Anon and found it to be a source of support and a safe environment within which to confide and seek advice and feedback for their disclosures about domestic violence. These narratives support the idea that clinical social work services and recovery or self-help resources can be a powerful adjunct to advocacy and case management services for abused Appalachian women.

Of those interviewed, four respondents had been residents in shelters, with mixed results. Two found the experience an important source of transitional support and guidance. Two others, however, felt nearly as much additional stress and anxiety as relief from their contacts with shelters because of the requirement that older children be left behind. A social worker whose clients encountered this situation would do well to assist them in exploring the reasons for this policy and advocating for flexibility, or locating an alternative shelter, even in another community, that allowed mother and older children to remain together. These women also tended to view the climate within the shelter system as somewhat officious, hierarchical, or rule-bound, conveying an unspoken expectation that residents should feel exaggeratedly humble and grateful; they perceived this posture as oppressive or unsupportive. This atmosphere is incongruent with the Appalachian cultural value of egalitarianism, and a social worker whose clients encounter this attitudinal barrier should be prepared to advocate (diplomatically) for a change in the system. Alternatively the social worker could interact directly with clients by means of coaching, communication skills training, and perhaps role play to enable them to advocate for these changes themselves.

The remaining 11 women interviewed had had no contact with any professionals within the system of advocacy or shelter resources; they expressed no awareness of the existence of these institutions. Their unqualified belief was that apart from the mobilization of inner resources or the good fortune of discovering support among emotionally significant others, every victim of domestic violence is essentially alone and without meaningful recourse from local resources.

Although training in the dynamics of domestic violence for professionals who respond to victims has been mandated by law in some areas of the country, these respondents' stories demonstrate that full realization of the intent of this legislation is not yet realized. To date, knowledge in some rural areas about shelter and advocacy resources may only have penetrated to a relatively limited extent. Clearly much work remains to be done in this area.

None of the respondents attributed her success in leaving abusive situations to the support and encouragement of family members, although several reported unexpected outpourings of support once making the break. The consistency of these results suggests that the sense of shame and of needing to keep intimate partner abuse secret from family members remains very powerful among these rural residents (Smith 2003). This is ironic, because family-centeredness is a strong Appalachian value, and yet these rural women all felt that, in their situation, the preserving secrecy and family pride mattered more than their own needs. This suggests, in turn, that advocates and counselors working with clients may need to prioritize options for support and concrete assistance first among friends, neighbors, coworkers, and institutions, rather than among family members.

When asked what most helped them to break away and start to recover, the respondents offered a wide array of answers. The range and uniqueness of these factors were noteworthy. Many were intensely personal, consistent with the Appalachian values of individualism and self-reliance.

One woman largely credited the comfort and support she perceived from her two cats. Another woman reported having videotaped herself describing her situation in poignant detail in order to create a documentary record "in case anything happened" to her. Yet once having made this videotape, she was struck in a new way by how pitiable yet evidently unnecessary her own circumstances appeared; this served as a pivotal motivation in her determination to break away. One woman gave a lot of credit to having taken a martial arts training class, which she found highly empowering. Another was finally mobilized by rage, which triggered homicidal ideation and a recognition about the need to leave, since "I wasn't going to jail for him." One woman felt that establishing a program of regular exercise had been a turning point, since this raised her self-esteem. Another gave the most credit to starting a part-time job, which enveloped her in a network of supportive contacts and enhanced her sense of worth. One respondent attributed her success primarily to the power of prayer, and another primarily credited the supportive counsel received during an initially hesitant or tentative consultation with a lawyer. The last two responses involved the use of self-help resources. One woman attributed her success primarily to self-guided bibliotherapy. The other ardently praised motivational audiotapes for the help they gave her; she played the tapes so frequently that several copies eventually became unusable. Years later, although doing better, she still missed these tapes and continued to wish that she had been able to locate a fresh set.

For us, the salient commonality among these apparently disparate and idiosyncratic answers is that each woman, who primarily kept her own counsel, determinedly created whole architectures of support and motivation out of deceptively simply resources, despite significant obstacles of socio-economic disadvantage or isolation. This suggests that, although a working relationship of supportive partnership with this population may be desirable, any approach that these clients perceive as imposed or driven by a worker's professional pride or faith in expert systems of thinking may miss the mark and, ultimately, may underestimate these women's needs and abilities to find their own answers. In the end, one of the women stated that, although she realized others meant well on her behalf, "I was the only one that could do it."

ONGOING NEED FOR MORE COMPREHENSIVE SERVICES

For rural women, the perceived need to rely mostly on inner resources and the support of friends and neighbors, rather than "the system," may also result from lingering limitations of traditional social service resources. Shelters and transitional programs can be extremely helpful for some women, yet many rural residents lack job skills and educational attainment that augur well for achieving economic independence within months or years of leaving abusive partners; most programs are not designed to sustain and nurture residents through such prolonged intervals (Few 2005; Websdale and Johnson 1997; Liang et al. 2005).

To combat this tendency, social workers in macro practice must continue to employ skills of advocacy, community development, and grantsmanship in order to improve funding and service availability in underserved areas. Meanwhile, practice experience suggests that mobilizing mutual aid and peer support resources among abused women may help considerably. One of the authors, for instance, has had success linking survivors together to pool child care needs and income, in order to secure shared housing, transportation, and other vital resources that none could have afforded on her own.

In many areas, needed services may also operate in self-contained silos lacking coordinated care with other potential client resources, such as mental or behavioral health-care and substance-abuse treatment services. In addition, professionals within each service system may operate from different philosophical or theoretical orientations and may respond to women in an inconsistent manner. Others, for instance, have acknowledged the disparate opinions among domestic violence advocates, researchers and scholars, and behavioral health providers regarding essential definitions of and causal attributions about intimate partner abuse (Carlson and Choi 2001; Smith and Randall 2007a).

The advocacy community, in particular, is more likely to view the matter from a feminist perspective and attribute offensive behaviors to patriarchy, masculine entitlement, and the desire to preserve male privilege and structures of power and control. Behavioral health professionals, in contrast, may often see issues arising from the multigenerational transmission of developmental pathologies, psychological conflicts, and unmet emotional needs, possibly, in some cases, on the part of both partners (Loseke 2005; Dutton and Bodnarchuk 2005; Yllo 2005). The former stance tends to argue for more sociopolitical interventions, whereas the latter suggests a rehabilitative approach involving, where possible, the family system in addition to therapeutic interventions tailored to the needs of individual family members.

Conducting seminars, focus groups, or continuing professional education events, possibly using Public Deliberation methodology (Levine, Fung, and Gastil 2005), are all avenues available to social workers interested in engaging human services workers on both sides of this issue in dialogue toward information sharing and consciousness raising. Improving the congruence and reducing the dissonance that an abused woman may encounter, regardless of the particular portal for entering the system of care, are crucial for all who work within the system to be as effective as possible.

As described above, small communities in rural Appalachia are often relatively conservative, both socially and politically. These factors often may influence women who are considering seeking help to think first of confiding in a clergyman, and asking for advice or guidance. From the perspective of domestic violence advocates, this may sometimes be a mixed blessing; clergy may not always be well informed concerning issues of domestic violence and therefore may assign priority to the sanctity of marriage vows over other considerations, even in high-risk situations.

Logan et al. (2005) found that protective orders were more difficult to obtain for rural women:

> Results suggest that (a) nonservice rates were much higher in rural areas; (b) rural women were charged for the orders to be served; (c) fewer cases were adjudicated during the time period of study in the rural areas, possibly suggesting women must come to court more often to obtain an order; (d) a greater proportion of cases were classified into the preadjudication category in the rural areas; and (e) there was a greater amount of leg work to obtain a protective order on the part of the victim in the rural areas. (p. 899)

Subcultures within rural Appalachian communities (e.g., people of color, gay men, or lesbian women), however, may perceive a worse response than that received by non-minority rural women. Few (2005) reported that black rural Appalachian women did not use police for temporary safety because they expected a poor response; they felt racially discriminated against by the police. In contrast, white rural Appalachian women perceived sex discrimination by the police. Rural women of color may also expect racism and discrimination from service providers (Grama 2000; Murdaugh et al. 2004).

For social workers, multidirectional public awareness efforts are needed to address misperceptions and prejudices on all sides of this issue. Rural citizens in general, and women at risk of abuse in particular, must be made aware of their rights, of the progressive nature of recent legislation, and of the availability of advocacy services so as to empower them to access services, if needed. At the same time ongoing work with judges, magistrates, and law officers is needed to raise consciousness that confronts prejudicial attitudes and disregards "duty" when such has occurred. Some police departments have a domestic violence ombudsman or liaison officer; when this is in place, social workers in all fields of direct practice should get to know this officer and apprise him or her of untoward or illegal practices reported by rural clients. Social workers should also maintain contacts and make common cause with the domestic violence advocacy community in their communities in order to address client issues of discrimination and denial of rights collaboratively.

In many parts of the country, domestic violence within gay, bisexual, lesbian, or transgender (GBLT) relations may go unrecognized by law enforcement or service providers. GBLT persons, however, may have more peer connections and be somewhat more organized than abused rural women generally. In regions where gay and lesbian activists have formed coalitions and support organizations, social workers can engage with them for collaborative work on issues of social justice.

ETHICAL ISSUES

Three important ethical dilemmas or concerns revolve around compromising confidentiality, faith, and children. An important ethical dilemma in rural Appalachia relates to confidentiality issues that arise in communities where "everyone knows everyone," while responders are trying to provide a coordinated community response. Such a response includes "pro-arrest or mandatory arrest policies; follow-up support and advocacy for victims; aggressive and prompt prosecution; active monitoring of offender compliance with probation conditions; court-mandated participation in batterer intervention programs; strengthening of civil remedies; and monitoring of the system-wide response to domestic violence cases" (Shepard 2005, p. 439). Under the circumstances of small-town life, how do domestic violence advocates strengthen the safety net for battered women? When team players meet, it may be difficult to talk about an issue without inadvertently or inappropriately revealing an individual's identity. If team players choose discretion to honor the identity and do not disclose information, they may be viewed negatively by their peers. Perhaps disclosing information would be helpful, but who decides: the social worker or the client? When a woman is in crisis and presents for services, should she be asked to sign a blanket release form so that information may flow between players in an effort to help her? Or should a client be presented with a form to share particular items of information when a need arises? Is it possible to know this in advance or even to be able to locate her?

A second concern relates to the role of communities of faith. Communities of faith are in need of considerable education about domestic violence, and this is just beginning to happen. Wolff et al. (2001) have worked to educate rural clergy, and the results are hopeful: respondents reported seeing themselves as active, supportive, informed, and important responders to domestic violence. Ongoing education may also include providing materials for child and youth programs, as well as organizing informal pastoral networks for training sessions. To overcome barriers to continuing education, Wolff et al. suggest keeping an up-to-date mailing list for the governing boards and clergy of rural congregations.

An important ethical dilemma concerns the mandatory reporting of child abuse in homes where domestic violence exists, when the children themselves are not the direct victims. A critical objective is to protect the child's best interests. How do advocates accomplish that goal? Advocates and other helping professionals strive to provide free, confidential, and voluntary services, but at the same time they are mandated to report child abuse or neglect. If a social worker files a report with the state, this may jeopardize the client-worker relationship, endangering the client should she drop out of services. In some states, reporting exposure to domestic violence may not automatically be mandated; rather, the reporter may use his or her discretion to determine whether witnessing violence or being exposed to it is harmful to the child. Social workers should seek consultation or training on the latitude for professional judgment that exists in their state or territory.

Some states require social workers to attain continuing education credits in ethics. Those working in the area of domestic violence are well positioned to organize continuing education seminars or workshops designed to bring colleagues together to explore ethical decision-making processes in situations similar to those described above. Local branch organizations within state chapters of the National Association of Social Workers (NASW) can provide the platform for members to organize themselves into peer consultation groups to deliberate ethical dilemmas. In rural areas where distance seriously impedes face-to-face meetings, conference calls may be available. Real time, Web-supported electronic discussions, such as those in "chat rooms") or an e-mail listserve are other options.

CASE STUDY

The following case study using fictional names illustrates some features a social worker might encounter when working with a woman caught in an abusive domestic situation in a rural region such as Appalachia.

Sarah Prentiss, MSW, was working as a therapist for a nonprofit agency under contract to the state's Department of Family and Children's Services to provide in-home services for families at risk for the removal of children because of possible abuse or neglect. Her new client family, the Clanahan-Mercers, consisted of a mother, Janine Clanahan, 29 years of age; her domestic partner Bo Mercer, 37; and two children, Sam Clanahan, 13, and Liss Mercer, 7. Janine and Sam were white, Bo was multiracial, and Liss was Janine and Bo's multiracial child. Sam's father, Janine's ex-husband Micah, 42, lived out of state and maintained no contact.

The family was reported to a child protective worker, Bethany Tandy, BSW, by school authorities who were concerned about the children's inconsistent school attendance, seasonally inappropriate attire, and poor hygiene. Upon investigation, Bethany found no immediate grounds for the children to be removed from the home, but she did refer the family to Sarah for in-home services.

DEVELOPING A COLLABORATIVE RELATIONSHIP

Sarah's first home visit impressed her with Janine's marked isolation. The family's mobile home was miles from the nearest small town along an unpaved rural road. During their first meeting, Janine seemed sullen, defiant, or uncommunicative, but Sarah was careful to refrain from interpreting Janine's apparent demeanor. Janine's

"CONTINUED"

long silences and repetitive questioning ("What do you need to know that for?") hampered Sarah's efforts to complete her agency's standardized assessment and data collection protocols. Sensing Janine's hunger for simple conversation, Sarah put aside her own interests in eliciting structured and categorical information to concentrate simply on getting to know Janine as a person. Expressing curiosity with minimal prompts and reflections of content and feeling, she encouraged Janine to talk about herself, her worldview, and her experiences at her own pace and on her own terms (Gross 2005; Paradine 2000). This approach, given that Janine was more comfortable with a more personalized style of communication, increased her trust and cooperation markedly.

PSYCHOSOCIAL ASSESSMENT

Janine was estranged from her family, in her view, because they disapproved of Bo. Sam and Liss, despite the family's isolation, had been doing adequately in school until recently, when Sam began acting out and Liss became withdrawn and disengaged from teachers as well as peers. Janine admitted that for several months she had become increasingly depressed and fatigued, finding it a huge effort to keep up with "householding" and parenting responsibilities. Prior to the onset of this precipitous decline in her mood and energy level, Janine's parenting and attentiveness to the children's school adjustment had been adequate, and her relationships with her children had been close and affectionate; these relationships had now become somewhat more distant. Janine was expressive concerning her loneliness and isolation, and yet she defended Bo, stating that he was misunderstood, that he loved her, and that their relationship was "the second best thing" in her life (after her children).

Resources were a constant struggle, and food and fuel were sometimes hard to procure. There was no phone in the home, and Janine did not drive. School- and church-related activities were important sources for contact and socialization for most community residents, but the Clanahan-Mercer family rarely participated. Bo had some male friends, but Janine was almost completely without social outlets and only attended church about once every month or month and a half.

Strengths and sources of resiliency for Janine were her loving memories of her maternal grandmother (Gran), now deceased; her love of traditional music and her skill with her harmonica; and the comfort she derived from the knowledge that kinfolk had been living in close harmony with nature in the region for more than 200 years. She also considered herself very handy and talented in crafts such as candle-making and working with clay, which had been elective classes during her GED studies and in which she still maintained an interest.

Bo came home unexpectedly during Sarah's third visit. Although he knew about the referral and about the open file on the family established by Bethany (the referring social worker), he reacted with considerable surprise and hostility to Sarah's presence. Janine's fearful reaction was evident.

Sarah returned the next day and gently commented on Janine's fearfulness, inviting her to discuss whether this was a common event in her relationship with Bo. Janine began to confide that Bo had "a terrible temper" and was prone to violence,

"CONTINUED"

although he had never been violent in front of the children nor directed his anger at them. During his most recent attack, Bo had come home in a rage and pushed Janine down the front steps, causing her to twist her ankle and break two toes. Weeping, Janine said that she was deeply ashamed and that, above all, she did not want kinfolk or members of the community to know about the violence (Smith 2003). Sarah wrestled with her conscience over whether she was obligated to disclose this information to the referring social worker. Recognizing that this ethical dilemma fell into a grey area, she consulted her supervisor and together they decided that she was free to withhold the information for now unless it became more apparent that Bo's propensity to violence rose "to the level of harm to the child" (J. Cook, personal communication, October 19, 2006).

GOAL SETTING AND CONTRACTING

Sarah's initial goals centered on the issues of parenting and family functioning that had triggered the original referral. In light of these disclosures, however, her priorities shifted, and she began working with Janine immediately on safety planning, lest Bo become enraged again and subject Janine to his temper because of the social workers' involvement in "family matters." Initially resistant and in considerable denial of the need for a plan, Janine ultimately took courage from Sarah's reassurances that Bo alone was responsible for the violence, and that Janine had a right to protect herself and live without constant fear.

Identifying a workable safety plan for Janine was initially very difficult until she remembered that she still had the key to a little-used hunting cabin within hiking distance of the family home, dating back to when she had served as a part-time caretaker for this property on behalf of the absent owner. She decided to stash some belongings there and flee to the cabin in case of a crisis, blocking the windows so no visible light would show from the rural road.

After much thought and emotional agonizing, Janine also gave Sarah permission to contact a distant cousin, Carl. Sarah placed a call to Carl on Janine's behalf and recruited Carl as a source of support for Janine. Janine also confided in the driver of the children's school bus, whom she had known most of her life, and the driver agreed to notify Carl in the event that Janine should place a given prearranged signal marker (a certain dented bucket) along the rural road so that he could see it while driving his route. If he spotted the bucket, Carl agreed to come for Sarah at the cabin and offer her a place to stay, and also to take her to pick up Sam and Liss who would join her. Sarah also advised Janine about services such as shelters and advocates for abused women, although the nearest facility was miles away. Sarah explained to Janine that she could obtain a protective order, but Janine was deeply mistrustful of this process and would not consider it.

CULTURALLY CONGRUENT SERVICES

Sarah was tempted to try to "talk Janine into" leaving Bo. However, she honored Janine's right to self-determination and, instead, engaged with Janine in clarifying

"CONTINUED"

her own beliefs about gender roles, spirituality, and family values. It emerged that Janine was comfortable with patriarchal views to an extent comparable with regional norms: "I've never been one of those women that thought they were equal to men," Janine said. "The man is supposed to be in charge, and I accept that." "Although," she added, "his dominion is supposed to be loving and benevolent, the pastor says, so maybe if he breaks that part of the deal, does that maybe mean the deal is off?" Janine pondered how her beloved grandmother would have counseled her to resolve this, and decided Gran would have advised her to seek an answer to this question in personal prayer. She also decided that Gran would have counseled that her commitment to Bo was possibly less sacred given that she and Bo had never married.

With Janine's safety plan in place, Sarah turned her attention to the original reasons for the referral. Janine agreed to consult her general practitioner in a rural health clinic concerning her depression. Janine was now feeling a little better and paying more attention to the children's needs for parental guidance and help with their school adjustment. With Janine's permission, Sarah contacted their teachers, who offered reassurances that the children's problems with peers did not seem to be about racial issues but rather about their inappropriate attire. Again consulting Janine first, Sarah next contacted Janine's pastor, who suggested a volunteer from Janine's small church to help Janine procure clothing vouchers from the Department of Family and Children's Service and use these to select new school clothes for Sam and Liss.

Meanwhile, Janine's anxiety remained very evident. Sarah now felt that assessment and treatment for possible lingering symptoms of stress and trauma were appropriate for Janine, but she felt that this work was beyond the parameters of the original referral. She preferred to transfer Janine's care to a grant-funded therapist specializing in such issues under contract with the regional domestic violence service agency. Janine agreed to give this a try, and she successfully prevailed upon Bo to drive her weekly into the small town where this therapist maintained an office, on the pretext that she wanted to enroll in an adult education crafts class. Conferring with the social worker who referred the case, Sarah reduced her own level of contact with the Clanahan-Mercer family to that of ongoing assessment and supportive counseling around any remaining parenting and school adjustment issues.

Janine now began working with her new therapist, Leanne, on issues of core self-esteem and trauma recovery. Because of inconsistent cooperation from Bo, Janine's attendance was spotty, but Leanne refrained from attributing this to resistance. During the course of this work, Bo again attacked Janine quite violently, causing her to flee in accordance with the safety plan she had worked out with Sarah. Bo was arrested briefly, yet they were reunited again after this incident several more times, as Janine continued to wrestle with the hope that love would conquer all and that Bo would change. Sensing her gradual gains in self-confidence and assertiveness, Bo began pressing Janine for a wedding date, although for years he had scorned the idea of marriage. This notion now alarmed Janine considerably, presenting her with frightening visions of legal as well as physical entrapment. Guided and supported through it all by Leanne, and by her inner dialogue with her memories of Gran, Janine decided instead to locate an affordable mobile home of her own, using secret money given to her by the hunting cabin's owner for a deposit. Her family finally learned of this and

"CONTINUED"

rallied to her support. Carl taught her to drive. Ultimately she left Bo and worked as a waitress, holding a second job as an adult education instructor of traditional music and crafts, until she attained a level of self-sufficiency enabling her to "make it" completely on her own, without ever having to leave her beloved hills of home.

MONITORING AND EVALUATING

By the time Janine finished working with both Sarah and Leanne, her mood and self-esteem had improved considerably. Using their skills with personal practice assessment, Sarah and Leanne monitored Janine's progress over the course their work with her by means of repeated administrations of two rapid-assessment instruments: the Generalized Contentment Scale and the Index of Self-Esteem (Hudson and Faul 1998). By using individualized rating scales that Leanne and Janine had developed collaboratively to capture Janine's circumstances in a contextually congruent manner (Bloom, Fischer, and Orme 2006), Leanne was also able to demonstrate that Janine's psychosocial functioning and involvement in community life were considerably improved as well.

COLLABORATIVE STRATEGIES

Opportunities abound for social workers wanting to make a difference in the area of domestic violence to work toward improving services for all who may be affected. The system of care is still very much a work in progress and continues to evolve. An advocacy organization in one Appalachian state, for instance, recently convened a Domestic Violence and Mental Health Initiative to study issues of commonality and divergence of professional opinion among domestic violence advocates and mental health professionals. The Initiative's goals were sharing perspectives and working collaboratively to improve the continuity and coordination of services to clients. Work by this task group of advocates, clinicians, scholars, and other interested professional constituencies has been under way for four years and is still vibrant. Although much remains to be done, participants are pleased with the results obtained to date. According to Sue Julian, the director of this advocacy agency, mutuality of interests and points of view are evolving and each "camp" that comes to the table is becoming more aware of and comfortable with one another's essential truths and potential contributions to the common mission of curtailing family violence: "We are all becoming much less black and white now in the way we see things" (S. Julian, personal communication, October 19, 2006).

SUMMARY AND CONCLUSION

Violence against women is physically harmful and spiritually corrosive wherever it occurs, but many social scientists often believe it is likely to be particularly dangerous in rural areas, where perpetrators are protected by long-standing cultural values that may also conspire to disguise or minimize their actions as well as by marked seclusion. As one abused rural woman put it, "When you're out on a farm at night, there's no one to hear you scream. And there's nowhere to go except out on a dark road" (Pennsylvania Coalition Against Domestic Violence [PCADV] 2002, p. 6). In rural areas, victims of domestic violence are often confronted by daunting barriers to much needed services, including long distances, scarce resources, lack of transportation, difficulty accessing telephone service, and, in some regions, difficulty believing that the abuse is neither their fault nor their exclusive responsibility simply to cope with. Also, higher rates of unemployment and poverty and lower levels of vocational opportunity and experience with the larger world may contribute to significant limitations on the rural women's ability to envision alternatives or to engage in effective problem solving.

Many rural women have intense regional ties and loyalties, and social workers should be mindful of the possibility that, in some cases, significant geographic flexibility may not be an option to clients in finding safety and freedom from a life of peril. Also, many rural women greatly value self-reliance and may ultimately only succeed in achieving a permanent solution in a manner that taps a unique inner source of strength and creativity. If so, the most effective social work role in many instances may be that of helping the client in a highly flexible and collaborative way to achieve the self-awareness and empowerment needed to mobilize such inner resources, rather than providing traditional service brokering or referral to more structured, proscribed, or programmatic resources.

Social change often comes more slowly to rural areas compared to the nation as a whole. The need remains great for advocates to raise public awareness that domestic violence is against the law and is not a private affair. Much has been achieved in many rural areas, but much more remains to be done so that, in the future, an increasing number of resilient rural women will be able to regain their lives and raise their families in nonviolent homes, and in peace.

RESOURCES

Appalachian Regional Commission (ARC)
1666 Connecticut Avenue, NW
Suite 700
Washington, DC 20009–1068
Phone: (202) 884–7700
Web site: http://www.arc.gov/index.jsp

Rural Assistance Center
School of Medicine and Health Sciences Room 4520
501 North Columbia Road Stop 9037
Grand Forks, ND 58202–9037
Phone: 1 (800) 270–1898
Fax: 1 (800) 270–1913
E-mail: info@raconline.org
Web site: http://www.raconline.org/info_guides/public_health/domesticviolence.php

Rural Technical Assistance on Violence Against Women
Praxis International
5402 North Shore Drive
Duluth, MN 55804
Phone (218) 525–0487
Fax (218) 525–0445
Web site: http://www.praxisinternational.org/rural_ta_frame.html

REFERENCES

Adler, C. (1996). Unheard and unseen. Rural women and domestic violence. *Journal of Nurse-Midwifery*, 41(6), 463–466.

Appalachian Regional Commission. (2006). Retrieved April 19, 2009, from http://www.arc.gov/index.do.

Bloom, M., J. Fischer, and J. G. Orme. (2006). *Evaluating Practice: Guidelines for the Accountable Professional* (5th Ed.). Boston: Allyn and Bacon.

Blakely, E. H., and B. L. Locke. (2005). Rural poverty and welfare reform: Challenges and opportunities. In R. Lohmann and N. Lohmann (Eds.), *Rural Social Work Practice* (pp. 25–40). New York: Columbia University Press.

Burns, S. L. S., S. L. Scott, and D. J. Thompson. (2006). Family and community.

In R. Abramson and J. Haskell (Eds.), *Encyclopedia of Appalachia* (pp. 149–154). Knoxville: University of Tennessee Press.

Carlson, B. E., and D. Choi. (2001). Intimate partner abuse. In A. Gitterman (Ed.), *Handbook of Social Work with Vulnerable and Resilient Populations* (2nd Ed.) (pp. 687–714). New York: Columbia University Press.

Cox, H., P. Cash, B. Hanna, F. D'Arcy-Tehan, and C. Adams. (2001). Risky business: stories from the field of rural community nurses' work in domestic violence. *Australian Journal of Rural Health*, 9(6), 280–286.

Davis, K. B. Taylor, and D. Furniss. (2001). Narrative accounts of tracking the rural domestic violence survivors' journey: A feminist approach. *Health Care for Women International*, 22(4), 333–347.

De Jong, P., and I. K. Berg. (2007). *Interviewing for Solutions*. Belmont, CA: Brooks/Cole.

Dutton, D. G., and M. Bodnarchuk. (2005). Through a psychological lens: Personality disorder and spousal assault. In D. R. Loseke, R. J. Gelles, and M. M. Cavanaugh (Eds.), *Current Controversies on Family Violence* (pp. 5–18). Thousand Oaks, CA: Sage.

Few, A. L. (2005). The voices of black and white rural battered women in domestic violence shelters. *Family Relations*, 54(4), 488–500.

Fiene, J. I. (1991). The construction of self by rural low-status Appalachian women. *Affilia*, 6(2), 45–60.

Goeckermann, C., K. Hamberger, and K. Barber. (1994). Issues of domestic violence unique to rural areas. *Wisconsin Medical Journal*, 93(9), 473–479.

Grama, J. L. (2000). Women forgotten: Difficulties faced by rural victims of domestic violence. *American Journal of Family Law*, 14(3), 173–188.

Gross, C. (2005). To listen is to learn: The social worker in rural Appalachia. In S. E. Keefe (Ed.), *Appalachian Cultural Competence. A Guide for Medical, Mental Health, and Social Services Professionals* (pp. 75–88). Knoxville: University of Tennessee Press.

Hall, E. (1999). If there's one thing you can tell them, it's that you're free. In D. B. Billings, G. Norman, and K. Ledford (Eds.), *Confronting Appalachian Stereotypes* (pp. 191–199). Lexington: University Press of Kentucky.

Hayden, W., Jr. (2004). Appalachian diversity: African-American, Hispanic/Latino, and other populations. *Journal of Appalachian Studies*, 10(3), 293–306.

Hilbert, J. C., and S. P. Krishman. (2000). Addressing barriers to community care of battered women in rural environments: Creating a policy of social inclusion. *Journal of Health and Social Policy*, 12(1), 41–52.

Hudson, W. W., and A. C. Faul. (1998). *The Clinical Measurement Package: A Field Manual* (2nd Ed.). Tallahassee, FL: WALMYR.

Jones, L. (2006). Values and religion in Central Appalachia. In *Encyclopedia of Appalachia* (pp. 1356–1358). Knoxville: University of Tennessee Press.

Kalmuss, D., and M. Strauss. (1982). Wife's marital dependency and wife abuse. *Journal of Marriage and Family, 44*, 277–286.

Keefe, S. E. (2000). Mountain identity and the global society in a rural Appalachian county. Paper presented at the Center for Ethnicity and Gender in Appalachia's National Conference. Huntington, WV, March 5, 2000.

———. (2001). Appalachian Americans: The formation of "reluctant" ethnics. In G. R. Campbell (Ed.), *Many Americas : Critical Perspectives on Race, Racism, and Ethnicity* (pp. 129–153). Dubuque, Iowa: Kendall/Hunt.

Levine, P., A. Fung, and J. Gastil. (2005). Future directions for public deliberation. *Journal of Public Deliberation, 1*(1), Article 3. Available at http://services.bepress.com/jpd/vol1/iss1/art3 (retrieved February 10, 2007).

Liang, B., L. Goodman, P. Tummala-Narra, and S. Weintraub. (2005). A theoretical framework for understanding help-seeking processes among survivors of intimate partner violence. *American Journal of Community Psychology, 36*(1/2), 71–84.

Logan, T. K., R. Shannon, and R. Walker. (2005). Protective orders in rural and urban areas. A multiple perspective study. *Violence Against Women, 11*(7), 876–911.

Lohmann, R. A., and N. Lohmann. (2005). Introduction. In R. Lohmann and N. Lohmann (Eds.), *Rural Social Work Practice* (pp. xi–xxvii). New York: Columbia University Press.

Loseke, D. R. (2005). Through a sociological lens: The complexities if family violence. In D. R. Loseke, R. J. Gelles, and M. M. Cavanaugh (Eds.), *Current Controversies on Family Violence* (pp. 35–48). Thousand Oaks, CA: Sage.

Miewald, C. E., and M. O'Quinn. (2006). Women's roles. In *Encyclopedia of Appalachia* (pp. 195–197). Knoxville: University of Tennessee Press.

Murdaugh, C., S. Hunt, R. Sowell, and I. Santana. (2004). Domestic violence in Hispanics in the Southeastern United States: A survey and needs analysis. *Journal of Family Violence, 19*(2), 107–115.

Paradine, K. (2000). The importance of understanding love and other feelings in survivors' experiences of domestic violence. *Court Review* (spring 2000): 40–46.

Pennsylavania Coalition Against Domestic Violence. (PCADV). (2002). Helping battered women and their families: A guide for leaders and religious communities. Available at http://www.pcadv.org (retrieved October 4, 2007).

Pollard, K. M. (2003). Appalachia at the Millennium: An overview of results from Census 2000. Available at http://www.arc.gov/images/reports/census2000/overview/appalachia_census2000.pdf.

Purnell, L. D. (2003). People of Appalachian heritage. In L. D. Purnell and B. J.

Paulanka (Eds.), *Transcultural Health Care: A Culturally Competent Approach* (2nd Ed.) (pp. 73–89). Philadelphia: F. A. Davis.

Randall, E. J., and M. Aldred-Crouch. (2006). The uncertain future of public mental health systems: A West Virginia case study. In J. Rosenberg and S. Rosenberg (Eds.), *Community Mental Health: Challenges for the 21 st Century* (pp. 233–245). New York: Routledge.

Randall, E. J., and D. Vance. (2005). Directions in rural mental health practice. In R. Lohmann and N. Lohmann (Eds.), *Rural Social Work Practice* (pp. 171–186). New York: Columbia University Press.

Saleeby, D. (2005). *The Strengths Approach to Social Work Practice.* New York: Longman.

Shannon, L., T. K. Logan, J. Cole, and K. Medley. (2006). Help seeking and coping strategies for intimate partner violence in rural and urban women. *Violence and Victims,* 21(2), 167–181.

Shepard, M. (2005). Twenty years of progress in addressing domestic violence. An agenda for the next 10. *Journal of Interpersonal Violence,* 20(4), 436–441.

Shepherd, J. (2001). Where do you go when it's 40 below? Domestic violence among rural Alaska native women. *Affilia,* 16(4), 488–511.

Shoaf, L. C. (2004). Domestic violence in Appalachian Ohio: The victim's perspective. Columbus, OH: Office of Criminal Justice Services. Retrieved April 26, 2009, from http://www.ocjs.ohio.gov/Research/rural%20vawa.pdf.

Smith, M. (2003). Recovery from intimate partner violence: A difficult journey. *Issues in Mental Health Nursing,* 24, 543–573.

Smith, M., and E. J. Randall. (2007a). Batterer intervention program: The victim's hope in ending the abuse and maintaining the relationship. *Issues in Mental Health Nursing,* 28, 1045–1063.

——. (2007b). Batterer intervention program: The perpetrator's and victim's perceptions. Paper presented at the West Virginia Summit on Violence Against Women. Charleston, WV, October 2, 2007.

Sudderth, L. (2003). An uphill climb: The challenge of collaboration in response to family violence in rural America. *Journal of Aggression, Maltreatment, and Trauma,* 8(4), 17–35.

U.S. Census Bureau. (2006). State and county quick facts. Available at http://quickfacts.census.gov/qfd/states/54000.html (retrieved February 10, 2007).

Websdale, N. (1995). An ethnographic assessment of the policing of domestic violence in rural eastern Kentucky. *Social Justice,* 22(1), 102–121.

Websdale, N., and B. Johnson. (1997). Reducing woman battering: The role of structural approaches. *Social Justice,* 24(1), 54–81.

West Virginia Council Against Domestic Violence. (2007). Domestic violence and West Virginia law. Available at http://www.wvadv.org/dv_wv_law.htm (retrieved February 10, 2007).

Whitener, L. A., B. A. Weber, and G. J. Duncan. (2001). Reforming welfare: Implications for rural America. *Rural America* , 16, 2–10.

Whitener, L. A., G. J. Duncan, and B. A. Weber. (2002). *Reforming Welfare: What Does It Mean for Rural Areas?* U.S. Department of Agriculture Economic Research Service, Food, and Nutrition Report No. 26–4. Washington, DC: U.S. Government Printing Office.

Wolff, D. A., D. Burleigh, M. Tripp, A. Gadomski. (2001). Training clergy: the role of the faith community in domestic violence prevention. *Journal of Religion and Abuse Advocacy. Pastoral Care and Prevention,* 2(4), 47–62.

K. Yllo. (2005). Through a feminist lens: Gender, diversity, and violence: Extending the feminist framework. In D. R. Loseke, R. J. Gelles, and M. M. Cavanaugh (Eds.), *Current Controversies on Family Violence* (pp. 19–34). Thousand Oaks, CA: Sage.

14

Taking an Ecological Approach to Dating
Violence Prevention

Barbara Ball and Barri Rosenbluth

THIS CHAPTER describes the dynamics and prevalence of teen dating violence. We consider how youth form their identity and expectations for intimate relationships in the context of family, peer group, school, and community. Our discussion of risk and protective factors for dating and sexual violence is based on this ecological model. Cultural beliefs and norms, and the exposure to violence in the home or in the community, increase the risk that teenagers will experience and perpetrate dating violence. Based on a review of pertinent research, we examine promising strategies for prevention that are relevant and engaging for teenagers and the school community. We present the Expect Respect program, a comprehensive school-based dating violence program built on the collaboration between a community agency and a school district. Expect Respect offers school-wide awareness activities, a youth leadership component, and support groups for at-risk students.

UNDERSTANDING TEEN DATING VIOLENCE

DATING NORMS AND DEFINITIONS

It is critical to be attuned to adolescents' unique experiences as they begin to explore romantic relationships, especially when developing a prevention program for dating violence. Romantic relationships during adolescence encompass a wide range of actions that indicate different levels of intimacy and commitment, such as spending time together at school, having a partner for a single event, "hanging out" in mixed-gender groups with a special friend, talking on the phone, going to movies, meeting each other's family, having sexual relations, and having a long-term boyfriend or girlfriend (Hickman, Jaycox, and Aronoff 2004; Avery-Leaf and Cascardi 2002; Fredland et al. 2005). When asked to describe their romantic relationships, adolescents often use the terms "hanging out," "talking," "chillin'," "playing around," or "going with someone." Other words imply a sexual connotation such as "messing with you," "hooking-up," and "having a friend with benefits" (Fredland et al. 2005). "Dating" is more often used by older adolescents to describe a "steady" or "couple-like" relationship. Terms vary by geographic region and cultural group, and change quickly with time. It is therefore imperative that prevention educators, social workers, counselors, and school staff listen carefully to the students' choice of words and attached meanings when asking students about their dating experiences.

PEER GROUP AND PEER PRESSURE

The peer group exerts a powerful influence on how and when adolescents begin exploring romantic relationships. Adolescents are eager to separate themselves from their parents and find a sense of belonging and identity within their peer group. However, norms of adolescent peer groups frequently support rigid gender stereotypes, for example, the expectation that boys are to be sexually forceful, aggressive, and in control of decisions in the relationship and girls are to be supportive and responsible for the success of the relationship (Sousa 1999). In addition, norms in the peer group exert pressure to have a boyfriend or girlfriend. Peer pressure also extends to sexual activity. According to Fredland et al. (2005, p. 103), "pressure on girls was not just from the boys wishing to be with them, but from girlfriends encouraging increased sexual involvement."

Intense levels of feeling, lack of experience, peer pressure, insecurity, and fear of rejection is a confusing mix. Consider the contradictory messages adolescent girls might get from their parents, friends, and dates about "love," as reported by a member of an Expect Respect support group:

> *Mom always says:* Never fall in love.
> *Dad always says:* I don't want to see you hurt.
> *Friends always say:* Have you had sex yet?
> *My dates always say:* I love you and I'll never leave.
> *My belief:* I'll find it some day just not now.

Some teenagers have difficulty identifying warning signs for abuse, as they are just beginning to explore the complexities of intimate relationships, often idealize their partners, and confuse jealousy with love and control with care. For example, Fredland et al. (2005) found that "'playing' was a word used frequently by boys and girls that seemed to define an acceptable level of being physical toward a partner." Yet, the term "playing" may obscure actual physical violence. Teens find it particularly difficult to recognize emotional abuse, such as efforts to control a partner's dress, friends, and activities; yelling; spreading rumors; and disrespectful "put-downs." How do youths know whether to consider these behaviors "minor"? When do these behaviors "cross the line" and become hurtful (Price et al. 2000)? The following comments came from two male members of an Expect Respect support group: "Guys call girls bitches, sluts. It's just calling that naturally. It's so common for guys to do this, I guess I never really pay attention to that"; "You can't stop people from expressing theirselves [*sic*]. I think that's minor. If it adds up and a girl gets fed up with it, then that's a problem."

ONSET AND IMPACT OF TEEN DATING VIOLENCE

Teen dating violence demonstrates patterns of physical, sexual, or emotional violence used to hurt or gain power and control over a partner in an intimate relationship. Violence can escalate in frequency and intensity—from early incidents of verbal and emotional abuse to increasingly severe physical and sexual violence. The most serious and life-threatening acts of violence are often committed during or after the relationship ends, when the abuser experiences a loss of control and power over the partner.

Teens are vulnerable to experiencing violence beginning with their earliest dating relationships. Many youths report having had their first boyfriend or girlfriend between 9 and 12 years of age (Avery-Leaf and Cascardi 2002). Among those who experience dating violence, 29 percent report that they first experienced dating violence at 12 to 13 years of age; 40 percent, at 14 to 15 years of age; and 29 percent at 16 to 17 years of age (Burcky, Reuterman, and Kopsky 1988).

The impact of dating violence on youths' lives can be severe. Physical and sexual dating violence against adolescent girls is associated with increased risk of substance use, unhealthy weight-control behaviors, sexual risk behaviors, pregnancy, and suicidality (Silverman et al. 2001). Abusive relationship patterns established in adolescence, moreover, may endure into adulthood, resulting in increasingly severe physical and emotional harm.

TRIGGERS FOR TEEN DATING VIOLENCE

When asked the reasons for using violence (Foshee 1996; Jackson, Cram, and Seymour 2000; O'Keefe 1997), the most frequent response from males and females is anger. Males, however, are more likely than females to report the desire to gain control over their partner, whereas females are more likely to report acting in self-defense. Jealousy is the third most frequently reported reason for violence between dating partners.

Interviews with adolescents provide a vivid picture of situations that trigger fights. Boys are particularly sensitive to perceived public disrespect, as illustrated in the following quote: "If you take your girl out and [she] sees another man and she don't pay attention to you and . . . you catch her walkin' over to that table and talkin' to the man, she just is disrespecting" (Fredland et al. 2005, p.106). This example also conveys the cultural beliefs that objectify women and assert male dominance and control. Similar triggers for boys include insults or the violation of a rule, such as "I told you not to . . ." (Motivational Educational Entertainment (MEE) Productions 1996). Disrespect, jealousy, and the desire to maintain control prompt and predict many violent responses.

Girls have a different view of what starts fights, stating that their partners are drunk or under the influence of drugs at the time (Molidor, Tolman, and Kober 2000; Fredland et al. 2005). Molidor and colleagues also found that "a large percentage of girls are being abused because they are refusing unwanted sexual advances" (2000, p. 3).

PREVALENCE OF TEEN DATING VIOLENCE

Prevalence research on teen dating violence has been hindered by the lack of a standard definition (O'Keefe 2005). Some researchers include psychological and emotional abuse in their definition of dating violence, whereas others use a more restrictive definition that includes only physically violent acts. Further, gathering data on sexual violence is not always the aim of a study. Studies also use different time frames—prevalence in one's lifetime or incidents over the past 12 months. The ability to compare studies is further hindered because of the great variation in the instruments used, ranging from single questions to detailed scales for each type of dating violence. Rates of dating violence tend to be highest when youths are asked multiple questions about emotional and physical violence—such as on the Conflict Tactics Scale (Straus 1979)—instead of single, global questions, for example, "Have you ever been hurt physically by your partner?" (Avery-Leaf and Cascardi 2002). As a result, published prevalence rates vary widely across studies—from between 10 percent and 20 percent (Grunbaum et al. 2002; Silverman et al. 2001) in large-scale surveys with one or two summary questions, to more than 30 percent in studies with multiple questions (Foshee 1996; O'Keefe 1997; Malik, Sorenson, and Anehensel 1997). Without question, however, teen dating violence is a common and serious problem.

PREVALENCE RATES FOR BOYS AND GIRLS

Most in-depth surveys of teen dating violence report rates of physical violence perpetration as high or higher for girls than for boys, suggesting that teenage dating violence is reciprocal (Foshee 1996; O'Keefe 1997; Hickman, Jaycox, and Aronoff 2004; Malik et al. 1997). In a study of eighth and ninth graders in a primarily rural school district in North Carolina, 38 percent of *dating* adolescents reported being the victim of dating violence and 21 percent reported perpetrating it (physical and/or sexual); this corresponds to 27 percent and 15 percent of the total sample, respectively, for victimization and perpetration (Foshee 1996). In this study, females reported perpetrating more mild, moderate, and severe physical violence than males, even when controlling for violence perpetrated in self-defense. Among high school students in Los Angeles, 43 percent of females and 39 percent of males reported that they had inflicted some form of physical aggression on their dating partners at least once (O'Keefe 1997). In this study, the strongest predictor of inflicting dating violence for males and females was having been the recipient of violence. As O'Keefe (1997) points out "every violent action creates a risk for a violent response or future violent acts" (p. 6).

Findings in both studies, however, were dramatically different for sexual violence. In the North Carolina study, males reported perpetrating more sexual dating violence (4.5% vs. 1.2% of females), and females were twice as likely to report sexual victimization (14.5% vs. 6.9% for males) (Foshee 1996). Sexual violence perpetration rates were higher in the Los Angeles survey, with 12.7 percent of males and 3 percent of females reporting having inflicted forced sexual behaviors on a partner (O'Keefe 1997).

Most studies have focused on perpetration rates for boys and girls. Fewer studies have explored the emotional and physical consequences of dating violence. Molidor, Tolman, and Kober (2000) found that the majority of boys in their sample were not hurt at all by the worst reported incident of dating violence victimization (56%). Only nine percent of the girls, however, reported not being hurt at all. Almost half the girls (48%) but only 4 percent of the boys reported that the incident "hurt a lot." Most commonly, boys (54%)responded that they "laughed" about the violence compared to only 10 percent of girls. For girls, the most common reactions were to cry (40%) and to fight back (36%). These findings suggest that girls are more seriously threatened and hurt when violence occurs.

RISK AND PROTECTIVE FACTORS FOR TEEN DATING VIOLENCE IN THE ECOLOGICAL MODEL

In exploring risk and protective factors for teen dating violence, we need to look beyond the individual and consider the context within which the person lives, develops his or her identity, and finds models for relationships. The context includes family, peer group, school, and youth culture, membership in ethnic minority groups, the religious community, the political environment, and broader social norms. Risk factors exist at each level of this social ecology and can have cumulative effects. At the same time, protective factors may increase a young person's resilience in the face of adversity. Two major risk factors permeate all levels of the social ecology and increase youths' vulnerability for dating violence: (1) cultural norms and beliefs that accept violence within intimate relationships and model relationships based on power and control; and (2) exposure to violence in the home or community. The following sections examine these risk factors in detail.

ADOLESCENTS' ATTITUDES TOWARD DATING VIOLENCE

Overall, survey research indicates that neither adolescent boys nor girls accept dating violence (O'Keefe 1997; Price, Byers, and the Dating Violence Research Team 1999). However, Price and colleagues (1999) note that "a substantial minority of students agreed that specific abusive behaviors are appropriate in dating relationships" (p. 370). This acceptance of dating violence is associated with the use of violence with a dating partner, regardless of gender (Price et

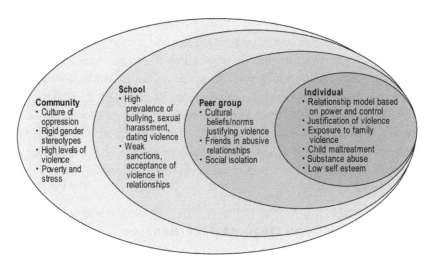

FIGURE 14.1. Risk factors for teen dating violence in the ecological model.

al. 1999). In addition, beliefs that endorse male dominance and privilege, and hostile and negative sexual attitudes toward women, are associated with the use of physical and sexual aggression by males (Flood 2005–2006).

A qualitative study with young African American men illustrates this issue. Although most boys agree that "it is unacceptable to hit women," they state that there are situations when "'it is OK to keep a woman in check' with aggressive or violent behavior, for example if she is 'acting out' in some way" (MEE 1996, p. 6). Young men and women agree that there are situations when a woman "brings it [abuse] on herself," most often when she is perceived as unfaithful and disrespectful. Motivational Educational Entertainment Productions also finds that there are no sanctions in the peer group when young men violate the "don't hit rule."

The situation is further complicated by different standards for the use of violence by boys and girls. Both the male and female survey respondents are more accepting when girls use violence than when boys use violence (O'Keefe 1997; Price et al. 2000, 1999). Price and colleagues hypothesize that "due to their smaller size, girls' use of physical violence may not be seen as a genuine physical threat to boys" (1999, p. 371). The same patterns hold true for Latino youth. Rayburn and colleagues (2007) found that Latino teens perceive the violence as more serious when the perpetrator is a boy; condemn violence by male perpetrators more than by female perpetrators; tend to show "sympathy" toward the female perpetrator; fear that a male victim will retaliate; and ridicule male victims. These mixed messages, in which adolescents are taught that a man should never hit a woman but romanticize a woman slapping a man, cause problems (O'Keefe 1997). These beliefs may contribute to the higher levels of physical violence perpetrated by girls, which also place them at higher risk of male retaliation. Furthermore, different standards for violence by boys and girls may be distorting prevalence studies of physical violence, should boys underreport aggressive behavior out of fear of more severe social sanctions.

FAMILY VIOLENCE AND CHILD MALTREATMENT

A history of child maltreatment (sexual, emotional, or physical abuse) is a pronounced risk factor for male adolescents becoming perpetrators or victims of physical violence and threats, and for female adolescents becoming victims of such violence (Wolfe et al. 2001).

Witnessing parental violence is often cited as another risk factor for teen dating violence, although research has produced mixed results (e.g. Schwartz, O'Leary, and Kendziora 1997; Malik et al. 1997). Witnessing parental violence has more consistently been associated with males' than females' use of dating aggression (O'Keefe 1997). In O'Keefe's (1998) study of the 232 adolescents who reported exposure to high levels of violence between parents, 51 percent reported that they had never inflicted violence against a dating partner, and 49 percent reported that they had done so at least once. More than half (55%) reported that they had experienced at least one incident of dating violence. Thus the majority of those who have observed or experienced family-of-origin violence do not later use violence against their dating partners.

Additional protective and vulnerability factors in the adolescents' environment may influence whether violence is transmitted from the family-of-origin to the next generation. O'Keefe (1998) found several variables that produced a protective effect on this at-risk population. For males, self-esteem emerged as a significant protective factor distinguishing males who inflict dating violence from those who do not, which is consistent with research on resilient children (Rutter 1990). For females, success in school produced a protective effect for inflicting or receiving dating violence. In contrast, acceptance of violence in dating relationships, exposure to community and school violence, lower self-esteem, and lower socioeconomic status represented additional risk factors for the adolescents in the study.

PEER INFLUENCE

Arriaga and Foshee (2004) explored whether having friends in violent relationships or interparental violence more strongly predicted dating violence perpetration and victimization. Their findings indicated that "the effect of friend dating violence was more important than the effect of interparental violence" (p. 178). It is likely that adolescents form norms for dating relationships based on peer observations. It is also possible, however, that there is a selective process by which adolescents with histories of family violence and maltreatment, and who experience interpersonal problems, gravitate toward peers with similar histories (Dodge et al. 2003) forming groups that reinforce violence and aggression toward dating partners (Capaldi et al. 2001). In contrast, positive experiences in the peer group are a protective factor for children from violent homes. Peer acceptance and pro-social skills are related to overall positive adjustment for children who have experienced family adversity, witnessed domestic violence, or experienced abuse (Criss et al. 2002; Rutter 1990).

SEXUAL HARASSMENT AND VIOLENCE IN THE SCHOOLS

School environments may contribute to dating violence by providing weak sanctions against disrespectful behavior, bullying, sexual harassment, and peer aggression (Olweus, Limber, and Mihalic 1999; Pellegrini 2002). Insufficient sanctions against sexual harassment and violence in the schools add to the perception that this is acceptable and normal behavior (Stein 1995). As the survey by the American Association of University Women (1993) documented, sexual harassment is widespread in schools, with 83 percent of girls and 79 percent of boys in grades 8 to 11 indicating that they have been sexually harassed.

The prevalence of dating and sexual violence in schools is unknown because of the paucity of survey data and the general difficulty of acquiring data on dating and sexual violence in schools (Stein 2005). However, 42 percent of boys and 43 percent of girls report that their worst incident of dating abuse occurred in a school building or on school grounds (Molidor et al. 2000). Other people were present 40 percent of the time when the female experienced abuse and 49 percent of the time when the male experienced abuse. Molidor and colleagues concluded that dating violence is a form of school violence that needs to be addressed in order to maintain a safe and equitable learning environment for all students.

VIOLENCE IN THE COMMUNITY

Malik et al. (1997) reported that exposure to multiple forms of violence most strongly predicted involvement in violence—in the community or in dating relationships. They further noted that being exposed to violence in one context appeared to carry effects over to other contexts, both as victim and perpetrator. In their study, African Americans reported higher rates of dating violence perpetration and victimization than whites, Hispanics, or Asians. Not surprisingly, the effects of ethnicity were accounted for by exposure to community and family violence—highest among African Americans—which was concordant with other studies (O'Keefe 1997; U.S. Department of Justice, Office of Justice Programs 2004).

Research on youth violence (Guerra and Williams 2006) demonstrates that concentrated disadvantages, danger, inequality, and oppression rather than ethnicity produce the heightened rates of violence in many ethnic minority communities. Guerra and Williams further state that "aggressive scripts can be seen as an adaptive response to social interactions marred by potential danger" (p. 31). In such an environment, displays of "toughness" become necessary for self-preservation and self-affirmation. The MEE (1996) places teen dating violence among African American youth in the larger context of disadvantage and oppression. Young African American men lack opportunities that build a healthy self-concept. Respect and a sense of power usually derive from productive contributions in school, the community, and society. When this is not possible, young men may need to get "respect," power, and control in their home (MEE 1996). Media and youth culture, particularly Hip Hop lyrics, amplify the problem by characterizing manhood as being about violence and conquest. The search for love then becomes confounded with a search for power and control; any perception of disrespect can lead to violent reactions.

SUMMARY

Current research shows how multiple risk factors can increase a young person's vulnerability for dating violence. Experiencing violence in the home and the community, growing up with adults and peers who justify violent relationships, and violent messages in popular youth culture represent cumulative risk factors. Nevertheless, it is important to remember that dating violence, just like domestic violence, occurs in all ethnic, racial, and socioeconomic groups. Although risk factors help us identify particularly vulnerable youths, young people who appear well adjusted and do not have any of the markers may become involved in dating violence and be at serious risk for harm. Based on our observations with teens, types of dating violence need to be differentiated. Although a majority of abusive teen dating relationships may be characterized by mutual violence, very serious abusive relationships also occur with clearly differentiated roles between the perpetrator and the victim. At this point, we do not have sufficient research on these different dynamics and the associated risks.

ADOLESCENTS' HELP-SEEKING BEHAVIORS AND BARRIERS TO SERVICES

ADOLESCENTS' HELP-SEEKING BEHAVIORS

Many teens are reluctant to seek help from anyone when they are in abusive relationships. Seeking support and protection is often fraught with shame, fear, and doubt; about 20–30 percent of teens state that they have talked to no one about the abuse (Ball 2006; Black and Weisz 2003; Jackson et al. 2000; Jaycox et al. 2006; Molidor et al. 2000). When teens share their experiences, it is most likely with one of their peers (about 60%). However, Koval 1989 (cited in Black and Weisz 2003) found that the majority of social support and advice adolescents received from their friends was unhelpful and tended to blame the victim. Furthermore, confiding to peers may have negative consequences for teens such as retaliation from the abuser and his or her friends, the loss of mutual friends and acquaintances, rumors, loss of respect, and loss of the status of having a boyfriend or girlfriend (National Resource Center on Domestic Violence [NRCDV] 2004).

Only between 5 and 30 percent of teens are likely to talk to a parent or family member, between 5 and 15 percent of students talk to a teacher or a school counselor, and even fewer confide in authorities. Adults often minimize teens' violent relationships as "drama" and "misbehavior," fail to understand the emotional intensity of teen relationships, and do not realize the danger of teen dating abuse. Teens are particularly wary that parents will demand that they end the relationship and that they will lose their parents' trust and their own hard-earned independence. Thus research indicates that most teens never report dating violence to adults or seek supportive services in the community.

CONCERNS ABOUT CONFIDENTIALITY

Teen victims of dating violence considering disclosure to school staff, counselors, social workers, or prevention educators may have important concerns about confidentiality (NRCDV 2004). They know that the adults may be legally bound to report to law enforcement, notify their parents, or encourage them to seek services. As the NRCDV report points out, mandated reporting of abuse and requiring parental notification and consent for services create barriers for teens accessing the support they need. Therefore, some states, such as Texas, permit minors to consent to counseling without parental consent for (1) suicide prevention; (2) chemical addiction or dependency; or (3) sexual, physical, or emotional abuse (Philip 2005). Texas state law, however, also mandates that any adult must report suspected child abuse or neglect either to child protective services or local law enforcement.

Philip (2005) advises that it is in everyone's best interest for minors to know exactly where they stand with respect to confidentiality when they disclose abuse and dating violence to an adult. Minors need to clearly understand confidentiality limits; Rosenbluth (2004) recommends that "whenever possible inform a student in advance when you intend to break his or her confidentiality. Give the student the opportunity to participate, for example, by making the report with you or by being present during discussion of the incident with authorities, parents, law enforcement, etc." (p. 19).

ACCESS TO PROTECTIVE ORDERS

Most teens know little about their legal rights as victims of partner violence and generally do not report violent incidents to the police (Jaycox et al. 2006). Therefore, Break the Cycle's three-session prevention curriculum, *Ending Violence*, addresses legal issues and teens' rights. Jaycox and colleagues (2006) evaluated the impact of this program and found increases in knowledge and perceived helpfulness and likeliness to seek help from attorneys and police.

Teen victims, however, still do not have the same access to protective orders as adults. Regulations vary by state and may require that a parent or guardian file the petition on behalf of the teen or restrict access to protective orders to partners who have a child in common or who have lived together. At this point, only 19 states and the District of Columbia allow teen victims of dating violence to request a protective order without representation by a parent or a legal or appointed guardian. The National Center for Victims of Crime (NCVC) provides information about each state's regulations on protective orders for teens (see the resource list at the end of the chapter). The authors contend that for many teens "a requirement of parental or guardian consent becomes an insurmountable obstacle to accessing the justice system. As a result, victims may remain in dangerous relationships simply because they do not want to tell or involve their parent" (NCVC 2005, p. 3).

EFFECTIVE STRATEGIES FOR THE PREVENTION OF TEEN DATING VIOLENCE

"Prevention efforts should ultimately reduce risk factors and promote protective factors. Additionally, prevention should address all levels that influence youth violence: individual, relationship, community, and society" (Centers of Disease Control and Prevention, National Center for Injury Prevention and Control 2006).

The analysis of risk and protective factors in an adolescent's environment shows that the focus of prevention must extend further than individual change. Prevention strategies are needed that engage the family, peer group, school, and community. And prevention programs and services must be accessible to all youth.

THE NEED FOR SCHOOL-BASED PROGRAMS

Research documents that sexual harassment and dating violence occur in the schools and threaten the safety of all students. "Dating violence is a form of school violence. . . . To address the issue, school systems need to create an environment of dating violence prevention by setting policies, developing intervention plans, and encouraging student input." (Molidor et al. 2000, p. 4). Support among educators is critical for changing social norms that underlie sexual harassment and dating violence on school campuses (Peacock and Rothman 2001). Learning about healthy relationships needs to be an important component of students' education that can improve the school climate and provide a safe and equitable learning environment for all students (as required by federal law under Title IX).

If prevention is to take an ecological approach and involve the major systems within which adolescents form their identities and relationships, then schools are indeed the ideal and central place to anchor a dating violence prevention program. School-based programs have several advantages including increased access to diverse youth and the opportunity to work with youth in their social environment (Wolfe et al. 2003). Molidor and colleagues (2000) suggest that school-based prevention programs have an additional important function in providing a gateway for counseling and other services, including legal advocacy.

BEST PRACTICES IN SCHOOL-BASED TEEN DATING VIOLENCE PREVENTION

As Meyer and Stein (2004) point out, "best practices" for school-based dating violence prevention have yet to be established. However, the following characteristics of effective prevention programs are offered in the literature (Ball, Kerig, and Rosenbluth 2009; Flood 2005–2006; Kerig, Ball, and Rosenbluth 2006; Meyer and Stein 2004; Nation et al. 2003; Thornton et al. 2002; Schewe 2002). To be effective, dating violence prevention programs must

- take a comprehensive, ecologically informed approach and engage all members of the school community;
- be implemented in middle school and the early high school years;
- involve boys and girls, perpetrators and victims, and are mindful that most teen dating violence entails the reciprocal use of violence;
- include significant contact with students and multiple points of contact with reinforcing messages;
- address cognitive, affective and behavioral domains;
- offer various teaching methods that stimulate an active and involved learning process and that develop skills;
- provide opportunities for teens to develop strong, positive relationships through mentoring and leadership opportunities;
- involve teens in program development;
- focus on positive messages and reinforce healthy relationship skills; and
- provide programming for the general student population as well as support for students who have already experienced violence in their lives.

Effective programs also need to be culturally relevant to the audience, engaging, and sustainable. Since most youth violence prevention interventions occur in multicultural contexts, it is important that they address culture in general and allow participants to provide meaning relevant to their own ethnicity or culture (Wright and Zimmerman 2006). A program targeting adolescents must also consider popular youth culture. As Wright and Zimmerman (2006) suggest, "it may even be the case that youth culture is more important as the referent group than the youth's ethnic culture. . . . The youth culture, however, may provide a common denominator for multicultural contexts and may be the central focus for making an intervention culturally sensitive" (p. 242).

Prevention programs will have a greater chance for success when they are framed and presented in ways that are appropriate to participants and when they can build on participants' cultural strengths. These programs must be culturally sensitive, paying particular attention to the school culture and climate, the teen culture, and the culture of the community. The following description of the Expect Respect Program illustrates how these strategies can be implemented.

THE EXPECT RESPECT PROGRAM

The Expect Respect Program aims to reduce the incidence and prevalence of relationship and dating violence among youth (Ball and Rosenbluth 2008; Ball, Rosenbluth, and Aoki 2008; Ball, Randolph, and Rosenbluth 2008; Rosenbluth and Ball 2008). Expect Respect implements an ecologically informed program by engaging all members of the school community, teachers, parents, and students. Schools are a central place for raising awareness about characteristics of healthy and abusive relationships among adults and youth, establishing policies that articulate clear expectations for respectful relationships, directly engaging youth in leadership programs, and providing accessible support services to vulnerable youth who have already experienced violence. Expect Respect consists of three program components, as shown in Figure 14.2.

The *School-wide Prevention Strategies* encompass working with the school system and school personnel to prevent bullying, sexual harassment and dating violence at school. Strategies include developing school policies, trainings for teachers and staff, a school climate survey, classroom activities, and seminars for parents and community members.

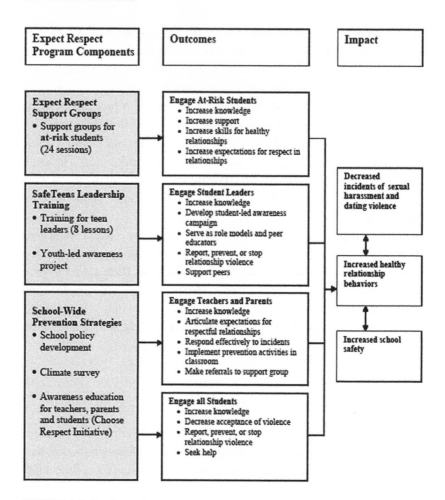

FIGURE 14.2. The Expect Respect program logic model.

The *SafeTeens Youth-Leadership Training* invites youths in school and in the community to become actively involved in preventing sexual harassment and teen dating violence.

The *Expect Respect Support Groups* are tailored to students involved in or at-risk for dating violence. The 24-week program engages boys and girls in gender separate groups. Support groups are offered during the school day to maximize accessibility.

COLLABORATION BETWEEN THE SCHOOL DISTRICT
AND A COMMUNITY-BASED AGENCY

The Expect Respect program is based on the collaboration between a school district and a community-based agency. Over the past twenty years, SafePlace, a sexual and domestic violence intervention and prevention agency, and the Austin Independent School District (AISD) have developed a partnership that has increased the district's commitment to prevention and supported the development of a comprehensive dating violence prevention program. In 2004–2005 SafePlace provided 28 support groups at 20 schools in the Austin area for youth at risk for perpetration and victimization in their dating relationships. The school-wide prevention activities, including staff training on school policies, parent seminars, youth leadership training, and educational programs, reached thousands of students and adults.

Expect Respect program staff work to increase awareness and knowledge about dating violence within the school system and respond in a flexible manner to the school's needs that are identified in the process. We recommend conducting a school-climate survey among students that assesses the prevalence of sexual harassment and dating violence; bystander behaviors; students' comfort in reporting sexual harassment and dating violence; their outreach to peers and adults; and their ability to identify abusive behaviors. Schools then choose to implement one or all three components of the Expect Respect program tailored to their needs. This flexibility in program design is critical for implementing and sustaining a successful program in the schools.

SCHOOL POLICY DEVELOPMENT AND STAFF TRAINING

An important milestone in the history of the program occurred when the Austin Independent School District's Board of Trustees adopted, in 2004, a district-wide policy for preventing dating violence, sexual harassment, and bullying. This policy, drafted in consultation with SafePlace, defines forms of abuse in students' relationships and provides a detailed protocol for students and staff to report incidents. Students are explicitly encouraged to report incidents and may request a conference with the principal or principal's designee. In addition, a student or staff member can submit a complaint to school authorities and request a stay-away agreement. The *Notice of Parent and Student Rights* (AISD 2006) describes the process as follows:

1. Students and staff members will complete a Complaint Form available in the school's main office.
2. The Complaint Form will be submitted to the principal immediately.
3. The principal or his/her designee will investigate complaints by meeting *separately* with each student involved in the situation.
4. The principal will conference with the targeted student and parent to discuss safety.
5. The principal will conference with the accused student and parent to discuss appropriate behaviors and consequences. With the prior consent of the targeted student, the principal may issue a School-Based Stay Away Agreement to the accused student during the parent conference.
6. Documentation of all Complaint Forms, follow-up actions, and Stay Away Agreements will be available to the General Counsel at all times.

A policy, to be effective, must be widely publicized and all responsible parties have to be trained to implement the policy properly. Thus the policy has become an important tool for raising awareness, increasing effectiveness and consistency of responses throughout the district, and motivating school administrators to address these problems proactively through comprehensive prevention strategies.

At the state policy level, Expect Respect program staff and AISD helped pass legislation in 2007 related to promoting healthy and respectful relationships among teens. Texas Code TEC 37.0831 (formerly H.B. No. 121) requires all school districts in Texas to amend their school safety codes to include a definition of dating violence and to address related counseling, protection, education, and training issues. The Texas Dating Violence Prevention Team, a committee of state organizations in collaboration with SafePlace, developed information and resources to assist school districts in developing their policies and addressing teen dating violence through training, curriculum, and other strategies (See http://www.healthyteendating.org [accessed April 30, 2009]).

SCHOOL-WIDE PREVENTION ACTIVITIES: CHANGING SOCIAL NORMS

The involvement of educators is essential for reducing violence and promoting a positive school climate (Rosenbluth and Ball 2008). Educators can positively influence social norms on campus and foster a culture of respect by modeling respectful relationships, responding effectively to incidents, and integrating prevention curricula into their regular classroom lessons. Advocates from community-based organizations have traditionally used their limited staff resources to make classroom presentations on dating and sexual violence prevention. Although this approach has some advantages (for example, the information is presented by an expert and awareness of community services is increased), the disadvantages are significant. Advocates are in short supply and cannot effectively reach all students with the number of sessions necessary to change attitudes and behaviors. Most important, presentations by outsiders do little to impact the day-to-day relationships on campus.

Instead, advocates can provide training for school personnel, and then the teachers can integrate prevention curriculum into regular classroom activities. Educators are experts at teaching. They are also authorities and often trusted adults on campus who can model positive relationship skills and support students in learning and practicing new behaviors. Indeed, Meyer and Stein (2004), in their review of existing school-based prevention programs, strongly recommend integrating relationship violence curricula into the classroom and to avoid add-on or peripheral programs.

In this spirit, the Expect Respect staff provides trainings to assist teachers with implementing *Choose Respect*, a teen dating violence prevention initiative developed by the Centers of Disease Control and Prevention (2006) in collaboration with SafePlace. *Choose Respect* consists of educational materials targeting 11- to 14-year-old youths that can be used in school and community settings. The centerpieces of this initiative are a 13-minute educational video for teens titled *Causing Pain, Real Stories of Dating Abuse and Violence* and a 30-minute version for parents and other adults. A *Video Discussion Guide* (Teachers' Manual) accompanies the video. Other components include television and radio public service announcements, posters, pocket guides, parent magnets, and an interactive Web site. Forthcoming materials include online teacher training and a community playbook designed to engage youths and adults in promoting respectful dating relationships. Many of these materials are available in English and Spanish and can be downloaded free from the *Choose Respect* Web site, http://www.chooserespect.org (accessed April 30, 2009). SafePlace also encourages teachers and student leaders to work together on designing additional campus-specific prevention activities during the designated National Teen Dating Violence Prevention Week and throughout the school year.

SAFETEENS YOUTH LEADERSHIP PROGRAM: ENGAGING TEENS AND CHANGING LIVES

Youth violence prevention research has shown that engaging teens in identify-ing personal and community needs and taking on leadership activities is an effective prevention strategy (Nation et al. 2003). Training teens to be leaders in dating violence prevention can directly influence peer group norms (Ball, Randolph, and Rosenbluth 2008). Educating teens to become leaders and role models also addresses the important issue of teens disclosing their abuse most frequently to friends. Peers, in reality, are the first responders. Therefore, teaching them how to respond effectively and empathically, without blaming the victim, fills a critical need.

The SafeTeens youth-leadership program invites teens on campus to become involved in preventing sexual harassment and dating violence. The program consists of two phases, a training based on an eight-lesson curric-ulum and a youth-led project. The training offers education about healthy relationships and can be integrated into health and social science classes or into existing leadership programs. Students learn about bullying, sexual harassment, sexual assault, and dating violence and practice skills needed for peer support, advocacy, and community action. After completing the lessons, students identify a problem relating to violence in their school or community and develop materials and interventions that are directly and specifically rel-evant and engaging for their peers. Because every SafeTeens group is unique, every project looks different. A key benefit of this approach is that youth-led projects are generally relevant and appealing to other youth.

SafeTeens youth leadership groups have been especially successful in creat-ing public service announcements (PSAs). For example, a girls' group created a PSA (running time 17 seconds) on sexual harassment (see Figure 14.3). They wanted to change their peers' attitudes about using synonyms for prostitutes as insults. The group wrote the script, acted it out in several different ways, and then decided that the impact was the greatest when the words were spoken by two girls supporting each other back-to-back. The group mentor assisted with editing the film. Furthermore, SafePlace collaborates with artists and art organizations in the community to develop creative ways in which teens can reach and mobilize their peers.

"Movement, rhythm, image, sound, color, spoken word—these are all components of the dynamic vocabulary of the contemporary voice of youth. Arts-based educational messages about critical thinking and making healthy

When you call her:		People start to think that they can:
prostitute	hooker	hurt her
ho	slut	sexually assault her
whore	wench	treat her badly
tart	floozy	
working girl	tramp	
call girl	show girl	**and you are sexually harassing her.**
trick	popper	

FIGURE 14.3. The Expect Respect public service annoucment.

choices created by and delivered by peers have a significantly greater chance of being heard and making an impact on young audiences" (Cleveland 1997).

The Expect Respect Program also partners with a local theater company to engage youth in educational theater. After receiving the SafeTeens training, youths devise scenes based on their own experience and create a play that is performed at schools and in the community. The *Changing Lives Youth Theatre Company* is highly effective in engaging teen audiences and reaching a wide group of teenagers, including those that resist messages delivered by adults. In addition to informing peers, program participants receive appreciation for their creative talents—a recognition that builds self-esteem and reinforces leadership skills.

EXPECT RESPECT SUPPORT GROUPS: ACCESSIBLE PREVENTION AND SUPPORT FOR VULNERABLE YOUTH

Most school-based dating violence prevention programs are intended for the general student population (see Meyer and Stein 2004), but programs must be equally sensitive to the needs of students who have experienced family violence and abuse or those who are currently experiencing dating violence. The Expect Respect support groups address these students' important needs for safety, social support, and learning healthy relationship skills (Ball, Rosenbluth, and Aoki 2008; Ball, Kerig, Rosenbluth 2009). By bringing these services into the school, we allow teens to access an age-appropriate intervention in a non-stigmatizing manner. In addition, Expect Respect support groups can provide effective gateways for further services, including protective orders and mental health services.

Expect Respect facilitators are employed by SafePlace and are trained in working with teens on the topic of healthy relationships. Facilitators offer an orientation to the program for all school personnel and advertise the groups in the schools with flyers, newsletters, and public service announcements. Support groups specifically target youths who have experienced violence in their families and in their peer and dating relationships. Typically teachers and counselors refer students to groups, although self-referrals also occur. Expect Respect facilitators conduct an intake interview, during which they explain rules about confidentiality and mandated reporting, assess eligibility, obtain student consent to participate, and provide a parent notification letter. Boys and girls are invited to separate gender groups for intensive group work, thus providing space and safety to talk openly and honestly, and share real feelings and concerns. The support group program is based on the 24-week *Expect Respect Support Group Curriculum* (Ball, Rosenbluth, and Aoki 2008; Rosenbluth 2004), which includes the following broad topics:

- Developing group skills
- Choosing equality and respect
- Recognizing abusive relationships
- Learning skills for healthy relationships, and
- Getting the message out.

The Expect Respect support groups focus on creating an emotionally safe and respectful group environment. Various learning strategies are used including videos, guest speakers, interactive group games, role play, creative expression, and a mixed gender discussion at the end of the group. Facilitators use examples from youth culture and media, such as hip-hop lyrics, to engage participants in a culturally relevant way.

The quotes given in Table 14.1 are excerpted from our focus group research with five male groups and five female groups (see also Ball, Kerig, and Rosenbluth 2009). Consider how participants describe the experience with the group facilitator and the relationships with other group members, and how they transfer this experience to their relationships outside the group.

TABLE 14.1 Examples from Focus Group Research on Expect Respect Support Groups

RESPONSES FROM BOYS' GROUPS	RESPONSES FROM GIRLS' GROUPS
THE GROUP FACILITATOR AS ROLE MODEL	**THE GROUP FACILITATOR AS ROLE-MODEL**
▪ "He always respected the way you feel. He'll never put you down. He'll correct you on something but he'll never put you down." ▪ "He doesn't make himself better, no better than us." ▪ "I liked the fact that he wanted to hear what we had to say and felt."	▪ "I think she [the facilitator] made us all feel like we're actually worth something." ▪ "She took all our feelings in consideration." ▪ "We couldn't keep anything back just because we knew that she didn't judge us."
THE GROUP PROCESS	**THE GROUP PROCESS**
▪ "What I like about the group is that I can express myself cuz [sic] my peers won't disrespect me. We respect each other. And that's something that helps me out." ▪ "Your peers are going to help you understand stuff and help you through the situation. It's like a big group of help."	▪ "You don't have to worry about people judging you, or anyone saying anything about you behind your back." ▪ "You can trust everyone in here." ▪ "I think everyone in this group truly grew in the fact that they can talk to people."
LEARNING ABOUT HEALTHY RELATIONSHIPS	**LEARNING ABOUT HEALTHY RELATIONSHIPS**
▪ "It is not one relationship. It is about what other people want, too." ▪ "I don't just think about me, but I think about her, too, and how she feels." ▪ "I learned how much it affects a girl's future if you mistreat her. How she feels after she's been talked down [to], violated. I can see how a girl feels."	▪ "It lets you know when to stop a relationship, when it is going too far. When to get help from somebody and to expect them [boys] not to do certain things." ▪ "We got confidence to stand up for ourselves now." ▪ "I learned how to talk to people and not be embarrassed or ashamed."

The comments in Table 14.1 illustrate how a support group format addresses the teens' needs for close peer relationships. Participants learn through building relationships with one another. Support groups create a positive and safe group environment, "*a family, but better because you can actually trust each other*," based on norms of respect, tolerance, and mutual acceptance. Expecting, giving, and receiving respect are important learning experiences that directly address some of the triggers youths commonly report for using violence: perceived disrespect and the desire to gain control. Participants' statements in focus groups indicate that they transfer these norms and expectations to their personal relationships outside the group.

EXPECT RESPECT PROGRAM EVALUATION

Expect Respect was selected in 2003 to participate in an empowerment evaluation project sponsored by the Centers for Disease Control and Prevention (CDC) for programs designed to prevent first-time male perpetration of sexual violence. As part of this project Expect Respect program staff received technical assistance for program development and evaluation. Preliminary results for the quantitative, uncontrolled pilot evaluation of Expect Respect support groups (Ball et al. 2009) demonstrated that groups have immediate positive effects. At program completion participants reported significant increases in healthy conflict resolution skills. Among participants who reported perpetration of physical violence or victimization in the three months prior to the intervention we found a significant reduction in emotional and physical abuse perpetration and victimization.

Preliminary results for the evaluation of the Choose Respect initiative (CDC 2008) revealed that middle school students who were exposed to the initiative showed positive and significant changes in knowledge and beliefs, and also in behavioral intentions. For example, after participating in Choose Respect activities there was a decrease in the number of students who thought a healthy relationship was one where a dating partner wanted to know where the other one was every minute or became jealous when the partner talked to other people. Students were better able to identify the warning signs of abuse and showed stronger beliefs that abuse in relationships was unacceptable.

CONCLUSION

Teen dating violence is best understood when we consider the environments in which youth grow up and form their relationships. Cultural beliefs and attitudes about dating violence, as well as exposure to violence in the home and the community, increase youths' vulnerability for dating violence. The Expect Respect program is presented as an example of an ecologically informed school-based teen dating violence program. Expect Respect engages all members of the school community in changing social norms on campus and articulating clear expectations for respect in relationships. Expect Respect aims to decrease the acceptance of gendered violence and increase the adults' and students' willingness to act as active bystanders when they witness harassment and abuse. Further, Expect Respect involves youth groups in prevention activities and gives them the opportunity to design culturally relevant awareness campaigns, and become role models and leaders in their community. Support groups provide much needed and accessible services for at-risk youths who have already experienced relationship violence. By working with school personnel, parents, the general student population, and at-risk groups, Expect Respect aims to maximize the effectiveness of its interventions.

Note: Sections of this chapter have been previously published in the Expect Respect Program Manual by SafePlace, Austin, Texas.

RESOURCES

The National Teen Dating Abuse Helpline operates via telephone and online 24 hours a day and is staffed by both teen and adult advocates. Teens (and parents) anywhere in the country can call toll-free, 1 (866) 331–9474, or log on to the interactive Web site, http://loveisrespect.org, and receive immediate, confidential assistance. The Web site offers secure, live interactive chat to teens. While online or on the phone, teens are given support as well as referrals to local resources in their hometown to provide them with the help they need.

ONLINE RESOURCES

Break the Cycle
2009 State-by-State Teen Dating Violence Report Card. Retrieved May 1, 2009, from http://www.breakthecycle.org/resources-state-law-report-cards-2009.html.

National Sexual Violence Resource Center
Sexual Violence and the Spectrum of Prevention: Towards a Community Solution (2006). Retrieved May 1, 2009, from http://www.nsvrc.org.

National Center for Victims of Crime and the National Crime Prevention Council, Teen Victim Project
Reaching and Serving Teen Victims: A Practical Handbook (2005). Retrieved May 1, 2009, from http://www.ncvc.org.

Texas Dating Violence Prevention Team
http://www.healthyteendating.org
Comprehensive toolkit available on the Web site to help schools and communities address dating violence.

Women's Law.org
Information for Teens. Retrieved May 1, 2009, from http://www.womenslaw.org/teens.htm.

SafePlace
Information about the Expect Respect Program and other resources is available on the Web site: http://www.SafePlace.org.
Teen Dating Violence Prevention Campaigns
Break the Cycle
Website: http://www.breakthecycle.org

Choose Respect Initiative (Centers for Disease Control and Prevention)
Website: http://www.chooserespect.org

Love Is Not Abuse (Liz Claiborne)
Website: http://www.loveisnotabuse.com

Men of Strength Campaign (Men Can Stop Rape)
Website: http://www.mencanstoprape.org

National Teen Dating Violence Prevention Initiative. Toolkit. (American Bar Association)
Website: http://www.abanet.org/unmet/toolkitmaterials.html

That's Not Cool
Website: http://www.ThatsNotCool.com
This Web site provides interactive, Web-based tools and resources to prevent teen dating violence by promoting positive friendships and relationships, raising awareness about the signs of abuse, and most importantly, educating teens about "digital gray areas."

REFERENCES

American Association of University Women Educational Foundation (AAUW). (1993). *Hostile Hallways: The AAUW Survey on Sexual Harassment in America's Schools.* Washington, DC: Author.

Arriaga, X. B., and V. A. Foshee. (2004). Adolescent dating violence: do adolescents follow in their friends' or parents' footsteps? *Journal of Interpersonal Violence,* 19(2), 162–184.

Austin Independent School District (AISD). (2006). *Notice of Parents' and Students' Rights.* Austin, TX: Author.

Avery-Leaf, S., and M. Cascardi. (2002). Dating violence education: Prevention and early intervention strategies. In P. Schewe (Ed.), *Preventing Violence in Relationships: Interventions across the Life Span* (pp. 79–105). Washington, DC: American Psychological Association.

Ball, B. (2006). Prevalence rates for sexual harassment and dating violence in 4 middle and high schools. Unpublished report. SafePlace, Austin, Texas.

Ball, B., P. Kerig, and B. Rosenbluth. (2009). "Like a family but better because you can actually trust each other." The Expect Respect program: Dating violence prevention with at-risk youth. *Health Promotion Practice,* 10(1), 45S–58S.

Ball, B., R. Randolph, and B. Rosenbluth. (2008). *Expect Respect Program Manual Part II: SafeTeens Youth Leadership Curriculum and Facilitator Guide.* Austin, TX: SafePlace.

Ball, B., and B. Rosenbluth. (2008). *Expect Respect Program Overview.* Austin, TX: SafePlace.

Ball, B., B. Rosenbluth, and A. Aoki. (2008). *Expect Respect Program Manual Part I: Support Group Curriculum and Facilitator Guide.* Austin, TX: SafePlace.

Ball, B., A. Teten, R. Noonan, and B. Rosenbluth. (2009). Preliminary evaluation of Expect Respect support groups: Dating violence prevention for at-risk youth. Unpublished manuscript.

Black, B., and A. Weisz. (2003). Dating violence: Help-seeking behaviors of African American middle schoolers. *Violence Against Women,* 9(2), 187–206.

Burcky, W., N. Reuterman, and S. Kopsky. (1988). Dating violence among high school students. *The School Counselor,* 35, 353–358.

Capaldi, D. M., T. J. Dishion, M. Stoolmiller, and K. Yoerger. (2001). Aggression toward female partners by at-risk young men: The contribution of male adolescent friendships. *Developmental Psychology,* 37, 61–73.

Centers for Disease Control and Prevention, National Center for Injury Prevention and Control (2006) *Youth Violence: Prevention Strategies.* Retrieved April 25, 2007, from http://www.cdc.gov/ncipc/fastsheets/yvprevention.htm.

Centers for Disease Control and Prevention (CDC). (2006). *Choose Respect. Cam-*

paign to Promote Healthy Relationships and Prevent Dating Abuse. Retrieved April 25, 2007, from http://www.chooserespect.org.

——. (2008). Choose Respect 2007–2008 Final Report. Unpublished.

Cleveland, W. (1997). What is, and what can be: Artists helping young people. In National Endowment of the Arts (Ed.), *Art Works! Prevention Programs for Youth and Communities.* Rockville, MD: National Clearinghouse for Alcohol and Drug Information.

Criss, M, G. Pettit, J. Bates, K. Dodge, and A. Lapp. (2002). Family adversity, positive peer relationships, and children's externalizing behavior: A longitudinal perspective on risk and resilience. *Child Development,* 73(4), 1220–1237.

Dodge, K. A., J. E. Lansford, V. S. Burks, J. E. Bates, G. S. Pettit, R. Fontaine, et al. (2003). Peer rejection and social information-processing factors in the development of aggressive behavior problems in children. *Child Development,* 74, 374–393.

Flood, M. (2005–2006). Changing men. *Women Against Violence,* 18, 26–36.

Foshee, V. (1996). Gender differences in adolescent dating abuse prevalence, types and injuries. *Health Education Research,* 11(3), 275–286.

Fredland, N., I. Ricardo, J. Campbell, P. Sharps, J. Kub, and M. Yonas. (2005). The meaning of dating violence in the lives of middle school adolescents: A report of a focus group study. *Journal of School Violence,* 4(2), 95–114.

Grunbaum, J., L. Kann, A. Kinchen, B. Williams, J. Ross, R. Lowry, et al. (2002). Youth risk behavior surveillance: United States 2001. *Journal of School Health,* 72(8), 313–328.

Guerra, N., and K. Williams. (2006). Ethnicity, youth violence, and the ecology of development. In N. Guerra and E. Smith (Eds.), *Preventing Youth Violence in a Multicultural Society* (pp. 17–46). Washington, DC: American Psychological Association.

Hickman, L.J., L. H. Jaycox, and J. Aronoff. (2004). Dating violence among adolescents: Prevalence, gender distribution, and prevention program effectiveness. *Trauma, Violence, and Abuse,* 5, 123–142.

Jackson, S., F. Cram, and F. Seymour. (2004). Violence and coercion in high school students' dating relationships. *Journal of Family Violence,* 15, 23–36.

Jaycox, L. J., D. McCaffrey, B. Eiseman, J. Aronoff, G. Shelley, R. Collins, et al. (2006). Impact of a school-based dating violence prevention program among Latino Teens. *Journal of Adolescent Health,* 39, 697–704.

Kerig, P. K., B. Ball, and B. Rosenbluth. (2006). Expect Respect: Process and outcome associated with a successful dating violence prevention program. Department of Psychology, Miami University, unpublished manuscript.

Malik, S., S. Sorenson, and C. Anehensel. (1997). Community and dating violence among adolescents: Perpetration and victimization. *Journal of Adolescent Health,* 21, 291–302.

Meyer, H., and N. Stein. (2004). Relationship violence prevention education in schools: What's working, what's getting in the way, and what are some future directions. *American Journal of Health Education*, 35(4), 198–204.

Molidor, C., R. Tolman, and J. Kober. (2000). Gender and contextual factors in adolescent dating violence. *Prevention Researcher*, 7(1), 1–4.

Motivational Educational Entertainment (MEE) Productions. (1996). *In Search of Love: Dating Violence among Urban Youth*. Philadelphia: Center for Human Advancement.

Nation, M., C. Crusto, A. Wandersman, K. Kumpfer, D. Seybolt, E. Morissey-Kane, et al. (2003). What works in prevention: Principles of effective prevention programs. *American Psychologist*, 58, 449–456.

National Center for Victims of Crime. (2005). *Dating Violence: Can Teen Access Protection Orders?* Retrieved April 25, 2007, from http://www.ncvc.org/ncvc/AGP .Net/Components/documentViewer/Download.aspxnz?DocumentID=41372.

National Resource Center on Domestic Violence (NRCDV). (2004). *Teen Dating Violence: Overview*. Retrieved April 25, 2007, from http://www.nrcdv.org and http://www.vawnet.org.

O'Keefe, M. (1997). Predictors of dating violence among high school students. *Journal of Interpersonal Violence*, 12, 546–568. Document retrieved electronically from InfoTracOne File. Thomson Gale Document Number A19732565.

——. (1998). Factors mediating the link between witnessing interparental violence and dating violence. *Journal of Family Violence*, 13(1), 39–57.

——. (2005). Teen dating violence: A review of risk factors and prevention efforts. *VAWnet Applied Research Forum*. National Electronic Network on Violence Against Women. Retrieved January 7, 2006, from http://www.vawnet.org.

Olweus, D., S. P. Limber, and S. Mihalic. (1999). *The Bullying Prevention Program: Blueprints for Violence Prevention*, Vol. 10 (Boulder, CO: Center for the Study and Prevention of Violence).

Peacock, D., and E. Rothman. (2001). Working with young men who batter: Current strategies and new directions. *VAWnet Applied Research Forum*. National Electronic Network on Violence Against Women. Retrieved January 7, 2006, from http://www.vawnet.org.

Pellegrini, A. D. (2002). Bullying, victimization, and sexual harassment during the transition to middle school. *Educational Psychologist*, 37(3), 151–163.

Philip, D. (2005). *Youth Rights in Family Violence/ Domestic Violence: Basic Legal Information concerning Texas Minors*. Training provided for Texas Council on Family Violence, Criminal Justice System Response Training.

Price, E., E. Byers, and the Dating Violence Research Team. (1999). The attitudes towards dating violence scales: Development and initial validation. *Journal of Family Violence*, 14(4), 351–375.

Price, E., S. Byers, J. Whelan, and M. Saint-Pierre, (2000). *Dating Violence Amongst New Brunswick Adolescents: A Summary of Two Studies.* University of New Brunswick, Canada, Muriel McQueen Fergusson Centre for Family Violence Research, Research Paper Series 2.

Rayburn, N., L. Jaycox, D. McCaffrey, E. Ulloa, M. Zander-Cotugno, G. Marshall, and G. Shelley. (2007). Reactions to dating violence among Latino teenagers: An experiment utilizing the Articulated Thoughts in Simulated Situations paradigm. *Journal of Adolescence*, doi:10.1016/j.adolescnce.2006.11.005.

Rosenbluth, B. (2004). *Expect Respect: A Support Group Manual for Safe and Healthy Relationships.* Austin, TX: SafePlace.

Rosenbluth, B., and B. Ball. (2008). *Expect Respect Program Manual Part III: School-Wide Prevention Strategies Facilitator Guide and Resources.* Austin, TX: SafePlace.

Rutter, M. (1990). Psychosocial resilience and protective mechanisms. In J. Rolf, A.S. Master, D. Cicchetti, K. H. Nuechterlein, and S. Weintraub (Eds.). *Risk and Protective Factors in the Development of Psychopathology* (pp. 181–214). Cambridge: Cambridge University Press.

Schewe, P. (2002). Guidelines for developing rape prevention and risk reduction interventions: Lessons from evaluation research. In P. Schewe (Ed.), *Preventing Violence in Relationships: Interventions across the Life Span* (pp. 107–136). Washington, DC: American Psychological Association.

Schwartz, M., S. G. O'Leary, and K. T. Kendziora. (1997). Dating aggression among high school students. *Violence and Victims, 12*, 295–305.

Silverman, J., A. Rai, L. Mucci, and J. Hathaway. (2001). Dating violence against adolescent girls and associated substance abuse, unhealthy weight control, sexual risk behavior, pregnancy, and suicidality. *Journal of the American Medical Association, 286*(5), 572–579.

Straus, M.A. (1979). Measuring intrafamily conflict and aggression: The Conflict Tactics Scale (CTS). *Journal of Marriage and the Family, 41*, 75–88.

Sousa, C. (1999). Teen dating violence: The hidden epidemic. *Family and Conciliation Courts Review, 37*(3), 356–374.

Stein, N. (1995). Sexual harassment in school: The public performance of gendered violence. *Harvard Educational Review, 65*(2), 145–162.

——. (2005). A rising pandemic of sexual violence in elementary and secondary schools: Locating a secret problem. *Duke Journal of Gender Law and Policy, 12*, 33–52.

Thornton, T., C. Craft, L. Dahlberg, B. Lynch, and K. Baer. (2002). *Best Practices of Youth Violence Prevention: A Source Book for Community Action.* Atlanta, GA: Centers for Disease Control and Prevention, National Center for Injury Prevention and Control.

U.S. Department of Justice, Office of Justice Programs. (2004). *Research in Brief. Violence against Women: Identifying Risk Factors.* Washington, DC: National Institute of Justice.

Wolfe, D., K. Scott, C. Wekerle, and A. Pittman. (2001). Child maltreatment: Risk of adjustment problems and dating violence in adolescence. *Journal of the American Academy of Child and Adolescent Psychiatry,* 40(3), 282–289.

Wolfe, D. A., C. Wekerle, D. Reitzel-Jaffe, and L. Lefebvre. (1998). Factors associated with abusive relationships among maltreated and nonmaltreated youth. *Development and Psychopathology,* 10, 61–85.

Wolfe, D., C. Wekerle, K. Scott, A. Straatman, C. Grasley, and D. Jaffe. (2003). Dating violence prevention with at-risk youth: A controlled outcome evaluation. *Journal of Consulting and Clinical Psychology,* 71(2), 279–291.

Wright, J., and M. Zimmerman. (2006). Culturally sensitive interventions to prevent youth violence. In N. Guerra and E. Smith (Eds.), *Preventing Youth Violence in a Multicultural Society* (pp. 221–248). Washington, DC: American Psychological Association.

NOTES

CHAPTER 1. CULTURAL COMPETENCE AND INTERSECTIONALITY

1. Although Lum's model focuses heavily on racial/ethnic groups, it can equally be applied to other culturally diverse groups. The model also promotes an ecological systems perspective of culturally competent social practice with a discussion of the intersectionality of diversity that acknowledges within-group variations consistent with the theme of this chapter and this book.

CHAPTER 4. A LILY OUT OF THE MUD

1. This excerpt is from a collective poem generated from 120 API domestic violence advocates at the conference, Engendering Change: Addressing Violence against Asian Women, held in St. Paul, Minnesota, in July 2005, by the Asian and Pacific Islander Institute on Domestic Violence (APIDV). Originally developed by Pualani Enos, the poem was re-created at this conference and compiled by Quynh Dang, Beckie Masaki, and Yanin Senachai.

2. The Asian and Pacific Islander Institute on Domestic Violence offers a definition of Asian and Pacific Islander that includes Central Asians: Afghani, Azerbaijani, Kazakh, Kyrgyz, Tajik, Turkmen, and Uzbek; East Asians: Chinese, Japanese, Korean, Okinawan, Taiwanese, and Tibetan; Hawaiian and Pacific Islander: Carolinian, Chamorro, Chuukese, Fijian, Guamanian, Hawaiian, Kosraean, Marshallesse, Native Hawaiian, Nieuean, Palauan, Pohnpeian, Samoan, Tokelauan, Tongan, and Yapese; Southeast Asians: Burmese, Cambodian, Filipino, Hmong, Indonesian, Laotian, Malaysian, Mien, Papua New Guinean, Singaporean, Timorese, Thai, and Vietnamese; South Asians: Bangladeshi, Bhutanese, Indian, Maladivian, Nepali, Pakistani, and Sri Lankan; and West Asians: Bahrain, Iran, Iraq, Israel, Jordan Kuwait, Lebanon, Oman, Palestine, Qatar, Saudi Arabia, Syria, Turkey, United

Arab Emirates, and Yemen (Asian and Pacific Islander Institute on Domestic Violence [APIIDV] 2008).

3. Estimated count from Asian and Pacific Islander Institute on Domestic Violence (2005).

4. In 2007 the Oakland, California-based East Bay Asian and Pacific Islander Coalition to End Domestic Violence and the California Partnership to End Domestic Violence formed a working group to address rising wrongful domestic violence arrests of immigrant women. Asian Women's Shelter, one of the member organizations, documented that, for several months in 2007, more than half the shelter residents entered the shelter upon release from wrongful incarceration for domestic violence offences.

CHAPTER 5. SOCIAL WORK PRACTICE WITH ABUSED PERSONS WITH DISABILITIES

1. The authors of this chapter use the terms "people with disabilities" and "disabled people" interchangeably, though we acknowledge that each term has been criticized by those within and outside the disability communities.

2. For example, consider the definition of "family" or "household member" according to the Code of Virginia §16.1–228 (Virginia General Assembly Legislative Information System 2004):

> Family or household member" means (i) the person's spouse, whether or not he or she resides in the same home with the person, (ii) the person's former spouse, whether or not he or she resides in the same home with the person, (iii) the person's parents, stepparents, children, stepchildren, brothers, sisters, half-brothers, half-sisters, grandparents, and grandchildren, regardless of whether such persons reside in the same home with the person, (iv) the person's mother-in-law, father-in-law, sons-in-law, daughters-in-law, brothers-in-law, and sisters-in-law who reside in the same home with the person, (v) any individual who has a child in common with the person, whether or not the person and that individual have been married or have resided together at any time, or (vi) any individual who cohabits or who, within the previous 12 months, cohabited with the person, and any children of either or them then residing in the same home with the person. (para. 23; http://leg1.state.va.us/cgi-bin/legp504.exe?000+cod+16.1-228)

3. Nonresidential places where persons with disabilities learn empowerment and develop the skills necessary to make lifestyle choices.

4. Among working-age men with disabilities, 60 percent were employed compared to 80 percent of nondisabled men. For working-age women, the percentages were 51 percent for women with disabilities and 67 percent for those without (Waldrop and Stern 2003).

5. A safety plan is often a pre-established form a victim will complete in order to list the steps she can take to remain safe during possible future incidents of abuse as well as resources in her community to assist her (National Coalition Against Domestic Violence 2007).

6. An "incapacitated person" is any adult who is impaired by reason of mental illness, mental retardation, physical illness or disability, advanced age, or other causes to the extent that the adult lacks sufficient understanding or capacity to make, communicate, or carry out responsible decisions concerning his or her well-being (Code of Virginia, §63.2–1603).

7. Training manuals that may assist practitioners have been developed by domestic and sexual assault service providers (for example, National Coalition Against Domestic Violence 1996; Safe Place Disability Services ASAP, 2002).

CHAPTER 7. DOMESTIC ABUSE IN LATER LIFE

1. This number is an accurate report, not a typing error.

CHAPTER 9. OUTING THE ABUSE

1. We use the term "intimate partner violence" in this chapter, as it is gender neutral and does not rely on a heterosexual model of "domestic violence," where "domestic" implies an opposite sex couple, usually married, sharing a living space together. We use the more common term "domestic violence" when talking about the service delivery system.

2. As noted in Table 9.1, many different terms can be used to refer to persons with non-dominant gender identity or sexual attractions. We use the term "LGBT," understanding that it is limited and potentially obscures people who are also gender/attraction nonconforming but who do not relate to these labels. The term "queer," while broader in scope and used by many members of LGBT communities, continues to carry derogatory implications for some LGBT people. A comprehensive listing of terms and definitions related to LGBT communities is available at http://www. safeschoolscoalition.org/ElevenAspectsofSexuality.pdf, accessed October 12, 2007.

CHAPTER 12. A COMMENTARY ON RELIGION AND DOMESTIC VIOLENCE

1. For additional information on many of these traditions, see Jean Anton (Ed.), Walking Together: Working with Women from Diverse Religious and Spiritual Traditions (Seattle: FaithTrust Institute, 2005). Available at http://www.faithtrustinstitute.org.

2. See Susan Yarrow Morris, Opening the Door: A Pastor's Guide to Addressing Domestic Violence in Premarital Counseling (Seattle: FaithTrust Institute, 2006).

3. Kiddushin 39b.

4. See Lev, 19:16.

5. Jerusalem Talmud, Pe'ah 1:1.

6. Midrash Tanchuma, Exodus, chap. 14.

7. For some examples of this teaching, see Qur'an verses 18:7, 22:11, 29:2, 34:21, 47:31, and 64:15.

8. "A man who has no wife lives without joy, without blessing, and without goodness" (Talmud, Yevamot 62b).

9. Talmud, Kiddushin 41a and Niddah 17a.

10. Gates of Repentance (High Holy Days Prayer Book), Central Conference of American Rabbis, 1978, p. 67.

11. Maimonides, Hilkhot Ishut 14:2.

12. Maimonides, Hilkhot Ishut 14:8.

13. Qur'an 4:1.

14. Qur'an 4:21.

15. Qur'an 2:187.

16. Qur'an 4:34.

17. Qur'an 4:128.

18. Maurice Lamm, The Jewish Way in Love and Marriage (New York: Harper and Row, 1991), p. 157.

19. Talmud, Baba Metzi'a 32a.

20. Kitzur Shulhan Arukh, ch. 143; Yoreh De'ah 240:25.

21. Mishnah, Yoma 85b.

22. See also Marie M. Fortune and Joretta Marshall (Eds.), Forgiveness and Abuse: Jewish and Christian Reflections (New York: Haworth, 2002).

23. Qur'an 5:45.

INDEX

Abugideiri, Salma Elkadi, vii, 318–40
Abuse, Rape and Domestic Violence Aid and Resource Collection, 263
Abuse Assessment Screen-Disability (AAS-D), 143
Abusers. *See* Batterers/abusers
Accessibility issues, 133, 150
Activism, 145
Activity-limited persons. *See* Disabled abused women
Adolescents. *See* Teen dating violence
Adoption, 235, 239, 245, 251, 292
Adult Protective Services (APS), 193, 203
Advocacy for persons in abusive relationships: Asian and Pacific Island women, 118–21; community level, 56; disabled women, 135–36, 145–48; immigrants and refugees, 163–77; Latinas, 216–17; LGBT (lesbian, gay, bisexual, and transgender) persons, 240–41, 248–53; local, state, national, and international level, 56; military women, 278–79; Native American women, 300–302; organizational level, 55–56; rural women, 348–49, 354–56, 362; state laws and policies, 44; teen dating violence, 381–92; through Legal Momentum, 43–44; through TANF, 43; through VAWA,

42–43; through Victims of Crime Act, 43
African American women in abusive relationships: diversity, 68–69; domestic violence as primary public health issue, 67–68; economic, employment, and network embeddedness issues, 70–71; establishing helping relationship, 83–84; historical context, 69–70; intersectionality of oppression, 73–74; literature review, 68; references, 91–99; resources and web sites, 89–91; service disparities, discrimination, and injustices, 72–73, 77, 78, 80; sexism and sex-role perceptions affecting, 71; teens' attitudes towards violence, 375, 378; trauma's impact, 72
African American women in culturally sensitive practice: assessment strategies, 84–85; case study, 82–83, 84–86, 87, 88; community involvement and influences, 75, 81–82; cultural competence, 77–79; ending helping relationship, 87–88; familial influences, 74–75; goal setting and contracting, 85–86; help seeking, 76–77; intervention selection, 86, 87–88; lack of comprehensive or geographically accessible services, 78–80;

Race and ethnicity issues. *See* Ethnicity/race
Ramona (Mexican immigrant case study), 168–71
Ramos, Blanca M., xvii, 209–27
Randall, Elizabeth, xvii, 343–63
Rape Abuse and Incest National Network (RAINN), 57
Red Cross Armed Forces Emergency Service Centers, 283–84
Red Lake Band of Chippewa's Family Advocacy Center of Northern Minnesota (FACNM), 307
Refugees. *See* Immigrants and refugees
Religion and domestic violence: avoiding assumptions, 300–301; Christian view of nature of marriage relationship, 328–30; Christian view of suffering as theological issue, 325–26; Confucianism, 165; cooperative roles for religious leaders and secular workers, 321–22; faith-based communities (FBC), 75–76, 81, 357; faith-based communities' importance, 75–76; Jewish view of nature of marriage relationship, 330–31; Jewish view of suffering as theological issue, 326–27; marriage relationship, 328–33; misuse of sacred texts, 320–21; Muslim view of nature of marriage relationship, 331–33; Muslim view of suffering as theological issue, 327–28; Native American view of unity of creation, 296; need for education of rural clergy, 357; as positive and negative influences, 110, 318–21, 355; references, 342; religion as pervasive aspect of cultural diversity, 4, 318, 319; resources and web sites, 340–42; role of clergy, 323; role of secular advocate, 322; for rural women, 347, 355; shared views on confession and forgiveness, 336–38; shared views

on marriage covenant and divorce, 333–35; shared views on parents and children, 336–38
Research gaps, need for knowledge: Asian and Pacific Island women, 106–7, 122; disabled abused persons, 128; elder abuse, 188–89; immigrants and refugees, 160; Latinas in abusive situations, 216; LGBT communities, 236, 239–40; Native American women in abusive situations, 294; teen dating violence, 372–73, 377, 379
Respeto, 210–11
Restraining orders, 52–53
Rodgers, Selena T. Antá, xvii, 67–89
Rosebud Sioux Tribe's White Buffalo Calf Woman's Society, 308
Rosenbluth, Barri, xviii, 369–93
Rural Assistance Center, 364
Rural regions—abuse in Appalachia: barriers faced by victims, 348–49, 363; case study, 358–62; collaborative strategies, 362; cullturally sensitive practice, 349–51; cultural factors, 346–47, 363; definitions, geography, and demographics, 343–45; ethical issues, 356–58; historical issues, 345; isolation exacerbating, 189–90, 345–46, 363; narratives of survival and discovery, 351–54; need for more services, 354–56; older women, 189–90; policy and community response, 348–49; references, 364–68; resources and web sites, 364; teen dating violence, 373–74
Rural Technical Assistance on Violence Against Women, 364

Sacred Circle National Resource Center, 313
Safe and Fear-Free Environment (SAFE) (Bristol Bay Native Association), 305
SafePlace (Austin, Texas), 385, 395

Foundations of Social Work Knowledge
Frederic G. Reamer, Series Editor

CPSIA information can be obtained
at www.ICGtesting.com
Printed in the USA
JSHW051416140820
7303JS00001B/3